The Human Perspective

Readings in World Civilization

VOLUME II

The Modern World
Through the
Twentieth Century

THE
HUMAN
PERSPECTIVE

READINGS IN WORLD CIVILIZATION

VOLUME II

The Modern World
Through the
Twentieth Century

EDITED BY

Lynn H. Nelson

University of Kansas

HARCOURT BRACE JOVANOVICH, PUBLISHERS

San Diego   New York   Chicago   Austin   Washington, D.C.
London   Sydney   Tokyo   Toronto

In memory of LYNN ARTHUR NELSON

ISBN: 0-15-540393-1
Library of Congress Catalog Card Number: 86-80748
Printed in the United States of America

Preface

A steadily shrinking world has led history departments to increase their offerings of world history at the introductory level. But many instructors who teach these courses have received little formal training in non-Western areas. Moreover, most of their students have had little exposure to history other than that of the United States and could profit from materials that offer greater depth and interest than a traditional core text. *The Human Perspective* grew out of a personal frustration at the unavailability of such materials. These two volumes seek to remedy this problem by providing an assortment of readings that both supplement the basic course materials and, through the attention given to non-Western subjects, compensate for the Western and European emphases of many texts.

The 24 essays in each volume are drawn largely from secondary accounts and fall into the general category of social history. They deal with the everyday lives of average men and women rather than the great deeds of leaders and heroes, with continuing patterns of activity rather than great events, and with the concrete rather than the abstract. Core texts in world history generally establish the traditional political, institutional, and economic framework of history quite well. They are less satisfactory in fleshing out that framework and lending the study of history its proper human perspective. These volumes are intended to perform that function.

A special feature of *The Human Perspective* is a system of presentation that combines chronological, cultural, and topical criteria. In each volume, the readings appear in chronological order within three major historical divisions. In each historical division four readings concern Western and four non-Western cultures. All the readings relate to four topical categories: the life and times of individuals, technological innovations and their effect on societies, women and minorities, and education and recreation.

This second volume covers the period from 1660 to the present, and its three historical divisions are "The Early Modern Period: 1660–1789"; "Industrialism and Democracy: 1789–1914"; and "The Twentieth Century: 1914 to the Present." Each of the parts opens with a chronological chart and a brief historical introduction that, together, outline the important movements of the age and place the readings in their historical context. Every reading has its own short introduction and is followed by a brief annotated bibliography. A set of discussion questions closes the part.

The parts all contain two readings on each topical theme, one

Western and one non-Western in emphasis. This organization allows the instructor a variety of approaches. To follow a chronological order within a given topic, for example, one might investigate the status of minorities in the West by reading "Response of Slaves," "Irish Servant Women: The Irish 'Biddy,' " and "Democracy and Hypocrisy: The American Homefront During World War II." Or one could take a comparative approach to the development of technology in the early modern world by reading "An Early Energy Crisis and Its Consequences" and "Skills and Resources in Late Traditional China."

The organization is not rigid, however, since many of the readings relate to more than one topic. To take just one of many examples, "Two Parsons" can be read as a portrait of two individuals, an account of the diversions of the English middle class at the turn of the eighteenth century, or a picture of the effect of the Industrial Revolution on English rural life. In other words, the readings do not stand alone in any category, but reinforce each other in various ways. The discussion questions are helpful in pointing out many such connections, as is the "Topical Table of Contents," which lists each reading not only under the category that is its main focus but under other categories to which it is relevant.

This volume and its companion should be useful at whatever level the instructor cares to employ them. One might assign individual selections simply as supplementary readings, or topical or chronological groups of readings as subjects for papers or discussions. One or more selections, along with their bibliographies, might serve as starting points for term papers. Finally, the discussion questions offer topics for student papers and reports, or they might suggest themes around which to structure classroom presentations. In short, *The Human Perspective* is intended as a useful and rewarding tool in teaching and learning about the history of our world.

I acknowledge the valuable assistance and counsel I have received from Steve Drummond of Harcourt Brace Jovanovich in the conception and preparation of these volumes. Those who helped in the initial stages of the project include John Dardess, University of Kansas; Bruce Garver, Richard Overfield, and Michael Tate, University of Nebraska at Omaha; Judith Shaw, Pittsburg State University; Sister Georgia McGarry, Benedictine College; and James Falls and John Stack, University of Missouri at Kansas City. I am especially grateful to Stanley Chodorow, of the University of California at San Diego, who reviewed both volumes, and to James Summers for their advice and guidance, which helped significantly in shaping the text, and to Drake Bush and Catherine Fauver of Harcourt Brace Jovanovich for their encouragement and aid. Finally, my largest debt of gratitude is to my students, past and present, whose inquisitive minds provided the stimulation for this work.

Lynn H. Nelson

Contents

PART III   The Twentieth Century: 1914 to the Present

Topical Table of Contents

Each reading is listed here under its major topical area. "Related Articles" lists readings that are not primarily focused on the general topic but are relevant to it.

Individuals

Technological Innovations

Women and Minorities

Recreation and Education

The Human Perspective

Readings in World Civilization

VOLUME II

The Modern World
Through the
Twentieth Century

PART I

THE EARLY MODERN PERIOD

1660–1789

	1600	1625	1650	1675
EUROPE	**ca. 1550–1700** AN EARLY ENERGY CRISIS **1602** Dutch East India Company founded **1618–1648** Thirty Years' War	**1624–1642** Richelieu **1640–1649** Puritan Revolution	**1660–1688** Stuart Restoration **1661–1715** Louis XIV	**1685** Edict of Nantes revoked **1687** Newton's Law of Gravitation **1688** Glorious Revolution **1689–1725** Peter the Great **1690** Locke, *Two Treatises of Civil Government*
SOUTHWEST ASIA AND AFRICA	**ca. 1600–1800** THE AFRICAN SLAVE TRADE **ca. 1600** Fall of Kongo		**1652** Dutch found Cape Colony	
SOUTH AND SOUTHEAST ASIA	**1619** Dutch colonize Indonesia	**1641** Dutch capture Malacca from Portuguese	**1653** Taj Mahal completed	**1690** British found Calcutta
EAST ASIA	**1600–1868** Tokugawa shogunate **ca. 1600–1750** SKILLS AND RESOURCES IN LATE TRADITIONAL CHINA **ca. 1600–1800** SOCIAL ENVIRONMENT OF TOKUGAWA KABUKI	**1630** Japan closed to foreigners **1644–1911** Qing dynasty	**ca. 1660** THE DEATH OF WOMAN WANG **1662–1722** Emperor Kangxi	**ca. 1675–1725** Golden age of Edo urban culture, Japan
THE AMERICAS AND THE PACIFIC	**1607** Jamestown settled **1608** Quebec founded **1609** Henry Hudson explores Hudson River **1620** Puritans land in Massachusetts	**1642** Dutch discover New Zealand	**1664** British seize New Amsterdam	

PART I: 1660–1789

1700	1725	1750	1775	1789
ca. 1700–1850 UNIVERSITIES AND THE SCIENTIFIC REVOLUTION **1701–1714** War of Spanish Succession **1708** WOODES ROGERS: PRIVATEER AND PIRATE HUNTER	**1740–1780** Maria Theresa **1740–1786** Frederick the Great	**ca. 1750** THE RESPONSE OF SLAVES **1756–1763** Seven Years' War **1756–1791** Mozart **1762–1796** Catherine the Great **1769** James Watt's first steam engine	**1770–1827** Ludwig van Beethoven **1776** Adam Smith, *Wealth of Nations*	**1789** French Revolution begins
ca. 1700 Rise of Ashanti, West Africa	**1737–1747** Nadir Shah, decline of Safavid Empire			
ca. 1700 Sikhs form militant order		**1751** French control Deccan **1757** Battle of Plassey	**1773** Regulation Act **1784** East India Act	**1786–1793** Cornwallis in Bengal
	1736–1795 Emperor Qianlong			
	1728 Bering explores Alaska	**1756–1763** French and Indian War **1765** Stamp Act **1768–1780** Cook explores Pacific Ocean	**1773** Boston Tea Party **1774** Quebec Act **1775–1783** American Revolution **1776** Declaration of Independence	

THE world historian's attention is drawn primarily to European affairs during the early modern period because change and development were concentrated in Europe. Although the other civilizations of the Old World were unable to challenge European superiority or to halt Western expansion, they were strong enough to dictate the terms on which they interacted with the West. They used that temporary advantage to limit Western influences and to maintain strong and stable regimes that preserved their traditional social and cultural patterns from contamination by Western ideas. While these civilizations retreated into traditionalism and conservativism, the Europeans tightened their control over the rest of the world and increased their military and technological superiority.

Such a pattern was particularly evident in Japan, where, after 1636, the ruling Tokugawa warlords virtually sealed off the islands from any foreign contact and withdrew their subjects from maritime pursuits. In this isolation, which lasted for more than two centuries, the state's attempts to preserve traditional aristocratic ways of life met with imperfect success. The authoritarian Tokugawa regime brought an era of peace that permitted the growth of an enlarged and dynamic Japanese middle class. One aspect of this development, the emergence of new forms of theater and a new moral climate in Japanese society, is treated in "The Social Environment of Tokugawa Kabuki."

China, by contrast, allowed limited and closely regulated European contacts and even adopted some Western products, such as the sweet potato and the pendulum clock. However, these influences appear to have had little effect on traditional culture. The basic patterns of peasant life, of the sort depicted in "The Death of Woman Wang," remained unchanged, as they were to do until the mid-twentieth century. The conservative Chinese society's successful resistance to the technological and industrial innovations pioneered by the Europeans was the result of complex forces, which are analyzed in "Skills and Resources in Late Traditional China." Although content with their prosperity and peace, the Chinese steadily fell further behind the Europeans in real power.

The Islamic lands, which, at the time, included much of India, also enjoyed a general prosperity during this period. Control of Indian Ocean commerce was lost to the Europeans, and new European trading stations along the Indian coast were able to tap some of the resources and markets of the interior, but the net effect of these activities was relatively small. The Muslims turned their attention inland and inward. The era saw such great achievements as the building of the Taj Mahal and the model city of Isfahan, as well as an accommodation of the religious conflicts between the Sunni and the Shi'a sects that had wracked Islam during the 1500s. The Muslims' prosperity and relative stability made it unnecessary, at least for the moment, for them to confront the challenge posed by the increasing Western presence throughout the world.

Meanwhile, the structure of European expansion was evolving. On a political level, the hegemony in overseas exploration and trade that Spain and Portugal had established in the sixteenth century was being challenged by the English, the French, and the Dutch in the seventeenth century. The era saw a struggle for colonies that was to occupy the European powers until the nineteenth century. The complexities of that imperial competition are illustrated by the career of "Woodes Rogers: Privateer and Pirate Hunter." On the economic and social level, European exploitation of new lands evolved from the early explorers' hunt for gold and silver to more complex and sophisticated patterns. The new lands, particularly those of the tropics, were cultivated and harvested to produce sugar, chocolate, spices, cotton, coffee, quinine, and a number of other products for European consumption and trade. The great obstacle in this process was a lack of labor. The Europeans were too few and too susceptible to tropical diseases to meet their own labor needs, and they had imported into the tropics diseases that the indigenous inhabitants were unable to resist and that quickly depleted local labor sources. The difficulty was finally overcome when the Europeans began to tap an African source of labor, through the system described in "The African Slave Trade." Western exploitation of the tropics shortly became a biracial endeavor, some of whose peculiarities are described in "Response of Slaves."

Internally, Europe emerged from the struggles of the so-called Age of Religious Wars to enjoy the relative peace and security of the Old Regime. Beneath the apparent stability, however, movements were under way that would eventually transform the European society and economy and firmly establish Europe's superiority in wealth and power throughout the globe. One of those movements was the Scientific Revolution, which began around the middle of the seventeenth century. Starting from an interest in natural philosophy centered in mathematics and astronomy, the movement steadily widened its scope and expanded its methodology. Europe soon was benefiting from innovations that originally were mere spinoffs of scientific speculation: microscopes and telescopes, thermometers and barometers, and others. By the end of this period the Scientific Revolution had become institutionalized in European society, through a slow process that saw the universities taking responsibility for scientific inquiry, a process discussed in "Universities and the Scientific Revolution."

A less clearly defined movement was under way in industry and manufacture. As is shown in "An Early Energy Crisis and Its Consequences," advances were being made in sources of energy, in industrial machinery, and in economic organization. These innovations were laying the foundation for what would emerge by the close of the era as the Industrial Revolution.

An Early Energy Crisis
and Its Consequences

John U. Nef

Important technological innovations seldom occur in isolation. Generally, they are the culmination of a gradual preparatory process. Such was the case when nineteenth-century Europe underwent that period of unprecedented technological development called the Industrial Revolution. The spectacular and rapid technological improvements during that era resulted in the transformation of Europe's agrarian economy to an economy dominated by industry and machine manufacture. The Industrial Revolution, which began in England and spread to continental Europe, profoundly altered the nature of Western society and its relationship with the other peoples of the world.

Although the technical discoveries and improvements of the nineteenth century were tremendous by comparison with changes that had occurred at any earlier time in history, the transformation from agriculture to industry was a very gradual process. The Industrial Revolution's agricultural and mechanical innovations were the products of a long evolution, an almost unbroken continuity of change starting in the late Middle Ages. Many technological improvements were possible only after advances in associated fields. The first article in this part, "An Early Energy Crisis and Its Consequences," by John U. Nef, treats one of the most important of the early changes that were to make the Industrial Revolution possible, the replacement of wood by coal as the primary source of artificial power.

The earliest coal-burning economy was established first in England, then in Scotland, between 1550 and 1700. The author maintains that this substitution of coal for wood initiated a chain of events that culminated 200 years later in the Industrial Revolution. He examines the reasons for the transition from wood to coal and why it first occurred in Britain, citing the depletion of Britain's wood supply and the ensuing energy crisis as the primary factors in the transition. The importance of coal in the development of new methods of manufacturing, in the expansion of existing industries, and in the exploitation of new natural resources receives special attention, and serves to illustrate the evolutionary nature of the technological developments that led to the Industrial Revolution.

I n medieval Europe wood was utilized not only in many types of construction but also in most domestic and industrial heating. Then in Britain in the second half of the 16th century coal came into widespread use as a substitute for wood as fuel. The earliest coal-burning economy the world has known was established first in England and then in Scotland between about 1550 and 1700. This transition from woodcutting to coal mining as the main source of heat was part of an early British economic revolution. The first energy crisis was a crisis of deforestation. The adoption of coal changed the economic history of Britain, then of the rest of Europe and finally of the world. It led to the Industrial Revolution, which got under way in Britain in the last two decades of the 18th century. The substitution of coal for wood between 1550 and 1700 led to new methods of manufacturing, to the expansion of existing industries and to the exploitation of untapped natural resources.

To make these assertions is not to belittle the role of other changes during the Middle Ages and the Renaissance in the coming of our industrialized world. The century before Britain's wood crisis—the 100 years from about 1450 to 1550—was characterized by a new spirit of expansion. Voyages of discovery were launched, carrying explorers to the ends of the earth. The art of printing with movable type spread across Europe, and the production of paper expanded; millions of books were printed and put in circulation. In central Europe, where the major centers of mining and metallurgy were to be found, the output of ores, particularly silver-bearing copper ores, multiplied severalfold. The years between 1494 and 1529 have been described as bringing about a "revolution in the art of war." With the help of the new firearms Spain conquered Mexico and Peru.

These and other innovations increased, directly or indirectly, the need for all existing kinds of energy: the heat provided by wood and

AN EARLY ENERGY CRISIS   By John U. Nef, from *Scientific American*, November 1977, pp. 140–51.

Before the advent of coal wood was the main source of heat energy in Europe. Industrial power was provided by wind, animals and running water. It was often necessary to convert the wood to charcoal by partially burning it in furnaces such as the ones shown here. The wood was piled in stacks, covered with earth and powdered charcoal dust and then burned. The covering kept combustion at a minimum so that the end product was charcoal rather than ashes. For some manufacturing processes charcoal was preferred to wood because it is mostly pure carbon and so yields a greater amount of heat per unit volume of fuel. Illustration is from Diderot's Encyclopédie, ou Dictionnaire Raisonné des Sciences, des Art et des Métiers.

the power provided by wind, animals and running water. The need for larger amounts of wood for construction and for heating, particularly for the smelting and refining of ores, called for a substantial increase in the felling of trees.

All Europe felt these pressures, and yet the first large area to experience an acute shortage of wood was Britain. Why did the fuel revolution that led to new uses of heat energy begin in that particular place? Was wood particularly scarce there? It seems to be true that the most populous parts of Scotland (the areas surrounding the Firth of Forth) were barren of trees; a wit from England is said to have observed in the reign of James I that if Judas had repented in the king's native land (Scotland), he would have been hard put to find a tree on which to hang himself! Such an explanation does not fit England. The wood crisis there has to be attributed to the requirements of expanding agriculture, industry and commerce, all stimulated by a growing, shifting population.

It appears that Sweden and the Netherlands were the only other European countries to experience anything comparable to the growth and resettlement of the British population in the period from 1550 to 1700. The population of England and Wales, about three million in the early 1530's, had nearly doubled by the 1690's. The resulting demand for wood for various purposes was further increased by changes in the distribution of the population. In this period the inhabitants of London multiplied at least eightfold, from some 60,000 in 1534 to some 530,000 in 1696.

According to Gregory King's estimate for the latter year, the British capital had by then become the largest city in Europe and perhaps the world. King estimates that England's other "cities and . . . market towns" had a total population of about 870,000. This means that although only one person in 10 was a "townsman" in the 1530's, one person in four was a townsman in the 1690's. Larger towns meant heavier demands on nearby wood supplies. Moreover, outside the towns there was much migration of the unemployed across the country in search of work. Wherever they found employment, shelter had to be provided, putting still another strain on the forests.

During the reigns of Elizabeth I (1558–1603) and James I (1603–25) this pressure on the supply of trees was reflected in the soaring cost of firewood and lumber for construction. The period from 1550 to 1640 was a time of inflation throughout Europe, but the price of wood in England rose very much faster than that of any other commodity in general use anywhere. Complaints of deforestation came from all parts of the kingdom.

Wherever coal seams outcropped in Europe, coal had been burned in small quantities since the 12th century. (It had been more extensively burned in China earlier than that and also to some degree in Roman Britain.) In Europe during the later Middle Ages peasants had occasionally warmed their homes or stoked their lime kilns and smithies with these "black stones." Why then was coal not widely adopted as a fuel on the Continent and in Britain before the forests were seriously depleted?

In societies earlier than the one that arose in western Europe in medieval times mining was looked on with disfavor. It was often regarded as robbery, even as a kind of rape. Unlike the plow, which made the earth fertile, the pick and shovel removed what seemed to be irreplaceable soil and subsoil.

By the early 16th century a different attitude toward the exploitation of the more valuable underground resources found expression in two books. In *De re metallica* (1556) Georgius Agricola (1494–1555)

The wood crisis of the 16th century coincided with the expression of a changed attitude toward mining. Until the Middle Ages mining had been widely considered an affront to nature. In De re metallica, *published in 1556, however, Georgius Agricola expressed a new respect for mining. This careful account of metallurgy and mining gives a good picture of those industries at about the time when it was first necessary to increase coal production. In the illustration on the opposite page from* De re metallica *a tunnel, D, has been cut into a hill and three shafts have been dug from above. Although the mining was facilitated when a shaft connected with the tunnel, not all the shafts were meant to do so. In this case the shaft at A will be mined only from the surface; the shaft at B connects with the tunnel, and the tunnel will soon connect with the shaft at C. Material was hauled vertically out of a shaft with a windlass, which was usually covered with a shed to keep rain out of the shaft.*

ranked the miner's calling higher than "that of the merchant trading for lucre." And in *Pirotechnia* (1540) Vannoccio Biringuccio (1480–1539) advocated an all-out assault on these underground riches. He advised "whoever mines ores . . . to bore into the center of the mountains . . . as if by the work of necromancy or giants. They should not only crack the mountains asunder but also turn their very marrow upside down in order that what is inside may be seen and the sweetness of the fruit despoiled as soon as possible."

The new dignity attached to mining was reserved for metallic ores. It did not extend to coal. The medieval craftsmen who needed fuel wanted their work to be beautiful, whether it was for their church or for rich laymen. The unpleasant smoke and fumes of coal therefore limited the market for it. There was little incentive before the mid-16th century to dig deep into the soil in search of this dirty fuel as long as wood was available, and there seemed to be an abundance of that. Biringuccio himself believed the forests of Europe could fill all conceivable future demands for fuel. In *Pirotechnia* he wrote: "Miners are more likely to exhaust the supply of ores than foresters the supply of the wood needed to smelt them. Very great forests are found everywhere, which makes one think that the ages of man would never consume them . . . especially since Nature, so very liberal, produces new ones every day." Coal is mentioned only once in his long treatise and then just to dismiss it: "Besides tres, black stones, that occur in many places, have the nature of true charcoal, [but] the abundance of trees makes [it] unnecessary . . . to think of that faraway fuel."

Less than a generation later the English turned to coal under pressure from the high price of wood. By the early 17th century efforts by the government to stop deforestation were felt to be imperative because the shortage of lumber for shipbuilding seemed to threaten Britain's existence. A royal proclamation of 1615 laments the former wealth of "Wood and Timber," the kind of wood that is "not only great and large in height and bulk, but hath also that toughness and heart, as it

is not subject to rive or cleave, and thereby of excellent use for shipping, as if God Almightie, which had ordained this Nation to be mighty
by Sea and navigation, had in his providence indued the same with
the principall materiall conducing thereunto." By the middle of the
17th century coal had proved so useful and was already so widely burned
that the British had come to make necessity a virtue. They reconciled

themselves to the disappointing failure of their explorers to locate sources of precious metal and of their miners to find much of it in Britain itself. In spite of the smoke and fumes of coal and in spite of a widespread distaste for it, by the time of the civil war in the 1640's Londoners were dependent on the coastwise shipment of coal to keep warm. In 1651 the anonymous author of *News from Newcastle* wrote verses in praise of the new fuel. "England's a perfect World! Has Indies too! / Correct your Maps; New-castle is Peru! . . . / Let th' naughty Spaniard triumph, 'til 'tis told / Our sooty mineral purifies his gold."

Even earlier, as is made clear by William Harrison's *Description of Britain* (1577) and by a petition London brewers addressed to Sir Francis Walsingham, Queen Elizabeth's secretary of state (1578), coal was acquiring a new and important place in domestic and industrial heating. The surviving records of customs officials at Newcastle-on-Tyne (and later records of other towns) reveal a continuous and rapid growth in the shipments of coal between 1550 and 1700, first from Newcastle-on-Tyne and then from other ports. These records suggest that the coastwise shipments increased at least twentyfold between 1550 and 1700. Coastwise imports to London grew even faster, probably more than thirtyfold, which is not surprising in view of the multiplication of the city's population in that period. Lord Buckhurst, who became Queen Elizabeth's lord treasurer at the end of the 16th century, required the customs officials during the 1590's to determine the "rate of growth" in coal shipments from Newcastle, thereby introducing a new concept into human affairs. The calculations on which Buckhurt insisted indicated that taxes on coal shipments could be counted on to provide a continually increasing source of revenue, and so taxes on coal shipments were imposed in 1599 and 1600.

The most impressive rises in the growth rate of coal production occurred in the second half of the 16th century and at the beginning of the 17th. In fact, the growth rate in the volume of coal mined between 1556 and 1606 may even exceed the growth rate (computed from less incomplete statistics) in the volume mined during the first part of the 19th century, that is, at the height of Britain's Industrial Revolution. The actual quantities involved in the rapid growth of coal production in the earlier period may seem insignificant today, but it is the viewpoint of the Elizabethans and their immediate successors that needs to be recaptured. To them the expansion in the output of coal must have seemed extraordinarily rapid.

Coal was not only a source of energy but also a spur to technological development. Most products that could be manufactured with open wood fires were damaged by contact with coal fumes. John R. Harris has commented that as a result "coal was hardly ever adopted without significant alteration of industrial processes." Indeed, the technological advances of the Industrial Revolution were largely the culmination of the innovative period associated with the conversion to coal.

New methods of firing had to be developed in which the materials to be heated were protected from direct contact with the burning coals and the gases evolved in their combustion. Otherwise the coal would have had to be reduced to coke and so purged of its noxious properties. After about 1610 glass began to be manufactured with mineral fuel in a variant of the reverberatory furnace, a system that later played an important role in the growth of other major industries. In this type of furnace an arched roof reflects the heat of the burning coal onto the material to be heated, thereby preventing the contamination of the material by substances originating with the fuel. The potash and sand to be melted down to form glass were enclosed in a clay crucible to further protect them from the fumes. Like the reverberatory furnace, the crucible was later employed in many other manufacturing processes.

Over the decades following 1610 new technology brought coal into many kinds of manufacturing. The cementation process for converting wrought iron into steel with coal was introduced between 1612 and 1620. By 1618 a method of baking bricks in coal fires near London was described by the Venetian ambassador in words showing that Italians were no longer disposed to ignore this "faraway fuel" as Biringuccio had recommended. Before the British civil war of the 1640's coke was introduced for the drying of malt in connection with the brewing industry, which had expanded rapidly during most of the 16th century with the spread of hop gardening from the Netherlands.

One of the most important applications of coal following the restoration of the British monarchy in 1660 was in the adaptation of the reverberatory furnace for smelting nonferrous metals. This innovation of the 1680's made it possible to smelt the lead, copper and tin ores of Britain with coal. By the end of the 17th century only the production of pig and bar iron remained dependent on wood. Although the problem was not completely solved until the 1780's, an important step toward its solution was taken in 1709, when coke was introduced by Abraham Darby the elder at his blast furnace in Shropshire. In this kind of furnace the fuel and the ore are in contact. The trouble with Darby's process was that it yielded a kind of pig iron that, unlike the pig iron produced with wood, could not be converted to wrought iron, the form of iron then most in demand. In 1784 Henry Cort invented the puddling process, in which pig iron (even pig iron from a blast furnace) is remelted and manipulated in a coal-fired reverberatory furnace to produce wrought iron. Until Cort's invention the making of iron remained largely dependent on charcoal. Thus although iron production in England had increased several times between 1540 and about 1620, this growth had been arrested by the shortage of wood for making charcoal in the 1620's. Beginning in that decade, however, an increase in iron imports, notably from Sweden, made possible a continuous slow growth in the output of finished iron wares, which were already produced by processes utilizing mineral fuel.

Samuel Eliot Morison has observed about innovations in ship-building and navigation that there is always "a gap between the invention of a device and persuading owners to supply it or sailors to use it." The same can be said about the spread of inventions connected with the introduction of coal in Britain after 1550. It took a substantial period of experimentation to make the new coal-based methods efficient. For example, in brickmaking (as also in the baking of clay tobacco pipes) there was much waste through breakage when coal-burning furnaces were introduced. Before the end of the 17th century, however, few bricks were lost in the course of coal firing.

As it became clear that coal could mean cheaper and more efficient production more industries turned to it as a fuel. Before the end of the 17th century in Britain's growing textile industry, where processes such as steaming and dyeing called for large quantities of fuel, that fuel was usually coal. Before 1700 the expanding manufactures of salt, alum, copperas (vitriol, or ferrous sulfate), saltpeter, gunpowder, starch and candles depended on coal. Coal was then also being employed extensively in the preparation of preserved foods, vinegar and Scotch whisky, and in brewing, soap boiling and sugar refining. A French visitor studying English technology in the Midlands in 1738–39 reported that the new coal-burning kilns (made of coal-baked bricks) had produced such a superior lime fertilizer that the yield of arable land had tripled. He considered coal "the soul of English manufactures."

The spread of coal into British homes that began early in Elizabethan times was continuous throughout the 17th century. This was not the only residential change brought about by the conversion of Britain to mineral fuel. The kingdom was extensively rebuilt under Queen Elizabeth and her Stuart successors. Brick and stone structures (with mortar made from coal-burned limestone) were replacing wood ones. Windows made of glass (produced in coal furnaces) were installed in buildings to retain the heat from the new coal-burning fireplaces (which had iron grates and brick chimneys manufactured with coal). In spite of its grime and stench coal had brought a new comfort to Britain's damp, chilly climate. Already in 1651 the author of *News from Newcastle* observed that the sacks of coal had heightened the joys of intimacy!

Coal had been so successfully incorporated into the British technology and economy that during the last four decades of the 17th century wood prices stopped rising. Some years ago I ventured a rough estimate of three million tons for Britain's annual coal production in the 1690's. In Harris' opinion that figure "may eventually prove conservative rather than excessive." It appears that at least as much as four times more heating was done at that time with coal than was done with wood. Never before had a major country come to depend on underground resources for the bulk of its fuel.

Although the exploitation of coal had largely solved the fuel shortage before 1700, there was still a wood shortage because other demands for wood had increased. In 1618 a traveler from London described his time as a "rattling, rowling, rumbling age" and remarked that "the World runnes on [wood] Wheeles." Great quantities of lumber were required for the construction of the growing number of ships and horse-drawn vehicles needed to transport people and goods across water and land. Moreover, although there was some reforestation during the 17th century, more and more forest was being cleared for farms and pastures. In addition smaller areas were being cleared for the growing metallurgical industries and for the expansion of mining, particularly of coal mining. Britain's forests simply could not keep up with the island's demand for wood.

The British were forced to supplement their domestic supply with imports, mostly from the American colonies and from the Baltic region. (In his *Wealth of Nations,* published in 1776, Adam Smith remarked that in his native Edinburgh "there [was] not perhaps a single stick of Scotch timber.") The imports of wood were paid for in part by the mounting exports of coal and probably in greater part by the mounting exports of textiles manufactured in varying degrees with coal fuel. This foreign trade, and even more the rapidly expanding coastwise trade, had already resulted in the 17th century in the development of a large British merchant marine. New colliers, or coal ships, were designed to carry more coal with a smaller crew, and the coastwise coal trade was considered the chief training ground for seamen, a major factor in Britain's emergence as a sea power.

Yet in some instances coal made Britain less dependent on imported commodities, for example salt. As Robert Multhauf explains in his recent book *Neptune's Gift: A History of Common Salt,* this commodity was an essential one in Europe during the 16th and 17th centuries. In Britain, where food from the sea was coming to occupy a more important place in an increasingly abundant diet, salt was indispensable for preserving fish. In southern and western France salt was obtained by allowing the sun to evaporate seawater in shallow pans, or ponds, but this method was impractical in Britain's climate. By the early 16th century two-thirds of the salt consumed in England had to be imported, mostly from France. Britain's almost total conversion to coal changed the situation. At the end of the 17th century some 300,000 tons, or nearly 10 percent of the coal mined annually in Britain, was burned to evaporate water for the production of salt in England and

Scotland. As a result the country had become virtually self-sufficient in terms of salt.

The conversion to a new kind of fuel might have had less effect on the British economy if Britain had been poorly, or even only moderately, endowed with coal. Before the end of the 17th century, however, it had become clear that Britain possessed enormous coal reserves. A piece of coal-inspired technology provided new and reassuring information. The device, called a boring rod, was introduced at the beginning of the 17th century. Early boring-rod surveys were inaccurate, but before the 17th century had ended mining experts were able to determine the thickness and quality of coal seams without sinking shafts. Boring rods had become reliable tools and had revealed a newfound land of plenty under the soil and even under the surrounding seas. Much of the island was seen to be underlain with coal. This trove of energy resources began to exert a pull in the direction of a quantity production that had not been equaled in previous history.

It was not until the middle of the 19th century, after an unprecedented acceleration in the rate of growth of production had begun, not until the publication in 1865 of William Stanley Jevons' *The Coal Question,* that some became aware that the coal deposits were exhaustible. By this time resources of petroleum and natural gas were known outside Britain, although neither were much exploited until later in the 19th century. It was not until the 1920's that a few people began to realize the supplies of all fossil fuels had distinct limits.

The shift to fossil fuel in the 17th century led on after 1785 to the aggressive exploitation of the world's vast stores of iron ore. Without the coming of the first coal-burning economy the age of iron and steel might never have developed. The conversion to coal that began in Elizabethan England had further consequences in bringing into being the modern mechanized age. The utilization of steam power and of travel by rail were also vital to the coming of that age. Attempts to build steam engines and to introduce railed ways with horse-drawn wagons in Britain go back at least to the reign of James I, but it was not until 1712 that Thomas Newcomen installed at a colliery in Staffordshire a steam engine that actually worked. It was to no small extent the needs of coal mining and coal transport that led to the steam engine and the railroad. Britain's damp climate made the damage of water in the multiplying coal mines a serious problem. Power from horses (which ate costly fodder) and from running water (which required capital for dams and overshot wheels) was diminishing the profits from coal mining throughout the 17th century. The compelling need for more efficient drainage systems in the British coal mines in that early age played an important part in the development of the Newcomen engine. Once these "fire engines" were invented, as John S. Allen and Alan Smith have shown, they spread rapidly across Britain between 1712 and about 1730.

It should be mentioned that coal appears to have been burned for many industrial purposes in China in the Sung era, in the 10th and 11th centuries. The episode was largely forgotten. It clearly did not lead, as it did in Europe much later, to an industrial revolution.

Studies made over the past 50 years, since I published my own two volumes on coal, have shown that the period of Britain's energy crisis—the late 16th and 17th centuries—was also the period of what has come to be called the scientific revolution. The revolution in thinking that brought modern science into being was an even more important factor than coal in the establishment of the mechanized age. By the 1620's and 1630's Europeans were becoming aware of the immense growth in production promised by the development of the new fuel. It was in those two decades that Francis Bacon wrote *The New Atlantis* (1627) and René Descartes his *Discourse on Method* (1637). Bacon's imaginary island over the seas was provided with a great institution of scientific research presiding over human destiny, and he was confident that a new abundance, made possible by the growth of scientific knowledge, would solve intellectual and moral problems as well as economic ones. And Descartes in his *Discourse* was no less confident. Even more specifically than Bacon he foresaw greater output, lighter labor and longer life for human beings everywhere. Even at that time there was talk of airships, submarines, devastating explosives and journeys to the moon. It was the scientific revolution in the late 16th and 17th centuries, together with the economic transformations brought about by the introduction of coal, that gave birth to the industrial world in which we live.

In Britain the period of the onset and resolution of the energy crisis (1550–1700) was characterized by increased returns from labor in all kinds of production. The British statesman and historian Lord Clarendon (1609–1674) was referring to this prosperity when he wrote that during the period before the 1640's the English "enjoyed . . . the fullest measure of felicity, that any people in any age for so long time together have been blessed with; to the wonder and envy of all the parts of Christendom." Clarendon did not base his assertion on what would today be considered reliable statistics, and indeed it is not possible to provide such statistics. Yet the new information on English economic growth contained in recent books of Eric Kerridge's and of mine supports Clarendon's statement. Britain, which lagged behind the rest of Europe in many economic areas during the later Middle Ages, was probably ahead of the other European countries in per capita agricultural and industrial output by 1700.

Kerridge has shown that whereas it has been thought that British agriculture was transformed in the 18th and early 19th centuries, the transformation actually took place between the late Middle Ages and the end of the 17th century. In this period, he writes, "the improvement of yields [from farming] must have been enormous. Corn [that is, grain] and grass yields rose about fourfold, and the yields of the fallows [the land not previously tilled] increased out of recognition. All told it is difficult to resist the conclusion that yields rose up to tenfold and fivefold on the average."

In the 1920's and 1930's most students of the coming of industrialism (myself included) accepted the explanations of Karl Marx, Sir William Ashley, Max Weber, Henri Hauser and others. The works of these scholars suggested that the advent of capitalism and of the "capitalist spirit" was the main factor leading to the overwhelming increase in the output of goods and services in the 19th century. I now think that an even more important factor was a growing faith in quantitative progress, in the multiplication of output.

Late in the 16th century a new attention came to be focused on concepts of quantity. The effects of this new concern could be seen in the more exact measurements employed in the developing natural sciences and in the replacement of the Julian calendar by the far more accurate Gregorian calendar. It was also reflected in a series of inventions designed to speed up numerical calculations, one made by Galileo (1564–1642), another made by the Dutch mathematician Simon Stevin (1548–1620) and two more by the Scottish laird John Napier (1550–1617), the originator of logarithms. A sophisticated mathematics—the calculus—was developed first in France after 1620 and more fully later in the 17th century by Newton and Leibniz. The idea of rates of growth introduced during the Elizabethan age brought a fresh precision to economic studies. The new point of view emphasized the probable value of quantitative goals to humanity. The transformation of industrial aims constituted a major advance toward an industrialized world.

In 1697 an Englishman named James Puckle wrote: "Our artisans [are] universally allow'd the best upon Earth for Improvements." This was certainly true in manufacturing that called for efficiency and quantity production. Yet a different evaluation needs to be made of the state of the arts and the luxury crafts in Britain following the conversion to coal. At the juncture of the 17th and 18th centuries Europe was eager to learn more efficient production methods from the British, but the British were equally eager to learn ways of fashioning beautiful products and environments from the Italians, the French and the Dutch. (Nowhere in 17th-century Europe was the quest for beauty and harmony in buildings and furnishings as remarkable as it was in the Netherlands of Rembrandt and Vermeer.) Harris has shown that in the 18th century the British, in spite of their aspirations to high fashion, had great difficulty copying the methods of making high-quality glass that were employed by the French at Saint-Gobain. In Britain the rise of the coal industry had weakened the position of craftsmanship and art as the heart and soul of production.

Moreover, the rise of coal mining had cast a shadow over the laborers connected with coal. Coal miners and coal carriers, stained by the black mineral, were often outcasts. They were seen as black men, and in the 17th century, when real black men were being shipped as slaves from Africa to America, coal laborers were being subjected to a new form of slavery in Scottish collieries and coal-burning salt pans.

As coal spread from Britain to the rest of Europe in the late 18th century and afterward the concern for beauty in manufactures and in the human environment weakened. Throughout history this kind of dedication to beauty has been important in setting reasonable limits to economic growth. The advent of coal seems to have diminished such dedication. The exploitation of the earth's resources has often violated the bounds of good taste. To make the most of these resources calls not only for ingenuity but also for restraint. At present man's dependence on fossil fuels is as problematic as his dependence on wood was some 400 years ago. The best hope for the fruitful exploitation of fuel resources may lie in a renewal and an amplification of the standards of beauty. If humanity is to advance, the making of history must become an art, that is, a search for beauty.

Suggested Readings

John U. Nef, *The Rise of the British Coal Industry* (London: George Routledge & Sons, Ltd., 1932), is a two-volume history of the British coal industry. Phyllis Dean, *The First Industrial Revolution* (Cambridge: Cambridge University Press, 1965), is a scholarly work that recreates the atmosphere of England on the eve of the Industrial Revolution. Much of the study is devoted to demographic, agricultural, commercial, and transportation changes. Dean evaluates the consequences on labor, government, and the standard of living. A comprehensive study of the social results of the Industrial Revolution is Peter Stearns, *European Society in Upheaval* (New York: Macmillan, 1967). Lewis Mumford, *Technics and Civilization* (New York: Harcourt Brace Jovanovich, 1963), is a classic analysis of the "machine" in Western history. A valuable study of the Industrial Revolution is David S. Landes, *The Unbound Prometheus: Technological Change and the Industrial Revolution in Western Europe from 1750 to the Present* (Cambridge: Cambridge University Press, 1969).

The African Slave Trade

Paul Bohannan and Philip Curtin

Economic factors significantly influenced the character of the New World colonial societies established by Europeans during the 300-year period from the beginning of the sixteenth to the end of the eighteenth century. A new type of colony was created, whose primary function was to produce goods desired by the Europeans. The first New World colonies were the sugar islands of the Caribbean; later came the tobacco, tea, and coffee colonies.

The colonial economies were largely based on a plantation system requiring vast numbers of workers. To acquire the labor power needed to work the plantations, the Europeans—in particular the Portuguese, English, Dutch, and French—initiated a system of importing slaves from West Africa that rapidly assumed a vast scale and directed to the New World a steady and substantial stream of migration from Africa. This forced migration, although economic and not racial in its intention, eventually created substantial racial minorities in many of the New World countries.

The following selection by Paul Bohannan and Philip Curtin briefly describes the origin of Negro slavery and of the slave trade that perpetuated such a ruthless system. The involvement of both Europeans and Africans is emphasized by the authors, whose description of the commercial slavery networks existing in Africa prior to the arrival of the Europeans is of particular interest. This examination of the impact of the slave trade on Africa clearly shows the dire consequences the system had for African societies.

It is one of the ironies of African history that the end of isolation, made possible through the maritime revolution, should have led in less than a century to a new commerce in which Africa's chief export was its own people. Historians have long disputed the causes and consequences of the slave trade—both for Africa and for the world—and the debates are far from finished.

Recent research nevertheless makes it possible to dismiss some of the older myths about the slave trade, myths that originated in the eighteenth- and nineteenth-century European image of Africa with all its racist overtones. Where the slave trade was once explained by the "primitive" condition of African societies and the "natural docility" of the Africans, it is now clear that Africa was not primitive and African slaves were far from docile. Slave revolts were a standard feature in the American tropics. Not only were the Afro-Americans of Saint Domingue (now the republic of Haiti) the first non-Europeans to overthrow colonial rule; other, less known, revolts were also successful. Communities of runaways and rebels were scattered through the back country of South America and in the tangled mountains of the larger Caribbean islands. Several such communities maintained their independence of European control until the end of slavery itself ended their need for isolation.

The Origins of Negro Slavery

Other new research helps to explain why Africans came to make up the majority of slaves in the Western world. In southern Europe—unlike northern Europe, where the slavery of the Roman period changed gradually into various forms of inequality generally categorized as serfdom—slavery continued throughout the Middle Ages and down to the eighteenth century in some places. Mediterranean slavery had nothing to do with the race of the slaves. It was a matter of religion; Christians enslaved Muslims, and Muslims enslaved Christians. Black Africans were present among the Mediterranean slaves, but not in large numbers until the fourteenth century. Before that time, the principal external source of slaves for Christian Europe was the northern and eastern coasts of the Black Sea.

In the fourteenth and fifteenth centuries, slavery in southern Europe served three purposes—to furnish domestic service, to provide oarsmen for the galleys that were the principal naval craft, and to concentrate people for new enterprises. Wherever mines or plantations were established in places with an insufficient supply of labor, the institution

THE AFRICAN SLAVE TRADE   From Paul Bohannan and Philip Curtin, *Africa and Africans* (Garden City, N.Y.: Doubleday, 1971), pp. 261–76.

of slavery was a convenient way of mobilizing labor, especially for sugar plantations on the Mediterranean islands, southern Spain, or Portugal.

Even before the discovery of America, Europeans began to set up similar plantations on Atlantic islands like the Canaries or Madeira. By the early sixteenth century, they had moved as far as São Thomé in the Gulf of Guinea, and these moves were followed later in the century by similar establishments in the Caribbean and Brazil. At each step, the existing population was too small to provide enough workers for a labor-intensive crop like sugar, and the previously isolated populations lived in disease environments that lacked many of the common diseases of Africa and Europe. This meant that the people had no immunities derived from childhood infection or inheritance. With the introduction of Afro-European diseases, they passed through a series of devastating epidemics of diseases like measles, smallpox, typhus, malaria, or yellow fever. The result was a population disaster, sometimes ending in the effective extinction of the original population, especially in the tropical lowlands of the Americas—the region best suited for plantation agriculture. Europeans already had the institution of slavery as a way of forcing labor mobility; they used it in the Atlantic just as they had done in the Mediterranean.

Some form of slavery or forced labor was useful for other reasons as well. The natural conditions of a frontier region, with plenty of land and few people, made for high wage rates, and high labor costs made for labor-extensive use of the land—often pastoralism or simply hunting wild cattle. It was tempting in these conditions to use force in order to make people work some of the land more intensively. As the Indian populations declined in Mexico and Peru, the Spanish turned increasingly to various forms of peonage. On the eastern frontiers of Europe, the landed class tightened the bonds of serfdom. The solution found for America's tropical lowlands was slavery.

But Africans were not the only enforced immigrants to the New World. Convicts, unsuccessful rebels against the government, and indentured workers who bound themselves more or less voluntarily to serve for a period of years were shipped off to the Americas in large numbers. Indians were also enslaved and used for plantation agriculture, especially in Brazil. Of the three sources of labor—Africa, America, and Europe—it was soon clear that the Africans survived best in the tropical American environment. At the time, African superiority in this respect was attributed to some special quality of the Negro race, but modern knowledge of epidemiology shows that early environment rather than race is the true explanation. Europeans died in large numbers in the American tropics, just as they died in even larger numbers in the African tropics. Indians also died on contact with Afro-European diseases, but Africans were comparatively immune both to tropical diseases and to the ordinary range of diseases common on the Afro-

Eurasian land mass. Migration from Africa to the Americas brought higher death rates for the first generation, but lower rates than those of Europeans who made the equivalent move.

Given the choice of slavery as a labor system and the fact that Africans were the most efficient workers, the problem of supply remained. A large-scale slave trade would have been impossible if Africa had been truly primitive; European death rates on the coast guaranteed as much. But Africa was not primitive. Developed commercial networks were already in existence before the discovery of America, both in West Africa and the southern savanna. African rulers often enslaved war prisoners, and the prisoners were sold into the slave trade—often for shipment to distant places where escape was less likely. Some were exported across the Sahara to North Africa, and the Portuguese were briefly in the business of buying slaves in one part of Africa and selling them in another, even before the demand from American plantations drew the focus of the slave trade across the Atlantic.

But slavery in Africa was different from slavery on an American plantation. A slave was without rights at the moment of his capture; he could be killed or sold. He continued without rights until he was sold to an ultimate master in Africa—or else to the Europeans for transportation overseas. If he ended up on an American plantation, his rights would be few and he was treated as a mere labor unit. But in Africa, slavery was not mainly an economic institution. The object in buying a slave was to increase the size of one's own group, more often for prestige or military power than for the sake of wealth. Women were therefore more desirable than men, but men and women alike were assimilated into the master's social group. They had rights as well as obligations. In many cases, a second-generation slave could no longer be sold. And slaves belonging to important people could often rise to positions of command over free men.

The Slave Trade in Africa

The Atlantic slave trade thus tapped an existing African slave trade, but in doing so it sent people into a very different kind of slavery. Over the centuries, it diverted increasing numbers to the coast for sale to Europeans. The organization of this trade varied greatly from one part of Africa to the next. In some regions, Europeans built trade forts; twenty-seven were constructed on the Gold Coast over a distance of only about 220 miles. African authorities allowed the Europeans to exercise sovereignty within the forts themselves, but they often charged rent for the land the fort stood on. Other trading posts were nothing more than a few unfortified houses onshore for the storage of trade goods and a tightly fenced yard for slaves awaiting shipment. In that case, the Europeans who stayed onshore between ships' visits did so with the permission of the African ruler, and under his protection. Another form of trade was the "ship trade," in which Europeans sailed down the coast, calling at likely ports, but without leaving European agents permanently stationed onshore.

Whatever the point of trade, elaborate customary procedures had come into existence by the end of the sixteenth century. Trade normally began with a payment to the local authorities, partly a gift to demonstrate good will and partly a tax. Each section of the coast had its own trade currency of account—the "bar" (originally an iron bar), the "ounce" (originally an ounce of gold dust), a form of brass currency called manillas, or cowrie shells from the Indian Ocean. Various European commodities were customarily valued at so many bars or ounces. Bargains were struck in terms of the number of bars or ounces to be paid for a slave and then once more in terms of the "sorting" of different European goods that would be used to make up that value.

The internal trade to the coast was more diverse. In some African kingdoms, such as late-eighteenth-century Dahomey, the slave trade was a royal monopoly, tightly controlled for the profit of the state. Other states, such as Futa Toro on the Senegal River, sold few slaves themselves but charged heavy tolls for the privilege of shipping slaves through the country on the way to the coast. Still other states expanded by conquest in order to be able to control the passage of slaves. The kingdom of Akwamu followed a pattern of expansion in the late seventeenth century, moving to the east and west of the Volta River in present-day Ghana, but some distance back from the coast. After a period of growing strength based on revenue from the flow of trade across the kingdom, Akwamu was able to reach down to the coast itself in the 1680s and dictate terms to the coastal trading states and the European garrisons alike.

Other African societies adjusted to the demand for slaves, changing their own social and political institutions. Along the fringes of the Niger delta, the Ijo had been settled for centuries as fishermen and exporters of salt to the interior. Early in the eighteenth century, a series of new city-states like Nembe, Bonny, and Kalabari came into existence, with a commercial and political organization designed expressly to serve the demand for slaves. Each city-state was divided internally into a series of "canoe houses," in effect a commercial firm based on the extended family plus domestic slaves. The houses operated large trading canoes, vessels that might have fifty to a hundred paddlers and mount a small cannon. Trade was highly competitive between houses, and within a house command went to the most successful traders. A slave might rise to become head of the house. The Ijo canoes on the creeks of the delta were supplied, in turn, by other trade networks leading to the waterside. The Aro subgroup among the Ibo, for example, had small colonies of Aro settled in towns throughout Iboland. Slaves were passed from one Aro community to another until they were sold to the Ijo and finally to the Europeans. The Aro enjoyed this special position partly because they also controlled an important religious shrine, and many of the slaves they collected were originally given as sacrifices at the shrine, though in fact they ended in the Americas.

African societies south of the tropical forest also adjusted to the trade in slaves. By the late seventeenth century, the Jaga, who had first appeared as destructive raiders a century earlier, turned to commerce. Their kingdom of Imbangala, inland from the Portuguese post at Luanda, drew slaves from a wide range of central Africa. A little later, the Ovimbundu in the hinterland of Benguela took the same course. Bihé and Mbailundu in particular among the Ovimbundu states became wealthy on the basis of trade routes reaching far into the interior, ultimately as far as Katanga. Like Imbangala to the north, the Ovimbundu states were far too strong to be threatened by Portuguese power on the coast. In time, a rough alliance came into existence, in which the Portuguese acquiesced to the trade monopoly of the inland kingdoms for the sake of having a regular and plentiful supply of slaves delivered to the coast.

East Africa also made a small contribution to the slave trade, especially the hinterland of Mozambique City. (To the north of Cape Delgado, slaves from the Swahili coast were almost all directed toward Arabia and Persia, though this trade was small until the early nineteenth century.) The principal African carriers of the trade within southeastern Africa were the Yao from the vicinity of Lake Malawi. They first went into the long-distance ivory trade and then shifted to slaves as demand increased in the course of the eighteenth century. For southeastern Africa, the most important destination of that period was the Mascarene Islands in the Indian Ocean, where the French developed sugar plantations on the pattern of the West Indies. A few thousand nevertheless found their way around the Cape of Good Hope into the slave trade of the Atlantic.

The Growth and Incidence of the Slave Trade

The European demand for slaves grew slowly and steadily; over many decades African institutions adapted to meet the demand. From an annual average of less than 2000 slaves imported into the Americas each year in the century before 1600, the trade grew to about 55,000 a year for the eighteenth century as a whole. The peak decade for the whole history of the trade was the 1780s, with about 70,000 to 75,000 slaves arriving in the Americas each year; deliveries reached more than 100,000 in a few individual years. At least for the crucial period from

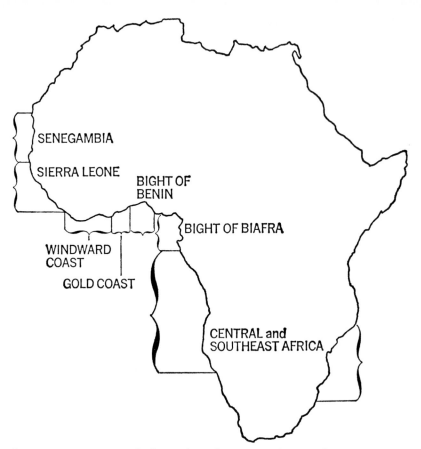

Approximate sources of the eighteenth-century slave trade, 1711–1810. Sample based on combined Anglo-French-Portuguese exports.

Senegambia	192	(3.7%)
Sierra Leone	113	(2.2%)
Windward Coast	396	(7.7%)
Gold Coast	475	(9.2%)
Bight of Benin	1005	(19.5%)
Bight of Biafra	824	(16.0%)
Central and Southeast	2148	(41.7%)
(Total)	5153	

Source: P. D. Curtin, *The Atlantic Slave Trade*, (Madison: University of Wisconsin Press, 1969), pp. 221, 228.

1711 to 1810, it is possible to estimate the drain of population from various regions of Africa by taking the combined estimates of the exports carried by the three most important carriers—England, France, and Portugal (see map). While the map represents the origins of something more than half of all those carried, it also leaves out some important aspects of the trade. During that century, the sources of the trade shifted dramatically from one part of the coast to another. The Gold Coast, for example, supplied almost a quarter of the Anglo-French exports in the 1720s, but only about 8 percent in the 1790s. Meanwhile, the Bight of Biafra rose with the development of the Ijo-Aro trade network from about 2 percent of the trade in the 1720s to 42 percent in the first decade of the nineteenth century. Or again, the exports from central Africa doubled between the 1770s and the 1780s. In short, while the demand for slaves was relatively steady, it was met by rapid shifts from one source of supply to another, depending on African political conditions or the development of new trade routes from the interior.

North Americans, with a view of world history that centers on their own country, often think of the slave trade as a flow of people from Africa to the United States. In fact, about one third of all slaves landed in the Americas went to Brazil; about a half went to the Caribbean islands and mainland; no more than a twentieth came to the United States. Yet the Afro-America population of the United States today is one of the largest in the New World. The explanation lies in a sharp and important demographic distinction between North America and the American tropics. While the Negro population of the North American colonies began to grow from natural increase at a very early date, the slave population of the tropical plantations suffered an excess of deaths over births. This meant that the slave trade could not be a one-shot affair, importing a basic population that could then maintain its own numbers. It had to be continuous merely to maintain the existing level of population; any growth of the plantation economy required still more slaves from Africa.

Several factors help to account for this demographic peculiarity. Disease environment was important in the first generation, since both morbidity and mortality rates were higher among slaves raised in Africa than they were among the American-born. Planters also imported about two men for every woman, and they worked the women in the fields along with the men, preferring to have their labor rather than creating the kind of social setting in which they would be willing to have children.

The planters may have been correct, on strictly economic grounds, in believing that it was cheaper to import new labor from Africa than to allow the leisure, additional rations, and other privileges that might have encouraged a high birth rate among the slaves. The real cost of slaves was very small indeed before the middle of the eighteenth century. In 1695, for example, a slave could be bought in Jamaica for about £20 currency, or about the same value as six hundred pounds of raw sugar sold on the London market, or the European cost of sixteen trade guns for sale in Africa. All things being equal, a new slave could be expected to add more than six hundred pounds to the plantation's production in a single year. Yet a prime slave on the coast of Africa cost only about eight guns or a half ton of iron in bars—little enough to allow a handsome profit on the slave trade itself.

But the real price of slaves in Africa rose steadily during the eighteenth century. One result was to make planters think twice about their policy of importing slaves, rather than allowing them to breed naturally. By the 1770s, several Caribbean planters began to readjust by balancing the number of men and women on their estates, granting special privileges to child-rearing mothers and time off for child care. It is uncertain how generally these new polities were applied, but some of the older colonies, such as Barbados, began to achieve a self-perpetuating slave population by about 1800. Even where slaves were still imported, the demand tended to drop as the local birth rate rose, and the total number imported dropped in each decade from 1790 to 1820. When the United States, Great Britain, and Denmark abolished their own part of the slave trade in the first decade of the nineteenth century, the planters complained, but the really serious need for continued slave imports was nearing its end—at least in the older plantation areas.

The slave trade nevertheless continued well into the nineteenth century. In spite of British efforts to halt the trade by a partial blockade of the African coast—and by diplomatic pressure on Portugal, Brazil, and Spain—a sugar boom in Cuba and a coffee boom in southern Brazil brought a new demand for slaves from places where the plantation economy was newly introduced in that century. The slave trade therefore lasted until Brazil decided, in 1850, to enforce its own anti-slave trade laws and Spain made a similar decision for its Cuban colony in the 1860s.

The Impact of the Slave Trade on Africa

Leaving aside the unanswerable question of what Africa might have become over these centuries without the slave trade, some evidence for assessing the impact of the trade is available. We know that most of the slaves sent to the Americas were captured in war. Some warfare took place in order to supply slaves to the trade, and all warfare produced captives who could be sold. Thus, the rise and fall of African states, contested successions, or periods of chronic warfare between states attracted slave dealers who followed the armies and purchased the prisoners. Famine was another cause of enslavement in the regions of unreliable rainfall, where a series of bad harvests forced people to sell their domestic servants, or even their kin and themselves. Judicial condemnation for crime or political dissent also sent some people on their way to the Americas.

But the knowledge that warfare was the principal cause of enslavement in Africa is not as useful for assessing the impact of the trade as one might suppose. If a war took place with the specific and sole aim of capturing slaves, then the slave trade can be blamed for the damage to society at large. When, however, people were enslaved in the course of wars that took place for other reasons, the slave trade was a neutral factor. It might even have been beneficial; all wars are destructive, but a war fought so as to maximize the number of prisoners might well be less destructive than most. Our present knowledge is enough to indicate that both types of warfare took place in Africa, but not enough to tell which type was more common. On one side, historians can point to spectacular events like the collapse of the empire of Oyo in present-day Nigeria, a political change which led to a whole series of wars lasting for many decades in the early nineteenth century. It is clear that these wars were fought over real issues, not merely to supply the slave trade—yet they supplied more slaves to the trade than any other source in their time. In other cases, historians have detected what appears to have been a "gun-slave cycle," where an African state armed itself with guns, used them to capture unarmed neighbors, who were sold for still more guns. Once caught in this cycle, it was hard to escape. Sooner or later, the neighboring peoples would have guns as well; at that point, slave raiding to buy guns might be necessary for survival. Cases can be found where African states, like Dahomey in the late eighteenth century, reorganized as a military machine for the supply of slaves. But the gun-slave cycle may have been comparatively rare. The long reloading time of the typical eighteenth-century muzzle-loader limited its advantage against rapid-fire bowmen in the forest or wooded savanna. In the open savanna, cavalry was still the dominant military arm far into the nineteenth century.

Still another problem in assessing the impact of the trade is the obvious variation from one African society to another. Some societies were completely destroyed, others may have become wealthy by selling their neighbors to the Europeans, still others were never seriously involved in the trade at all—either as sellers or as victims. We might be able to arrive at a better assessment if we knew more about the level of African populations during the period of the trade; we could thus make some estimates as to the per capita drain of population. But it could still be argued that the underlying influence of the trade was far more profound than any mere drain of population or change in the incidence of warfare. Having been isolated from the intercommunicating zone, the Africans of the western coasts had, in the arrival of seaborne Europeans, both an opportunity and a challenge. If they had responded by seeking new products to sell in return for the Indian textiles and European hardware offered by the maritime trade, they might well have been led to new economic institutions, technological innovations, and a more rapid rate of economic development than ever before. As it was, the Europeans wanted slaves, and the challenge of meeting this demand diverted African creativity to an essentially unproductive enterprise. When the slave trade finally ended, African societies took up the challenge of supplying products rather than people, but time was already running out; the European invasions came before the adjustment could be completed. It seems clear from this point of view that, at the very least, the slave trade forestalled some of the possible fruits of more intense contact with the outside world.

On the other hand, it is hard to sustain the view that the slave trade destroyed African civilization or set Africa back on its path to progress. African civilization was not destroyed, and Africa made progress during this period in spite of slave trade. Literacy spread in the western sudan with the spread of Islam. Literacy in English and Portuguese spread along the coast, where slave dealers learned to read and write and sometimes sent their children to Europe for education. Recent studies of African states like Ashanti show a continuous development from small-scale, kinship-based political units to the institutions of a large state, capable of assimilating its conquered territories and exercising administrative control that was at least as effective as that of feudal monarchies in western Europe before the thirteenth century. Metallurgy and textile production also improved, and hand-loomed cotton cloths were sold into world trade during the eighteenth century, before the cheaper machine-made cloth from Europe drove them from the market. In short, measured by technology, there is no doubt that African societies advanced during the period of the slave trade, though it is equally certain that the advance was too slow to close the gap between African technology and that of the intercommunicating zone.

Suggested Readings

Two scholarly works that provide vivid coverage of the European slave trade are Basil Davidson, *Black Mother: The Years of the African Slave Trade* (Boston: Little, Brown, 1961), and Philip D. Curtin, *The Atlantic Slave Trade: A Census* (Madison: University of Wisconsin Press, 1969). Eric Williams, *Capitalism and Slavery* (New York: Capricorn Books, 1966), attempts to place in historical perspective the relationship between early capitalism as exemplified by Great Britain and the Negro slave trade, Negro slavery, and the general colonial trade of the sixteenth and seventeenth centuries. Readings on slavery from ancient times to the present are available in *Slavery: A Comparative Perspective,* ed. Robin W. Winks (New York: New York University Press, 1972).

Skills and Resources in Late Traditional China

Mark Elvin

Until the fourteenth century, China led the world in technological development. Gunpowder, silk manufacture, the compass, printing, paper-making, and a host of other Chinese innovations spread throughout the Old World, stimulating economic development and adding to the world's store of learning. The Chinese leadership came to an end at the close of the thirteenth century, from which time it was Western Europe that led in technological advances, in a steady movement that led directly to the Industrial Revolution and European world dominance. Although Chinese civilization did not become stagnant, the subsequent innovations that were made in China seemed to have relatively little effect on its society and economy.

This reading selection investigates the degree to which China abandoned the path of progress through technology and the reasons for China's failure to maintain its position of technological leadership. The author finds that, although numerous advances were made during the period, they were directed primarily toward allowing more productive use of existing resources, and that the increased production these advances facilitated was quickly absorbed by a growing population. If anything, China lost technological leadership to the Europeans because the Chinese were too practical. They regarded "excessive ingenuity" as a vice and valued technology only as a means to a concrete end. The Europeans, on the other hand, often viewed innovation as an end in itself and brought to technology a playful and enthusiastic spirit that was lacking in the Chinese.

By the later Middle Ages both Europe and China had mechanized manufacture. By this I mean they had machines that could be substituted for a complex operation by the human hand and perform many such operations simultaneously, using inanimate power if appropriate. In both areas these machines were approximately identical. They were devices with multiple spindles for twisting and doubling silk and other thread. The European version is the *filatorium* or *torcitorium* of Lucca, invented in the thirteenth century. Its Chinese contemporaries were the water-powered machines for twisting hemp and silk described in Wang Chen's *Treatise on Agriculture* of 1313.

They were destined for very different careers. The filatorium was the direct ancestor of Arkwright's spinning-frame and the textile machinery of the first Industrial Revolution. The Chinese machines were without direct progeny, except perhaps the hand-operated silk-doubling and twisting machines of a somewhat different design that were used in the nineteenth century and are discussed below.

These contrasting fates are the key to the central concern of this paper. In Europe there was a period of several centuries of increasingly active technical experimentation and innovation, such that the advances embodied in the characteristic triumphs of the first Industrial Revolution were, in purely technical terms, relatively slight. This was even true of the railway and the steam engine. It was the economic aspects that were revolutionary. In their impact on supply, and indirectly on demand, these advances brought the new technology across some sort of qualitative threshold.

During the same period, from the fourteenth to the eighteenth century, China did not remain inactive in the field of technology, though creating nothing to compare in world-historical significance with earlier contributions like printing and gunpowder. What is puzzling is why this activity added up to so little in terms of qualitative change. The problem is approached here in three steps.

The factual picture is still so hazy that our first concern must be to establish at least the outlines of technological progress in China during Ming and Ch'ing times. This is really too big a task for so short a paper, and the reader is cautioned that every conclusion in this poorly documented area is more than usually provisional. Since a technical evaluation of a machine or a process is necessary before we can test any economic hypothesis about its use, diffusion, or neglect, many of the arguments advanced below rest perforce on insecure foundations.

Our second concern will be to try to find a way of accounting for

SKILLS AND RESOURCES IN LATE TRADITIONAL CHINA   By Mark Elvin, from *China's Modern Economy in Historical Perspective*, ed. Dwight H. Perkins (Stanford: Stanford University Press, 1975), pp. 85–114.

the pattern of changes that emerges from the preceding survey. Here I shall argue that much of what happened, and much of what did not happen, may be explained by a greater interest on the part of the Chinese in improving the return from already accessible natural resources than in making labor or capital more productive. But there is at least one major obstacle to such a simple approach. This is the almost unchanging state of hydraulic technology. Given the enormous pressures that were almost certainly operating for better methods of pumping both in agriculture and in mining, sectors where advances could have yielded a spectacular payoff in food, metals, and fuels, it is astonishing that nothing was accomplished. What is more, inhibition due to restraints associated with the high-level equilibrium trap seems to have only the most limited relevance here. There *were* better methods that did not involve science-based inputs. Cultural factors would seem, by a process of elimination, to have played an important part in retarding invention and diffusion.

The third objective is to evaluate what impact the technical advances made in the late traditional period had on output. Except for restricted localities and periods, the nonhomogeneity of resources across both space and time renders misleading any attempt to estimate the impact of improvements from the scattered statistics that exist. The fertility of land varies from place to place; as exploitation progresses, deposits of metallic ore become harder to mine. We have therefore to rely in good part on the evidence of our impressions, and this suggests that technological change was just about sufficient to stabilize the standard of living as the population grew and the average quality of resources suffered a long-term Ricardian decline. Looking at the question from the standpoint recently made familiar by Richard Wilkinson, we might equally hypothesize that population growth stimulated only sufficient technological growth to preserve a familiar equilibrium.

Progress: Certain, Probable, and Possible

In our analysis of technological change we need to make two sets of distinctions. The first is tripartite: between Chinese inventions and improvements, the adoption of new methods from abroad, and the diffusion of superior practices already well known in one region during the preceding age. The second is along a sliding scale: estimating the differing degrees of probability that a given technique was adopted in the late traditional period. Only rarely is it possible to be confident that we know when something was done for the first time; and many of the machines and methods listed below may eventually turn out to have a more venerable ancestry than they are credited here with having.

Perhaps the most spectacular addition to the post-Mongol countryside was the Chinese type of windmill, which resembled a cross between a small sailing-ship and a merry-go-round. The earliest surviving description comes from the first half of the seventeenth century:

> In some cases [pallet-] pumps are turned not by men but by an ox. A [horizontal] wooden plate, like a cartwheel but with a larger circumference, is fitted with cogs that turn the driveshaft of the pump. This economizes on the [human] energy needed to make the pump go round, and is twice as effective. In some cases not even an ox is employed; rather the wind is used to turn the pump. The method of construction resembles the ox-powered pump, but the sails are set on the wheel [on masts mounted vertically around the rim], and advantage is taken of the wind to make it rotate. This is the most ingenious of all the machines used in farming. It is not suited to common use, however, for when great winds blow the pump is liable to be smashed.

In central Kiangsu in the present century, wind-pumps of this sort were said to be able to irrigate 50 mou in a day, given a good wind.

Another advance in pneumatic technology was the adaptation of the closed-in rotary fan to the ventilation of mineshafts. This machine, used until this innovation for winnowing grain, consisted of a paddle-wheel turning in a circular box with an air intake at its hub and a peripheral vent. The earliest illustration and description seem to be those in Wu Ch'i-chün's *Illustrated Summary of the Mines of Yunnan,* published in 1845, so this may be a Ch'ing development.

Progress was made in various forms in the control of heat and humidity: in incubators for poultry eggs, the killing of silkworm pupae for the temporary preservation of the cocoons, greenhouses and the forcing of plants, and cellars for the spinning of cotton yarn in a suitably moist atmosphere. Only the last of these, however, can be indubitably dated as late traditional.

According to Pao Shih-ch'en, writing in the first half of the nineteenth century:

> If one puts [eggs] in a basket, places it high up and covers it with grass, so causing them to incubate, they will hatch out of the basket in 15 days. (The present-day method is for everyone to use heating by fire. . . . The old method is as I have described. It is definitely not unfounded gossip, so I have preserved a record of the theory to facilitate its experimental use.)

How old was the "old method"? The earliest reference to incubation by fire that I have found is in a Ming miscellany compiled by T'ien I-heng and quoted in Ch'en Yüan-lung's early-eighteenth-century *Reflected Sources on the Sciences:* "In Kwangtung they hatch ducklings by warming ducks' eggs in hot water. In Chekiang they hatch them in a different fashion, by warming ducks' eggs over a fire." The first proper description of an incubator seems to be in Ch'ü Ta-chün's *New Discourses on Kwangtung,* published in 1700:

> Many of the people of Kwangtung are skilled at incubating ducks. They take five or six hundred ducks' eggs to each basket and put them in a clay hut, cover them with coverlets, and encircle them with woodchips in which they kindle both slow and quick fire [probably fire smothered with ashes for controlled burning]. Once the eggs are slightly warm, they switch the positions of the high and low baskets and continue to change them back and forth about six or seven times in every day-and-night period. On the eleventh day they put them up onto a rack, the slats of this rack likewise being covered with coverlets, which are reduced according to time. After a month has elapsed, the ducklings diligently peck through their shells and emerge.

From this we can establish that there was probably a diffusion of advanced incubation technique from Chekiang to Kwangtung in the late traditional period. But it is not clear when the Chekiang poultrymen abandoned the haybox for the charcoal-fired double-shelled earthenware incubators described by Franklin King and other modern observers. On the strength of Pao Shih-ch'en's observations and the general timing of the somewhat analogous methods described in the following passages, we may guess that it was in Yüan or Ming times.

Only about ten days are available for reeling the silk off live cocoons. After this point the moths emerge and tear the filaments. When modern filatures were introduced late in the nineteenth century, it became essential to preserve the cocoons so that the machinery could be operated round the year. But even before this, killing some of the pupae before reeling could usefully take pressure off the reelers. The two major agricultural compendia of the Yüan dynasty, Wang Chen's *Treatise* and the officially sponsored *Essentials of Farming and Sericulture,* describe three ways of doing this: steaming, sunning, and soaking in brine. During late traditional times, two more methods were added to the repertoire: packing with salt in an air-tight jar and killing by heat-drying. The first of these is mentioned in Pao Shih-ch'en's *Four Arts for the Governance of the Common People* from the early nineteenth century and also, with some minor variations, in Wei Chieh's *Collected Notes on Sericulture* of 1898(?). Wei recommends the Yüan steaming technique except in humid weather, when drying is a problem. Then the following practice is preferred:

> *Drying Cocoons.* When there is not the time to reel many of the cocoons, and so reason to fear that moths will break out, drying the cocoons on a brick bed warmed by fire will ensure that no moths emerge. If the brick bed has an extensive surface, it is possible to dry several hundred catties of cocoons in a day. In the

north, where the brick beds are kept very warm, it is necessary for the heat to be evenly distributed and for the cocoons to be turned over from time to time so that they are dried through to the appropriate degree and do not become too scorched. Smoky fuel should not be used. The best way of drying cocoons is that found in eastern Szechwan: hot air is brought into the brick bed from outside, so there is no trouble from damp heat and no anxiety that they will be dried up. But when silk filaments undergo drying by heat, the color and sheen inevitably suffer.

It was probably the concern with quality apparent in this last sentence that limited the use of these techniques before the coming of the modern filature. Even with modern steam-killing the silk is easily damaged.

I have made no systematic inquiry into the origins of the Chinese type of greenhouse, but its association with the luxury horticultural market generated by the new northern capital at Peking suggests that it may have been a Yüan or Ming development. Hsieh Ch'ao-che, writing in late Ming times, disapproved of the uses to which it was put:

> Out-of-season flowers are regularly among the items presented these days at Court. All of them, however, have been produced in earthen cellars where they have been forced by fires placed around them. Thus peonies can blossom in the depths of the winter. It is reckoned that this work costs a dozen ounces of silver or more per plant. This is merely esteeming what is hard to obtain; and, in truth, things out of season are proper neither to Heaven nor to Earth.

There is a full description of these "cellars" in the *Mémoires concernant les Chinois,* written by missionaries in eighteenth-century Peking. They were partially underground structures, sunk to a depth of seven to twelve feet, with stepped floors so that all the plants had equal access to the sunlight, and thick walls on three sides rising to ten or twelve feet above ground. The fourth side, which was always the one facing south, was entirely covered with paper windows backed by heavy matting blinds that could be raised or lowered as desired. Heating was provided by brick stoves or charcoal braziers; and humidity was maintained by distributing vases of water about the interior. The growth of plants could be forced by filling the houses with steam, and there were special techniques (whose efficacy awaits trial by experiment) for opening the buds. One such method was to place the plants on racks over a trench full of compost blended with ox or goat urine and pour boiling water onto this mixture.

One by-product of this sort of expertise was the use by northern Chinese of cellars to create the humid atmosphere needed for the spinning of cotton yarn. This was fairly certainly a Ming development, since cotton was hardly spun at all in the north under the Yüan. According to Hsu Kuang-ch'i's *Encyclopedia of Agricultural Policy* of 1639:

> In recent times much cotton has been grown in the north; but it is not convenient to spin or weave it there, the north having an arid climate such that the cotton fibers snap and it is impossible to get a continuous filament. . . . The south is low-lying and humid. Therefore the filaments are tight and fine, and the cloth likewise strong and substantial. These days many people in Hsien-ning [in Ho-chien county, central Hopei] make underground cellars several feet deep and build houses over the top of them, the eaves being only two feet or so above ground. They pierce windows to let in the sunlight. People live in them and make use of the humidity to spin and weave. . . . It would be unusually interesting to know who began this.

Some useful existing machines were improved. Thus a treadle was added to the Yüan cotton gin. This made it necessary to have a flywheel (or bobs on spokes serving the same purpose), which in turn imposed such a torque on the upper roller that it had now to be made of metal rather than wood. A more complicated case is that of the silk-spinning machine, which Wang Chen, writing in 1313, said had been "recently" created on the same lines as the hemp-spinning machine, being "particularly saving of effort as compared to doubling filaments by means of the horizontal board on the open ground." The hemp-spinning machine subsequently went out of use altogether, and a silk-spinning machine does not surface again in the literature until more than 500 years later, in Wei Chieh's book on sericulture written at the end of the nineteenth century. Moreover, Wei's machine differs substantially from Wang's. In place of vertical spindles surmounted by bobbin-rollers (rotating hollow cylinders halfway between fliers and the rings used in ring-spinning), it has simple horizontal pirns (cone-shaped spindles) and draws the threads either around a horizontal roller through a trough of water or across pads of moistened felt. In structural terms, we have here a development analogous to the seventeenth-century European flax-retwisting mills (which also had horizontal pirns and no fliers), unless we are dealing with a fresh start or an unacknowledged borrowing.

There were probably one or two advances in metallurgy. The extraction of pure zinc may have been one of these. Analysis of the content of Chinese coins shows that the first virtually pure zinc specimens date from the fifteenth century, and the percentage of zinc in alloy coins rises sharply after this time. It is known that coal was used in China for iron smelting by means of a crucible process long before Sung times, and some scholars believe that coke, invented during the T'ang dynasty for cooking food, was not long afterward also employed in ferrous metallurgy. If so, the practice seems not to have survived into late traditional times, although anthracite continued to be used in the ironworks of Shansi and Szechwan. This is a curious development, since coke, in a variety of grades and large quantities, was used for smelting silver and copper in the Ch'ing period. Presumably the use of crucibles, whose successful manufacture eluded Europeans trying to smelt iron with coal in the seventeenth century, made it unnecessary to use a refined fuel, except perhaps for extra heat.

Agriculture is the most difficult sector to evaluate. The Ming and Ch'ing periods saw the introduction of new crops, new fertilizers, and new varieties of familiar food plants, but it is possible that the biggest economic impact came from refinements in the application of long-known basic principles regarding rotations, intercropping, and soil preservation. There seems to have been a slow shift from a mixture of monoculture and polyculture toward a symbiotic farming in which every plant was a part of a deliberately designed interlocking whole. A further contribution was made by the diffusion of superior local methods, sometimes the length and breadth of the empire, and often through official or semiofficial initiative.

The new food plants introduced from the Americas were maize, peanuts, and sweet and white potatoes. At the same time tobacco, also from the New World, and opium, long known as a medicine, became widely cultivated cash crops. Here, as an illustration of this process, is the seventeenth-century scholar Yeh Meng-chu describing how tobacco came to his native Shanghai:

> *Smoke leaves.* These . . . originally came from Fukien. When I was young I heard my elders say that in Fukien there were some who smoked them by inhaling, and that doing this made people drunk. They were called "dry wine." But there were none in this locality. At the end of the Ch'ung-chen reign [1628–44] a man surnamed P'eng in the county capital got some seeds from I know not where, and grew them here. He picked the leaves and dried them in the dark. Then those who worked at this business cut them into fine shreds, and they were sold to merchants from places far away. The local people still did not dare to try them. Later a severe prohibition was issued by the authorities. . . . People were not allowed to grow them or merchants to traffic in them. Those who disobeyed were to be punished in the same way as those who had dealings with foreigners. . . . Tobacco cultivation therefore came to an end. At the beginning of the Shun-chih reign all the soldiers smoked tobacco; and in next to no time dealers gathered and cultivators multiplied, obtaining redoubled profits.

The new fertilizers were oilseed cakes (made from soya, rape, and cotton) and green fertilizers such as clover that were turned over and spaded into the soil or worked into a mud-and-clover compost. Pao Shih-ch'en describes the benefits of planting some acreage in rape:

When growing wheat or barley [as a winter crop] would use up too much fertilizer and labor, one should divide one's land into three sections. Plant two of these with wheat or barley, and the other with rape. Rape is harvested for use as a vegetable in the late winter and early spring. Much of it can be sold. One mou yields two piculs of seeds from which 80 catties of oil may be pressed and 120 oilcakes obtained. These will fertilize three mou of land and their [fertilizing] power will safeguard the harvests. Rape is as profitable as wheat or barley; the fertilizer and labor needed are similar; and the stalks will serve as fuel just as wheat-stalks do. But the fertilizer obtained can revitalize the exhausted wheat-fields.

An example of a new strain of a known grain developed in late traditional times is the salt-resistant rice of Ch'üan-chou.

The late traditional concern with the design of rotations and combinations of crops is evident in Pao Shih-ch'en's *Four Arts for the Governance of the Common People.* Turnips and cabbages should be used to restore the fertility of fields where cereals had been grown. In shallow-pit cultivation, "one grows in sequence beans, millet, taro, and potatoes." "Growing beans beneath mulberry trees is also of benefit to the mulberries." "Barley and broadbeans make a suitable base for a rice-seedling field." In other sources one finds a sharp awareness that cotton and sugarcane should be alternated with rice or other grains. A sort of inverted rotation involved moving the soil rather than the crops. King noted that the Chekiang farmers periodically exchanged the soil of their mulberry orchards with that of their paddy-fields. As Pao Shih-ch'en observed, in discussing the "recent" adoption of transplanting for taro: "Plants all like a change of soil and receive fertility [from the move]."

Intercropping was also intensified in this period, and Pao describes a characteristic system of double-cropping with intercropping for either the first or second harvest:

> Two harvests [of rice] are common in the southern regions. For the first harvest [the farmers] transplant the rice-shoots just as for early-ripening rice elsewhere. In the middle of the sixth moon, ten days before reaping, they broadcast seed beneath the stalks of grain. When the first crop is cut, the sprouts of the second are four to five inches high. They are weeded with a hoe as in dry farming. At the end of the eighth moon they are harvested and barley planted as usual. . . . After the early-ripening rice has been harvested it is [also] possible to plant buckwheat for reaping in the eighth moon, and before this harvest to scatter-sow mud-beans beneath the grain-stalks in the same way as the second rice crop is sown. So long as there is plenty of fertilizing power, the fields are not damaged.

Other possibilities were planting cotton under millet or mud-beans under rice, mixing garden peas with wheat, and sowing early- and late-ripening rice at the same time for two separate crops, at the cost presumably of doing without transplanting. There were also some minor changes in the ways of growing indigo, sorghum, and hemp.

The most impressive example of late traditional skill in soil preservation is to be found in Pao's account of how to open up marginal hill lands and prevent erosion:

> From the summit of the hill downward divide [the land] into seven levels. The fifth level and those below it may be opened up for cultivation. One begins with the lowest level. (In general, hills shaped like mounds are opened up like upland fields. Stony hills that are opened up are 70 to 80 percent rocks, and 20 to 30 percent soil. Whenever there is a heavy rain the mountain streams break forth in torrents and sweep the rich topsoil away downstream. Therefore [the land] becomes unusable after three years. Furthermore, the richness of the hills adheres to the surface; once streams have been opened up to flow through them, the richness dries up within and one is constantly afraid of drought.) One starts by cutting down the undergrowth and grasses on the spot, and burning them. Then one opens up [the soil] with a heavy wedge-shaped hoe, using one chopping blow to every two pounding blows.
>
> When one first opens up land, no matter whether in summer or winter, one begins by planting a crop of turnips everywhere. These plants are good at loosening the soil and at guaranteeing a harvest. Their roots serve as vegetables, and the leaves can be fed to pigs or used as fertilizer. . . . Next one plants maize and darnel mixed together with sweet sorghum. Where the topsoil is relatively heavy one may also grow cotton. In every case one must [also] choose some moderately level ground and dig ten or more pits in which to grow taro, yams, melons, and greens to serve as vegetables, and to prepare [the soil] for grains. (If there are many people in the mountain hut there will be no shortage of manure. Therefore one should prepare lots of pits for growing crops.) After every two years one changes one level, proceeding gradually upward. What is more, the fertility of the soil moves downward from above. If the upper half of the land is not opened up, the fertility will flow from its surface and be retained by the lower levels, making it fertile everywhere. Furthermore, one should estimate the point at which the mountain streams are at about the same height as the ground that has been opened up, and excavate winding [contour-line] ditches to these streams, using stones and mud to dam the water. . . . When the fifth level has been reached, the richness from the top four levels will flow down every day to the lower levels, and one can start the cycle again from the beginning, reaping harvests without end.

The effect of such skills must have been greatly to extend the area accessible to cultivation.

The interregional diffusion of agricultural techniques had analogous consequences. An example of a very long-distance transmission may be found in a Ch'ing dynasty poem written by Ch'i Chung. It describes his feelings on seeing wet-field paddy growing in Tz'u-chou, in what is now southern Hopei:

> Some people say the lands of the northeast
> Have soil so porous that water easily runs short.
> Flooded in the morning, they are parched by nightfall.
> How then can one lightly talk of irrigation?
> Success in farming—according to my view—
> Lies in weeding and hoeing to the limit.
> If mud's well blended, cracks won't open in the tilth;
> With plenty of manure, soil becomes like an alluvial deposit.

He adds the following explanatory note:

> Some time ago I helped Ch'iu Wen-ta manage water-conservancy in Chihli [Hopei]. Our talk turned to the farmers' fields, and this is what he told me: "When Kao An-hsiang was managing fields he thought the soil [here] too porous to retain water, and this matter [of wet-field paddy] was neglected. Recently I was reading the section on double plowing in Chou Shih-hsun's gazetteer of Lien-chou prefecture [Ho-p'u, Kwangtung]. He says: 'At the beginning of spring, plow for the first time and then, when the time has come for transplanting, plow and hoe again. The reason for this is that the first plowing is only capable of making the soil open and scatter. It is therefore necessary to plow and hoe again, after which the cracks and leaky crevices in the fields will be filled up and blocked, and they will be resistant to drought.' I tried this out with [two] fields that were as close as the upper and lower lip. The one that had been plowed and hoed only once was the first to dry out when there was a period of drought. The field plowed twice was easily kept from drying up. The appearance of the paddy, flourishing in the one and withered in the other, was quite different in each case."

Two points are worthy of note in this passage. One is that literary sources served to spread technical knowledge. The other is that Kao An-hsiang understood the principle of the controlled experiment.

Presumably, technology usually traveled by means of the movements of skilled workers. This emerges from the proposals made in the fourteenth and fifteenth centuries to bring southeastern methods of water-control in coastal areas to the northeastern seaboard:

> During the T'ai-ting reign-period [1324–27] of the Yüan dynasty, when Yü Chi was an Auxiliary Han-lin Academician, he made the following proposal: "There are reed-swamps to the east of the capital along several thousand li of coastline, reaching northward to the gulf of Liao-yang, and southward bordering on Ch'ing and

Ch'i [Shantung]. The tides that come in every day from the sea have silted them up, so that they are now rich land. We should use the technique of the men of Che [southern Kiangsu and Chekiang] to build dikes to keep the water out, and turn them into fields. We should allow rich persons who want to obtain official rank to gather their followers together and be allocated land. . . . Those able to farm with ten thousand men should be given land for this number, and be the leaders of ten thousand. Similar measures should be adopted for those with a thousand or a hundred. . . . If for five years they have accumulated reserves of grain, they should be given official rank . . . and if they show no failing for ten years, this rank should be made hereditary, as with the system for military officials."

Yü's proposals were not taken up at the time, but in 1352 the Mongol Chancellor Toqto revived them with an added suggestion. Farmers, he said, should be recruited from Kiangnan together with "one thousand each of those able to farm wet-field paddy, and those able to build and repair polders and embankments, who will serve as agricultural instructors." Once again, nothing happened. About a hundred years later, the idea was taken up again, this time by Ch'iu Chün, who also thought that official rank should be bestowed on those leading the enterprise. He advised that people from Chekiang and Fukien with a good knowledge of farming should investigate the possibilities before anything was done on a large scale. Hsü Kuang-ch'i, writing in the first half of the seventeenth century, noted that no progress had been made until the Wan-li reign (1573–1619), and then only on a modest scale. He urged further efforts, but was opposed to people "acquiring official rank by contributing funds for the opening up of land." This phrasing of the last point was a misrepresentation of the original scheme, and together with Hsü's attitude throws an interesting light on the changed nature of land tenure by the late Ming.

The Wan-li breakthrough was inspired by a certain Wang Ying-chiao and accomplished in the military colony lands near Tientsin.

When I saw the region around Tientsin and Ko-hu [Wang wrote], everyone told me that this land had hitherto been saline and un-farmed. Here and there, near the rivers, where it was fertile, there were people growing beans but getting only two piculs a mou. It was my opinion that it was alkaline where there was no [fresh] water, but fertile where there was [fresh] water. If one used the methods of Fukien and Chekiang for dealing with the land along the coast, dug canals, and irrigated with water, it would no doubt be fit to become paddy-fields. For a time, however, neither the civil nor the military authorities were willing to respond. This year they bought cattle and built machinery, cut ditches and constructed embankments, everything being done at one and the same time. . . . Where plenty of manure was used and the men worked hard, yields were from four to five piculs a mou. . . . The dry-field rice, however, withered at once because of the alkalinity. . . . With this the local soldiers and civilians have for the first time learned to trust the methods of land-management of Fukien and Chekiang.

Unfortunately, neither Wang nor Hsü gives any indication of where the know-how came from.

It was probably in late traditional times, too, that animal and human manures were used to fertilize fish ponds. The carp, the foundation of traditional pisciculture, was also to some extent replaced by the pai-lien and the ts'ao, fish that fed off grasses tossed into their pool.

Although Katō Shigeshi argues that there were improvements in the organization of locust-control in late traditional times, there is no evidence that these amounted to much. In the summer of 1269, for example, we already find the relief administrator Ch'en Yun-kung mobilizing more than 2,000 men for locust-catching in Pao-ti county (Hopei). The method they used was the following: "The edge of the field was plowed by an ox to form an extended moat, and in the middle of the moat a small well was dug; one side of the moat was walled with rush matting, and the locusts were driven into it, killed, and buried." This is virtually identical with the late traditional method described in a long poem by Ch'iu Yueh-hsiu in the eighteenth century. Another argument against Katō's hypothesis of better organization in later times is that official incompetence often resulted in any grain spared by the insects being trampled down by the locust-catchers; and official help was often made the pretext for all sorts of exactions on the peasants. Possibly, though, the use of ducks to eat up unfledged locusts was new. Flocks of these birds were also relied on to control the land crabs that infested the newly opened polders of Kiangnan and Kwangtung.

Finally, in regard to our list of improvements originating in China, it seems likely that there was some progress in the art of seafaring north of the mouth of the Yangtze. It is not possible to prove this, but a tentative argument may be constructed on the following lines: (1) Up to and including early Ming times the northern seas were regarded as more dangerous than they were later; (2) there is no obvious reason for the improvement in the safety of navigation in later times; (3) in addition, some fragmentary collateral evidence suggests that the type of boat mainly used, the *sha-ch'uan,* or "sand junk," was either a new creation or greatly improved. These points are developed below.

(1) Sung writers such as Lu I-hao emphasized the dangers of the northern seas. The frequency of disasters was one of the reasons the sea transport of grain from Kiangnan to Peking was discontinued by the Ming government early in the fifteenth century. It is possible that

the institutional arrangements increased the hazards. Fleets set off too early in the year to avoid the bad weather; government ships may have been less sturdily built than private ones, if warships are to be taken as a guide. Yet by the eighteenth century there was an enormous maritime trade between Shanghai and Manchuria; the junks routinely sailed through the icy fogs and the gales of the northern waters in winter; and in spite of occasional major disasters the annual loss of vessels did not exceed 1 percent.

(2) The *Record of the Sea Transport of the Great Yüan Dynasty* indicates that the mariner's compass was used early in the North China sea. Unless its early use was restricted to government ships, greater knowledge of the compass would not seem to be the key to the safer navigation of late Ming and Ch'ing times. One possibility, though, is the official system of inspection and licensing. Boats had to be seaworthy and carry adequate crews for their size, and a record was kept of the number of voyages made. But this is a thin explanation for a major change.

(3) The most important type of ship on the run from Shanghai to Manchuria was the sand-junk. Its tumble-home construction, with gunwales that curved back in toward each other, gave it the strength to resist the undertows and currents off the North China coast. Lee-boards gave it an exceptional maneuverability, as a seventeenth-century gazetteer for Sung-chiang prefecture indicated:

> Only the sand-junk's system of maneuvering on the water is such that it can, by adjusting its lee-boards, advance when it wants, go back when it wants, hover and wheel as if flying, and sail with the wind on the quarter or ahead. Next best are ships like the *ts'ang-chung,* which uses both sails and oars, and is also able to maneuver. Ships like those from Kwangtung and Fukien do not have oars, relying entirely on sails. These ships are large and go with the wind abaft. They are unable to go back in the face of a contrary wind or an opposing tide, and are not convenient for advancing, retiring, or turning.

This is part of a discussion of naval warfare, and a little later it is noted that the sand-junk's lee-boards allowed it to move upwind of larger Japanese pirate vessels—the smaller ones were simply rammed— before attacking with firearms.

Assuming that the sha-ch'uan was the key to safe sailing in the northern seas, what reason is there to think that it was new? Previous scholarly opinion—not lightly to be dismissed—has held that the hull embodied one of the oldest designs in China. Lee-boards were also being used on warships, though with a different hull design, in the late T'ang and Sung. Three points offer a basis for a revisionist hypothesis, though not for any firm conclusion, First, the sand-junk, which never held more than 3,000 piculs of cargo, was much smaller than many of the ships used for the Yüan dynasty sea-transport, which often held up to 9,000 piculs. This in itself hints at some change in design. Second, Nishikawa Jōken, a Japanese astronomer and geographer who was a native of Nagasaki, a regular port of call for these ships, thought that the sand-junks, which he called "Nanking junks," were derived from the flat-bottomed boats that plied the Grand Canal from Nanking to Peking. Since any name containing the word Nanking must be of Ming vintage or later, and this particular canal, whose most elevated reaches were shallower than those of the quite differently aligned T'ang and Sung canals, was of early-fifteenth-century origin (with brief Yüan antecedents), our suspicion of a late date is strengthened. Third, there is clear evidence that new types of junks were produced in late traditional China. One such was the Chekiangese vessel called "Unlike the Three Others," first built in 1699 and used mainly in northern waters. So far as I know, the term sha-ch'uan does not appear until Ming times, which is at least consistent with our hypothesis.

Last of all, we have to look at techniques imported from abroad, concentrating for the moment only on those that found widespread practical use. Outstanding among these were corrective lenses for defective vision. Ming accounts mention only spectacles for farsightedness and middle-aged sight, but Yeh Meng-chu in the early Ch'ing also refers to those for nearsightedness:

> *Spectacles.* When I was young I sometimes chanced to see old people wearing them. I had no idea, however, how much they cost. Later on I heard that those made in the West were the best, and cost from four to five ounces of silver the pair. Glass was used for the body and elephant hide for the stems. Only the very rich could afford them. After the Shun-chih reign [1644–61] the price gradually fell, and a pair cost no more than .5 or .6 of an ounce of silver. Recently many people in Soochow and Hangchow have been making them. They are on sale everywhere, and everyone can get them. At the most expensive a pair is only .007 or .008 of an ounce of silver, or even .002 or .003. All of these are suitable for the general purpose of brightening vision. There is another kind in the West, however, with lenses thicker than leather [presumably convex], which enable the nearsighted to see clearly the minutest details. Farsighted and elderly persons who wear them will, on the contrary, find their vision blurred. There is still no one selling them in the markets, but I suspect that in a few more years the cunning artisans of this region will be making them in large numbers.

John Larner has suggested that spectacles were a major factor in the growth of textual scholarship in Italy after the beginning of the fourteenth century. It is intriguing, in this comparative perspective, that the rise of the school of "empirical research" in China, with its delight in the minutiae of textual criticism, should have coincided with the spread of spectacles in the seventeenth century.

The use of the cylinder-and-piston pump with inlet and outlet valves for projecting a jet of water for fighting fires was probably, but not certainly, introduced by the Jesuits. There is the following description in the *Illustrated Account of Remarkable Machines from the Distant West,* dictated by Schreck (Terrentius) to Wang Cheng in 1627:

> This water-gun puts out fires. . . . Its merit lies in [alone being of any use when] the power of a conflagration rapidly becomes overwhelming and people cannot get near it. What is more, it does not waste a drop of water and it can reach anywhere, no matter how high or far away. . . . It is neither difficult to make nor very expensive. Every city and village should install two or three of these machines, which are advantageous for warding off disasters. We have already made a small version and tried it out with great success.

A century later Chu Hua, who wrote a poem on the use of these "water-dragons" against a fire in his native Shanghai, gave a different version:

> In times past we had only water-bags and tubes for carrying water to fight fires. The present-day method of using the water-dragon was obtained at the beginning of the dynasty from the Japanese by a certain T'ang who lived in Ch'iao-nan in the county capital. After a time it gradually spread to other areas. . . . Its fire-fighting power is a hundred times greater than that of any other device.

Whichever version we adopt, the device was clearly of foreign origin.

The case of the "pulling dragon," the only type of cylinder-and-piston pump used in premodern Chinese mines, is more doubtful. Since it resembles the pumps used in sixteenth-century German mines, and a comparable pump was not introduced into Japan until 1618, presumably as the result of Western contacts, it may well have been imported. But there are other considerations that suggest it may have been an indigenous development. It was of the most rudimentary description, consisting of a circular valved shoe fixed to a long handle working up and down a short travel inside the lower end of a cylinder, into the bottom of which the water could flow freely. The operator kept the shoe below the level of the water in the channel from which it was being pumped; he forced water in through the shoe-valve on the downstroke and pulled it up with the upstroke, hence the Chinese name.

Wu Ch'i-chün provided this description in his mid-nineteenth-century book on the mines of Yunnan: "It is from eight to sixteen feet long, hollow inside, and with a diameter of four to five inches. There is also a wooden or iron rod *of the same length* [sliding inside] and tipped with a piece of leather cut to make a base. It is used to draw up the water." In other words, it was only a little more than a reversed form of the piston air-blower used in the Yunnan mines,* and embodied a principle long known to the Chinese in the buckets with flap-valves on their lower ends used in the brine-wells of Szechwan, a source of inspiration much nearer to Yunnan than the southeastern seacoast. On the other hand, Joseph Needham mentions "piston pumps" employed to drain the bilge-water from junks after the late sixteenth century. It would be interesting to know if they were also of this very simple type.

The Pattern of Technical Change

It is not easy to characterize the trend of technological advance described in the preceding section in terms both appropriate to the subject and acceptable to the modern economist. Broadly speaking, the kind of progress that was best understood, and the only one that was more or less consciously aimed at, was a more effective adaptation to the natural environment, an extension of the range of useful resources. Two minor "improvements" on existing practice epitomize this approach. In Fukien, the Ming dynasty saw the abandoning of salt-boiling in caldrons in favor of solar evaporation, with economies in expenditure on increasingly costly fuel. Sometime in the seventeenth century a Shantung peasant discovered that spirit could be distilled from moldy grain that was useless for any other purpose. Such instances are a reminder that a useful definition of "technical advance" is possible only with reference to the relative cost of resources.

And late traditional China was caught in a severe shortage of resources for its enormous and growing population. The desperate ecological adaptation described by the Ch'ing writer Chou Hsi-p'u was an extreme case but one that dramatized widespread pressures and hazards:

> I was returning to Ning-hsia from Chung-wei in Lan-chou, when I received orders from the prefect to inspect a disaster caused by hail in the Hsiang mountains. These are 80 li south of Chung-wei city, but it was a journey of several hundred li to the site of the disaster, and a weary tramp over huge sand dunes. When I brought out cash to exchange for grain and fodder, none was forthcoming. On asking the reason for this I learned that it was because the people who lived in the mountains ate *p'eng* grasses, some of which were shown to me. There were three kinds: sand p'eng, water p'eng,

---

* There is no reference to a valve halfway up the cylinder, such as was found on German pumps; and the statement that the rod was "of the same length" as the cylinder tends to argue against the existence of such a valve. Thus no use was made of the partial vacuum created beneath the piston on the upstroke.

and soft p'eng. They are prepared for eating by boiling them once in water, straining them out, putting them in water again, and cooking them into a broth. This serves as breakfast and supper, morning and night. Large quantities are dried in readiness for the winter. . . . I ordered some to be boiled and presented to me. So rank and acrid was the taste that I almost could not swallow them. Yet these frontier people eat them all year round.

Behind this there was a story, which Chou disclosed in a poem:

> Their forebears in times past built terraces for farming;
> Ten thousand hoes chopped at the hills till the hills' pulses shifted
> Saline flakes appeared on the sprouts and early stems,
> And they speak of mosquito larvae as big as silk cocoons.
> Onto the ground like rushes they tossed the state-provided hoes;
> And now the sons and grandsons live by chewing grass.

Failure to maintain adequate moisture deep in the soil to prevent salt being drawn to the surface by evaporation had made the land unfit for farming. The colonists had to eat grasses, and to rely on raising the cattle and sheep that were mentioned later in the poem as having suffered from hail. This story reminds us of an important fact about development projects in the late traditional period: they sometimes damaged as much as they developed. The overly dense building of lake-polders could increase the danger of floods by reducing the size of the intervening channels. New irrigation schemes sometimes robbed existing schemes of much of their water.

Understandably, experiment in agriculture was directed at increasing yields per acre. An example of this is the adaptation by P'an Tseng-i, early in the nineteenth century, of the old technique of cultivation in shallow pits to wet-rice paddy. The idea was to do away with the transplanting of rice seedlings, which he held was apt to harm the sprouts, especially in a multiple-crop system which imposed a timing that was less than ideal, and also to do away with the usual secondary wheat crop in such a system, compensating for its loss with heavier yields. Trials by P'an and by Ch'i Yen-huai in the Soochow area reportedly produced exceptional results in the range of 180 to 200 bushels of rice per acre.

Why, then, was this practice not widely adopted? There are two possible technical reasons, and one probable social one. The basic objective of shallow pits, which had been known and used since antiquity, was to conserve moisture. They were found in Yüan and Ming times for growing dry-land crops in areas without adequate well or river water, and sometimes for cotton in years of drought elsewhere. It is not clear what advantage they would have had in wet-rice cultivation in the Yangtze delta; and one wonders if the good results were not due to unusually good soil or especially intensive care. Further, the absence of a supplementary crop reduced the safety margin of the ordinary peasant in the face of bad weather. Finally, tenants in Kiangnan were charged rent only on their rice crop and not on their wheat crop; switching to the exclusive cultivation of rice would have been disastrous for them.

This concern to squeeze the utmost out of resources was combined in the Chinese with a well-developed appreciation of economy of effort. A characteristic illustration of this may be found in the comments of P'eng T'ing-mei on the revival in Ch'ing times of the long-neglected Sung technique known as the "wooden dragon." This was a sausage-shaped raft that could be moored against an embankment on the outer bend of a river to protect it from erosion, and to retain a fill of earth and stones placed between it and the bank. According to P'eng: "The wooden dragon is able to deflect the water so as to protect the dike on one side of a river, and by deflecting the water cause it to cleanse away the silt on the other bank. Compared with installing [temporary] embankments and [draining and] dredging, it is half as much trouble and twice as effective. It is a good method of river protection and should not be forgotten again."

The Chinese appreciation of labor-saving practices was not limited to cases like this, where nature was, with a little art, persuaded to do man's work for him, but also extended to machinery. An example of this is Wei Chieh's praise of the multi-spindle silk-spinning machines:

> Only Kiangsu, Chekiang, and Szechwan have sophisticated methods of spinning. In northeast China they use the technique of "striking the thread," and this is also employed in Shansi, Shensi, Yunnan, and Kweichow, one person drawing the filament and another walking away from him using a small turning device to twist it in such a way that five to eight filaments are joined to form one thread. This costs much energy and yields little thread. The method of spinning used in Chekiang requires one person to work the horizontal bar at the front of the machine. . . . With one session at this machine a single person can obtain fifty threads, and a hundred threads from two sessions. Compared with the method of twisting silk used in the various [other] provinces, one person does the work of a hundred.

It is notable that this sort of economy is virtually always discussed in terms of energy or effort, not of costs, that is to say, from the point of view of the operator rather than of the entrepreneur. One is inclined to associate this with the fragmented nature of the productive structure of late traditional Chinese industry, in which merchants coordinated a multiplicity of small producers but rarely organized production directly themselves. One of the few exceptions I know of to this generalization is Wu Ch'i-chün's observation on the use of "pulling dragon" pumps in series to drain the government's Yunnan mines. When there were more than 10 to 12 pumping stations "it is always the case that the cost of the workers' upkeep is too great for one to recover one's outlay, and the only long-term solution is to select a place to cut a drainage channel."

It is thus easy to point to a strong trend toward making the land yield more and to a much weaker one toward slight reductions in the labor needed for a given output or operation. (The flywheel cotton gin, for example, could be worked by one person if necessary, whereas the older version required at least two.) What is difficult is to contrive a satisfactory conceptual scheme for the analysis of the advances described in the first section of this paper. One or two, such as the greenhouses for forcing out-of-season plants, provided new capabilities that had not existed before, but cannot be shown to have economized on any factor of production. Others, such as the humid cellars used in the north for cotton spinning, may have been valuable because they used labor that would otherwise have been subject to seasonal unemployment. (Of course, we should not overlook the savings on the labor previously used to transport the cotton to other spinning centers.) Spectacles were somewhat comparable; by allowing people with defective vision to do work that they could not otherwise have done they enhanced the quality of the labor supply. Firefighting pumps and better navigation in the northern seas reduced the loss of houses, ships, and human life, which I suppose must be defined as economizing on both labor and capital. Mineshaft ventilators and "pulling dragon" pumps made ores accessible that could not otherwise have been mined. What was saved, here, ultimately, were the capital and labor that *would have had to be* used to prospect and open new mines; but in practical terms these innovations are best compared to the new fertilizers that, at the cost of some extra labor and expense, increased the output of the fields. I am therefore inclined to believe that a straightforward approach on the basis of factors of production is likely to contain so much artificiality and to require so many arbitrary decisions as to which categories are appropriate for which data that it will lead to nothing useful.

We have also to account for what did *not* happen. As we have just seen, silk-spinning machinery was not used in several parts of China. Similarly, the three- and four-spindle treadle-operated wheels of the Sung-chiang cotton region seem to have been confined to this area. Iron wire, which required a special technique of repeated annealing, was produced only in Fo-shan, where in its heyday it provided work for more than 1,000 men. There were obviously barriers to diffusion, though their nature is by no means clear. But the most important problem concerns water technology. There should have been enormous benefits from more efficient pumping devices both in irrigated agriculture and in mining, which was beset by drainage problems. Yet for half a millennium almost nothing was done to improve on the methods inherited from the past.

The need for better techniques was perceived, if only by an imaginative minority. Early in the nineteenth century, Ch'i Yen-huai experimented with the Archimedean water-screw, which had been known in the literature at least since the *Western Hydraulics* dictated by the Jesuit De Ursis to Hsu Kuang-ch'i some 200 years earlier. In spite of a method of manufacture adapted to materials available in China, it seems to have been hardly used. Here are some lines from a poem written by Ch'i on his efforts:

Kiangnan farmers have few reserves in store.
Ten days they can pedal the pumps and still fear shortage.
They brush the grime away and piteously sigh,
For the springs are dry, the moisture gone, and in due course there
    will be famine.

Now see how this dragon's tail* goes down into the stream,
Producing a flooded expanse from a mere foot of water!
Within, it never runs backwards; outside, it never leaks.
By early morning a hundred mou will look as if heavy rain had
    fallen.

Five to ten people may be served by one machine,
And the smallest effort yields very great results.
Eight families who share a well and one of these pumps
Need never fear drought or flood will rob their fields of grain.

    . . .

The high officials and provincial governor are worthy men
Who study water control and make plans for farming.
Having heard my account of this pump, they urgently wanted to
    see it.
So two were set up in a boat on the Ching-ch'i River.†

When we tested them by the Hay Bridge at noon,
We were watched by a throng of entrancing ladies
Who came, their excitement all bubbling over
And the ground trembling like thunder with their calls of
    welcome.

The pool covered ten mou and was two feet deep.
In three-quarters of an hour the pumps drained seven inches.
With a laugh the provincial governor said to me:

* The "dragon's tail pump" was the Chinese name for the screw.
† Probably the river of this name in south Kiangsu.

"This will help more than just fields and gardens.
The lakes are rising just now and lap the skies.
Long have Huai and Huang been a burden to our people;
If we drained with a thousand [ordinary] pumps and dredged the
　　yellow stream,
The two haulovers and three rivers might be closed for a long time.

"The Liu River is choked with silt; I have long wanted to clear it.
But pumping out water is slow, and I have feared to squander
　　funds.
If we used a hundred of these instead, installed by the rivers and
　　marshes,
We could mobilize workers with baskets and spades, and finish the
　　job in days."

An equally clear indication of an awareness of need is the passage of
the *Western Hydraulics* (reprinted both in Hsü Kuang-ch'i's *Encyclopedia of Agricultural Policy* of 1639 and in the *Comprehensive Examination of Seasonal Practices* of 1742) on a more developed type of cylinder-and-piston pump. In this pump the upstroke of the piston creates a partial vacuum in a chamber and so draws in water through a flap-valve from below; the downstroke expels it from the chamber by pressure and through another valve up a pipe. It is a more sophisticated and efficient mechanism than the "pulling dragon":

> The cylinder-and-piston pump is a machine for raising water from wells and springs. When one is far away from rivers it is necessary to depend on wells for sustenance. Drawing water from wells is mostly done by means of a rope and an earthenware container. From breakfast until supper, from dawn till dusk, people [will do this], unaware of how troublesome it is. In upland areas that I have seen, where wells are used to irrigate the fields, the people use either the windlass and bucket or the well-sweep. Although these appear to be convenient, one may look up and down all day without managing to water all of a mou of land. I have heard that in Shansi and Honan the people work extremely hard to irrigate fields with water drawn from wells. In a year of drought, eight people toiling night and day can manage only several mou. In other areas it is the custom to be lazier. Having seen the difficulties involved, people no longer inquire into the method of watering the fields from wells. . . . If the machine shown here is made, there is no need for a well-rope and an earthenware container, or for a windlass or a well-sweep; and one man using it can do the work of several men. Used for irrigating fields, it can save about four-fifths of the labor needed.

It can hardly be argued in the light of this that "cheap" labor was an obstacle to all sorts of technical progress. Yet, so far as I know, this type of pump was never used by farmers in premodern China. Since we have already shown, in the simpler case of double plowing for water retention, that farm techniques were sometimes successfully taken from books (and P'an Tseng-i was another technologist who delved into old writings), it is permissible to be surprised.

We conclude this demonstration of economic pressure on hydraulic technology with an account of the problems that beset mining. The accumulation of water as shafts grew deeper drove up the price of coal in eighteenth-century Peking. Wu Chen-yü, governor-general of Yunnan and Kweichow in the first half of the nineteenth century, spoke of the "hundreds of stratagems" tried to drain the copper mines, and of the "limitless expense" of the work. Wang Tsai-yo observed that "what in times past could be obtained in a morning now needs ten days" as ores grew less accessible. As the Reverend Williamson observed in the course of a journey through Shantung in 1867: "The Chinese system of mining misses the lower and better strata. . . . A pit is dug down, or a hole is made, at a more or less acute angle in the side of a hill, and they work until the water rises; they then leave that place, and open another pit." Yet pumping equipment remained rudimentary. Lu Shih, who investigated the Shantung mines in 1720, mentions in a poem that "in deep shafts they have installed well-sweeps." Chao Lei-sheng noted of the Chien-yang lead mines that "the springs flow in the deep pits, so they smash an opening from above and lower in a water pump," but he did not specify what kind. The "pulling dragon" was the only innovation, and we know from a competition arranged in Japan in the seventeenth century between this kind of pump and the Archimedean screw that the latter was more efficient. Yet Chinese at the level of Wu Chen-yü and Wu Ch'i-chün had easy access to information about the screw.

There was another simple pump that could have helped the Chinese. This was the paternoster pump, in which circular pallets or balls fixed at intervals along a continuous chain pull the water up through a pipe. Needham has pointed out that this pump, more than any other, has ousted the traditional square-pallet chain pump from the fields of China in recent decades, a tribute to its efficiency and economy. This pump figures prominently in such Western works as Agricola's *De Re Metallica* of 1556, but it is not mentioned in either the *Western Hydraulics of* De Ursis and Hsü or the *Illustrated Account of Remarkable Machines from the Distant West* of Schreck and Wang Cheng. There was thus no need here for inputs based on modern science or industry to break through the sort of ceiling that late traditional technology had reached in agriculture and inland water transport. In other words, in the case of hydraulic techniques there was a situation in which there were relatively few constraints imposed by the high-level equilibrium trap; a strong and perceived need for progress existed; and yet there was minimal advance. We are thus inescapably drawn to ask if this could have been due to cultural factors.

Any explanation based on cultural factors, however, will have to be a subtle one. Inventions were appreciated in China. Shrines were even put up to innovators, as may be seen from Chu Hua's eighteenth-century *Cotton Manual*:

> The Taoist nun Huang was a native of this country [Shang-hai] but went to live on the rocky islands off the coast of Yai-chou. During the Yüan-cheng reign-period [1295–96] of the Yüan dynasty she returned home with spinning and weaving equipment and taught the techniques to the people of Wu-ni-ching. Everyone profited greatly thereby. When she died a shrine was erected at which sacrifices could be made to her spirit and a statue of her displayed. An image of her was also made for the Ning-kuo Temple. At the present time there is also a small temple for sacrifices to her on a little street to the northwest of the Tu-ho-lou in the county capital. The women workers of the county gather here in crowds at harvest time to pay her their respects, and call her "Mother Huang."

Evidence of another kind for the appreciation of technology may be found in the anthology of Ch'ing poetry about everyday life entitled *The Bell of Poesy of the Present Dynasty,* which contains numerous poems on machines and techniques. Ch'i Yen-huai's lines on the paradoxical mechanism of the water-screw is characteristic of the delight in useful ingenuity shown by many of the authors:

> Eight bands spiral about a central post.
> Winding back and forth, they form a revolving streambed
> Like a bottomless bucket open at both ends.
> The waist is slightly constricted and girt with a ring.
> The stream flies thirty thousand feet straight down,
> Quite unaware of having been lifted up!

Poems were written to propagandize better methods. Thus P'eng K'ai-yü, a native of Kiangsu who lived in the K'ang-hsi reign (1662–1722), tried by this means to popularize a bizarre but apparently effective two-man reaping combine he had seen in the wheatfields round Tsinan in Shantung. Nor were the lower levels of society rigidly conservative in their ways. A late Ch'ing gazetteer for Nan-hui county tells how aquatic grasses had recently become popular as a fertilizer for cotton because the use of pig manure tended to give rise to weevils, and concludes that this change had taken place "because the farmers seek out the principles to be derived from their experience over many years and gradually introduce improvements."

One criticism that might perhaps be leveled against popular Chinese attitudes toward technology is that they were, if anything, *too* practical. There was intense competition between artisans, and the tastes of their customers were uncompromisingly utilitarian, with the result described by one of the French missionary-authors of the *Reports on the Chinese:* "Since no one here looks for anything in necessities except what is necessary, or for anything in objects of use except what is useful, no one ever pays—or hardly ever—for additional charm. For this reason, fortune never favors the arts of taste, imagination, and fantasy, which is just as the government would wish." He speaks of how the continually increasing population "puts merit ceaselessly in competition with merit, diligence with diligence, and work with work, in a manner that prevents great fortunes." It is easy to imagine how, under such circumstances, experiment with its attendant errors and reflection with its consumption of time to little apparent profit were luxuries that were not easily afforded.

Artisans may also have disapproved of cheaper methods of production, understanding that their adoption could lead to the loss of jobs. It is not possible to show this at present for the period before the Opium War, but there is evidence for it afterward. Ch'en Ch'i-yüan, who pioneered modern silk-reeling in Kwangtung in the 1870's, would have had his factory destroyed by a Luddite mob but for official intervention. An even more interesting case, though complicated by the interweaving of antiforeign sentiment, was recounted in the *North-China Herald* of July 22, 1867:

> *Beancake Manufacture.* An experiment is about to be made in the north of China, the progress of which will be watched with great interest. A Newchwang firm has conceived the project of establishing at that port machinery for crushing beans, and making the cake and oil which form so important a staple of local trade. . . . A similar experiment was tried, some years ago, in Hong Kong, but resulted in complete failure, through native combination against it. A slight spurt at the commencement led to the conception of gorgeous hopes. Good oil was manufactured and profitably disposed of. But as soon as the importance of the innovation was appreciated by the Chinese hitches of every kind began to arise. The machinery was good, and in San Francisco, where it was purchased, had worked well; yet it was always getting out of order. Precisely as in the case of the beans imported here in foreign vessels, the oil could not be sold. There was no more rational objection to oil turned out of a foreign mill than to cake imported in a foreign ship. But influence was successfully exerted to bring about the rejection of both. Another experiment in machinery, once tried in Shanghai, had a very

similar result. An adverse combination was got up, and the enterprise had to be abandoned. The washermen, here, established such a terrorism that the Steam Washing Company could get no workmen. . . . A like opposition to the new experiment will, we fear, be met in Newchwang. . . . With all their readiness to adopt mechanical contrivances, the Chinese seem to dread the higher appliances of European science, as tending to subvert and ruin their own slow process of labour.

Where such attitudes prevailed, probably only an innovator with official backing would have had much chance of long surviving the jealous egalitarianism and organized obstruction of those whom he had put at a disadvantage in his chosen line of business.

When the Chinese gift for practical invention reappeared in the early modern period, the entrepreneurs pioneering the practical use of new machines regularly sought official backing and rights of exclusive usage equivalent to a patent. This was the case, for example, with the three major Chinese inventions of 1904: a new type of wooden loom in Fukien, the use of crushed sugarcane pulp for paper manufacture in Szechwan, and Yen Chung-lun's method of extracting gas, oil, and tar from coal in conjunction with the brine-boiling traditionally practiced for the recovery of salt. It is interesting to note in passing that the gas container used in Yen Chung-lun's invention needed good quality foreign iron imported through Shanghai, an illustration of how international trade helped technical advance in a multitude of small ways.

Superstition seems to have had no inhibiting effect on economic enterprise, with the exception of geomantic objections to mining. Even here it is hard to be sure how far the fear that cutting the veins of the earth would bring misfortune was the real reason for opposition. In northern Taiwan in the eighteenth century the chief opponents of coal mines were gentry; the local commoners had no hesitation in digging as the market for the fuel expanded. Moreover, we know of at least one case where geomantic pretexts were used as a smokescreen: the campaign mounted in the fifteenth century against the extension of the Grand Canal from T'ung-chou to Peking by those who had vested interests in carting and porterage.

Government policy is harder to evaluate. Some measures did substantial damage. Obvious examples are the early Ming paper money policy and the ban on the raising of horses by commoners, which was lifted only in 1690. Possibly the most disastrous was the interdict placed on coastal shipping during the Yung-lo reign (1403–24). Although this ban was relaxed in 1567, it was reimposed at the end of the Ming with renewed unfortunate consequences for the coastal economy. An already bad situation became still worse under the Ch'ing with the forcible removal of much of the coastal population inland until the war with Coxinga was over.

In regard to mining, policy fluctuated. Ever since the miners' rising fomented by Yeh Tsung-liu in the 1440's, there was a fear that as ores ran out unemployed miners would turn to brigandage or worse. At the same time there was a genuine if intermittent concern with the people's welfare, exemplified by a decree in 1740 encouraging private coal mining throughout the empire—a relaxed attitude that had disappeared again by the beginning of the nineteenth century. The positive effects of state action were most often at a local level. Thus in 1629 Lu Chen-fei, county magistrate of Ching-yang in Shensi, opened up a water route previously thought too dangerous for continuous navigation in order to provide the inhabitants with cheaper coal. But attitudes were generally benign toward anything that had a positive effect on the people's welfare. Pao Shih-ch'en spoke for a long tradition of physiocratic concern when he justified his own contribution to the study of technology: "The most important matters in ruling the prefectures and counties are agriculture and sericulture."

Certain Chinese criticisms of Europe point up the most significant cultural aspects of our problem. Here is Ch'eng T'ing-tso, writing around the middle of the eighteenth century: "Far-off Europe! . . . Its people are known for their many-sided cleverness, excelling particularly at mathematics. Apart from this, *everything else is excessive ingenuity,* enough to amaze those of little knowledge. Often to play around with things is to bring myriad burdens on oneself. They have investigated to the utmost such cruel things as firearms."

His phrase was echoed some 100 years later by Hsüeh Shih-yü in his poem on "The Fire-Wheel Ship," or Western paddle-steamer:

> When the ancient sages fashioned tools they forbade excessive ingenuity.
> Boats and carts were everywhere the same.
> In the hills and marshes exploitation was not unrestrained.
> In each skilled art men obeyed the Supervisor of Works.
> In handling fire they did not give it dominion over water.
> How could they ever have put wheels upon a warship? *
> Their intelligence was in no way inferior,
> But they would not pit their human skill against the gods' achievements.

Both comments have an element of justice. As one can see from the treatises of men like Besson (1573), Ramelli (1588), and Böckler (1662), enthusiasts for the new technology in early modern Europe were sometimes carried away by the prospect of the seemingly impossible

---

* Forgetting that this is what his fellow countrymen had done in Sung times, though without the benefit of the steam engine.

feats that could be accomplished by gears, pulleys, and levers. And as Hsüeh noted—though he used a different mythology—there was an element of Promethean striving and Promethean impiety in the Western quest for power over nature.

With hindsight we can see that the exuberant European imagination served a useful long-run purpose even if it was (perhaps almost because it was) intermittently impractical in its pursuit of perpetual-motion machines and other follies. But Ch'eng T'ing-tso missed something more important than the payoff of "excessive ingenuity," for all that he appreciated Western mathematics. By the eighteenth century it was already evident that the spirit of analytical calculation inspired by Euclid and Archimedes had permeated the work of practical engineers. In a sense, the new machinery was geometry set in motion. When the French hydraulics expert De Bélidor was confronted with a startling variation in efficiency in two square-pallet chain pumps used at Strasbourg—typically Chinese machines, and borrowed from China—he reacted in a way that was quintessentially un-Chinese:

> It would appear that so far no one has followed any exact rule for the construction of pallet chain pumps, judging by the variety of proportions that has been given to their parts, two such machines that were perfectly similar having never perhaps existed. Yet there is no doubt that there must be a perfect construction. The example of the two pumps that I have just been discussing is a most convincing proof of this, since the one that drains twice as much as the other in the same time, and holds this advantage very likely from luck rather than reasoning, must approach this perfection more closely. Let us try to find out whence it comes, so as to derive a general rule therefrom that will leave nothing to be desired so far as this matter is concerned.

He then showed that the pallets should be at least as close to each other as a distance equal to their height, calculated the theoretical flows of the pumps on the basis of their proportions, and found that the ratio between them agreed closely with the reality (actual flow, of course, depending on how hard the cranks were turned).

It was this capacity to see ghosts in machines, those abstracted skeletons of lines and angles that appear increasingly as diagrams in technical books from the seventeenth century on, that differentiated modern Europeans from Chinese. Chinese pumps were subtly varied to suit different conditions. In Sung-chiang, for example, pallets 1.3 to 1.5 feet wide but only .5 feet high were used for low-angle lifts, and pallets .7 feet wide and .8 feet high for steep angle lifts. Yet so far as I know the Chinese never sought a quantified rationale for what they were doing.

The Economic Effects

Estimating the economic contribution made by late traditional technical advances is close to impossible. At best we can hazard a few informed guesses. Thus humid cellars made possible a new regional cotton-textile industry. Better navigation in the northern seas brought cheap Manchurian beancake to fertilize the cotton fields of Kiangnan, and so helped keep down the price of raw cotton. The improved gin halved the labor needed to remove the seeds from the same material. Incubators made a helpful contribution to the supply of protein. Spectacles extended the useful life of the elderly and the scholarly. Slightly better drainage and ventilation of mines restrained the rising prices of minerals. A new power source—the wind—was of great importance locally, but limited in its use to the coastal belt from Chekiang to Hopei.

But the main problem concerns agriculture. It may well be that over the centuries a number of individually slight improvements added up cumulatively to a significant advance. What makes it hard to tell is that technology is here so intermixed with other inputs, such as land and labor, that its effect cannot be isolated, given the simple materials at our disposal. As the quantity of land in cultivation grew, its average quality must have fallen. Thus a considerable number of technical refinements may have been needed just to maintain existing yields per acre. In fact, yields improved in late traditional times. But this may have been due to increased inputs of labor using time-honored methods. It is my impression that farm work, as opposed to small-scale trading, was not often done by women in Sung times. It was certainly quite common in many regions by the Ming and Ch'ing. The poet Wang Mien wrote of Kiangsu women who "follow their husbands to work in the fields during the day, and spin hemp at night without going to bed." Chi Ch'i-kuang tells of women in the Huai region who "work at their looms by night and exert themselves in the fields by day . . . with sickles and hoes at their waists and babies on their backs." Such instances can easily be multiplied, and no evaluation of the contribution of technology to farming can be made until such questions as the possible long-term increase in female participation in the agricultural labor force have been resolved.

Broadly speaking, it seems likely that technological change in late traditional China was a stabilizing factor. As population grew and pressure on resources became sharper, it helped to keep output per person from sinking or sinking too rapidly. A lesser or a greater measure of change would probably have provoked a social and political crisis. This conclusion, if it is correct, is a significant one, for it helps to explain both the immobility and the resilience of the last few centuries of the empire.

Suggested Readings

The standard work on Chinese science and technology is Joseph Needham, ed., *Science and Civilization in China* (Cambridge: Cambridge University Press, 1959–). A work of more limited scope is E-tu Zen Sun and S. C. Sun, *Chinese Technology in the Seventeenth Century* (University Park: Pennsylvania University Press, 1966). A general study of the period is provided by Albert Feurwerker, *State and Society in Eighteenth Century China: The Ch'ing Empire in Its Glory* (Ann Arbor: University of Michigan Press, 1976).

The Social Environment of Tokugawa Kabuki

Donald H. Shively

Kabuki is perhaps the most internationally popular of Japan's theatrical forms. It originated during Japan's last premodern era, called the "Tokugawa" or "Edo" (1615–1868). Like any other art form, kabuki reflects something of the cultural values and attitudes of the period in which it developed. The erotic and emotional atmosphere of the early kabuki greatly appealed to a population restricted by a rigid social system embodying a strict ethical code.

The socioeconomic conditions of Tokugawa Japan made possible the rapid development and acceptance of kabuki. Sixteenth-century Japan experienced continuous civil warfare and destruction. Under those conditions, it is understandable that individuals sought new means of diversion and amusement. The vast majority of the population was seldom allowed to attend a performance of Nō, for that theater was the court entertainment of the aristocracy. The creation of kabuki provided the emotional outlet the common people needed. Equally important was the emergence of a powerful new mercantile, urban society, which patronized early kabuki. The popular kabuki theater of today originated as a response to the changing social conditions of Tokugawa Japan.

Kabuki's reflection of the new urban society is clearly apparent in the following article by Donald H. Shively. The author uses the close connection between prostitution, with its pleasure quarters, and kabuki to illustrate his assertion that kabuki's development was a product of the changing social environment of Tokugawa cities. Particularly interesting is his description

SOCIAL
ENVIRONMENT
OF TOKUGAWA
KABUKI

61

of the physical organization of the theater and its surroundings, which allowed for a close rapport between actors and audience.

Tokugawa Kabuki and Kabuki Today

The audience of "classical kabuki" in Tokyo today witnesses a production which closely approximates its eighteenth-century prototype. If the new play is indeed a classical piece, the text was written during the latter half of the Tokugawa period and hence in subject matter and language remains an artifact of that time. The actors, all descendants of professional theater families, seem to have preserved in mime, dance, and elocution, the conventions of their predecessors. Instrumental and singing styles, handed down from father to son by rote imitation, are probably faithful transmissions of the Tokugawa art. Costumes and props follow those depicted in early woodblock prints. Many of the staging techniques also date from premodern times. In short, today's viewer sees on the kabuki stage a world familiar to his Tokugawa forebears.

Although he may enjoy the performance and empathize with the dilemmas enacted on the stage, the modern Japanese brings with him attitudes and experiences substantially different from those of a Tokugawa observer. A more modern logic and a changed ethical orientation separate him from the action on the stage. A considerable part of the kabuki repertoire consists of history plays which, while they concern events of a much earlier era, depict a moral system and feudal psychology ideally characteristic of the Tokugawa samurai class. The domestic tragedies deal with shopkeepers, artisans, prostitutes, farmers, and the tragic-mundane problems of their lives. Specific events in the city—a murder, a double suicide, an arson case, a swindle—were quickly given sensational treatment on the stage. Other plays treat the more fabulous social outrages—the vendetta of the forty-seven *rōnin* or scandals in the mansions of feudal lords. As it was forbidden to write about the affairs of the ruling families, these plays were cast in an earlier historical period as camouflage. Public curiosity and the daring of the playwright afforded them particular titillation. There are also plays which reflect the aspirations and fantasies of the drifters in society—masterless samurai, gangsters, gamblers, and above all, chivalrous commoners who defy their samurai superiors. This audacity of playwright and actor would be misinterpreted if it were considered an expression of protest against the social and political system. It was, rather, good box office to electrify an audience with bold passages and parodies which spoke to the experience of the commoner.

THE SOCIAL ENVIRONMENT OF TOKUGAWA KABUKI   By Donald H. Shively, from *Studies in Kabuki: Its Acting, Music, and Historical Context* (Hawaii: University of Hawaii Press, 1978), pp. 1–18, 53–54.

Both the history and domestic dramas assume inevitable capitulation to the ethical code which governed society. Characters entangle themselves in nets of loyalties and obligations which come into conflict with unexpected personal desires or sympathetic impulses. The code tolerates no generosity of interpretation. The hero transgresses, fully resigned to pay with his life. The fairness of the code remains unquestioned.

The conscientious, perhaps compulsive reenactment of these dilemmas suggests the importance of the plays as emotional outlets for an audience well disposed to weep over tragedies so suggestive of the conflicts in their daily lives. Kabuki taxes every feeling. It shifts from scenes of love or maternal solicitude to violent murders and graphic harakiri. This rather basic function of theater as response to a rigid social system with a relentless ethical code is little perceived by a modern audience. A substantial difference in the content of his moral difficulties isolates a present-day viewer from some of the deeper reactions of a Tokugawa audience to the plays.

The ambience of the theater and its social environment have also undergone fundamental changes. The theater itself has been transformed. Today's western-style building offers upholstered seating and all the amenities of a lavish opera house. The Tokugawa audience, which might have numbered slightly over a thousand, was less than half the size of a modern audience. Yet it was squeezed together on the floor of a hall only a fraction the size of a new theater. The stage was far smaller than those we know in kabuki today and, normally deprived of the use of even torches for lighting, the old theaters were quite dark.

Yet there was an intimacy between actor and audience, due not merely to physical proximity but to the familiarity of the audience with the actor and the freer interaction between them. Attending the theater was a more joyful, uninhibited experience than we know today. The theater was part of the world of sensual entertainment provided in the cities for the pleasure of the commoners. The origins of kabuki were deeply tied to both male and female prostitution, and although the government repeatedly attempted to forge clear separations between the two professions by banning women from the stage and concentrating houses of prostitution in designated quarters detached from the theaters and actors' residences, the distinction of function was not always cleanly drawn. Female dancers continued to perform kabuki dances and skits at private parties and many of the actors served as social and sexual companions.

In principle, at least, the theatrical and prostitution quarters became parallel facilities for amusement—the two wheels of the vehicle of pleasure. They were tolerated in the conviction that vulgar diversions for the lower classes, unprepared by education or lineage for more refined recreation, were necessary evils. It was further argued that while the three great cities—Edo, Osaka, and Kyoto—were under Tokugawa control, they would lose their commanding positions in population and hence in commerce without the presence of lively amusement areas. The two professions, therefore, received some official recognition insofar as they were licensed and relegated to separate quarters removed from the rest of society and treated as analogous groups.

Prostitutes and actors, like others who took money from performing, were classified by the officials as pariahs. The operators of houses of prostitution in Edo were placed under the jurisdiction of the head of the eta, Danzaemon, and denied certain privileges given to other residents of the city. They were known by the derogatory name *kuruwa mono.* Kabuki managers and actors, who were treated in much the same way, were called *kawara kojiki* (riverbed beggars) or *koya mono* or *shibai mono,* equally derisive terms. When they did go out of the quarter, they were required to wear woven hats made of sedge grass to hide their faces, the same type of hat worn by outcasts and criminals under arrest.

The common people, while regarding these members of the demimonde as somewhat disreputable, found them endlessly fascinating. They were admired for their beauty and their splendid clothes, their social poise and savoir faire. They were the purveyors of entertainment and pleasure for the nonaristocratic residents of the city, and provided the social stage on which the more prosperous could enjoy their wealth and make reputations as men of importance within their levels of society.

Both quarters were intended for the entertainment of commoners. Yet the excitement of the kabuki theater and the glamor of the pleasure houses were irresistible to the numerous samurai who visited these quarters exercising only a moderate degree of discretion in concealing their faces with large hats or scarves. Since involvement in any altercation would be embarrassing, they could ill afford to insist upon the prerogatives of their class. Muro Kyūsō (1658–1734), the Confucian scholar, lamented: "There are even feudal lords and district governors who like to enjoy themselves secretly in houses of prostitution, and there are warriors and great men who vie in learning the customs of the theater."

Prostitutes of the highest grades were reputedly accomplished entertainers, skilled in music or dance and surpassing in coquetry. The leading players of male roles had prodigious reputations as lovers. Some of the beautiful young actors were sought after as sexual partners, and women's roles were played by male actors *(onnagata)* who also had an erotic fascination for both men and women. In a society in which there was an easy acceptance of homosexual relations, the presence of actors on the stage who deliciously exploited sexual nuance occasioned far more excitement than it does today.

Confucian advisors to the government, who expected drama to edify the viewer, were distressed by the pernicious influence of kabuki. One of these scholars, Dazai Shundai (1680–1747) remarked: "Because our kabuki plays of today put on licentious and unrestrained matters which obtain among the people in present-day society in order to cater to vulgar sentiment, they all set examples of licentiousness. There is nothing worse than this in breaking down public morals."

Thus the kabuki performance in Tokugawa times was charged with a far more erotic atmosphere than it is today. The social environment in which the actors lived and the social role they performed off the stage conditioned both their private lives and their style of acting as well as the content of the plays. These were important factors in the shaping of early kabuki and must be taken into account to understand classical kabuki. With the profound changes that have transformed modern Japanese society, and the quite different private lives now led by actors, the sensual elements in the performance have paled and only faintly touch the present-day audience. With the "reform" of kabuki in the last decades of the nineteenth century, by which is meant primarily the ending of public prostitution by actors and the raising of their social status to the level of other artists, the special relationship between kabuki and the pleasure quarters finally ended. Kabuki was removed from the social environment in which it had developed, and it became "classical" theater.

The extent of this change can be appreciated if we recreate the proper social atmosphere of Tokugawa kabuki, describing the physical arrangement of the theater and its surroundings and the sexuality of the actors in the eyes of the Tokugawa audience. Of particular interest is the situation in the early eighteenth century when kabuki first flourished. By that time the style of acting of the various type roles, the structure of the plays, and most of the conventions and traditions of the theater had been established, although they were to be considerably refined and elaborated during the following century or more. To understand the social milieu of the theater and the many interconnections between the kabuki and the prositutes' quarters (a theme which will be developed later), a review of the early history of these quarters is instructive.

The Beginnings of Kabuki and Licensed Prostitution

The conventional account of the origins of kabuki opens with the appearance in Kyoto of Okuni in 1603 or perhaps earlier. An itinerant dancer who claimed association with Izumo Shrine, she was said to have performed suggestive dances and skits in the dry riverbed of the

Kamo River by Gojō Bridge, then the eastern edge of the city proper, which was given over to amusements and sideshows. Shrine dancers from earlier times had engaged in prostitution, and those who traveled around to solicit funds, frequently renegades who performed for their own profit, were called *aruki miko* (walking priestesses) or *uta bikuni* (singing nuns). Okuni's dances were probably standard contemporary skits dressed up with novel dramatic elements and a farcical or erotic twist. Her particular contribution to the development of kabuki may have been no more significant than that of similar entertainers, but it is at least certain that performances by small troupes of female dancers were popular in the first two decades of the seventeenth century. One of these troupes performed in 1608 at Sumpu (the present Shizuoka), where Tokugawa Shogun, Ieyasu, had retired. A brawl erupted, whereupon Ieyasu banned such groups from the town, setting aside a place for them next to the prostitutes' quarters outside the town at Abekawa.

Within a few years of Okuni's appearance in Kyoto, there were imitations of her performance by troupes of prostitutes. In 1612 Sadoshima Yosanji set up a stage on the riverbed at Shijō, and brothel proprietors in that vicinity followed suit in order to solicit patrons. These shows were known as *yūjo kabuki* (prostitutes' kabuki). Many of the skits demonstrated techniques used by prostitutes to approach prospective clients or mimed the style of gallants accosting a favorite. They were, in fact, a kind of burlesque with risqué lines and suggestive dance movements. Occasionally male performers assumed female roles, producing a great deal of sexually confused pantomime. A contemporary Confucian scholar Hayashi Razan (1583–1657) remarks: "The men wear women's clothing; the women wear men's clothing, cut their hair and wear a man's topknot, have swords at their sides, and carry purses. They sing base songs and dance vulgar dances; their lewd voices are clamorous, like the buzzing of flies and the crying of cicadas. The men and women sing and dance together. This is the kabuki of today."

Screens and handscrolls of the time depict the girls swinging their hips and throwing their arms about with an abandon not to be seen in later dancing. Descriptions of performances leave no doubt that they were prostitutes as well. The diary kept by Richard Cocks from 1615 to 1622, while he was head of the English trading post at Hirado, refers to them as "*caboques* or Japan players (or whores)." He mentions being entertained by a Japanese merchant who "provided *caboques,* or women plears, who danced and songe; and when we returned home, he sent eavery one one of them."

Early "theaters" copied the rudimentary structures found in amusement areas around the edge of Kyoto which were used for occasional performances of subscription *nō (kanjin nō),* staged to raise money from the general public for temple construction or repair. Only the small square stage was covered with a roof. Spectators paid admission to enter an enclosure formed by a high fence of bamboo palings covered with straw mats. There they stood or sat on mats on three sides of the stage.

Fights sometimes occurred among the more hotblooded samurai or footsoldiers in the audience. Many were *rōnin,* samurai who lost employment during the purges of daimyo in the first decades of the Tokugawa period. They drifted to the cities in search of new masters, employment, or excitement, and were often a disorderly element in the streets. Because brawls were touched off by rivalries over the performers, female players were banned from the kabuki stage in 1629. This ban was repeatedly issued, and after a few years actresses ceased to appear in the theaters of the principal cities. Their place was taken by young male actors.

The exile of women from the stage was, of course, the basic step in the separation of the professions of prostitute and actor. It served the government's objective of creating greater social order and stability by recognizing the various trades and affording them a degree of security and protection from competition by new operators.

The practice of licensing prostitutes began in the Muromachi period. At the end of the sixteenth century, Hideyoshi took the first steps to isolate their houses from good society by establishing a quarter in Kyoto at Madenokōji Nijō. It was moved in 1603 to Rokujō (Misuji-machi) south of the political and commercial areas. Yet prostitutes continued to scatter through all parts of the city. In 1641 an extremely large quarter called the Shimabara, replete with luxurious establishments, was founded in the fields of the southwest corner of the city. In the shogun's capital, brothels sprang up in various parts of the city in the early years of the Tokugawa rule, but in 1617 they were brought together to form the Yoshiwara, just east of Nihonbashi. Bathhouse girls and other prostitutes in competition with the Yoshiwara were rounded up repeatedly during the next few decades and deposited in the licensed quarters. After the Meireki fire of 1657 which destroyed two-thirds of Edo including the Yoshiwara, the houses were moved outside the city to the open fields beyond Asakusa Temple, some four miles from Nihonbashi. Two hundred houses were licensed there as the New Yoshiwara. In Osaka, Shimmachi was established in 1629, and in other cities and castle towns sections for prostitutes were also set aside.

The prosperous condition of the cities in the seventeenth century supported the creation of opulent houses of assignation in the licensed quarters. These *ageya,* or more popularly, *chaya* (teahouses), were tasteful parlors for drinking and dining where dancing girls, reciters, jesters, and other entertainers could be summoned. Prostitutes lived in separate houses called *okiya* to which they were indentured. Several ranks of prostitutes populated each quarter. A guidebook to the Yoshiwara of 1642 mentions 75 girls of *tayū* rank, 31 *kōshi*, and 881 *hashijorō*. By the next century the quarter distinguished among its 4,000 inmates at least six ranks representing a wide range of fees. A girl of the highest rank, indulged like an aristocrat, might refuse a client who did not interest her. Perhaps she would require considerable wooing—several visits and various gifts—before she would bestow her favors.

In addition to the official quarter there were other centers of prostitution, some of which came to be tacitly recognized but were not accorded the same status and privileges. Because of the great distance to the Yoshiwara from Edo and its theaters, unlicensed houses kept appearing in more convenient locations within the city. In 1673, 512 illegal prostitutes were seized in 74 houses near the theater quarter and sent out to the Yoshiwara. A decade later another 300 were rounded up at various unlicensed parlors. Such sweeps on a much larger scale were conducted during the Kansei and Tempō reforms of the late Tokugawa period. Since it proved too difficult to confine all prostitution to one quarter of the city, the authorities in later years permitted prostitution at Shinagawa, Fukagawa, Nakasu, and Ryōgoku, and in Kyoto at Gion, Nijō, Shichijō, and Kitano. There was also a considerable amount of less formal prostitution in public places of entertainment and relaxation. At many bathhouses, restaurants, and inns, female attendants liberally sold their fruits. The great variety and gradation among professional sexual practitioners is suggested by the over four hundred terms used to designate prostitutes. There were other female entertainers: dancers *(odoriko)* who entertained at private parties, and geisha who made their appearance in the 1750s. Prostitution was commonly practiced by entertainers of all kinds, both male and female—dancers, actors, jōruri reciters, musicians—as well as by young itinerants calling themselves nuns or monks, and youths who were peddlers of toilet articles and incense. Frequent prohibitions were issued against private prostitution, but the main concern of the authorities seems to have been the prevention of exploitation of girls and boys by unscrupulous panders. The young kabuki actors as public entertainers, like the actresses before them, could be engaged as sexual partners.

Even before the ban against actresses, at least as early as 1612, there were troupes made up entirely of boys or young men who performed *wakashu kabuki* (youths' kabuki). Homosexual practices had become extremely prevalent during the military campaigns of the fifteenth and sixteenth centuries and were also common in Buddhist monasteries. During the seventeenth century some of the shogun and feudal lords exercised their preference for beautiful youths. Homosexuality was, moreover, widely practised among commoners, following the example of their betters. The playlets performed in youths' kabuki were of two types: those in which homosexual love was acted out, emphasizing the loveliness of these boys *(shudō goto),* and those which demonstrated techniques to accost prostitutes *(keisei goto)*. The latter was, as mentioned earlier, a popular convention in women's kabuki. City officials attempted to curb the erotic effect of the young female impersonators as rivalries over these youths led to altercations between admirers. Homosexual prostitution was banned in 1648, but to little effect. Finally, in 1652, the authorities seized upon an incident to close the theaters in Edo and other cities and youths' kabuki, or at least kabuki by that name, came to an end.

Following repeated entreaties by theater owners, an agreement evolved which permitted kabuki performances to be staged again, henceforth known as *yarō kabuki* (fellows' kabuki). One basic change required female impersonators to dress their hair in the masculine fashion, shaving the forelock. Further, youths over fourteen were no longer permitted to use girls' clothes or hairstyles. Since men in the Tokugawa period had a shaven pate, a coiffured forelock was erogenous. The young actors were inspected periodically to make certain that they were closely shaved. They hid their bald spot with kerchiefs, although this too was prohibited, and later with patches of dark purple silk to give the impression of glistening dark hair. By the end of the century it became common practice to wear a wig on the stage. While this indicates the enduring concern over appearance, there was a gradual tendency to assign female roles to older performers who relied more on acting resources than on physical attraction, and the art of the *onnagata* (female impersonator) developed. Government repression, ironically, had inspired the transformation of these popular performances from burlesque into a more serious art form.

The beneficial effects of the reforms of 1652 were realized only gradually. For some years the most characteristic scenes continued to be the prostitute-accosting routines, known as Shimabara *kyōgen*. In fact, kabuki was frequently called "Shimabara" until these plays were banned in 1664.

The reforms of 1652 were intended to separate homosexual prostitution from kabuki and to relegate the kabuki theaters and actors' residences to one or two quarters of the cities. In the first respect the reform was only partially successful. It did remove from the stage those youths who were more prostitute than actor. These continued their service in separate sections of the city. Yet in the "reformed" *yarō kabuki,* young actors, especially those apprenticed to the role of *onnagata,* continued to be sought after. *Yarō,* a somewhat derogatory term for "fellow," carries the connotation of homosexuality. An account in an Edo guidebook suggests that even in this form of kabuki there was at first excessive interest on the part of the audience in these beautiful boys:

> When these youths, their hair beautifully done up, with light make-up, and wearing splendid padded robes, moved slowly along the runway, singing songs in delicate voices, the spectators in front

bounced up and down on their buttocks, those in back reared up, while those in the boxes opened their mouths up to their ears and drooled; unable to contain themselves, they shouted: "Look, look! Their figures are like incarnations of deities, they are heavenly stallions!" And from the sides others called: "Oh, that smile! It overflows with sweetness. Good! good!" and the like, and there was shouting and commotion.

The display of youths on the stage differed little from the line-up of prostitutes within the lattice fronts of the Shimabara houses.

Only four years after the reform, an incident in Kyoto again closed the kabuki theaters in that city for a time. The *onnagata* Hashimoto Kinsaku was drinking in a box with a samurai admirer when the latter, in a fit of jealousy, drew his sword, inspiring Kinsaku to leap into the pit to save himself.

The Development of Theater Buildings

The earliest kabuki performances, as noted, were staged in rudimentary enclosures which could be hastily constructed if subscription *nō* stages were not already available in the amusement quarters at the edge of the cities. From about 1617 Kyoto began issuing licenses to operate theaters. As was true of houses of prostitution, the theaters were increasingly restricted to certain quarters of the city. In Kyoto they were clustered in the area of Shijō, just east of the river, and although as many as seven licenses were issued by 1669, it is not clear how many were in operation at one time. This concentration parallels the establishment of the large prostitution quarters at Shimabara, several miles to the southwest, in 1641. The Shijō theater area and riverbank was a large amusement center in which kabuki was one of many dozens of diversions. There were smaller playhouses, puppet theaters, and a number of wayside entertainers who recited tales from military epics, the *Taiheiki* and *Heike monogatari*. There were fortune-tellers, dentists, *sumō* wrestlers, jugglers, and tightrope walkers. There were sideshows exhibiting such freaks as the female giant and the armless woman archer. There were exotic animals—tigers, bears, porcupines, eagles and peacocks, performing monkeys and dancing dogs. Teahouses, restaurants, and refreshment stands lined the streets. Paintings of the period show these establishments crowded together, thronged with people of every description.

Edo performances of women's kabuki and youths' kabuki took place as early as 1617 in the Yoshiwara and the nearby amusement area of Nakabashi. The first theater to be licensed was the Saruwaka-za in Nakabashi in 1624, later renamed Nakamura-za, which continued to operate at a succession of locations until 1893. It serves as a particularly remarkable example of the exercise of an hereditary license to operate a theater. This and later kabuki theaters were ordered to move from time to time and finally, after the Meireki fire of 1657 forced the Yoshiwara far outside the city, were restricted to Sakai-chō and Kobiki-chō and shortly limited to four in number. The Tokugawa government continued to follow a policy of treating the prostitution and theater quarters as parallel concerns. When the theater quarters burned in 1841, nearly two centuries later, they were ordered to move to Saruwaka-chō in Asakusa, close by the Yoshiwara. In Osaka too, where the issuing of regular licenses to theaters followed the Edo precedent, they were restricted from the 1660s to Dōtombori and Horie.

With the issuing of licenses permitting the construction of permanent theaters, the buildings became gradually more substantial. The mat fence was replaced by solid board walls, and a row of boxes *(sajiki)* was built along the two sides of the parquet *(doma)* for spectators who required more comfort and privacy. Later boxes were added at the rear of the parquet. City officials, seeking to keep kabuki a simple form of entertainment, forbade the construction of roofs over the parquet. But resourceful theater owners devised a method of stretching mats across the parquet to serve as makeshift shelters which provided shade from the sun and protection against light showers. Over a period of two centuries the theater buildings became gradually more elaborate and comfortable as the authorities made concessions, alternating between a resigned attitude and a stricter policy of sumptuary regulation.

Set back slightly from the street so as not to obstruct traffic, the theater facade was dominated by a tower on which ornamental spears were mounted to indicate possession of an official license. This spear (or drum) tower was draped with a cloth bunting featuring the large design of the theater's crest. The Nakamura-za first used the wheeling crane *(maizuru)* design. The Ichimura-za chose a rounded crane within an octagon. Most theaters placed large billboards on the tower, the center board announcing in bold characters the name of the proprietor, those on either side the names of leading actors. Lower billboards, typically four in number if the offering was a four-act play, gave the titles of each act. From the 1720s a tableau from each act was painted above the title.

Before these signs stood low platforms where barkers waved their fans to attract the attention of passersby and entice them into the theater. In addition to the cruder techniques of whistling and calling to onlookers, they would attempt to draw a crowd by staging impersonations of the leading actors, imitating their voices as they recited tantalizing lines from the play, and parodying their characteristic poses and gestures. Contemporary paintings record the remarkably exuberant commitment of these *kido geisha* (entrance performers) to their task.

The early theaters had only one entrance, located in the center of the building under the drum tower. It was a small opening with a high threshold which the customer had to step over while ducking under a low overhead. Aptly called the mouse-entrance *(nezumi kido),* it was a holdover from the enclosures used for subscription *nō* and was presumably designed to make it difficult for anyone to slip in quickly without paying. As the theaters grew larger in the eighteenth century, an entrance was provided on each side of the drum tower for admission to the parquet. The stoop entrance was abandoned and a short curtain *(noren)* hung across the top of the doorway, as is customary in Japanese shops. Tickets were purchased outside and other fees paid within for the rental of a reed mat *(hanjō)* and a length of smoldering cord to light one's pipe. On each side of the front of the building an entrance was added for guests going to boxes in order to avoid jostling by the plebs. Inside, stairs led to the upper level of boxes.

The price of tickets ranged widely between the cheapest and the best seats. In 1714, boxes in Edo theaters commanded 1200 *mon,* single spaces 200 *mon.* Parquet tickets averaged 64 *mon.* When space was available, single-act tickets were sold for 12 *mon.* Rental of a mat was 6 *mon* additional. These prices increased rather steadily through much of the Tokugawa period, probably following the general inflationary trend, but exacerbated at certain times by the excalating salaries of the star actors. Attending a major theater was not cheap. The cost of a box seat in 1828 was 1 *ryō* 2 *bu,* the equivalent of 3 bales *(hyō)* of rice or a servant's salary for three or four months. When a performance was popular, the price of tickets rose abruptly.

While the Nakamura-za in Edo provides a detailed illustration of the physical design of a theater, it should be noted that no two were identical. Theaters were, moreover, periodically rebuilt, for fires frequently ravaged Edo. In the 1690s the outer dimensions of the Nakamura-za were 71.5 feet by 97.5 feet, or 6,971 square feet. At its largest in 1809, it measured 80 feet by 138.5 feet, or 11,080 square feet. The structure remained a fraction the size of the present Kabuki-za in Tokyo which has 39,000 square feet of space on the ground floor, seating 1,078 people, approximately the same number as the Tokugawa structure. But the modern building has five floors with 120,000 square feet of floor space and accommodates an additional 1,522 people on the mezzanine and balconies. The Nakamura-za of 1720 had a row of boxes along the two sides and across the back. Although only one tier was allowed at that time, by 1724 a second tier of boxes had been added. It was repeatedly forbidden to hang bamboo blinds across the front of the boxes and to install screens or other partitions which would provide privacy for the occupants. However, a number of paintings from this period show such items in use, partially concealing from the gaze of the populace ladies-in-waiting of the shogun's or daimyo's households, members of the Buddhist clergy, and rich merchants.

The parquet *(doma)* of the Nakamura-za, 52 feet wide and 82.4 feet deep in 1720, had a capacity of 800 persons. Later, the front half with its better seats was divided into partitions *(masu)* not quite five feet square which narrowly accommodated seven or eight people. Rear parquet space was unreserved. The last back seats, called the *ōmukō* (greatly beyond) were so far from the stage that they were also known as the "deaf gallery." Thus including boxes and the cheapest parquet seats the theater held about 1,200. Operating policy was to crowd in as many as possible. According to a book of 1703: "The people came in pushing and jostling, and eight persons sat knee over knee on a mat. It is very pleasant to see them pressed together like human *sushi.*"

By the early eighteenth century, wooden roofs occasionally sheltered part of the pit, although not officially sanctioned until 1724. Thereafter tile roofs were recommended to decrease the danger of fire from flying embers. Even after the theaters added roofs, artificial lighting remained proscribed because of the danger to the wooden structure from the open flame of oil lamps and candles. Performances, expected to end about 5 P.M., depended on natural light from windows with translucent paper-covered *shōji* installed on both sides of the theater behind or above the upper row of boxes.

Dressing rooms, located directly behind the stage, were built in two stories by the 1670s. Before the end of the century the Morita-za in Edo added a third level. This section of the building was built high to take as little ground space as necessary from the stage and parquet. A passageway leading to the dressing room section was constructed behind the boxes. Though intended for use by actors to gain access to the end of the runway *(hanamichi)*, it was soon traveled by actors summoned to boxes or patrons visiting dressing rooms. The usual arrangement called for baths and quarters for musicians, writers, and *wakashu* on the first floor, *onnagata* on the second, and players of men's roles on the third. A large rehearsal area also occupied the third level. Leading players had individual dressing rooms, although partitions had not received official sanction.

The early kabuki stage basically recreated the square *nō* stage with pillars in the four corners supporting a thatched roof. The main platform had two narrow appendages, one to the right used by the chorus in the *nō,* the other at the rear for the musicians. Off the left of the stage a "bridge" *(hashigakari)* for entrances and exits extended back at an oblique angle with a railing on each side and a long roof. These features of the *nō* stage were gradually modified in the kabuki theater, although it is surprising how long they persisted. The stage itself was only nineteen feet square at the outset. Rather than alter its design, more space was gained by greatly widening the bridge and eliminating its handrails. It then emerged as a secondary performing area, a rectangle set back slightly from the main stage. A platform was appended to the front of the stage *(tsuke-butai)* which jutted into the audience. Though these changes were not completed until the first decades of the eighteenth century, some stages had already become quite large. That of the Nakamura-za measured 32.5 feet by 37.7 feet in 1724. Not until 1796, however, was the roof over the main stage eliminated.

One of the most distinctive inventions of the kabuki theater is the *hanamichi,* a five-foot-wide runway which extends from the left side of the stage to the rear of the audience. It is used for more dramatic entrances and exits and as an occasional pivot of activity. Its origins are unclear. The more obvious assumption, that it began as a second *hashigakari* directed through the audience, appears to be incorrect. Perhaps as early as the 1650s a small platform was attached to the stage slightly left of center where members of the audience placed gifts *(hana)* of money or goods for their favorite actors. These were called *hana* because the gift was attached to a flower *(hana)* branch. Such a platform appears in a drawing of the Nakamura-za in 1687. By 1724, at least, the *hanamichi* was a runway 52 feet long, set at an oblique angle, probably ending toward the rear end of the row of boxes on the left side of the hall. Although the word *hanamichi* may originally have meant "a path for gifts," by the 1720s and perhaps several decades earlier, it was used primarily as an extension of the stage. Woodblock prints of the next decade show actors standing or seated upon it. Occasionally a small platform called the *nanori-dai* was added about the midway point where an actor could stand almost dead center of the parquet to announce the name and pedigree *(nanori)* of the character he was portraying. After

Interior of the Ichimura-za in Edo in 1744. Woodblock print by Okamura Masanobu.

1780 another narrower runway was sometimes erected on the right side of the hall. Perhaps as a result, the main *hanamichi* was set at right angles to the stage, parallel to its narrower companion.

Most of the physical features of the theater discussed on the pre-

Plebs, packed into the "arhat dais" and "Yoshino" at stage right, revel in the action on the stage, while well-dressed ladies in boxes watch quietly. Detail of a woodblock print by Utagawa Toyokuni III.

ceding pages are illustrated in a woodblock print by Okumura Masanobu (1686–1764) of the Ichimura-za in Edo in 1744. The *nō* stage with its roof and front pillars, the appended *hashigakari* stage right and *tsukebutai* stage front and the *hanamichi* are clearly evident. There is a raised walk *(ayumi)* across the hall for easier access by customers and vendors to the front part of the pit. A tea and a food vendor pass through the audience. The stage curtain is drawn to stage right. Boxes of the first tier were known as quail boxes *(uzura sajiki)* because their wooden bars made them resemble crates for keeping quail. The second tier of boxes retained eaves from the days, a few decades earlier, when there was no roof over the pit. Sliding doors of translucent paper let in daylight above the boxes.

In such a theater the play moved easily into the audience. The tiers of boxes at the front of the hall were alongside the stage. Later in the eighteenth century a low balcony intruded behind the left corner of the stage (stage right). Known as the *rakandai* (arhat dais), its tightly lined-up spectators hovered over the stage like the five hundred arhats of a Buddhist painting. A seventeen-syllable satirical poem *(senryū)* observes: "The five hundred went home, having seen the actors' backs." A second balcony inevitably grew above this. It was called *tsūten* (passing through to heaven), or Yoshino (a mountain district noted for cherry blossoms), as its perspective barely penetrated the artificial cherry blossoms suspended from the ceiling of the hall. A woodblock print of the last decades of the Tokugawa period shows the plebs, crammed in these galleries at the edge of the stage, watching gleefully, mouths agape, as the actors perform, almost within reach. When the play was a great success, the management, not impervious to the potential boon, seated customers on the stage itself. This practice is recorded by the satirical poems: "A big hit—the action is performed in a six-foot square," and "Spectators and actors are lined up together—a big hit." With an audience thus gathered on three sides of the performers and cheap balcony seating available over one corner of the stage, no concept of a platform-framing proscenium arch emerged.

Conclusion

The interconnections between kabuki and the pleasure quarter illustrate how specifically the theater was a product of the social environment of Tokugawa cities. The physical presence of attractive youths acting out the roles of glamorous courtesans had more immediacy for an audience which was curious about or knew firsthand the sensual world of prostitute and catamite which was to be found in the cities. But the excitement of kabuki was not limited to such gross features. Kabuki was a stage on which to display many of the accomplishments of the new urban society. These were not limited to the immediate ingredients of drama, such as the elaboration of more subtle plots and variety in acting styles. Kabuki called for new musical forms, recitative styles, composition of songs, and especially choreography. It inspired innovation in fabric and costume design, hairstyles and personal ornamentation. Whatever was new and striking found its way quickly to the stage.

With kabuki as the most exciting form of entertainment, it is not surprising that fashions seen on the stage were copied and that the speech and mannerisms of the popular actors were emulated. Kabuki also provided subjects for painters and printmakers and inspired a new boldness in composition. The traditions and tales on which kabuki drew for its material were returned into the stream of literature to make stories with intricate plots and more dramatic structure. This continuous interchange between the theater and its social environment wove kabuki into the fabric of urban culture.

Suggested Readings

Two useful general surveys of kabuki theater are Earl Ernst, *The Kabuki Theatre* (New York: Oxford University Press, 1956; reprint, Honolulu: University of Hawaii Press, 1974), and A. C. Scott, *The Kabuki Theatre of Japan* (New York: Macmillan Co., 1966). Peter Arnott, *The Theatres of Japan* (New York: Macmillan Co., 1969), traces the development of the classical Japanese theatrical forms and shows their influence on modern productions. English translations of kabuki plays are available in Samuel L. Leiter, *The Art of Kabuki* (Berkeley: University of California Press, 1979). An informative study of kabuki music is William Malm, *Nagauta: The Heart of Kabuki Music* (Tokyo: Tuttle, 1963).

The Death
of Woman Wang

Jonathan D. Spence

The following reading comes from a book in which the author set himself the task of giving some insight into the lives of Chinese peasants of the early modern period by investigating "four small crises" in the lives of the inhabitants of the county of T'an-ch'eng in northeast China in the years between 1668 and 1672. The crises involved the collection of land taxes in the district, the struggle of a widow to protect her child and her property, a a local feud, and the murder of woman Wang. T'an-ch'eng was poverty-stricken, and the surrounding countryside was infested with bandits. Life was hard for all, worse for the poor, and worst of all for the wives and daughters of the poor. It was a life that woman Wang was unable to endure, and so, without any real chance of bettering herself, she ran away. Not long after she returned, she was murdered by her husband.

Perhaps the one great difference between writing history and writing fiction is that writers of fiction can add as many details and as much information as are necessary to make a complete story. Historians can present only that information for which they have secure evidence, and thus they can never tell a complete tale. There is, therefore, much missing in the story of woman Wang. We do not know what she thought she could gain by running away, where she thought she was going, why her lover abandoned her, or why she chose to return, and it is unlikely that we shall ever know. We can only imagine. It is extraordinary, therefore, that the author is able to tell us as much as he does, and the story of woman Wang gains poignancy from our knowledge that it all really happened.

W e do not know exactly when they married, though it must have been some time in the late 1660s, nor do we know their personal names. We do not even know how Jen could afford a wife, since there were many fewer women than men available in T'an-ch'eng due to a combination of factors: female infanticide, the lower levels of food supplied to girls, the presence always of several women in the homes of wealthier men. Jen might not have had to pay any cash, or even furnish the customary presents to get woman Wang as his wife, for she seems to have been an orphan—or at least to have had no surviving relatives living nearby—and since Jen's own father was a widower of seventy, she might have been brought in as a young girl to help with the household chores and married to Jen when she was old enough, as was often done with young girls in the country.

What we do know about the couple is this: By early 1671 they were married and living in a small village outside the market town of Kuei-ch'ang, eight miles southwest of T'an-ch'eng city. They were poor, and Jen made his living as a hired laborer on other people's land. They had a one-room house that contained a cooking pot, a lamp, a woven sleeping mat, and a straw mattress. We know too that for six months after the marriage woman Wang had lived with her husband and her seventy-year-old father-in-law, but that the old man finally moved to another house a mile away because he got on so badly with her. And we know that woman Wang was left alone much of the day; that she had bound feet; that she had no children, though there was a little girl living in a house next door who called her "Auntie"; that her house fronted onto a small wood; and that at some time, for some reason, as the year 1671 advanced, she ran away.

She ran away with another man, though we do not know his name, nor where the two of them intended to go. We can see from the map that they had three initial choices: they could move southwest and cross the border into P'ei; they could walk eight miles northeast to the county city of T'an-ch'eng and from there follow the post road, either south to Hung-hua fou and into Kiangsu, or north to I-chou and on into central Shantung; or they could walk eight miles northwest to Ma-t'ou, and from Ma-t'ou head west on the road that led to Chang-ch'eng market and on into T'eng and Tsou counties. Whichever route they chose, unless they could afford carriers or a cart, they would have to move slowly on account of woman Wang's bound feet.

P'ei would not have been a bad choice if they wanted to avoid pursuit. The way there was hilly, but the countryside had for years supported bandits and fugitives who had played the change of pro-

THE DEATH OF
WOMAN WANG

79

THE DEATH OF WOMAN WANG   From Jonathan D. Spence, *The Death of Woman Wang* (New York: Penguin Books, 1979), pp. 116–32.

vincial jurisdiction to their advantage. One could even travel part of the way by light boat down the River I in summer and autumn when the water level was high and the authorities in P'ei were unlikely to worry about one more fugitive couple. P'ei had been struck by catastrophes as serious as those in T'an-ch'eng—famine, locusts, and war, cycles of drought and flood. P'ei had also suffered from the earthquake of 1668, though less than T'an-ch'eng, but since P'ei was on the Yellow River, flood was a potential catastrophe, which it never was in T'an-ch'eng, with its smaller tributary rivers; and a month after the earthquake high winds and swollen water levels tearing at the banks had broken the land, and much of the city of P'ei fell beneath the waves. Only one or two hundred families escaped, and in the period when T'an-ch'eng slowly began to recover, in P'ei the population dropped by another third.

T'an-ch'eng city was in some ways an obvious goal, but the disadvantages were also obvious. As the site of the magistrate's yamen and the center of county administration, security was tighter than anywhere else. Regulations that remained only on paper elsewhere in the county were enforced here: there were regular patrols outside the city and checkpoints on the roads nearby. Travelers could be stopped for questioning and made to explain their reasons for wanting to enter the city, even refused entrance unless they had relatives living there. The inns were notorious for their dishonesty: many were run by dishonest owners who lured the unwary with displays of cheap food and wine; but once the country folk had registered, the bills began to climb, and outsiders and hangers-on charged items on their accounts. If the guests tried to move to other lodgings they found it impossible, since the innkeepers hired goons to threaten the owners of other places to which they might go. Even if the innkeepers were honest, those within the city walls were expected to keep a daily register of all travelers who lodged there, whether individuals or groups; they also had to note their origins and destinations, the goods they might have for sale, their mules or carts, their weapons if they had them. Armed horsemen without luggage or goods were forbidden to hire grooms or to stay in town overnight. Even lone foot travelers, whether armed or not, could be moved on if they had no baggage and no one in the city to vouch for them. No walking around in the city was permitted after nightfall, though during the hottest summer months the people whose homes had no halls or courtyards were allowed to have their doors ajar and sit on the stoops to enjoy the evening coolness. But the wooden gates that led from the alleys out to the main streets were closed and guarded at nightfall, and only those seeking emergency help from a doctor or midwife were allowed to pass—and then only if they had a regulation "night travel permit," duly authenticated, and if their residence and identity had been checked.

Certainly Ma-t'ou market would seem a more attractive choice for a couple seeking to hide out. Despite its size it had few garrison troops and no senior officials in residence. It had been attacked twice by bandits, in 1641 and 1648, but regained prosperity rapidly—as we can tell by a number of indices. Its major market days on the third and eighth day of every ten-day cycle, and the lesser market days on the fifth and tenth, dictated the market cycle of the surrounding areas. It was the only town with significant trade being moved by both road and water, trade that was worth taxing. It had a sizable urban working population, strong trade guilds, more temples than the other towns, more gardens, larger religious festivals. It was the only town in the county that supported a family of well-known physicians.

The couple needed somewhere to hide, for by the mere act of running away from her husband, woman Wang had become a criminal in the eyes of the law. Only if a wife was severely hurt or mutilated by her husband, or if she was forced by him to commit sexual acts with others, was she free to leave him. An example of a husband who by his actions put himself beyond the pale of the married relationship was furnished in Ning-yang, northwest of T'an-ch'eng (and also in Yen prefecture), in a case that was cited by jurists in the K'ang-hsi reign: a husband who sold his wife off as a prostitute and subsequently, having been forced by the magistrate to take her back, connived at her adultery with their lodging-house keeper, was considered to have "severed the bonds of marriage." But barring acts of this nature by the husband, the woman who ran away was classified as a fugitive and subject to a punishment of one hundred blows. All those who helped her or sheltered her—unless they could prove total ignorance of her fugitive status—could be subject to punishment in the same way as those who harbored fugitives or the wives and daughters of military deserters.

The act of adultery, furthermore, made both woman Wang and her paramour liable to serious punishment. The *Legal Code* stipulated that those having illegal intercourse by mutual consent were to be punished with eighty blows; if the woman was married, with ninety blows; if they intrigued to meet away from the woman's house, with one hundred blows, whether the woman was married or not. The man and the woman who had illegal intercourse, by mutual consent or after intriguing to meet away from the woman's house, received identical punishment. If the woman gave birth to a child after the illegal intercourse, the natural father met the expenses of raising it. The husband could sell off his adulterous wife or keep her, as he chose; but if he sold her in marriage to the adulterer, then both the husband and the adulterer were punished with eighty blows, the woman had to be divorced and returned to her family, and the price originally paid for her was forfeited to the government.

The punishment could be more serious than this, however, since the husband was considered justified in killing either his wife or the adulterer or both if he caught them in the act and slew them while in his initial rage. As in the case of killing to revenge a parent, the husband had to act swiftly, and in 1646 a rider had been added to the law, presumably to prevent vendettas or extended pursuit in the desire for revenge, stating that the husband was not justified in killing either of the adulterers if they merely were dallying before committing the sexual act, or if they had committed adultery but surrendered to him on their own, or "if he caught them in a place other than that where the adultery was committed." Thus by leaving Jen's house without being caught, woman Wang and her lover became legally more secure.

Not that life on the road can have been particularly secure, even if it was lively. The list of people technically under the supervision of the "Inspector of Humble Professions"—whose office like so much else in T'an-ch'eng had been burned down in the 1640s and not yet rebuilt—included such wandering specialists as fortunetellers, diviners, physiognomists and graphologists, jugglers, conjurers, actors, jesters and street wrestlers, storytellers and itinerant Buddhist and Taoist priests, woman dentists and midwives, the chiefs of the beggar groups, pipers, drummers, flute players, firecracker makers, tea sellers, and chair bearers. Huang Liu-hung's own reports often mentioned grooms, yamen runners, couriers and clerks from the post stations, the staffs of the state-managed hostels, and crowds of peddlers so poor and so numerous—their stalls under matting sheds in rows on the streets-that Huang gave up all attempts to tax them. Besides these there were refugees, fugitives from justice, and army deserters. Despite the regulations, such people could often find work, since farmers valued them as a source of cheap labor and asked no questions, while restaurant and lodging-house keepers would give them food and shelter if they could pay; making a living was more important than following the exact letter of the registration laws.

Indeed, there seems to have been a virtual fugitive subculture with its own rules and its own exploitations, inevitably involving the law-abiding civilian population because of the strict laws against harboring fugitives and the rigors of mutual responsibility under the *pao-chia* registration system. We see something of the fugitives' world from a case reported in T'an-ch'eng where a fugitive was used to harass an enemy in a private commercial feud. The police clerk Wei accused the inn-keeper Shih Wen-yü of hiring a fugitive for three hundred cash a month to work at his inn on the very steps of the T'an-ch'eng magistrate's yamen. Wei attempted to have Shih imprisoned on this charge; investigation showed, however, that the story was a trumped-up one (though the fugitive was real enough), fabricated by Wei so that he would not have to pay for the hundred or more cups of wine he had drunk on credit in Shih's inn over the previous year. Wei had blackmailed the fugitive into making the false charge. In such cases it was not so much that the fugitive's testimony had to be believed, but rather that his presence had to be disproved, which was not always easy; on this occasion Shih was luckily proved innocent, since the magistrate held an informal police line-up at which the fugitive could not distinguish Shih from a neighboring bean-curd seller. Other cases show that soldiers also harassed the innocent through a fairly subtle confidence game: Soldier A, pretending to be a fugitive, would go into a moored boat or some isolated village; other soldiers would then come and "arrest" him, pretending to be police runners, harassing the locals for harboring a fugitive, and robbing them as they left. Or perhaps they would briefly build up an identity in some village as hired hands and then, when all were drunk together one evening, cut themselves up, tear their own clothes, and claim they had been "robbed" in order to get hush money from the local villagers; if suspicions began to be aroused, one of their friends would come claiming to be a superior officer from the fugitive unit, and would reclaim them. At times it might be the ferrymen themselves running the rackets and claiming far more than the stipulated rate of one copper coin a person and two coppers per mule: demanding extra money in rain or snow or late at night, extra to allow a coffin on their boat, or holding passengers to ransom when out in the middle of the stream. While ashore the ferry guard might levy his own "taxes" and confiscate the goods of those who refused to pay, or fondle the women and make them pay to be released.

If it was hard for the two of them on the run, it must have been a nightmare for woman Wang after her lover abandoned her a short time later and left her alone on the road. The society of T'an-ch'eng did not supply many jobs for women, even if they were regarded as reputable: a few became midwives or diviners; some who were trusted and well known locally served as marriage go-betweens and as guarantors who would take responsibility for the women prisoners in the local jail. A few jobs were available in the orphanages and the homes for the totally indigent and the old, where women were employed as nurses, as children's companions, or as watchmen, as well as houseworkers to clean up and do laundry. For such work they would get their keep and an allowance of three hundred copper cash a month, or else a flat wage of six taels a year—roughly equivalent to the wages of men in the poorer positions in the local yamen. Those women who had the resources for a loom could spin and sell the product, but that was usually work done in one's own home, and woman Wang now had no home. If they were at the right place at the right time, they might get a job as a maid in one of the larger households. There was a slight chance of becoming a worker in a Taoist or Buddhist convent. Otherwise the main employment must have been in the gambling houses, teahouses, and brothels of T'an-ch'eng, of Ma-t'ou market, of Hung-

hua post station, even—according to Huang Liu-hung—in quite isolated rural villages, where local gentry set up brothels just as in the
urban centers, giving protection to the women and taking a percentage
of their money in return.

Woman Wang chose none of these alternatives, nor did she continue her flight alone. What she did was head back to her original
home in Kuei-ch'ang; but when she got near the house she was too
frightened to confront her husband Jen.

Near her village stood a Taoist temple to the Three Forces—the
heavens, the waters, and the earth—forces that could bring happiness
(heaven), remission of sins (water), and protection from evil (earth).
Here she was given shelter by the sole resident of the temple, a Taoist
priest; and here a former neighbor of hers, Kao, came to offer incense
one day in November 1671 and caught a glimpse of her in one of the
side rooms of the temple.

"You are in charge of a temple to the gods," he shouted to the
priest. "What do you mean by keeping women in here?"

"She's the wife of a man called Jen in the village," the priest
replied. "I heard that she ran off with someone, and Jen went out
looking for her to get her back. But she didn't dare return home and
took shelter here. Because she is one of our villagers, it would not have
been good to just send her away."

While they were still talking about her, Jen himself came into the
temple, having learned that woman Wang had returned and was hid-
ing there. "A fine kind of priest you are," he shouted angrily. "My wife
hides out in your temple and you don't even tell me about it."

"She's the wife from your house," countered Kao. "Why should
she end up at the temple? You don't even know that, and now you
want the priest to explain it to you?"

Even angrier, Jen shouted, "Oh, so in that case it must be you
who hid her out here in the temple," and at this insult Kao hit him
twice in the face. Jen swore at him and left, leaving his wife where she
was.

This sudden outburst of rage between the two men may have
been because of some long pent-up grievance—they were neighbors,
Kao was comparatively well off, with a covered porch to his house and
a wife named Ts'ao whom Jen also seems to have disliked. But Kao
should not have hit Jen, however severe the insult; the *Legal Code* was
strict about this and drew distinctions about fights of this kind with
such minute attention to detail that they were clearly regarded as a
major problem. Any person striking another with a hand or foot was
to be punished with twenty blows if he caused no wound, with thirty
blows if he caused a wound; any person striking another with an object
of any kind would receive thirty blows if no wound was caused, forty
if there was a wound—a wound being defined by discoloration or

swelling in the place struck, as well as by bleeding. Tearing out more than one inch of hair was punished with fifty blows, striking another so as to cause internal bleeding with eighty blows; eighty blows too for throwing ordure at the head of another, and a hundred blows for stuffing ordure into his mouth or nose, for breaking a tooth or bone, or injuring the eyes. In cases where permanent injury was caused, the offender forfeited half his property to pay the support of the injured party.

Jen now had a real grievance against Kao, one that would fester for months, but he did not press any charges against him—presumably the situation was too humiliating to air any more publicly. Yet the incident had been awkward enough for both Kao and the priest, and they decided it would be wiser to make woman Wang leave the temple, though they hesitated to send her back to her husband right away. Instead they took her to her father-in-law and explained what had taken place. The father-in-law gave the two men tea. "There's nothing at all that I can do about this bitch," said he, and called a fellow to take woman Wang back to his son's house.

The priest said that Jen had been "out looking" for woman Wang; but however strong Jen's desire might have been to have his wife back— whether because he missed her or because he was planning vengeance against her—he was not in fact entitled to keep her, because of the crime of flight and adultery she had committed. The law was complicated on this point. It did state clearly that a husband could divorce a wife on one of seven grounds: inability to bear sons, lascivious behavior, failure to serve her in-laws properly, talking too much, having a thievish nature, being overjealous, and suffering from serious illness. Divorce by mutual consent was also permitted under the law. If the wife did not want the divorce, the husband was not allowed to divorce her if one of these three factors applied: the wife had mourned her husband's parents for three years; the husband had risen from poverty to riches during the time of his marriage; the wife had no family of her own to go to. Since woman Wang did not have a family living that she could return to, the law seemed at first glance to show that she should stay with Jen despite her infidelity; but a substatute added in the Ming stated specifically that the three exemptions from divorce did not apply if the woman had been adulterous. Since another clause of the *Legal Code* also stipulated that a husband would be beaten with eighty blows if he refused to send away his wife after she had committed an act for which she should have been divorced, it appears that technically Jen could have been punished for taking her back. But in fact nobody in the county administration took any action, nor did Jen follow any of the legal channels open to him. He did not start divorce proceedings. He did not arrange to sell woman Wang. He did not report her bad conduct to the local headman, so that her shame would be aired publicly, as he was entitled to do. Instead, he bought a new woven sleeping mat to lay upon the straw that served as their bed.

The two of them lived together again, in their house outside Kuei-ch'ang market, through the last months of 1671 and into January 1672. They would have been cold, for the mean temperature in Shantung during January was in the twenties, and the houses of the poor were frail: the walls were of beaten earth, mud bricks, or kaoliang stalks; the few wooden supports were unshaped branches, often thin and crooked; roofs were thatched thinly with straw and reeds and were not true proof against either wind or rain. If there was fuel available, it was used primarily for cooking, and the warmth from the cooking fire was fed under the raised brick sleeping platform through a system of flues; this sleeping platform was covered with a layer of straw. In Jen's house it was here that he placed the new mat he bought for woman Wang's return.

On an evening toward the end of January 1672, the two of them sat at home. Jen had told woman Wang to mend his jacket, and she was darning it by the light of a lamp. Outside it was snowing. The neighbors could see the light of the lamp shining from their house, and later they heard the two of them quarreling. The neighbors could hear the anger in the voices, though they could not make out the words. They were still listening when the lamp went out.

Woman Wang took off her outer jacket and trousers and her heavy shoes. She drew, over her bound feet, a pair of worn bed shoes, with soft soles of red cotton. Her jacket was blue, her thinner under-trousers were white. She lay in these clothes on the mat in the straw, and Jen waited while she fell asleep.

In the world it is winter, but it is warm here. There are lotuses in bloom on the green waters of the winter lake, their scent reaches her on the wind, there are people trying to pick them, but the plants drift away as the boats approach. She sees the winter mountains covered in flowers. The room is dazzlingly bright, a path of white stones leads to the door, red petals are scattered over the white stones, a single branch of blossom pokes through the window.

The branch stretches out over the table, the leaves are far apart, but the blossoms are pressed thickly together, they are not yet opened, they are like the wings of a butterfly, like the wings of a damp butterfly, moistened and hanging down; the stems that hold them to the branch are fine as hairs.

She can see how beautiful she is, the lines are gone from her face, her hands are smooth as a girl's, not rough from work. Her brows are dark and perfectly arched, her teeth are white and perfectly spaced, she practices her smile and the teeth just appear, she checks the corners of the lips and the corners of the eyes.

The sleeping place is covered with furs thick as palm fronds, they are deep and soft, the coverlet is filled with shreds of cotton and powdered incense, the chamber is filled with its fragrance. The man is handsome but he looks ill, his face is bathed with tears. She rubs his temples, she brushes the dust from his clothes, she wipes the tears from his eyes; she can feel on his body the weals from his beatings and she rubs them gently with her fingers.

She unfastens the belt of his robe and slips her hand inside, she massages him lightly with her fists, but he cannot move from pain, there is a tumor growing out of his chest, it is as big as a bowl and gnarled like the growth at the foot of a tree. She slips a golden bracelet off her wrist and presses it down upon the tumor, the flesh rises around the outside of the bracelet, but the center of the tumor rises up through the metal, she draws a knife with a fine blade from her robe and slices it gently around the bracelet's edge. The dark blood gushes out onto the bed and matting, she takes a red pill from her mouth and presses it into the wound, as she presses into the wound it slowly closes.

She is tired. Her limbs feel delicate and heavy, her legs straighten and bend as if she has no force, but the beautiful women admire her, they cluster around her, their foreheads bound in red silk bands, their robes violet with sashes of green. They carry bows and quivers on their backs, they have been out hunting.

She passes through door after door until they reach the courtyard. The trees are tall enough to reach the red eaves of the buildings, the court is full of flowers, and the seed pods are drifting down off the trees in the light breeze, a swing is hanging down on slack cords. They are helping her up into the swing, she stands erect on the swing and reaches up her arms to hold the ropes, she is wearing a short-sleeved dress and her arms are shining, the ropes of the swing are hanging from the clouds, her dark hair swirls around her neck, she stretches up with her bright arms and light as a swallow swings up into the clouds.

There is a boat of many colors drifting toward her in the sky, it is draped with fine clouds. People are climbing aboard. There is only one oarsman, he holds a short wooden oar. The oar has no blade at the end, the end is thickly clustered with feathers like a giant fan; as the oarsman waves the feathers a light wind blows and they move ever faster through the clouds. There is no sound but the throbbing of the light wind. The clouds are all around, they press in on her like cotton wool, they are soft under her feet, and she is slightly dizzy as though still traveling on the boat. She looks up and sees the stars close to her eyes, they range in size from great jars down to tiny cups, they are neatly arranged like the seeds within a lotus flower; below is an infinite silver sea, through gaps in the clouds she sees whole cities big as beans.

In front of her is a flight of steps, the steps are shining like rock crystal, she is reflected in each step as in a mirror. Clear water is running over white sand. There are little pavilions with red windows, there are beautiful women moving in the pavilions, and young men in embroidered coats and red shoes. People are eating fruit from jade bowls, they are drinking wine from goblets a foot around the rim. The peonies are ten feet high, the camellias twice as high again. A girl with white fingers plays an instrument she has never seen before, another plucks a lute with an ivory plectrum and sings of women who weep. As the music sounds a light breeze blows, birds crowd into the courtyard and settle quietly in the trees.

She sits down at the foot of a high tree. The trunk of the tree is wide and smooth, a single thread of yellow sap courses through its center, the leaves grow thickly on its delicate branches. It casts a deep shade. Red blossoms shimmer among the leaves and tinkle like precious stones as they fall. A bird is singing in the tree. Its feathers are gold and green. It is a strange bird, its tail is as long as its body, and the song it sings is a sad song that makes her think of home.

She moves away on high, scented shoes with hurried steps through the morning dew, the dew makes her shoes and stockings glossy with moisture. The trees are growing thickly, but through the trees she can see the tower, the walls are of copper, there are tall pillars of iron supporting a shimmering roof. There are no doors or windows in the walls but there are deep indentations, placed close together, and she climbs up by placing her feet in these. Inside she is quiet, she is safe.

He kneels beside her. He is trembling and hugs his own body with his arms. "Eat this," she says, and with her bare feet she treads the delicacies into the ground. "Over here," she says, and he offers her the night-soil bucket, holding it out for her in his hands. "Clean these," she says, and gives him her tiny embroidered shoes, caked with mud.

She places a woman's cap on his head, with her make-up she paints his face, she paints his face like a warrior's. There is a light cotton football, she kicks it into the air and he scampers after it, the sweat is pouring off him. The ball is transparent and filled with a glittering substance, he kicks it up in a shining arc through the air, it whistles through the air like a comet, it falls into the water, its light goes out in the water with a gurgle. And she sees that there is no tower, there are no round walls supporting a shimmering roof, there is no forest; there is only a cheap ring lying on the ground, needles thrust through it on which the lid of a make-up box is resting, all lying abandoned among the briers.

He stands before her in his ragged clothes, the snot is dribbling down his face, he smiles at her. "Does the pretty lady love me?" he asks. He hits her. The crowd presses closer to watch. He rolls a ball from his snot and gives it to her. "Eat it," he says. She puts it in her mouth and tries to swallow, he laughs aloud, "The pretty lady loves me," he cries. She wants to answer but her mouth is full of earth, she is pinned, she is pinned by the snake's coils that enfold her, she struggles harder, her body is thrashing in the water, she can smell the filth in the water, the people are crowded along *the river bank, they are watching and laughing, they must help her, she must cry out, they will not help her.*

As Jen's hands drove deeply into her neck, woman Wang reared her body up from the bed, but she could not break free. His hands stayed tight around her throat and he forced his knee down onto her belly to hold her still. Her legs thrashed with such force that she shredded the sleeping mat, her bowels opened, her feet tore through the mat to the straw beneath, but his grip never slackened and none of the neighbors heard a sound as woman Wang died.

It was still snowing in T'an-ch'eng. Jen picked up his wife's body and drew her blue outer jacket around her shoulders. He opened the door and began to carry her through the woods, toward the house of his neighbor Kao. This was how he had planned it: when she was dead he would take her body to Kao's house and leave it in the gateway; he would say she had been having an adulterous affair with Kao and that Kao had killed her. The story would be plausible: she had already run away once, and Kao was a violent and quick-tempered man. The two of them could have been carrying on every day while Jen was away at work.

But Jen never reached Kao's house with woman Wang. As he walked through the dark wood a dog barked. Watchmen, sheltering in the porch, banged a warning gong. A light shone. Jen dropped the body in the snow and waited. No one came to investigate. The light went out and there was silence again. He left woman Wang lying where she was and returned to his empty house, locked the door, and went to sleep.

The body of woman Wang lay out in the snow all night. When she was found she looked almost alive: for the intense cold had preserved, in her dead cheeks, a living hue.

Suggested Readings

An excellent study of peasant life in China is Hsiao-t'ung Fei, *Peasant Life in China: A Field Study of Country Life in the Yangtze Valley* (London: G. Routledge and Sons, 1939). Nobel laureate Pearl Buck's novel *The Good Earth* (New York: John Day Co., 1931) portrays Chinese village life, emphasizing the roles of wife and mother, with considerable insight. Pearl Buck also translated the Chinese bandit epic *The Water Margin* under the title *All Men Are Brothers* (New York: John Day Co., 1933). Jonathan D. Spence, the author of this reading selection, has produced a number of excellent and readable works on seventeenth-century China that are well worth the student's attention.

Universities and the
Scientific Revolution

Eric Ashby

Universities during the twentieth century have been so much in the forefront of scientific and technological progress that it is difficult to realize that this has not always been the case. In fact, the Scientific Revolution of the seventeenth and eighteenth centuries was largely a non-university phenomenon carried forward by individual investigators and learned societies. This reading selection discusses the European universities' slow accommodation to the new currents of scientific investigation and the reasons why they had failed for so long to take a leading role in scientific development. It was not until the latter half of the nineteenth century that scientific studies were integrated into university curriculums and scientific research was recognized as a legitimate pursuit for university faculties. That required a virtual revolution in the philosophy and organization of higher learning, out of which emerged many of the characteristics of the modern university.

The university in modern society faces a constant problem. One of its accepted roles has been to protect and preserve traditional truths and values against passing fads and dogmas. It is also expected, however, to be open to change and ready to support and advance new movements, methods, and approaches. This reading illustrates how important freedom of inquiry and an open exchange of ideas are in maintaining the proper balance between those roles.

I t is legitimate to speak of a scientific revolution; for although there has been no age since the time of Aristotle without its scientists, there was, contained within two generations in the seventeenth century, a unique flowering of genius which re-orientated the thought of Western Man. A man born in the year when Charles I came to the throne could have seen, as a child, Kepler and Galileo; he could have talked with Harvey; Boyle would have been his contemporary; and in his old age he could have read Newton's *Principia*. The history of this scientific revolution lies almost completely outside the universities. It is true that Harvey did the best of his work in Padua, and Newton taught at Cambridge. But these circumstances were incidental to their discoveries. In no sense can the universities of Europe be regarded as instigators of the scientific revolution.

Already in the eighteenth century the new way of thinking had taken root in Europe. It was an age of reason, when men found that they could explain many things in the universe with the aid of a few simple abstractions, and what they could not explain they were content to reject. It was an age of invention, when men found that rule-of-thumb mechanical devices, like Newcomen's steam-pump and Arkwright's spinning frame, could increase production and wealth. It was an age which began to realise that science could be harnessed to industry: Euler published in 1760 a book on the mathematical treatment of gear-wheels, and, about the same time, Black's discovery of latent heat enabled James Watt to perfect the steam-engine. It was an age not without its own triumph of scientific imagination, for toward the end of the century Lavoisier began to do for chemistry what Newton had done for physics.

Science became a respectable leisure-time occupation for country gentlemen and townsmen of substance. The Marquis of Rockingham (for example), twice Prime Minister of England, entertained himself by conducting experiments on the production of oil from tar. At meetings of philosophical clubs and societies, such as the Lunar Society of Birmingham (founded by Erasmus Darwin in 1766) and the Literary and Philosophical Society of Manchester (founded in 1781), lectures on electricity, hydrostatics, gravitation, mechanics, and optics, with experiments, were given to fashionable and enthusiastic audiences. All over the country there were peripatetic lectures financed by public subscription, and for members of the middle classes who wanted a more systematic training in science there were courses offered by some of the dissenting academies. The universities shared little of this enthusiasm.

UNIVERSITIES AND THE SCIENTIFIC REVOLUTION

91

UNIVERSITIES AND THE SCIENTIFIC REVOLUTION   From Eric Ashby, *Technology and the Academics; An Essay on Universities and the Scientific Revolution* (New York: St. Martin's Press, 1958), pp. 4–27.

It is true that science was taught in the Scottish universities, but most of it was suited to the level of schoolboys. The Universities of Oxford and Cambridge, sleeping behind their ancient statutes, took even less account of this enthusiasm. Even at the threshold of the nineteenth century, 113 years after the publication of Newton's *Principia,* institutions for higher education in Britain were still making practically no contribution to scientific thought.

In the accomplishment of the scientific revolution British scientists played a notable and distinguished part. But British universities (except fortuitously and incidentally) played no part whatever. They had allowed the revolution to pass over their heads and still, a century later, they were providing no lead in scientific thought. They reflected yesterday: they did not illuminate tomorrow. This isolationism on the part of the universities cannot be attributed to any one cause; indeed, the causes differed from one university to another. To appreciate these causes we must deal separately with Oxford, Cambridge, and the Scottish Universities.

Oxford was weighed down by every imaginable device for inertia. Dissenters, who were the greatest enthusiasts for science and technology, were not admitted to the University. Power lay with the colleges, which were obliged by their statutes to elect fellows on all sorts of criteria other than that of intellectual distinction. The teaching staff was comprised of celibates in holy orders, members of the Church of England, committed to a curriculum drawn up in the time of Charles I. Such natural science as was taught was Aristotelian, dogmatic and desiccated. These circumstances alone would have been enough to prevent Oxford from adapting itself to the new scientific age. But there was a further circumstance which, had it not been for the University's wonderful powers of adaptation in the 1850's, might have threatened the very viability of Oxford as a university. This was the almost complete atrophy, in the eighteenth and early nineteenth centuries, of half the University's function.

On paper the pattern of Oxford was consistent with its generic status as a mediaeval university. It had a dual function: as a group of colleges where young men could study the trivium and quadrivium as a preliminary to their professional training; and as a group of professional schools providing advanced study in theology, medicine, and law. The first function was discharged by college tutors. Among these tutors there was scarcely any differentiation of teaching duties: each tutor was responsible for teaching his group of students all the subjects for the degree of B.A.: ancient history, Latin and Greek, poetry, philosophy and logic, mathematics. They were in fact schoolmasters. That this course of liberal studies was intended for boys was evident from some of the statutes still in force at Oxford in 1800, for example, a statute directing corporal chastisement for those who neglect their lessons.

It was an integral part of the pattern of the University that this preliminary liberal education should be followed by advanced study in a professional school; and it is clearly for this reason that Oxford had, in addition to college tutors, public university professors and lecturers in the faculties of theology, law, and medicine. Public teachers in science subjects were attached to the Faculty of Medicine. Thus chairs in medicine, natural philosophy, botany, and geometry had existed since the seventeenth century and (as a gesture toward the advocates of reform) chairs of chemistry and experimental philosophy were added in the early nineteenth century. But this second function of the University, though nominally recognised, was actually ignored. Even as late as 1852 the Regius Professor of Medicine reported that he had discontinued his lectures. He formerly had 10 students a year and the numbers had dwindled to 4. The Professor of Geometry gave tuition in his house to about 3 students a year. The Professor of Botany was obliged to give 12 lectures a year, but there were often no students to attend. The newly created chair of chemistry attracted only 12 students a year, even though the length of the course had been halved. There was actually a reduction in the numbers attending science lectures between the 1820's and the 1840's. This can be attributed partly to Oxford's preoccupation in the Tractarian movement and partly to the increasing competition for University honours, which could not be secured through scientific studies. The position in legal studies was similar. In brief, two of the professional schools in Oxford had atrophied, and science teaching (with the singular exception of lectures in mineralogy) was at a very low ebb. Lawyers went to London and medical men to Edinburgh or Leyden or to one of the hospital schools in London.

It needs no imagination to realise how formidable these barriers were to the introduction of science into Oxford. Most of the students who went there were candidates for the priesthood of the Church of England or were drawn from the upper classes, destined to preside over their country estates or to enter public life through politics. Those who aspired to academic life had to get fellowships, and in so far as election to fellowships depended upon intellectual qualifications, they were qualifications in the classics, not in science, not even in logic. Accordingly, eighteenth-century Oxford had become a self-perpetuating machinery for safeguarding the interests of college fellows; most of its teaching was concentrated upon what even a fourteenth-century university would have regarded as only the prerequisites of a university education.

In Cambridge the barriers to the introduction of science were less formidable, but it could not be said, even as late as 1852, that scientific work had taken root there. However, Cambridge had produced Newton and was proud of the fact; and even before the opening of the nineteenth century mathematics and mechanics were essential ingredients for a degree. The mathematics of those days had a strong Greek flavour. Consider, for example, this problem set in an examination at St. John's College in 1794:

> A countryman, being employed by a poulterer to drive a flock of geese and turkeys to London, in order to distinguish his own from any he might meet on the road, pulled 3 feathers out of the tails of the turkeys and 1 out of those of the geese, and upon counting them found that the number of turkey feathers exceeded twice those of the geese by 15. Having bought 10 geese and sold 15 turkeys by the way, he was surprised to find as he drove them into the poulterer's yard, that the number of geese exceeded the number of turkeys in the proportion of 7 : 3. Required the number of each.

When, in 1822, a classical tripos was introduced at Cambridge, aspirants to the tripos still had first to obtain honours in the mathematical tripos. In justice to Cambridge it should not be forgotten that the judges, statesmen, and bishops of that day who graduated in classics were more familiar with such concepts as mass, velocity, and inertia than most modern classicists are.

The lectures on applied chemistry by W. Farish (who succeeded to the chair of chemistry in 1793) were well attended, although they did not 'count' toward a degree or toward the elections to college fellowships. Furthermore, Cambridge, although it excluded dissenters from its degrees as rigorously as Oxford did, was not so prejudiced toward their thinking; and Cambridge was not so helplessly bound by the authoritarian teaching of the Anglican Church. Perhaps that is why it was able to abandon the Aristotelian tradition in science teaching, while Oxford still retained it.

Nevertheless, even a century after the death of Newton, it could not for one moment be said that Cambridge was alight with the flame of science. The overwhelming majority of students who read seriously read for holy orders. Even the mathematics and mechanics courses, suffering from a sort of Newtonian scholasticism, were not taking account of advances in knowledge since Newton's day. When a Royal Commission examined the affairs of Cambridge during 1850–52 they heard from the Professor of Chemistry (the Rev. J. Cumming, who was appointed in 1815):

> A course of about 28 lectures was given annually by the present Professor . . . until the year 1831. From that time thirty lectures were given in the Lent and twenty in the Easter Term. This was continued until 1845, but the attendance in the Easter Term was

so small, consisting of only four or five medical students, that the original plan was resumed of giving lectures only in one Term. . . . There is no residence, museum, library, collection, or apparatus attached to the Professorship . . . and there are no funds for this purpose. There are no opportunities afforded to students for instruction in the actual manipulation of instruments. . . . Hitherto the study of Chemistry has not only been neglected but discouraged in the University, as diverting the attention of pupils from what have been considered their proper academical studies.

This—we have to recollect—was evidence given a whole generation after Dalton had published his *New System of Chemical Philosophy* and after Berzelius had determined the atomic weights of 40 elements; it was over two generations after the researches of Cavendish (himself a Cambridge man) and after Lavoisier had established chemistry as a quantitative science.

The situation in other sciences was not much better: the Professor of Botany—the Rev. J. S. Henslow—could only attend to his subject during one term in the year, 'consistent' (as he put it) 'with my duties to my parish'. Responsibility for teaching physics was shared by the Lucasian professor of mathematics and the Plumian professor of astronomy. In astronomy there was practical work; indeed it was the only subject in which research was required of the professor. (The origin of this is that the founder, Dr. Thomas Plume, Archdeacon of Rochester, required the Trustees of his will to consult, among others, Sir Isaac Newton about the duties of the Chair.) In other branches of physics there was no practical work; there was no equipment except that privately owned by the professors (G. G. Stokes, Lucasian professor, had purchased the equipment of earlier professors because he had agreed to lecture on physics); and the Plumian professor said in evidence that there was 'more interest . . . in abstract mathematics than in attending to the experimental evidence on which the different departments of Natural Philosophy rest. . . . There may be reason to fear that the present system of mathematical studies in the University tends to become too abstract and too exclusive of the propositions and processes of reasoning required by the actual demands of science . . . a taste for Experimental Philosophy might be promoted by founding a complete Cabinet of Physical Apparatus.'

Apart from astronomy, which was part of the mediaeval quadrivium, only one scientific subject in Cambridge had caught the enthusiasm of the age. That was geology under Adam Sedgwick. He records that for eighty-eight years, up to 1818, 'no course of lectures was given by any of the Professors', and that this was due 'to the absence of all academic interest in subjects connected with the natural history of the earth'. But Sedgwick began in 1820 to lecture on geology to a mixture of students and townspeople, and his lectures were supplemented by observational work in the Museum.

To sum up: Oxford at the turn of the century was offering young men of 18 a course of study intended under the Laudian Code for boys. The more advanced studies in the professional faculties, which the Laudian Code assumed would follow the liberal education in the arts, had atrophied. Cambridge, though more sensitive to the age than Oxford, could not by any stretch of imagination be said to have responded to the scientific revolution. England's two ancient universities were—in Matthew Arnold's words—'places where the youth of the upper class prolong to a very great age, and under some very admirable influences, their school education . . . they are in fact still schools'.

The purpose of this analysis is not to pass judgment on early Victorian Oxford and Cambridge, still less to pass judgment on the merits of a classical versus a scientific education. It is simply to establish the fact that scientific thought, which by 1800 was already consolidated in the foundations of modern physics and chemistry (those of biology were still to be laid by Darwin), and which had caught the imagination of the general public (even of artisans, who crowded to Anderson's 'anti-toga' lectures in Glasgow), had scarcely influenced the universities of England. The scientific revolution had occurred not through, but in spite of, the English universities.

The Scottish universities were more sensitive to the spirit of the age. When Charles Lyell compared the Scottish and English universities in 1827 he was able to say that the elements of natural philosophy 'form an indispensable part of preliminary education in Scotland'. Edinburgh and Glasgow had flourishing medical schools, and the scientific subjects prerequisite to these were taught, under the aegis of medicine and usually by medical men, to large audiences. There was a rigorous examination system. The formal lectures were often punctuated by viva voce examinations. A picture of Scottish university teaching at its best is given by Lyell. He is referring to John Millar, a distinguished professor of law in Glasgow at the end of the eighteenth century:

> Every morning, before he began his address from the chair, he endeavoured to ascertain, by putting a number of questions to his pupils, whether they had been able to follow his reasoning on the preceding day; and it was his custom, when the lecture was over, to remain some time in his lecture-room to converse with those students who were desirous of further information on the subject. By engaging with them in an easy dialogue, he contrived to remove obscurities, and to correct any errors into which they might have fallen. This meeting was called among the students, familiarly, *the*

committee, from which they acknowledged that they reaped more benefit than from the lecture itself.

Most of the Scottish science professors of those days were part-time teachers, whose main preoccupation was medical practice; so, notwithstanding the fact that scientific subjects formed an integral part of the curriculum, the universities were not able to take the initiative in original scientific work. There were notable exceptions, for example Joseph Black, one of the great names in chemistry, who brought into the lecture theatre some of the spirit of scientific research, and who earned praise from no less a dignitary than the Lord Chancellor of England, Lord Brougham:

> The gratification of attending one of Black's last lecture courses exceeded all I have ever enjoyed. I have heard the greatest understandings of the age giving forth their efforts in their most eloquent tongues—have heard the commanding periods of Pitt's majestic oratory—the vehemence of Fox's burning declaration—but I would prefer, for mere intellectual gratification—to be once more allowed the privilege—of being present, while the first philosopher of his age was the historian of his own discoveries, and be an eye-witness of those experiments by which he had formerly made them, once more performed by his own hands.

One reason for the vitality of Scottish universities was that they remained throughout the eighteenth century in touch with scientific thought on the Continent. At a time when the English universities were closed shops for the Church of England and were therefore insulated against influences from abroad, the Scottish universities maintained a constant traffic of ideas, especially with the universities of Holland. In the early eighteenth century the University of Leyden became an important centre for the propagation of Newtonian physics through Europe. Scottish students were welcomed in Holland to study medicine and mathematics. Men like Black and Cullen, who put their imprint upon scientific studies in Glasgow and Edinburgh, were disciples of Boerhaave, and the historian of the University of Edinburgh records that at this period teaching in the University had become distinctively Dutch.

The most striking difference between the pattern of teaching in the Scottish universities and in Oxford and Cambridge in the 1820's was that in Scotland—through the method of professional lectures— each subject was taught by what was (for those days) a specialist; whereas in the English universities teaching was undifferentiated, in the hands of college tutors. For this reason alone Scotland had a far greater right to regard her universities as having maintained their traditional pattern. Furthermore the Scottish universities were complete: education was not (as in Oxford and Cambridge) truncated even before the end of the quadrivium. But nevertheless even the Scottish universities did not (except spasmodically) break new ground in scientific thought. Two circumstances contributed to this. In the first place, there were the extra-mural preoccupations of the professors. In the second place, there was the fact that the Scottish universities were *de facto* still both colleges and professional schools. Boys entered at 14, as in mediaeval times they entered the English universities; so a great many of the 4000 undergraduates in Scottish universities were virtually schoolboys.

Fewer than three generations lie between the impoverished science teaching, most of it without laboratories or equipment, in the British universities of the 1850's and the research schools of J. J. Thomson and Gowland Hopkins in Cambridge, Rutherford in Manchester, Baylis in London, and Robinson in Oxford. During these three generations the British universities learned not to drag their feet at the back of the procession of scientific thought. Today the procession has become a race, with universities as the pacemakers. They have adapted themselves to the contemporary environment; and none have accomplished the adaptation more efficiently than Oxford and Cambridge. Yet they remain in the genus university: indeed, functionally they are today truer to their mediaeval prototypes than they were at any time during the previous two centuries. In accomplishing this adaptation the universities have recovered their prestige and influence without losing their identity.

There was powerful and sustained resistance to any adaptation. For fifty years men of foresight battered against this resistance through books, through articles in the quarterly reviews, through speeches. Among the pioneers of complaint were Babbage and Brewster. Babbage's *Observations on the Decline of Science in England* (1830) was a somewhat petulant attack, largely directed against the Royal Society and complaining about the lack of public appreciation for scientists. Brewster wrote a belligerent review of Babbage's book, in which, after giving a list of British scientists whose work had been done outside universities (including Priestley, Cavendish, Rumford, Davy, Dalton, Herschel, Faraday), he went on to say, in the vein of overstatement which was tolerated in those days: 'nor need we have any hesitation in adding that within the last 15 years not a single discovery or invention of prominent interest has been made in our colleges, and that there is not one man in all the eight universities of Great Britain who is at present known to be engaged in any train of original research.' Pressure for scientific education became organised through the British Association for the Advancement of Science and the Society of Arts. By mid-century the Government itself was involved in applying pressure through the cautious and wordy mechanism of royal commissions and committees of inquiry. Finally, in the landslide of prejudices which followed the publication of *The Origin of Species* (1859) the battle was won, though it took some two more generations before science was admitted to its appropriate place in university education; indeed the process of assimilation is not complete yet.

Of the many environmental forces which injected scientific thought into British universities, two may be singled out as of special importance. Both came from outside Britain. One was an ideal. The other was an anxiety. The ideal was the German concept of *Wissenschaft:* the university as a centre for research. The anxiety was that continental countries by their vigorous application of science to industry would overtake Britain's industrial supremacy. Before describing the ecological play of these two forces on the British universities, we have to observe how the scientific revolution fared on the Continent.

Up to the middle of the nineteenth century the scientific revolution had left practically untouched the ancient universities of England. The Scottish universities had readily absorbed the new philosophy and faithfully transmitted it, but they did not have the opportunity to become creative centres of scientific thought.

The names of Bacon and Newton ensure to England a high place in the history of the scientific revolution. But it was France which first recognised the gigantic significance of Newton's work and which first put into practice Bacon's precepts. Why was this so? One reason, at any rate, is that France (unlike England) had the organisation for doing systematic scientific research. The Royal Society of London had to depend for its finances on the entrance payments and contributions of its own members. All it received from Charles II was its Charter. The Paris Academy, however, was in 1671 endowed for research by Louis XIV, and charged with the responsibility for doing experimental work and for disseminating the results of scientific enquiry. This responsibility it discharged with distinction throughout the eighteenth century, and when, under the genius of Lavoisier, the 'postponed scientific revolution in chemistry' (as Butterfield has called it) took place, Paris became the undisputed capital of scientific thought in Europe. The French Revolution (notwithstanding the fact that it was responsible for the deaths of such men as Lavoisier and Condorcet) was a great stimulus to science in France. In 1794 the new government set up the École Polytechnique with an allocation of some £12,000. It opened with 400 students. Its staff included the mathematicians Lagrange and Laplace, the chemist Berthollet, and the crystallographer Haüy. By 1800 the scientific spirit was firmly established in France and had permeated its education.

But there was no intellectual importation from Paris to Oxford and Cambridge. This can be attributed partly to the unpreparedness of the English universities, partly to the inevitable association of scientific thought in the minds of the English upper classes with the horrors of the Reign of Terror, and partly to the sinister shadow of Napoleon. By the time these obstacles had cleared away, French science, weakened by the over-centralisation first imposed by Napoleon's Université Impériale, had lost much of its authority.

France was the mother of organised scientific research. She was the first country to encourage the practice of experimental science on a large scale, systematically, and the first country to realise that (as Bacon had foretold) scientific work must not only be organised, it must also be summarised and propagated. The Academy, and the scientific schools closely associated with it, mobilised the intellect of the nation. Moreover, the popularisation of science (not for the common people—that began in England—but for the intelligentsia) began in France. Cuvier's *éloges historiques* are the forerunners of our Third Programme science talks. And it was France which led the way in the application of scientific principles to industry. The urge to apply science to industry did not, however, obscure the spirit in which what we now call pure science was studied. Here is Cuvier's buoyant view of science (written in a report presented to the Academy in 1808): 'Experiments alone, experiments that are precise, made with weights, measures and calculation . . . this today is the only legitimate way of reasoning and demonstration'. And as an example of the honour in which foreign scientists were held, there is the story about the visit to France of Charles Bell (the Edinburgh surgeon who first differentiated sensory and motor nerves and who is said not to have been properly appreciated in his own country). In France, Bell's name was so venerated that a professor of anatomy, when Bell visited his lecture room, dismissed his class of students with the words: 'C'est assez, messieurs, vous avez vu Charles Bell'.

The scientific spirit was unable to cross the Channel; but it did cross the Rhine, and it found in Germany a uniquely appropriate intellectual climate. The social prerequisites for the survival of science are finance, leisure, and freedom to pursue research, coupled with opportunities for scholars to associate together and to transmit ideas and techniques to their successors. All these were already present in Germany in the early nineteenth century. The German universities, founded and sustained by independent states, constituted an intellectual fellowship without parallel in Europe. Their teachers and students were constantly migrating from one university to another and continually interchanging ideas. Between one university and another there was a healthy rivalry. Of course liberalism did not prevail everywhere, but if one university was suffering through the illiberal interference or bigotry of some patron, there was always another university in the fellowship where persecuted professors might expect to be received and sheltered.

This unique network of institutions devoted to higher education had, after the turn of the century, recovered from a period of relative inactivity to become one of the major intellectual forces in Europe. At the beginning of the eighteenth century the German universities had indeed not emerged from the shadows of mediaeval scholasticism: they merely handed down a corpus of hallowed and unalterable knowledge. But during the eighteenth century Kant worked in Königsberg; the University of Halle awakened to a new age in scholarship under Christian and Friedrich August Wolf; and in 1737 the University of Göttingen was inaugurated.

Halle and Göttingen marked a new departure in the pattern of universities. The mediaeval German universities comprised the conventional faculties of philosophy, theology, law, and medicine. Hitherto the Faculty of Philosophy had served only as a handmaid to the professional faculties; in Halle and Göttingen, and subsequently in the other universities of Germany, it became the business of this faculty to pursue knowledge for its own sake, not merely as a prerequisite for the traditional professions. Philosophical studies were based on reason and not on dogma. There was *libertas docendi* and *libertas philosophandi*. Great scholars no longer worked only as individuals: groups of advanced students gathered round them to learn by apprenticeship, not by formal study. The idea arose that private study and research are essential qualifications for a university teacher; the scholar's dream was symbolised by a magic word: *Wissenschaft.*

It is always necessary to preface any discussion of *Wissenschaft* by saying that it is not translatable by the English word *science*. It covers the objective and critical approach to all knowledge. There could be no more vivid illustration of this than the fact that *Wissenschaft* became the guiding star of some German universities before the scientific revolution reached them. Apart from the physiologist Haller, who taught at Göttingen, most great German scientists of the eighteenth century worked (as their English counterparts did) outside the universities; but *Wissenschaft* flourished inside them, as an objective analysis of the classics, questioning, comparing, searching the ancient literatures for historical truth wherever it might lead. The first-fruits of this were authoritative editions of the classics, so much prized that they—and not English editions—were used by the classical scholars of Oxford and Cambridge. Then followed philology, the scientific study of language, the beginning of biblical criticism (exemplified by the publication in

1780 of Eichhorn's Old Testament exegesis from Göttingen), and the dispassionate, scientific approach to history (typified by Ranke's dictum of recording nothing but *wie es eigentlich gewesen).*

So the foundations of *Wissenschaft*—the empirical approach to knowledge—were laid in Germany not by scientists but by humanists, and they were laid in the universities. The German university, therefore, was a wonderfully fertile soil for the transplantation of the scientific spirit from France. Of course there was no dramatic moment when science suddenly became part of the university's life. But there was a time when it became obvious that all science had meant to French thought it was now going to mean also to German thought, and that the universities were to be its headquarters. Perhaps this time dates from the researches of Gauss at Göttingen and the writings of Alexander von Humboldt.

The adaptation of the German universities to experimental science did not take place without resistance. Just as the flow of scientific thought into Oxford and Cambridge was later to be held up for a generation by the mystique of 'liberal education', so the flow of scientific thought into German universities was for a time held up by another mystique: *Naturphilosophie.* This movement rejected the experimental approach to Nature in favour of a philosophy which assumed that some mysterious unity pervaded Nature, and which sought to understand the phenomena of science by speculating upon this unity. As a school of thought, guided by Schelling and influenced by Hegel, it became powerfully entrenched in many German universities. Its most fervent disciples regarded Newton with contempt and the notion of collecting data as futile.

But the experimentalists were succeeding in solving specific problems, and the disciples of *Naturphilosophie* were failing to solve them; so it was only a matter of time before the new scientific method displaced the old. In 1826 Justus von Liebig, whose eyes had been opened when he went to Paris to work under Gay-Lussac, established a chemistry laboratory in the University of Giessen; not the first chemistry laboratory in any university, but the first to offer a systematic training in chemical research, and therefore the first nucleus of a 'school' of chemistry. This is a critical event in the history of British science, for it was Liebig's laboratory, years later, which thrust the first powerful injection of the scientific spirit into English universities. We may catch the enthusiasm of that first University chemistry course from Liebig's own autobiographical memoir:

> The first years of my residence at Giessen were almost exclusively devoted to the improvement of organic analysis, and with the first successes there began at the small university an activity such as the world had not yet seen. . . . A kindly fate had brought

together in Giessen the most talented youths from all countries of Europe. . . . Every one was obliged to find his own way for himself. . . . We worked from dawn to the fall of night: there were no recreations and pleasures at Giessen. The only complaints were those of the attendant, who in the evenings, when he had to clean, could not get the workers to leave the laboratory.

Under the combined influences of German *Wissenschaft* and French empirical experimental science the German universities underwent a change of pattern. They still remained generically universities. Indeed they became more cosmopolitan than any universities had been since mediaeval times: students from abroad flocked to work with Liebig in Giessen or Bunsen in Marburg or Wöhler in Göttingen. But their pattern had irreversibly changed; in response to the tradition of *Wissenschaft* and the stimulus of scientific investigation the German university threw its energies into research and the training of research workers. The ideal put before the student was not the liberal humanism which had permeated the new University of Berlin under the leadership of Wilhelm von Humboldt; it was a single-minded, almost fanatical, devotion to the advancement of knowledge. It was an enthusiasm which excluded philosophy (for, they said, had not the impotent speculations of the nature-philosophers deprived Germany of years of precious time for experiments?); it excluded the applications of science, too (for technology was not admitted into the university pattern: even before the end of the eighteenth century it had been relegated to separate *Technische Hochschulen);* and it excluded any idea of education-for-life. Typical of the new German professoriate was Helmholz, and there is a vivid picture of his attitude to science in his Academical Discourse delivered at Heidelberg in 1862. Helmholz represents the full flowering of the German idea of the university as a centre for research, teaching through apprenticeship. In his Discourse he said:

> Whoever, in the pursuit of science, seeks after immediate practical utility, may generally rest assured that he will seek in vain. All that science can achieve is a perfect knowledge and a perfect understanding of the action of natural and moral forces. Each individual student must be content to find his reward in rejoicing over new discoveries, as over new victories of mind over reluctant matter, or in enjoying the aesthetic beauty of a well-ordered field of knowledge, where the connection and the filiation of every detail is clear to the mind, and where all denotes the presence of a ruling intellect; he must rest satisfied with the consciousness that he too has contributed something to the increasing fund of knowledge on which the dominion of man over all the forces hostile to intelligence reposes. . . . In conclusion, I would say, let each of us think of himself, not as a man seeking to gratify his own thirst for

knowledge, or to promote his own private advantage, or to shine by his own abilities, but rather as a fellow-labourer in one great common work bearing upon the highest interests of humanity.

And so there arose the disciple-fetish in Germany. For a century, graduates of Oxford have spoken of themselves as Balliol men, or Magdalen men, or Trinity men. In Germany they spoke of themselves as Bunsen's pupil, or Kekulé's pupil, or Sach's pupil. Of course there were grave dangers in universities which set such store by research: there grew up an arrogant impatience with the rank-and-file of students; lecture terms were regarded by some professors as a tiresome interruption of the vacation; the social purpose of the university became narrowed to the advancement of science by the master in company with his acolytes; teaching was not commonly regarded as a high art, and matters not susceptible to the scientific method were dismissed as unworthy of serious thought.

Nevertheless, once the reactionary resistance of *Naturphilosophie* had been overcome, the prestige of the German universities rose to unparalleled heights. They became the envy of Britain and America. British and American scientists in the 1880's eagerly completed their education by attending a German university for a semester. To the French habit of exact thought the Germans added thoroughness, patience, and an eagerness to acquire data not only within Germany but wherever science was studied. Their teams of scholars produced, in addition to meticulous research, mammoth histories of other nations, *Jahresberichte* which annually summarised the state of science, handbooks like that of Gmelin, translations of any notable work published elsewhere, and more footnotes than the world had ever seen before. By the middle of the nineteenth century, the universities of Germany had adapted themselves wonderfully to the scientific age. They led the world in research. They treasured their *Lern-* and *Lehrfreiheit*. They were a magnet for scholars everywhere. They were independent of one another yet united by a common ideal (almost a cause) of research. They acquired homogeneity through the continual migration of students and teachers from one centre to another.

By this time—by mid-century—the British universities were at long last ready to accept the scientific revolution and to adapt themselves to its consequences. It was too late to turn to France: the eighteenth-century splendours of French science had become tarnished. It was to Germany that Britain turned for a model.

Suggested Readings

Herbert Butterfield, *The Origins of Modern Science, 1300–1800,* rev. ed. (New York: The Free Press, 1965), is an excellent introduction to the intellectual history of the Scientific Revolution, while Alfred R. Hall, *The Scientific Revo-*

lution, 1500–1800: The Formation of the Modern Scientific Attitude, 2nd ed. (Boston: Beacon Press, 1966), considers the movement in its broader organizational and social aspects. Alan G. R. Smith, *Science and Society in the Sixteenth and Seventeenth Centuries* (New York: Harcourt Brace Jovanovich, 1972), is a good general introduction with excellent illustrations. The function of the scientific societies is recounted by Martha Ornstein, *The Role of Scientific Societies in the Seventeenth Century* (Chicago: University of Chicago Press, 1938).

Woodes Rogers:
Privateer and Pirate
Hunter

M. Foster Farley

The first rush of European expansion was based on Spanish and Portuguese control of the world's sea lanes, and Spain and Portugal used that control to found their great seaborne empires. During the course of the seventeenth and early eighteenth centuries, England, France, and the Netherlands successfully challenged the Spanish and Portuguese sea power. One of the most effective weapons in that struggle was the small, heavily armed— and often illegal—ships of the freebooters, or buccaneers. The Spanish and Portuguese merchant ships could do little against those specialized craft, and imperial trade was severely hampered. The victorious powers naturally portrayed their privateers in the best possible light, and today's romantic picture of the period was born.

This selection sketches the life of Woodes Rogers, an important but not atypical figure of the period. The details of his career provide an insight into a complex era during which a vast struggle for empire was under way. Rogers served his country well as privateer, explorer, colonizer, and administrator, but he received relatively little in return for his extraordinary exertions. The distinction between pirate and patriot was frequently unclear, and rewards and punishments were often unjustly distributed.

On October 14th, 1711, two ships, the *Duke* and *Duchess,* with its prize, under the command of Woodes Rogers of Bristol, docked at a wharf in London, completing a three year and some months voyage around the world, bringing back treasure worth almost a million pounds. Nothing like this had happened since the days of Sir Francis Drake, and his profits were puny compared to the wealth captured by Rogers. What occasioned this voyage, and why was this Bristol merchant the talk of the hour? In order to answer this question we must examine the international situation of the period.

In the last two decades of the seventeenth, and for the first twenty years of the eighteenth century, England was engaged in a series of wars with France and Spain. These conflicts were fought on land as well as on the sea. The principal method of fighting at sea (besides battles between the regular navies) was the use of privateers. A privateer was literally a private naval vessel of a country, privately owned and operated, and carrying a commission or letters of marque issued by a government. These vessels struck at the enemy's merchant shipping, and divided the spoils between the owners and the crew. Many owners and officers grew rich; but the worst evil of privateering was that once the conflict was over, the men, seeing the money to be made, turned pirate, preying on *all* merchant ships, including those of their own nation.

Woodes Rogers became angry as Spanish and French privateers looted his ships during the War of the Spanish Succession (1702–1713). So he decided to turn privateer and retaliate against them. Combining his own resources with those of other Bristol merchants, including 'three men who had been or were to be Mayors of the city, two sheriffs and a Town Clerk' (the names of the owners were Christopher Shuter, Sir John Hawkins, John Romsey, Captain Philip Freake, James Hollidge, Francis Rogers, Thomas Goldney, Thomas Clements, Thomas Coutes, John Corsely, John Duckinfield, Richard Hawksworth, William Saunders, John Grant, Lawrence Hollister, and Daniel Hickman), they outfitted two warships, *Duke* and *Duchess*. The investors were not only interested in privateering, but were also eager to take the British flag and trade into the Pacific Ocean.

For one hundred and fifty years Spain had the Pacific to herself. Now with a Bourbon on the Spanish throne, the French began to build a thriving trade in that part of the world. Why shouldn't England receive her share of this trade, reasoned Rogers and his associates? He repeated the same idea in the foreword to his book that was published after his return to Bristol, *A Cruising Voyage Round the World.*

> I make no doubt, it will be to your [the owners of the *Duke* and *Duchess*] lasting Honour, that such a voyage was undertaken from Bristol at your Expence; since it has given the Publick a sufficient

WOODES ROGERS: PRIVATEER AND PIRATE HUNTER

107

WOODES ROGERS: PRIVATEER AND PIRATE HUNTER   By M. Foster Farley, from *History Today,* 29 (1979), pp. 522–31.

Bristol, where Rogers had studied the 'complex art of seamanship'; Broad Quay in the early eighteenth century. Artist Anon.

Evidence of what may be done in these Parts, and since the Wisdom of the Nation has now agreed to establish a Trade to the South-Seas, which, with the Blessing of God, may bring vast Riches to GREAT BRITAIN.

Woodes Rogers, who was twenty-nine when he set out on his adventures in 1708, came from an East Dorset family. An ancestor, John Rogers, had been sheriff in Poole, Dorset, (Woodes' birthplace) during the reign of Elizabeth I, had been knighted by the Queen, and became a Member of Parliament. Rogers was Bristol-trained; he had served a seven year apprenticeship studying the 'complex art of seamanship with a respected captain' of Bristol. In 1705, Woodes married Sarah Whetstone, daughter of Admiral Whetstone, also of Bristol. Three children, Sarah, born 1706, William, born in 1707, and Mary born in 1708, who died, came of this union. With his marriage he became a Freeman of Bristol (a term in those days denoting that he was qualified to vote in Parliamentary elections—an unusual privilege, for only one Bristol male in ten had this status in 1708). Rogers had inherited from his father a house in Queen's Square and a small legacy, with which he bought a pottery 'across the Frome, at the foot of Brandon Hill'.

Why was Rogers, an inexperienced young man, put in command over several more competent Bristol mariners? The owners evidently could see in Rogers many things that escaped the average observer— we know now why he was chosen; for we have the hindsight to look at the reasons that came out during his voyage and, later, as governor of the Bahamas. Rogers had the knack of separating himself 'from the activities around him and acting on the purely practical grounds that his own good was therein included'. And blood will tell. This phrase means more than the experts will ever admit. His grandfather and father were sea captains and dependable men; and the family motto *je fera mon devoir*, found in the family church of Blandford in Poole, is also an indication of how much Rogers was to be trusted with this privateering enterprise. He never had a mutiny, or serious trouble with his crew; which was unusual, for even the Royal Navy kept discipline by floggings and hangings.

Next to Rogers, the most important man in the expedition was William Dampier, also of Bristol, the 'pilot for the South Sea'. Dampier had served in the Royal Navy, and was also a logwood cutter, a buccaneer and a privateer. He 'seemed forever to be bestriding the pirate line defined by law,' but never crossed over into outlawry. Like Drake and Hawkins, Dampier maintained the English custom of a long line of buccaneers, who, while seizing Spanish commerce, simultaneously played the role of 'explorer and cartographer in extending the domains of the British Empire' and expanding its navy.

Dampier did something unusual; he wrote two books, *A New Voyage Round the World* (1697), and *Voyages and Discoveries* (1699). But he was a turbulent and quarrelsome man, and 'twice quarreled with his officers and had been courtmartialled out of any naval command;' but 'no Englishman could match his knowledge of lands, currents, and winds in eastern waters'. Dampier acted as pilot for the expedition, and at times, master of the *Duke*. Steven Courtney was captain of the *Duchess,* and on one of the lesser grades of officers was Woodes Rogers' younger brother, John.

The two ships sailed on August 1st, 1708, on what was to be a voyage of almost three years. Their first stop was at Cork, Ireland, where forty of the crew jumped ship; so new crews had to be hired. When they left Cork, there were 181 men on the *Duke* and 153 on the *Duchess,* making a total of 334 of which 'one third were Foreigners from most Nations; several of Her Majesty's Subjects on board were Tinkers, Taylors, Hay-makers, Pedlers, Fidlers, etc. one Negro, and about ten boys. With this mix'd gang, we hop'd to be well mann'd, as soon as they learnt the Use of Arms, and get their Sea-Legs, which we doubted not soon to teach 'em, and bring them to Discipline'.

On September 18th, Rogers captured a Spanish bark of twenty-five tons with a cargo of wine and brandy—a godsend, as the expedition's quartermaster had neglected to lay in an ample supply of spirits. A short time later, the two ships put in at the Canary Islands where more spirits were purchased. Then ready to sail, Rogers, carefully concealing his destination from the Spaniards, said that they 'were bound to any other place than the *English West Indies'*. He noted in his journal that they were now well stocked 'with Liquor, and shall be the better

WOODES
ROGERS:
PRIVATEER
AND PIRATE
HUNTER

109

able to endure the Cold when we get the Length of Cape Horn, which we are informed has always very cold bad Weather near it'. On October 8th, they were at the Cape Verde Islands where they filled their water casks and replenished their supplies.

By November 16th, their ships needed careening; and, anchoring off Brazil at the Isle of Grande, for several days they careened their ships and made the repairs that were always necessary. The crew went ashore in batches, and soon recovered their energies after a month or more at sea. The ships' refitting was completed in a week's time; and, after entertaining the 'Governour and the fathers (friars) on board' the *Duke,* the two vessels sailed the next day for Juan Fernandez Island, a voyage of some six thousand miles.

Three weeks after leaving Brazil, they were inside the Falkland Islands, and the usual bad weather came upon them, murky water and fog, 'the great foreboding of Antarctica.' They now put on what heavy clothing they possessed; the ships' tailors were ordered 'to stitch faster than ever'; and extra clothes were made out of blanket cloth. From noon of January 6th, 1709, and for the two following weeks, the *Duke* and *Duchess* rounded Cape Horn 'through open water to Antarctica'; earlier circumnavigators had followed Magellan's route through the three hundred and thirty mile straits between the great island of Tierra del Fuego and the South American continent. After enduring rough seas, high gales and the 'unblinking day of Antarctic summer, on January 15th the expedition accounted themselves in the South Sea'. Two weeks later, on January 31st, Dampier, knowing that the crews were sick of the sea, sighted the island of Juan Fernandez. On arriving, they saw a huge fire blazing on the beach. The next day a landing party met a bare-footed man, heavily bearded 'cloth'd in Goat-Skins, who looked wilder than the first Owners of them'. It was soon learned that the castaway, who had been on the island for four years and four months, was Alexander Selkirk, a Scot. Captain Dampier recognized him.

This particular affair had begun over four years earlier, when Dampier was captain of a privateer, the *St George,* which was accompanied by the *Cinque Ports,* of which Selkirk was an officer. The *Cinque Ports* was beached on the island, undergoing repairs; and the captain, Stradling, and Selkirk, quarrelled about how well the repairs were proceeding. Selkirk said that the *Cinque Ports* was not seaworthy, and would sink in a rough sea; and in a fit of anger, he declared that he would rather stay on Mia a Tierra than risk his life in a leaky vessel. Captain Stradling, with approval of Dampier, dumped Selkirk and all his belongings and sailed away. (Actually, Selkirk came out the better of the two; for Stradling and his crew were later captured by the Spanish and spent six years behind bars in Lima, Peru, and in France, before he escaped). So it was with great rejoicing that Selkirk was received by the *Duke* and *Duchess;* and Rogers made a place for him among his crew. Legend had it that Alexander Selkirk told his story to Daniel Defoe; but whether the two men ever met is of no consequence, for Defoe wrote *Robinson Crusoe,* which for the next two hundred and fifty years gave delight to school boys and to all who have loved adventure.

The crews of the two ships soon recovered their strength and, on February 13th, made sail for the coast of Peru. There followed several weeks of patrol during which no prizes were sighted. By March 9th, about twenty-one miles off the Peruvian coast, Rogers commented that his men began to 'repine that to come so far, we have met with no prizes in these seas'. But their luck changed for the better, for on March 16th, they captured a small vessel of sixteen tons. Deciding to keep this vessel for a courier ship, they renamed it the *Beginning,* since it was their first prize in the Pacific. While the *Duchess* and the *Beginning* were sent out to search for prizes, the *Duke* was refitted on Lobos Island, where part of its crew, suffering from scurvy, recuperated. The two other ships returned later with a fifty-ton prize, which they kept and named the *Increase,* with Selkirk as its master. Two more prizes were added; but no wealthy ship had yet been captured. The small squadron was now in need of fresh water; and, on April 12th, it was decided that, since they were close to Peru, they would storm the port of Guayaquil. Two small pinnaces, led by Robert Frye, Edward Cooke, and John Rogers, chased a Spanish ship; but when it was engaged, John Rogers was killed with a bullet in his skull. Rogers wrote that 'my unfortunate Brother was shot thro the Head, and instantly died, to my unspeakable Sorrow'. He added, however, that he 'began this Voyage with a Resolution to go thro it, and the greatest Misfortune or Obstacle shall not deter me, I'll as much as possible avoid being thoughtful and afflicting my self for what can't be recall'd, but indefatigably pursue the Concerns of the Voyage, which has hitherto allow'd little Respite'.

With 195 men split into three groups—Rogers leading one group; the rest of the privateers stayed aboard the ships, ready to sail at a moment's notice—they attacked the Peruvian seaport. They had expected to surprise the city; but it had received news of their coming. When Rogers sent an emissary into the town, demanding a parley, the governor appeared. A deal was struck; the Spanish would ransom their town for fifty thousand pieces of eight. The privateers were elated; but the money didn't arrive; and then the governor announced that he could afford only thirty thousand pieces. So Rogers stormed the town; and within half an hour Guayaquil was taken. The city was ransacked in true pirate fashion, and much booty was captured. The governor, Don Hieronomo Boza y Soliz, was given six days to pay the ransom of thirty thousand pieces; or Rogers would burn the city. The money was paid by the deadline; but disaster struck the expedition. A plague, which attacked Guayaquil shortly before Rogers arrived, soon hit the English crews as they headed for the Galapagos Islands. There some men died,

WOODES
ROGERS:
PRIVATEER
AND PIRATE
HUNTER

111

After the capture of Guayaquil in 1709 Rogers reassures the Spanish ladies whom his men are searching for their jewels; a contemporary engraving.

though most recovered; and the *Duke* and *Duchess* were refitted, scraped, caulked, re-rigged, and re-stowed. Now for the next several months they awaited the treasure ship from Manila, growing more weary all the time, and the crews more restless. On December 22nd, off southern California, they sighted what they thought was the long sought Manila galleon; but they later learned that it was the lesser one; for two had already sailed. During the brief fight that resulted in the capture of the Manila galleon, *Incarnacion,* Rogers later recorded in his journal that 'I was shot thro' the Left Cheek, the Bullet struck away great part of my upper Jaw, and several of my Teeth, part of which dropt down upon the Deck, where I fell. . . .'

For the next few months poor Rogers had to write his instructions 'to prevent the Loss of Blood,' and because of the pain he 'suffer'd by speaking'.

Now unable to command, he had to delegate authority; and, when the prisoners from the *Incarnacion* were interrogated, it was learned that the larger 'Acapulco ship' was probably near by. Close watch was kept; and on December 26th the second Manila galleon was sighted. She was soon engaged by the English privateers and Rogers was again wounded 'in the Left Foot with a Splinter just before we blew up on the Quarter-Deck [some powder exploded, not his ship] so that I could not stand, but lay on my Back in a great deal of misery, part of my Heel-bone being struck out, and all under my Ankle cut above half thro', which bled very much, and weaken'd me, before it could be dressed and stopt'.

Rogers was paying a heavy price for the money that he would

make from this voyage. After suffering great loss of life and much damage to the *Duchess,* the larger Manila galleon made her escape, but the expedition had seized the other ship which was to bring the total amount captured to a great sum.

After refitting, the small English privateer fleet left the North American coast on January 11th, 1710. Fifty-eight days later, reduced to starvation rations, they reached the island of Guam. There they told its Spanish officials that they came in peace, but threatened 'Military Treatment, as we are with ease able to give you'. The Spanish willingly sold the English what they needed, and after putting their ships in order they 'hoisted' their 'Colours' and sailed on March 21st, 1710, for the 'Dutch East India station of Batavia,' in Java. After four months of sailing, down to eating rats, the English arrived at Batavia on June 20th. An inhospitable welcome awaited them, for although Holland and England were allies in the War of the Spanish Succession, the Dutch East India Company was extremely jealous of English competition. Grudging assistance was, however, given to the English expedition which spent four months in the area because some of the crew deserted, some died of fever, and a couple were bitten in two by sharks while they were swimming. As a result men had to be recruited to fill the depleted ranks, while the ships had to be refitted for their long voyage to the next station at Cape Town. Rogers' health was also a matter of concern. Rogers wrote

> I am still very weak and thin, but I hope to get Time and Leisure to recover my Health . . . 8 Days ago the Doctor cut a large Musket shot out of my Mouth, which had been there near 6 Months, ever since I was first wounded; we reckon'd it a Piece of my Jawbone, the upper and lower Jaw being much broken, and almost closed together, so that the Doctor had much ado to come at the Shot to get it out. I had also several Pieces of my Foot and Heel bone taken out, but God be thanked am now in a fair way to have the Use of my Foot, and to recover my Health. The Hole the Shot made in my Face is now scarce discernable . . .

Despite the pettiness of the Dutch, the *Duke* and *Duchess* and their one remaining prize—they had disposed of the other captured ships for a good price—left for Cape Town on October 12th. From then until December 28th, when they arrived off Cape Town, Rogers reported 'Nothing remarkable happened, except a sailor, John Long fell overboard and was drowned. Mr. James Wasse our chief Surgeon died . . . being a very honest, useful Man, a good Surgeon, and bred up at Leyden, in the study of Physick as well as Surgery.' Although the *Duke* had three feet of water in her hold, and her pumps were clogged, the three ships finally limped into Cape Town.

They spent the next three months at the Cape waiting for ships

WOODES
ROGERS:
PRIVATEER
AND PIRATE
HUNTER

113

from India, and other places in the East, so that they could sail in a convoy as protection against Spanish and French privateers. The stay at Cape Town did not improve Rogers' health. On April 6th, the three English ships sailed in the company of some twenty others. On approaching the British Isles the convoy decided to sail around the northern part of Ireland and Scotland and head for the Shetland Islands because of the presence of French privateers in the Channel. Arriving at the Shetlands on July 15th, they were joined by ten Dutch warships which escorted them to Texel, Holland, where they dropped anchor on July 23rd, 1711.

Legal complications now developed. Letters from the owners informed Rogers that the English East India Company was very angry because Rogers and his group had 'encroached upon their [English East India Company] Liberties in *India*'. Rogers retorted that they 'had been at no other places than' those they had earlier mentioned. Despite the legal problems, rather than spending a winter in Holland they sailed for London escorted by four British men-of-war. On October 14th, 1711, as Rogers wrote the last sentence in his journal, 'at 11 of the Clock, we and our Consort and Prize got up to Eriff [Erith] where we came to Anchor, which ends our long and fatiguing Voyage'.

There followed a five-year legal battle in which the owners' two-thirds of the profits 'was cut in half by an exasperating medley of court costs, bribes, custom duties'. Most of the crew realized no more than £50 each, Dampier was never paid in full, and Rogers received only £15,300, which after paying 'three years of family bills' left him broke. But his voyage was remarkable, for not only did he bring home his two original ships and the prize galleon, but he also captured about twenty prizes, and lost no more than fifty men on the whole voyage.

By 1717, Rogers' love of adventure once more manifested itself, and having 'fixed his eyes on the lovely, piratical Bahamas, and pictured them as green as Eden,' he and several partners entered into an agreement with, 'the islands' owners for a twenty-one year lease with Rogers as governor without salary.' The Bahama Islands, although claimed by Spain, had nominally belonged to Great Britain since 1670. Technically they were under the control of six Lords-Proprietors, much like Carolina, Maryland and Pennsylvania. They were uninhabited until the pirates of the Caribbean made them their headquarters about two years before Rogers became governor. With the help of his friend Joseph Addison, who was Secretary of State, Rogers detailed the reasons why he wished to administer the islands for the Crown. They would serve as a good base against the Spanish, and the danger of their falling into alien hands was very real. The lack of any government or defense on the Islands, as well as their infestation by notorious pirates, was a great challenge to Rogers. On February 6th, 1718, he was appointed 'Captain-General and Governor-in-Chief in and over the Bahama Islands.' With a little over one hundred men from the disabled lists of the Guards and other regiments, and nonambulatory patients from the Hospital at Chelsea, Rogers sailed for his new post on April 11, 1718, aboard the ship *Delicia,* accompanied by three other British warships. He was armed with Royal Instructions and an Amnesty Declaration dated September 5th, 1717 whereby all pirates could surrender to some official and receive a royal pardon provided they did so by September 5th, 1718.

News traveled fast and information about the Royal Pardon, as well as of Rogers' appointment, reached the Bahamas a year before he arrived. A great council was held by the leading pirates including Henry Jennings, the founder of the pirate colony. Jennings and his crew, together with one hundred and fifty others, decided to take the Royal Pardon. They sailed to Bermuda, took the amnesty, and returned to New Providence. Other crews from the island of New Providence surrendered to authorities at Charles Town, Barbados and Jamaica. Rogers arrived off Nassau, the principal town of New Providence and the future seat of the government of the Islands, on July 25th. Owing to the lateness of the hour, he decided to wait until morning to land. He also learned that all the pirates of the Island, who had not yet taken the Royal Pardon, were anxious to do so with the exception of Blackbeard (Teach) and Charles Vane and their men. Vane swore that he would not let Rogers land, 'except on his own terms' and these he spelled out in a letter to the new governor:

> Your excellency may please to understand that we are willing to accept His Majesty's most gracious pardon on the following terms, viz- That you will suffer us to dispose of all our goods now in our possession. Likewise, to act as we think fit with everything belonging to us. . . . If your Excellency shall please to comply with this, we shall, with all readiness, accept His Majesty's Act of Grace. If not, we are obliged to stand on our defense. We wait a speedy answer.

Rogers declined to answer the letter, and in anticipation of an attempt at escape by Vane, he placed two ships, the *Rose* and *Shark,* at the entrance to the harbour. Vane then sent out a fire ship, but the *Rose* and the *Shark* cut their cables and put out to sea. Vane and ninety of his crew then escaped in the confusion. Vane was later captured, tried and hanged in Jamaica.

The next morning Rogers and his party went ashore and were received noisily and joyously by the ex-pirates. The pardoned pirate-captains, Hornigold, Davis, Burgess, Clarke, Carter and Currant, together with their crews, formed a double line up from the beach, through which Rogers marched to the accompaniment of a running fire of muskets overhead. Rogers immediately placed the area under martial law

WOODES
ROGERS:
PRIVATEER
AND PIRATE
HUNTER

115

and established himself and his staff in the ruins of the old fort that faced the harbor. Soon a civil government was established, mainly from the ranks of the pirates, which included justices of the peace, lower magistrates, constables, and a militia of sorts. Work crews were sent out to clear the jungle, and before long Nassau became a large town of palm-thatched huts. The fort, now called Fort Nassau, was repaired and several guns were mounted. Each man could take title to a lot 100 x 25 square feet anywhere in the settlement while timber and other building materials would be provided free.

Many of the former pirates became disillusioned with their 'peaceful' lives and yearned for that of the open sea. Of some four hundred who had taken the pardon, more than half slipped off to return to piracy. By December, 1718, Rogers faced his first real crisis. A former pirate, John Augar, returned to his old calling and plundered two ships that Rogers had sent out to trade. Thirteen of the recidivists were captured by Rogers' men. Three died of their wounds and the other ten were sentenced to hang. At the last moment Rogers reprieved an eighteen-year-old youth, George Rounsivell from Weymouth, Dorset. Rogers told Secretary of State Addison in a letter his reason for doing so.

> I hope this unhappy young man will deserve his life, and I beg the honour of your intercession on his behalf.

But Governor Rogers' main threat came from the Spanish who were piqued at Britain for establishing a colony in what they considered their territory. The long expected Spanish attack took place in February, 1720, when Don Francisco Cornego, with four warships, eight sloops and 1,300 men sailed into Nassau. Rogers had only five hundred men to face the Spanish force. But the governor and the former pirates fought furiously and drove the Spaniards into the sea. Rogers not only reformed the 'pirate capital of America,' but persuaded the pirates to accept his leadership, as this crisis showed. But the 'shiftlessness of the islander' and lack of good soil severely hampered Rogers' administration. The British government rewarded Rogers' energy with insult and neglect. He had to use his own money to keep the colony going as well as pay its garrison. He wrote many letters to the Board of Trade, begging for aid and supplies, but they were not even answered. By February, 1721, Rogers was at the end of his patience. His health had

deteriorated due to stress and overwork. 'It is impossible,' he wrote, and resigned. After appointing William Fairfax Deputy Governor, he sailed for Charles Town in March to buy provisions for the colony which would keep it going until Christmas. He then sailed for Bristol, arriving in August. He later went to London to argue his case before the Lords of the Treasury. He told the authorities that he had saved the Bahamas from Spain, had spent £11,000 of his own money to keep the colony solvent, and requested that he be reimbursed. But his appeal fell on deaf ears. He was now bankrupt, his wife left him, and he had to spend time in a debtor's prison. 'Thus were the services of Nassau's saviour rewarded.'

It was not until 1726 that Rogers' fortune changed. George I granted him a small pension, and on October 18th, 1728, he was appointed Captain-General and Governor of the Bahamas, this time with a salary of £400 a year. He took up his post on August 25th, 1729. Between his departure in 1721, and his return in 1729, affairs at Nassau had gone from bad to worse. George Phenny, who had succeeded him as governor, was a fairly good administrator, but encumbered by a dictatorial wife. She interfered in everything: monopolised trade so that the inhabitants had to pay inflated prices; browbeat juries and insulted the judges. Phenny himself even dismantled the fort and sold the iron in the guns for his own benefit. So it was with great relief that Rogers was received by the populace when he arrived together with his son and daughter on that August afternoon in 1729.

Over the next three years he made the 'ragtag population' of the islands, 'into a respectable colony'. He convened an Assembly, and promoted sugar and cotton planting, shipbuilding and the production of salt. But he had trouble with the Speaker of the Assembly, John Colebrooke, who together with a group of associates, opposed Rogers' policies in the Assembly. When Colebrooke withheld certain papers demanded by the Governor, he was arrested and charged with treason. He was tried and found guilty. The difficulties were somewhat lessened in 1731, when the six Lords-Proprietors consented to sell out, transforming the Islands into a royal colony. But Governor Rogers did not live to see this change. He died at Nassau on July 15th, 1732, worn out by the difficulties that he faced. On July 20th, Richard Thompson, President of the Council, wrote to the Secretary of State

> Whereas it pleased Almight God to take unto himself the soul of Woodes Rogers Esq. our late Governor on the 15th inst. We acquaint Yr. Lordship therewith.

So died a great mariner and an illustrious patriot, who had 'deserved' well of his country. Rogers' family did not long survive him; his estranged wife died the same year in London, his son William died at Whydah on the west coast of Africa in 1735 while on a slaving expedition, and his daughter Sarah, died in 1743. Since neither children were married, he left no direct descendants of the family.

Suggested Readings

A standard study of the British Empire, although now considerably dated, is the *Cambridge History of the British Empire,* 9 vols. (New York: Cambridge University Press, 1929–59). The story of the Spanish Pacific trade is engagingly told in William L. Schurz, *The Manila Galleon* (New York: E. P. Dutton, 1939), while the decline of the Spanish Atlantic trade is the subject of Geoffrey J. Walker, *Spanish Politics and Imperial Trade, 1700–1789* (Bloomington: Indiana University Press, 1979). Of course the reader will want to consider Daniel Defoe's *Robinson Crusoe,* the classic inspired by Woodes Rogers' passenger, Alexander Selkirk.

The Response of Slaves

Gad Heuman

The New World plantation system was largely based on Negro slavery. It was a brutal and oppressive system, marked by the complete domination of the slave by the master. White stereotypes of the Negro slave depict a lazy, irresponsible, and dishonest character who passively accepted a subservient way of life.

Historical research over the last 25 years, however, has done much to refute this conception of the "docile slave." Despite the severity and rigidity of colonial slavery, the slaves were never completely subdued. Various methods of resistance, both passive and violent, were available to them. Numerous instances have been documented of slaves resisting their masters by running away, refusing to work, or exhibiting deliberate laziness or inefficiency. Oftentimes a slave resorted to such extreme measures of resistance as poisoning the master or joining in open rebellion. Throughout the Americas independent communities of Negro slaves stood out as a challenge to white authority.

The various methods of resistance employed by Negro slaves are vividly treated in the following article by Gad Heuman. His coverage of the communities formed by maroons, or descendants of fugitive slaves, depicts an especially important example of the slaves' attempts to combat the existing social and economic system. It is often difficult to evaluate the true extent to which a transplanted people retain their native heritage. Examining this problem with regard to the Negro slaves, the author maintains that in many ways they successfully resisted the imposition of European culture and managed to retain substantial elements of their African heritage.

> To be Sold: A Black Man, a native of St Kitts, a good postilion, groom, butler and taylor; sober and healthy. *He is averse to living in the country,* but might do for a single person, or a family residing in or near town. He had absconded some time from his present owner, and for this reason is offered for sale. (my italics)

> To be sold at private sale: A Barbadian Lad, about 18 years old; a good butler, and careful servant to attend a horse; he has been some time at the Cabinet Maker's business, and is a tolerable good workman, *but prefers being either a butler, or carpenter, to that trade;* which is the occasion of his being offered for sale. He will suit any person inclined to carry him from the Island, *as he has no objection to travelling.* (my italics)

> —*Advertisements in the* Barbados Mercury, June 7th and 21st, 1806

These slave advertisements may come as a surprise to many who equate slavery in the New World with oppression, cruelty and torture. Nor would it be possible to deny that slavery in the Americas was a brutal system in which Europeans exploited Africans and that life for many slaves was indeed 'nasty, brutish and short'. Yet the advertisements also suggest that there was another aspect to slavery which is often ignored. Slavery was not just a matter of masters dominating slaves; it was also a case of slaves having a significant impact on their masters.

How was this possible? In what ways could slaves have any autonomy or even control in a system which so regulated their daily lives? Part of the answer can be found in these two advertisements from Barbados. In the first, the slave, who is valuable as well as skilled, prefers to live in town. He has run away from his owner, probably to be hidden by friends or relatives in town, and the master has decided that he must part with the slave. But the owner carefully points out that the slave is 'averse to living in the country.' The slave has not merely expressed a preference about where he wants to live, but he has succeeded in having the master act in accordance with the slave's wishes.

Similarly, in the second advertisement, the slave, who also has a variety of skills, is for sale because he wants to do another type of work. He would *rather* be a butler or carpenter than train as a cabinet

THE RESPONSE OF SLAVES   By Gad Heuman, from *History Today,* April 1984, pp. 31–35.

maker. There is something else worth noticing in this advertisement. The master reports that the slave has no objection to travelling, suggesting perhaps that other owners may have found it unwise to take slaves abroad against their will. Again, the slave has succeeded in making his own choice prevail—in this case, the type of work he prefers or his willingness to live in another country.

These advertisements are indicative of a broad range of slave responses to their predicament. Most importantly, the slaves were not merely passive agents of their masters. Some slaves ran away, some rebelled, and some established separate communities of their own. Others turned to their African heritage, their religion and their songs to maintain a sense of independence, even within the framework of slavery. In all these activities, slaves denied the white man's denigration of blacks and reinforced more positive images of themselves than white society was prepared to allow.

All through the Americas, slaves resisted the imposition of European culture or incorporated it within their traditional African practices. In the process, they retained significant parts of their African heritage. Funeral rites were among the most noticeable of these African retentions in the New World. In West Africa and the Americas, the spirit of the deceased was often interrogated to ascertain the cause of death. The bearers of the corpse might point to the offending party, if the deceased had been poisoned or died because of witchcraft. Describing a Jamaican slave funeral, the poet and historian, Edward Brathwaite, reported on the ceremony associated with it. A wake was held, usually accompanied by 'dirges, drumming, horn-blowing in the West African style, praise-songs for the deceased, sacrifices of poultry and libations.' As in parts of West Africa, forty days had to elapse before a second, or final burial took place, when more earth was heaped over the grave. The forty days was the period of official mourning for the deceased.

African and New World slave religions also had many parallels. Slaves believed that dead ancestors reappeared as ghosts or duppies who could have a very important bearing on their lives and had to be placated. In Caribbean and African religions, the priest was the obeahman, but he was also a doctor and philosopher. Perhaps the most famous New World cult, voodoo or vodun, is a descendant of religious practices in Dahomey.

Even in the least African of all New World societies, the United States, historians, anthropologists and linguists have found traces of the African past. The Gullah dialect used by blacks on the Georgia-South Carolina sea coast was influenced by West African languages. Elsewhere in the Americas, language and religion was even more heavily African, as the slave trade continued much longer and was more important in the Caribbean and Latin America. These African retentions are significant, because they attest to the survival of African patterns of thought and behaviour. Rather than accept the white man's view of the world, slaves clung to aspects of their own culture or adapted it to the demands of their new situation.

Folk-tales and songs were another part of slave culture which was often independent of the whites. Some of the folk heroes, such as the spider figure Anansi in the Caribbean, originated in West Africa. But it is not only the African dimension of the folk-tales which is important. They could also help the slave develop strategies for survival as well as provide him with metaphorical victories over his white master. The Brer Rabbit stories of the American South are typical of such folk-tales. As the American historian, John Blassingame, has suggested, the hero—who is usually depicted as the small trickster—always defeated the larger animal. Thus the weaker animal, who could be equated with the slave, occasionally killed or injured the stronger one, who represented the master. This was one way of safely wreaking revenge on an abusive master.

Tales could also be instructive; they were teaching devices designed to enable slaves to survive in the slave system. Lawrence W. Levine, who has collected and analysed slave folk-tales in Afro-American society, regards this as an important function of the stories. They were not simply an expression of wish-fulfillment, as in the Anansi or Brer Rabbit stories; they were also didactic lessons on how to function in the society as a slave. One very telling tale may illustrate this point. In the story, a slave meets an animal who can speak. Astonished, the slave reports this to the master and encourages him to see the miracle for himself. The master threatens the slave with severe punishment if he is lying. When the master confronts the talking frog or turtle, the animal is silent, and the slave is beaten. After the master has left, the animal scolds the slave by saying: 'ah tol' yuh de othah day, niggah, yuh talk too much.'

Like folk-tales, slave songs had a variety of uses. Spirituals, for example, identified slaves as the Chosen People, 'as the people of God', who had no doubt that 'to the promised land I'm bound to go.' Equally, slaves were certain what would happen to many of their masters: they would be consigned to hell, while slaves would be saved. Levine recounts the story of a slave who was quite concerned when he learned that he was to be rewarded by being buried in the same vault as his master. 'Well, massa', said the slave, 'one way I am satisfied, and one way I am not. I like to have good coffin when I die [but] I fraid, massa, when the debbil come take you body, he make mistake, and get mine.' The message was not just a light-hearted one; it was also a way of responding to the white view that slaves were the lowliest of all races. Over and over again, slaves resisted this white stereotype of blacks.

Slave songs could also mock whites or even contain revolutionary ideas. Like most other New World slave societies, particularly in the Caribbean and Latin America, Jamaica was highly stratified and colour-conscious. Whites were at the top, whatever their education and wealth. Browns, who were the offspring of whites and blacks, were often in the middle of the society, while the overwhelming majority of the population, the blacks, were at the bottom. Yet slaves did not necessarily recognise this racial hierarchy. One observer in 1799 heard slaves in Jamaica singing:

One, two, tree
All de same;
Black, white, brown,
All de same:
One, two tree . . .

These singers may well have been affected by events in neighbouring Haiti, where in the 1790s a massive slave revolt had succeeded in freeing the blacks.

The successful slave revolution in Haiti was unique in the history of the Americas. But all over the New World, slaves responded to slavery by plotting to overthrow the whites, by running away, and by establishing independent communities of their own. The communities formed by maroons, or fugitive slaves, are a particularly important example of the slaves' attempts to create physical alternatives to the existing society. These maroon societies are also significant, since they extended all through the Americas, from Brazil to Colombia, from Surinam to Jamaica, and from Mexico to the present borders of the United States. Some of these enclaves, such as Palmares in Brazil, were effectively states within a state. Others were loose federations or isolated bands of slaves. In all cases, they were societies at war with their white masters.

The Maroons of Jamaica can provide a useful case study of such communities. Although there were Maroons in the island when it was a Spanish colony, their numbers grew considerably after the English conquered Jamaica in 1655 and imported large numbers of African slaves to work the new sugar plantations. Several hundred African slaves, who rebelled on various estates during the second half of the seventeenth century, retreated to the hills and added to the small communities of runaway slaves already in existence. Living in remote parts of the island, the Jamaican Maroons were almost inaccessible to outsiders.

These societies were composed largely of Africans, some of whom had escaped in a vain attempt to get back to Africa. Their internal organisation was highly authoritarian and their leaders had powers of life and death over the rest of the community. In view of their relatively small numbers and their state of war with white society, it should not be surprising that Maroons developed supernatural ideas about their leaders. One of them, an obeah woman named Nanny, was supposed

A maroon slave of Rio de Janeiro.

to have been able to catch bullets and make them harmless. Another
leader, Tacky, was said to have the power of catching bullets in his
hands and then firing them back at his opponents. Whatever the power
of their leaders, Maroons made use of guerrilla tactics in fighting the
European forces sent against them. Faced with superior firepower and
generally outnumbered, Maroons frequently were able to defeat their
enemy through their skill at camouflage and use of surprise attacks.
The tradition of British soldiers marching in their colourful uniforms
and announcing their presence by beating drums made it considerably
easier for Maroon marksmen who were hidden behind rocks, trees and

lush vegetation. Moreover, as one white resident of Jamaica remarked, the white soldiers 'disdained for a time to have recourse to rocks and trees as a shield against their enemies' fire, accounting it base and unmanly in a soldier thus to shrink from danger.' As a result, the graves of many British soldiers sent to fight the Maroons can still be found in the areas formerly controlled by them.

How does the reality of a war-like, independent Maroon community correspond with white ideas of the slaves' indolence and docility? For maroon societies were clearly a menace to plantation colonies; they could serve as a model for other slaves and as an inspiration to rebel. As an authority on the maroons, Richard Price, has written:

> Throughout Afro-America, such communities stood out as an heroic challenge to white authority, and as the living proof of the existence of a slave consciousness that refused to be limited by the whites' conception or manipulation of it.

The solution for Europeans was either to crush the Maroons or to sue for peace with them. Unable to accomplish the first of these objectives, the British opted for a treaty in 1739 which guaranteed freedom for the Maroons. But there was a price for this freedom: Maroons agreed to become slave-catchers. They became hunters of fugitive slaves rewarded by the whites for the number of slaves they caught. Maroon-slave relations thus undoubtedly deteriorated after the treaty with the English. Nonetheless, maroons have had a significant role throughout the Americas in contradicting the white image of slave passivity.

Of course, most slaves did not become maroons. But many did run away, usually to family or friends. One such slave, Betty Beck from Barbados, had escaped from her owner who placed an advertisement for her in the press. According to her master:

> She is supposed to be harboured in the plantation called Stepney where she was born, and many of her family belong, and has been frequently seen in the road from thence, carrying marketing to town.

Betty had not only escaped to see her family; she also seems to have been maintaining herself independently as a market-lady or huckster.

Betty was not alone in working outside of the plantation. In many slave societies in the Americas, slaves were encouraged to grow provision crops to supplement the food given them by their masters. In time, this alternative economic activity led to the development of internal marketing systems, controlled by slaves and designed to fill some of the needs of the plantation society. Slaves were also responsible for establishing important markets in towns and cities and were themselves sometimes able to accumulate property and cash. Although the slave was legally a piece of property, masters occasionally recognised slaves' property rights, including the land they cultivated. Such provision grounds were owned by the estates, but planters would in some societies permit the slave to bequeath the land they tilled as if it were their own.

The slaves' work on their grounds and in the markets demonstrates a high degree of initiative and enterprise, particularly since slaves had to tend their crops outside the long days devoted to the plantations. Yet white stereotypes of slave behaviour depicted them as Sambos or Quashees, who were inveterately lazy, irresponsible, inefficient, dishonest, childish and stupid. But how is it possible to reconcile what we have learned about the slaves with this description of them? One possibility is that many slaves who were behaving like Sambos were role playing. They were providing an image for their masters which was specifically unthreatening to their owners and which may have had the effect of reducing the amount of punishment directed toward the slaves. Such behaviour also may have allowed the slave to do less work for the master.

But Sambo or Quashee was not an accurate depiction of the slave in his community. However debased slavery was, slaves resisted it at home, in their communal life with other slaves, and in their maroon societies. The slaves' religion, culture and songs attest to their independence within an oppressive system. Indeed, Lawrence Levine has suggested that these factors prevented legal slavery from becoming spiritual slavery. It may be that historians will now follow the advice of two anthropologists, Sidney Mintz and Richard Price, and study 'the role of the powerless in affecting and even controlling important parts of the lives of the masters . . .'

One final example may point the way toward this approach and suggest how influential slaves could be. An agent writing to the absentee owner of several large estates in Jamaica was aware of the owner's increasing desire to sell his property in the colony. But the agent doubted whether it would be possible to find buyers for his plantations, because of the poor economic climate in the early 1820s. Moreover, he added, 'I am sure that your negroes would not approve of a change of owners'.

Suggested Readings

Some authors mentioned in the article are useful starting points: Edward Brathwaite, *The Development of Creole Society in Jamaica, 1770–1820* (New York: Oxford University Press, 1971); John Blassingame, *The Slave Community* (New York: Oxford University Press, 1979); Lawrence W. Levine, *Black Culture and Black Consciousness* (New York: Oxford University Press, 1977); and Richard Price, ed., *Maroon Societies* (Baltimore: Johns Hopkins University Press, 1979). For a comparative approach, see Laura Foner and Eugene Genovese, eds., *Slavery in the New World: A Reader in Comparative History* (Englewood

Cliffs, N.J.: Prentice-Hall, 1969). Additional reading on the slave population in Jamaica is available in Barry Higman, *Slave Population and Economy of Jamaica, 1807–1834* (Cambridge: Cambridge University Press, 1976). Richard S. Dunn, *Sugar and Slaves: The Rise of the Planter Class in the English West Indies, 1624–1713* (Chapel Hill: University of North Carolina Press, 1972), and Orlando Patterson, *The Sociology of Slavery* (Rutherford, N.J.: Fairleigh Dickinson University Press, 1969), present revealing coverage of slave conditions and revolts in the Caribbean.

DISCUSSION QUESTIONS: THE EARLY MODERN PERIOD

1. China often is portrayed as a conservative society, changing relatively little over time. Compare the status of women as portrayed in "The Death of Woman Wang" in this volume and in "The Position of Women in Han China" in Volume I. To what degree had the position of women changed in those 1,500 years? Why?

2. The point is made in "Universities and the Scientific Revolution" that, while science was accepted into the curriculums of the German universities in the nineteenth century, technology was relegated to technical schools. That distinction is preserved today, with certain subjects taught in the core of the university but "technology" restricted to schools of engineering and other professional schools. How legitimate is such a distinction? Why should introductory science be required in most university curriculums and not introductory engineering? Given the importance of technology to the Western tradition, why has it not been integrated, as a science is, into our concept of a liberal education?

3. "Skills and Resources in Late Traditional China" raises a basic question: after centuries of leading the world in technological innovation, China suddenly ceased to do so, not just because Europe became steadily more active in the field, but because China became less so. How do you account for that change? What should a society do to maintain its level of commitment to technological advancement? What should it avoid?

4. In "The Social Environment of Tokugawa Kabuki," consider the degree to which the government interfered with and regulated the theater. What were the various areas of regulation, and what were the purposes of governmental intervention?

5. "Skills and Resources in Late Traditional China" and "An Early Energy Crisis and Its Consequences" present two different sets of causes for the Industrial Revolution in Europe. What are these causes? Are the two views contradictory?

6. The term *revolution* has the connotation of sudden, often violent change. After reading "An Early Energy Crisis," how well do you think this sense of the term fits the Industrial Revolution? If it does not fit, in what sense does the Industrial Revolution deserve to be called a revolution? What about the Scientific Revolution?

7. In many ways, Woodes Rogers epitomizes the British imperial activity of the late seventeenth and early eighteenth centuries. What activities described in "Woodes Rogers: Privateer and Pirate Hunter" were important to Great Britain in establishing its overseas empire?

8. "The African Slave Trade" presents that trade in a somewhat unfamiliar light, as a cooperative enterprise between the European slave purchasers, on the one hand, and the African slave sellers, on the other. This raises

a number of questions. In what ways did the slave trade benefit Africa, and in what ways did it impede African development? What might have been the history of European overseas expansion if cheap African slaves had not been available? Finally, if the Westerners were dependent on African labor sources, how were they able to turn against the slave trade in the nineteenth century?

9. "The Response of Slaves" discusses, among other things, numerous revolts of dissident and runaway slaves. Why do you think there were only a few such revolts in the United States? How would you account for the relative backwardness, until recent times, of those areas that had relied on slave labor for their development?

10. In "Universities and the Scientific Revolution," the author notes that the faculties of German universities valued their *Lern-* and *Lehrfreiheit*— their freedom of inquiry and teaching, the basic elements in the modern concept of "academic freedom." In what ways do you think those freedoms were important to scientific advancement in the nineteenth century? How important do you think they are today? Why do university faculties protect these freedoms so jealously?

PART
II

INDUSTRIALISM
AND
DEMOCRACY

1789–1914

	1789	1800	1825
EUROPE	**ca. 1740–1839** TWO PARSONS **1798** Malthus, *Essay on the Principle of Population* **1780–1890** COTTAGE INDUSTRY AND THE FACTORY SYSTEM	**1800–1820** Rapid growth of spinning factories begins **1804–1814** Napoleonic Empire **1811** Luddite movement	**1825** First commercial railroad **1827** Commercial production of quinine **1830** France's "July Monarchy" **1832** Britain's Great Reform Bill
SOUTHWEST ASIA AND AFRICA		**1805–1848** Mohammed Ali founds dynasty in Egypt **1806** British control Cape Colony **1807** Slavery abolished in British Empire **1818–1828** King Shaka, apex of Zulu Kingdom	**1817–1900** QUININE AND THE EUROPEAN CONQUEST OF AFRICA **1836** Boers' Great Trek begins
SOUTH AND SOUTHEAST ASIA	**1796** British conquer Ceylon	**1800–1855** THE BUSINESS WORLD OF JAMSETJEE JEJEEBHOY **1819** British found Singapore	
EAST ASIA			**1825–1830** Java War **1839–1842** Opium War
THE AMERICAS AND THE PACIFIC		**1803** Louisiana Purchase **1807–1830** Latin American wars for independence **1820** Great immigration into the U.S. **ca. 1820–1860** IRISH SERVANT WOMEN **1823** Monroe Doctrine	**1835–1840** Alexis de Tocqueville, *Democracy in America* **1840** Britain annexes New Zealand **ca. 1842–1900** THE EMERGENCE OF TEAM SPORTS **1845** America's first organized baseball team, the Knickerbockers **1846–1848** Mexican War

PART II: 1789–1914

1850	1875	1900	1914
1848 *Communist Manifesto* **1848–1861** Unification of Italy **1848–1870** Napoleon III **ca. 1850** UNIVERSITY STUDENTS IN RUSSIA **1851** Crystal Palace Exhibition, London	**1854–1856** Crimean War **1859** Darwin, *Origin of Species* **1861–1871** Unification of Germany **ca. 1860** Turgenev, *Fathers and Children* **1870–1871** Franco-Prussian War	**1876** First internal combustion engine **1878** Congress of Berlin **1882** Triple Alliance **1894** Russo-French Alliance	**1905** Russian Revolution begins **1905** Einstein's Theory of Relativity **1907** Triple Entente **1912–1913** Balkan Wars
1860 French expansion in West Africa **1869** Suez Canal opens		**1886** Gold discovered in southern Africa **1889** Rhodesia colonized **ca. 1890** Cecil Rhodes	**1899–1902** Boer War **1910** Union of South Africa formed
1857–1858 Indian Mutiny **1859** French seize Saigon		**1885** Indian National Congress founded	**1906** Muslim League founded
1850–1864 Taiping Rebellion **1854** Perry opens U.S. trade with Japan **1868** Meiji Restoration, Japan **ca. 1873** PROTESTANT EVANGELISTS AND CHRISTIAN SAMURAI		**1893–1976** Mao Zedong **1894–1895** Sino-Japanese War	**1900** Boxer Rebellion **1904–1905** Russo-Japanese War **1911** Chinese Revolution **1912–1949** Chinese Republic
1861–1865 American Civil War **1867** Russia sells Alaska to U.S. **1867** British North America Act **1869** Opening of transcontinental railroad		**1889** First Pan-American Conference **1898** Spanish-American War	**1910** Mexican Revolution begins **1914** Panama Canal opens

THE century and a half covered in this part saw European power in the world reach its height. At the same time, great and sweeping changes were occurring within Western society. It was a period of both accomplishment and turmoil.

The very base of European civilization expanded as the processes of colonization and settlement begun in the previous era continued at an increased pace. North America and most of South America, the islands of the Caribbean, Australia, New Zealand, and southern

133

Africa all experienced an increase in their European populations and an intensified economic development that all but swept away any influences of their indigenous cultures, allowing the consolidation of societies that were European in organization, outlook, technology, and, often, descent. During the nineteenth century, more than 60 million Europeans emigrated to swell the ranks of these new Western societies. The selection entitled "Irish Servant Women: The Irish 'Biddy'" illustrates one small aspect of this mighty movement of people.

Improved communications and transportation, together with a commonality of interests and values, bound the new societies to Europe, in a community that, at least for a time, shared in the benefits and stresses of a swiftly advancing technology, as well as sharing the profits from exploiting peoples outside the community. It was during this period that the modern Western world took shape.

The Western peoples of the period confronted two movements of such magnitude and consequences that they well deserve the name of "revolution": the Industrial Revolution and the Democratic Revolution. The Industrial Revolution began in Great Britain in the eighteenth century with the development of new machinery and the utilization of new energy sources. Coal and steam powered new spinning machines, power looms, lathes, furnaces, forges, and a host of other tools that produced an increasing torrent of goods, which were then carried to all parts of the world in the new iron steamships and coal-fueled locomotives.

Unlike the handicraft process, these new machines turned out large quantities of virtually identical items. The machines made possible the standardization of manufacture, resulting in production on a scale and with an efficiency hitherto undreamed of. The new form of production made handicrafts obsolete and transformed the economic system of Western society. That the transformation was neither swift nor easy is illustrated in "Cottage Industry and the Factory System." Nor was that all. As the handicraft system of production was swept away, so, too, was the social structure that had been based on it. The entire way of life in the West was changed, and in the process numerous traditional values were lost. That loss is still felt keenly by some, and the selection "Two Parsons" shows the ambivalence many felt toward this aspect of the Industrial Revolution.

In the middle of the nineteenth century, the Industrial Revolution entered a new phase. For one thing, the Westerners were now so rich and powerful that previous obstacles to the expansion of their power no longer existed. "Quinine and the European Conquest of Africa" considers one phase of that further expansion, the opening up of Africa. The West came to dominate India more efficiently than before, as can be seen in "The Business World of Jamsetjee Jejeebhoy." China was forced open to Western commercial interests, and Japan had to accept a Western presence. Aspects of the latter event are discussed in "Protestant Evangelists and Christian Samurai." Many of the lands of Islam also were forced to accept Western political and military tutelage. Nowhere was there another power to challenge Western domination. Westerners seemed obsessed by a need to penetrate into all corners of the globe, and a new golden age of exploration began.

At the same time, technological innovation ceased simply to improve on old pursuits and began to create new products and new industries. Chemical plants, electrical manufacture, rubber processing, pharmaceuticals, and other new endeavors transformed business and industry as effectively as their products were transforming society. Population increased, the life span lengthened, and new wealth encouraged new forms of diversion. "The Emergence of Team Sports: Baseball's Early Years" illustrates one aspect of the swiftly changing pattern and quality of life in the West. Perhaps nowhere was the change so apparent as in the cities, where electric lights, trolley cars, and elevators allowed Western urban centers to begin taking on the characteristics of the cities we know today. Life in the West generally developed a dynamism and richness unparalleled in human history.

Concurrent with the technological progress was another great movement: the Democratic Revolution. Beginning with the revolution of the North American colonists in 1776 and reaching its fullest influence with the French Revolution of 1789, the movement successfully challenged the traditional view that existing political and social institutions were divinely established and, therefore, sacrosanct. It led to an era of turmoil, in which every segment of society worked either to preserve its position or to gain a greater share of wealth and power. "University Students in Nineteenth Century Russia" discusses one small aspect of a process under way throughout the West during the period. Although popular government and social equity had not triumphed everywhere by 1914, the principle was generally accepted that governments and social institutions were mere tools that could be altered, improved, or, if they proved ineffective, discarded. The other great discovery of the period was that the new governments, uniting all the citizens of a state in the common bond of nationalism, could generate a power and will far greater than those of the aristocratic states of the past.

By 1914, the wealth and power of the Western nations were greater than they ever had been, and the nations' ability to use their resources also was greater than ever before. Western society had been transformed, and, although there were some who disputed the proposition, the consensus was that the change was for the better.

Two Parsons

Virginia Woolf

The Industrial Revolution was one of the great watersheds of the modern era, affecting virtually every aspect of life. The quality of the changes it brought is a matter of dispute, with some viewing the era before vitamins, constitutional democracy, mass education, and penicillin as a better age, in which the individual was somehow in closer harmony with a simpler, more natural, and more human world. Debatable though that proposition may be, it has had a great influence on literature, art, and even politics and economics.

In this reading selection, Virginia Woolf, one of the most skilled English stylists of the twentieth century, has attempted to exemplify that watershed through her sketch of the lives of two obscure English clergymen. These are not biographies in any technical sense of the term. Woolf has tried to reconstruct, through their memoirs, the means by which these two men managed to relate to the world they lived in. Although she recognizes the shortcomings of her attitude, she clearly prefers her own vision of the eighteenth century, "one of the breathing-spaces in human affairs," to the realities of her contemporary world. The former was orderly and proper, the latter mad. It is poignant to remember that, like the Reverend John Skinner, Virginia Woolf one day left her house and took her own life.

James Woodforde

One could wish that the psychoanalysts would go into the question of diary-keeping. For often it is the one mysterious fact in a life otherwise as clear as the sky and as candid as the dawn. Parson Wood-forde is a case in point—his diary is the only mystery about him. For forty-three years he sat down almost daily to record what he did on Monday and what he had for dinner on Tuesday; but for whom he wrote or why he wrote it is impossible to say. He does not unburden his soul in his diary; yet it is no mere record of engagements and expenses. As for literary fame, there is no sign that he ever thought of it, and finally, though the man himself is peaceable above all things, there are little indiscretions and criticisms which would have got him into trouble and hurt the feelings of his friends had they read them. What purpose, then, did the sixty-eight little books fulfil? Perhaps it was the desire for intimacy. When James Woodforde opened one of his neat manuscript books he entered into conversation with a second James Woodforde, who was not quite the same as the reverend gentleman who visited the poor and preached in the church. These two friends said much that all the world might hear; but they had a few secrets which they shared with each other only. It was a great comfort, for example, that Christmas when Nancy, Betsy, and Mr. Walker seemed to be in conspiracy against him, to exclaim in the diary, "The treatment I meet with for my Civility this Christmas is to me abominable." The second James Woodforde sympathised and agreed. Again, when a stranger abused his hospitality it was a relief to inform the other self who lived in the little book that he had put him to sleep in the attic story, "and I treated him as one that would be too free if treated kindly." It is easy to understand why, in the quiet life of a country parish, these two bachelor friends became in time inseparable. An essential part of him would have died had he been forbidden to keep his diary. When indeed he thought himself in the grip of death he still wrote on and on. And as we read—if reading is the word for it—we seem to be listening to someone who is murmuring over the events of the day to himself in the quiet space which precedes sleep. It is not writing, and, to speak of the truth, it is not reading. It is slipping through half a dozen pages and strolling to the window and looking out. It is going on thinking about the Woodfordes while we watch the people in the street below. It is taking a walk and making up the life and character of James Woodforde as we go. It is not reading any more than it is writing—what to call it we scarcely know.

James Woodforde, then, was one of those smooth-cheeked, steady-eyed men, demure to look at, whom we can never imagine except in the prime of life. He was of an equable temper, with only such acerbities and touchinesses as are generally to be found in those who have had a love affair in their youth and remained, as they fancy, unwed

TWO PARSONS

137

TWO PARSONS From Virginia Woolf, *The Second Common Reader* (New York; Harvest Books, n.d.), pp. 83–96.

because of it. The Parson's love affair, however, was nothing very tremendous. Once when he was a young man in Somerset he liked to walk over to Shepton and to visit a certain "sweet tempered" Betsy White who lived there. He had a great mind "to make a bold stroke" and ask her to marry him. He went so far, indeed, as to propose marriage "when opportunity served," and Betsy was willing. But he delayed; time passed; four years passed indeed, and Betsy went to Devonshire, met a Mr. Webster, who had five hundred pounds a year, and married him. When James Woodforde met them in the turnpike road he could say little, "being shy," but to his diary he remarked—and this no doubt was his private version of the affair ever after—"she has proved herself to me a mere jilt."

But he was a young man then, and as time went on we cannot help suspecting that he was glad to consider the question of marriage shelved once and for all so that he might settle down with his niece Nancy at Weston Longueville, and give himself simply and solely, every day and all day, to the great business of living. Again, what else to call it we do not know.

For James Woodforde was nothing in particular. Life had it all her own way with him. He had no special gift; he had no oddity or infirmity. It is idle to pretend that he was a zealous priest. God in Heaven was much the same to him as King George upon the throne—a kindly Monarch, that is to say, whose festivals one kept by preaching a sermon on Sunday much as one kept the Royal birthday by firing a blunderbuss and drinking a toast at dinner. Should anything untoward happen, like the death of a boy who was dragged and killed by a horse, he would instantly, but rather perfunctorily exclaim, "I hope to God the Poor Boy is happy," and add, "We all came home singing"; just as when Justice Creed's peacock spread its tail—"and most noble it is"—he would exclaim, "How wonderful are Thy Works O God in every Being." But there was no fanaticism, no enthusiasm, no lyric impulse about James Woodforde. In all these pages, indeed, each so neatly divided into compartments, and each of those again filled, as the days themselves were filled, quietly and fully in a hand steady as the pacing of a well-tempered nag, one can only call to mind a single poetic phrase about the transit of Venus. "It appeared as a black patch upon a fair Lady's face," he says. The words themselves are mild enough, but they

hang over the undulating expanse of the Parson's prose with the resplendence of the star itself. So in the Fen country a barn or a tree appears twice its natural size against the surrounding flats. But what led him to this palpable excess that summer's night we cannot tell. It cannot have been that he was drunk. He spoke out too roundly against such failings in his brother Jack to be guilty himself. Temperamentally he was among the eaters of meat and not among the drinkers of wine. When we think of the Woodfordes, uncle and niece, we think of them as often as not waiting with some impatience for their dinner. Gravely they watch the joint as it is set upon the table; swiftly they get their knives to work upon the succulent leg or loin; without much comment, unless a word is passed about the gravy or the stuffing, they go on eating. So they munch, day after day, year in year out, until between them they must have devoured herds of sheep and oxen, flocks of poultry, an odd dozen or so of swans and cygnets, bushels of apples and plums, while the pastries and the jellies crumble and squash beneath their spoons in mountains, in pyramids, in pagodas. Never was there a book so stuffed with food as this one is. To read the bill of fare respectfully and punctually set forth gives one a sense of repletion. Trout and chicken, mutton and peas, pork and apple sauce—so the joints succeed each other at dinner, and there is supper with more joints still to come, all, no doubt, home grown, and of the juiciest and sweetest; all cooked, often by the mistress herself, in the plainest English way, save when the dinner was at Weston Hall and Mrs. Custance surprised them with a London dainty—a pyramid of jelly, that is to say, with a "landscape appearing through it." After dinner sometimes, Mrs. Custance, for whom James Woodforde had a chivalrous devotion, would play the "Sticcardo Pastorale," and make "very soft music indeed"; or would get out her work-box and show them how neatly contrived it was, unless indeed she were giving birth to another child upstairs. These infants the Parson would baptize and very frequently he would bury them. They died almost as frequently as they were born. The Parson had a deep respect for the Custances. They were all that country gentry should be—a little given to the habit of keeping mistresses, perhaps, but that peccadillo could be forgiven them in view of their generosity to the poor, the kindness they showed to Nancy, and their condescension in asking the Parson to dinner when they had great people staying with them. Yet great people were not much to James's liking. Deeply though he respected the nobility, "one must confess," he said, "that being with our equals is much more agreeable."

Not only did Parson Woodforde know what was agreeable; that rare gift was by the bounty of Nature supplemented by another equally rare—he could have what he wanted. The age was propitious. Monday, Tuesday, Wednesday—they follow each other and each little compartment seems filled with content. The days were not crowded, but they were enviably varied. Fellow of New College though he was, he did things with his own hands, not merely with his own head. He lived in every room of the house—in the study he wrote sermons, in the dining-room he ate copiously; he cooked in the kitchen, he played cards in the parlour. And then he took his coat and stick and went coursing his greyhounds in the fields. Year in, year out, the provisioning of the house and its defence against the cold of winter and the drought of summer fell upon him. Like a general he surveyed the seasons and took steps to make his own little camp safe with coal and wood and beef and beer against the enemy. His day thus had to accommodate a jumble of incongruous occupations. There is religion to be served, and the pig to be killed; the sick to be visited and dinner to be eaten; the dead to be buried and beer to be brewed; Convocation to be attended and the cow to be bolused. Life and death, mortality and immortality, jostle in his pages and make a good mixed marriage of it: ". . . found the old gentleman almost at his last gasp. Totally senseless with rattlings in his Throat. Dinner today boiled beef and Rabbit rosted." All is as it should be; life is like that.

Surely, surely, then, here is one of the breathing-spaces in human affairs—here in Norfolk at the end of the eighteenth century at the Parsonage. For once man is content with his lot; harmony is achieved; his house fits him; a tree is a tree; a chair is a chair; each knows its office and fulfils it. Looking through the eyes of Parson Woodforde, the different lives of men seem orderly and settled. Far away guns roar; a King falls; but the sound is not loud enough to scare the rooks here in Norfolk. The proportions of things are different. The Continent is so distant that is looks a mere blur; America scarcely exists; Australia is unknown. But a magnifying glass is laid upon the fields of Norfolk. Every blade of grass is visible there. We see every lane and every field; the ruts on the roads and the peasants' faces. Each house stands in its own breadth of meadow isolated and independent. No wires link village to village. No voices thread the air. The body also is more present and more real. It suffers more acutely. No anaesthetic deadens physical pain. The surgeon's knife hovers real and sharp above the limb. Cold strikes unmitigated upon the house. The milk freezes in the pans; the water is thick with ice in the basins. One can scarcely walk from one room to another in the parsonage in winter. Poor men and women are frozen to death upon the roads. Often no letters come and there are no visitors and no newspapers. The Parsonage stands alone in the midst of the frost-bound fields. At last, Heaven be praised, life circulates again; a man comes to the door with a Madagascar monkey; another brings a box containing a child with two distinct perfect heads; there is a rumour that a balloon is going to rise at Norwich. Every little incident stands out sharp and clear. The drive to Norwich even is something of an adventure. One must trundle every step of the way behind a horse. But look how distinct the trees stand in the hedges; how slowly the cattle move their heads as the carriage trots by; how gradually the spires of Norwich raise themselves above the hill. And then how clear-cut and familiar are the faces of the few people who are our friends—the Custances, Mr. du Quesne. Friendship has time to solidify, to become a lasting, a valuable possession.

True, Nancy of the younger generation is visited now and then by a flighty notion that she is missing something, that she wants something. One day she complained to her uncle that life was very dull: she complained "of the dismal situation of my house, nothing to be seen, and little or no visiting or being visited, &c.," and made him very uneasy. We could read Nancy a little lecture upon the folly of wanting that "et cetera." Look what your "et cetera" has brought to pass, we might say; half the countries of Europe are bankrupt; there is a red line of villas on every green hillside; your Norfolk roads are black as tar; there is no end to "visiting or being visited." But Nancy has an answer to make us, to the effect that our past is her present. You, she says, think it a great privilege to be born in the eighteenth century, because one called cowslips pagles and rode in a curricle instead of driving in a car. But you are utterly wrong, you fanatical lovers of memoirs, she goes on. I can assure you, my life was often intolerably dull. I did not laugh at the things that make you laugh. It did not amuse me when my uncle dreamt of a hat or saw bubbles in the beer, and said that meant a death in the family; I thought so too. Betsy Davy mourned young Walker with all her heart in spite of dressing in sprigged paduasoy. There is a great deal of humbug talked of the eighteenth century. Your delight in old times and old diaries is half impure. You make up something that never had any existence. Our sober reality is only a dream to you—so Nancy grieves and complains, living through the eighteenth century day by day, hour by hour.

Still, if it is a dream, let us indulge it a moment longer. Let us believe that some things last, and some places and some people are not touched by change. On a fine May morning, with the rooks rising and the hares scampering and the plover calling among the long grass, there is much to encourage the illusion. It is we who change and perish. Parson Woodforde lives on. It is the kings and queens who lie in prison. It is the great towns that are ravaged with anarchy and confusion. But the river Wensum still flows; Mrs. Custance is brought to bed of yet another baby; there is the first swallow of the year. The spring comes, and summer with its hay and strawberries; then autumn, when the walnuts are exceptionally fine though the pears are poor; so we lapse into winter, which is indeed boisterous, but the house, thank God, withstands the storm; and then again there is the first swallow, and Parson Woodforde takes his greyhounds out a-coursing.

The Rev. John Skinner

A whole world separates Woodforde, who was born in 1740 and died in 1803, from Skinner, who was born in 1772 and died in 1839.

For the few years that separated the two parsons are those momentous years that separate the eighteenth century from the nineteenth. Camerton, it is true, lying in the heart of Somersetshire, was a village of the greatest antiquity; nevertheless, before five pages of the diary are turned we read of coal-works, and how there was a great shouting at the coal-works because a fresh vein of coal had been discovered, and the proprietors had given money to the workmen to celebrate an event which promised such prosperity to the village. Then, though the country gentlemen seemed set as firmly in their seats as ever, it happened that the manor house at Camerton, with all the rights and duties pertaining to it, was in the hands of the Jarretts, whose fortune was derived from the Jamaica trade. This novelty, this incursion of an element quite unknown to Woodforde in his day, had its disturbing influence no doubt upon the character of Skinner himself. Irritable, nervous, apprehensive, he seems to embody, even before the age itself had come into existence, all the strife and unrest of our distracted times. He stands, dressed in the prosaic and unbecoming stocks and pantaloons of the early nineteenth century, at the parting of the ways. Behind him lay order and discipline and all the virtues of the heroic past, but directly he left his study he was faced with drunkenness and immorality; with indiscipline and irreligion; with Methodism and Roman Catholicism; with the Reform Bill and the Catholic Emancipation Act, with a mob clamouring for freedom, with the overthrow of all that was decent and established and right. Tormented and querulous, at the same time conscientious and able, he stands at the parting of the ways, unwilling to yield an inch, unable to concede a point, harsh, peremptory, apprehensive, and without hope.

Private sorrow had increased the natural acerbity of his temper. His wife had died young, leaving him with four small children, and of these the best-loved, Laura, a child who shared his tastes and would have sweetened his life, for she already kept a diary and had arranged a cabinet of shells with the utmost neatness, died too. But these losses, though they served nominally to make him love God the better, in practice led him to hate men more. By the time the diary opens in 1822 he was fixed in his opinion that the mass of men are unjust and malicious, and that the people of Camerton are more corrupt even than the mass of men. But by that date he was also fixed in his profession. Fate had taken him from the lawyer's office, where he would have been in his element, dealing out justice, filling up forms, keeping strictly to the letter of the law, and had planted him at Camerton among churchwardens and farmers, the Gullicks and the Padfields, the old woman who had dropsy, the idiot boy, and the dwarf. Nevertheless, however sordid his tasks and disgusting his parishioners, he had his duty to them; and with them he would remain. Whatever insults he suffered, he would live up to his principles, uphold the right, protect the poor, and punish the wrongdoer. By the time the diary opens, this strenuous and unhappy career is in full swing.

Perhaps the village of Camerton in the year 1822, with its coal-miners and the disturbance they brought, was no fair sample of English village life. Certainly it is difficult, as one follows the Rector on his daily rounds, to indulge in pleasant dreams about the quaintness and amenity of old English rural life. Here, for instance, he was called to see Mrs. Gooch—a woman of weak mind, who had been locked up alone in her cottage and fallen into the fire and was in agony. "Why do you not help me, I say? Why do you not help me?" she cried. And the Rector, as he heard her screams, knew that she had come to this through no fault of her own. Her efforts to keep a home together had led to drink, and so she had lost her reason, and what with the squabbles between the Poor Law officials and the family as to who should support her, what with her husband's extravagance and drunkenness, she had been left alone, had fallen into the fire, and so died. Who was to blame? Mr. Purnell, the miserly magistrate, who was all for cutting down the allowance paid to the poor, or Hicks the Overseer, who was notoriously harsh, or the ale-houses, or the Methodists, or what? At any rate the Rector had done his duty. However he might be hated for it, he always stood up for the rights of the down-trodden; he always told people of their faults, and convicted them of evil. Then there was Mrs. Somer, who kept a house of ill fame and was bringing up her daughters to the same profession. Then there was Farmer Lippeatt, who, turned out of the Red Post at midnight, dead drunk, missed his way, fell into a quarry, and died of a broken breastbone. Wherever one turned there was suffering, wherever one looked one found cruelty behind that suffering. Mr. and Mrs. Hicks, for example, the Overseers, let an infirm pauper lie for ten days in the Poor House without care, "so that maggots had bred in his flesh and eaten great holes in his body." His only attendant was an old woman, who was so failing that she was unable to lift him. Happily the pauper died. Happily poor Garratt, the miner, died too. For to add to the evils of drink and poverty and the cholera there was constant peril from the mine itself. Accidents were common and the means of treating them elementary. A fall of coal had broken Garratt's back, but he lingered on, though exposed to the crude methods of country surgeons, from January to November, when at last death released him. Both the stern Rector and the flippant Lady of the Manor, to do them justice, were ready with their half-crowns, with their soups and their medicines, and visited sick-beds without fail. But even allowing for the natural asperity of Mr. Skinner's temper, it would need a very rosy pen and a very kindly eye to make a smiling picture of life in the village of Camerton a century ago. Half-crowns and soup went a very little way to remedy matters; sermons and denunciations made them perhaps even worse.

The Rector found refuge from Camerton neither in dissipation like some of his neighbours, nor in sport like others. Occasionally he drove over to dine with a brother cleric, but he noted acrimoniously that the entertainment was "better suited to Grosvenor Square than a clergyman's home—French dishes and French wines in profusion," and records with a note of exclamation that it was eleven o'clock before he drove home. When his children were young he sometimes walked with them in the fields, or amused himself by making them a boat, or rubbed up his Latin in an epitaph for the tomb of some pet dog or tame pigeon. And sometimes he leant back peacefully and listened to Mrs. Fenwick as she sang the songs of Moore to her husband's accompaniment on the flute. But even such harmless pleasures were poisoned with suspicion. A farmer stared insolently as he passed; some one threw a stone from a window; Mrs. Jarrett clearly concealed some evil purpose behind her cordiality. No, the only refuge from Camerton lay in Camalodunum. The more he thought of it the more certain he became that he had the singular good fortune to live on the identical spot where lived the father of Caractacus, where Ostorius established his colony, where Arthur had fought the traitor Modred, where Alfred very nearly came in his misfortunes. Camerton was undoubtedly the Camalodunum of Tacitus. Shut up in his study alone with his documents, copying, comparing, proving indefatigably, he was safe, at rest, even happy. He was also, he became convinced, on the track of an important etymological discovery, by which it could be proved that there was a secret significance "in every letter that entered into the composition of Celtic names." No archbishop was as content in his palace as Skinner the antiquary was content in his cell. To these pursuits he owed, too, those rare and delightful visits to Stourhead, the seat of Sir Richard Hoare, when at last he mixed with men of his own calibre, and met the gentlemen who were engaged in examining the antiquities of Wiltshire. However hard it froze, however high the snow lay heaped on the roads, Skinner rode over to Stourhead; and sat in the library, with a violent cold, but in perfect content, making extracts from Seneca, and extracts from Diodorum Siculus, and extracts from Ptolemy's *Geography,* or scornfully disposed of some rash and ill-informed fellow-antiquary who had the temerity to assert that Camalodunum was really situated at Colchester. On he went with his extracts, with his theories, with his proofs, in spite of the malicious present of a rusty nail wrapped in paper from his parishioners, in spite of the laughing warning of his host: "Oh, Skinner, you will bring everything at last to Camalodunum; be content with what you have already discovered, if you fancy too much you will weaken the authority of real facts." Skinner replied with a sixth letter thirty-four pages long; for Sir Richard did not know how necessary Camalodunum had become to an embittered man who had daily to encounter Hicks the Overseer and Purnell the magistrate, the brothels, the ale-houses, the Methodists, the dropsies and bad legs of Camerton. Even the floods were mitigated if one could reflect that thus Camalodunum must have looked in the time of the Britons.

So he filled three iron chests with ninety-eight volumes of manuscript. But by degrees the manuscripts ceased to be entirely concerned with Camalodunum; they began to be largely concerned with John Skinner. It was true that it was important to establish the truth about Camalodunum, but it was also important to establish the truth about John Skinner. In fifty years after his death, when the diaries were published, people would know not only that John Skinner was a great antiquary, but that he was a much wronged, much suffering man. His diary became his confidant, as it was to become his champion. For example, was he not the most affectionate of fathers, he asked the diary? He had spent endless time and trouble on his sons; he had sent them to Winchester and Cambridge, and yet now when the farmers were so insolent about paying him his tithes, and gave him a broken-backed lamb for his share, or fobbed him off with less than his due of cocks, his son Joseph refused to help him. His son said that the people of Camerton laughed at him; that he treated his children like servants; that he suspected evil where none was meant. And then he opened a letter by chance and found a bill for a broken gig; and then his sons lounged about smoking cigars when they might have helped him to mount his drawings. In short, he could not stand their presence in his house. He dismissed them in a fury to Bath. When they had gone he could not help admitting that perhaps he had been at fault. It was his querulous temper again—but then he had so much to make him querulous. Mrs. Jarrett's peacock screamed under his window all night. They jangled the church bells on purpose to annoy him. Still, he would try; he would let them come back. So Joseph and Owen came back. And then the old irritation overcame him again. He "could not help saying" something about being idle, or drinking too much cider, upon which there was a terrible scene and Joseph broke one of the parlour chairs. Owen took Joseph's part. So did Anna. None of his children cared for him. Owen went further. Owen said "I was a madman and ought to have a commission of lunacy to investigate my conduct." And, further, Owen cut him to the quick by pouring scorn on his verses, on his diaries and archaeological theories. He said: "No one would read the nonsense I had written. When I mentioned having gained a prize at Trinity College . . . his reply was that none but the most stupid fellows ever thought of writing for the college prize." Again there was a terrible scene; again they were dismissed to Bath, followed by their father's curses. And then Joseph fell ill with the family consumption. At once his father was all tenderness and remorse. He sent for doctors, he offered to take him for a sea trip to Ireland, he took him indeed to Weston and went sailing with him on the sea. Once more the family came together. And once more the querulous, exacting father could not help, for all his concern, exasperating the children whom, in his own crabbed way, he yet genuinely loved. The question of religion cropped up. Owen said his father was no better than a Deist or a Socinian. And

Joseph, lying ill upstairs, said he was too tired for argument; he did not want his father to bring drawings to show him; he did not want his father to read prayers to him, "he would rather have some other person to converse with than me." So in the crisis of their lives, when a father should have been closest to them, even his children turned away from him. There was nothing left to live for. Yet what had he done to make everyone hate him? Why did the farmers call him mad? Why did Joseph say that no one would read what he wrote? Why did the villagers tie tin cans to the tail of his dog? Why did the peacocks shriek and the bells ring? Why was there no mercy shown to him and no respect and no love? With agonising repetition the diary asks these questions; but there was no answer. At last, one morning in December 1839, the Rector took his gun, walked into the beech wood near his home, and shot himself dead.

Suggested Readings

Two works that discuss economic conditions in Britain in the period are Eric Pawson, *The Early Industrial Revolution: Britain in the Eighteenth Century* (New York: Barnes and Noble Books, 1979), and Arnold D. Harvey, *Britain in the Early Nineteenth Century* (London: Batsford, 1978). The social processes of industrialization are extremely well surveyed in M. Dorothy George, *England in Transition: Life and Work in the Eighteenth Century* (New York: Penguin Books, 1953). Charles Dickens' novel *Hard Times* presents a striking contemporary view of an industrial town and of a perceived tendency to treat humans like machines.

Cottage Industry and the Factory System

Duncan Bythell

The common view of the Industrial Revolution focuses on the development of machinery and power sources, the growth of great factories, and the exploitation of urban laborers. The emphasis on these dramatic features obscures the true complexity of the process of industrialization and distorts some aspects of this period of social change. In the following selection, the author discusses one of the less dramatic features, the so-called "putting-out" arrangement that preceded the factory system and continued to act as an alternative to it.

It was inevitable that some stages of an industrial process were mechanized before others, causing disruption within the process as a whole. Thus, the first textile machines spun vast amounts of yarn. They did not weave cloth, however, and large numbers of weavers were needed to keep up with the increased supply of yarn. Some industrialists solved the problem by providing the raw material for many small processors—sometimes merely the heads of families—who did the work in their own premises. The factory operator then collected the finished product, paying the processor on a piecework basis. The system, although complex and cumbersome, was also efficient and flexible for many industries, and it was particularly effective in drawing women and children into the work force. Indeed, the cottage system functioned so well that it persisted in some industries far into the nineteenth century and must be considered as characteristic a feature of the Industrial Revolution as the factory is. The cottage system worked because the laborers, primarily women and children, could be paid so poorly that the cost of their

COTTAGE
INDUSTRY
AND THE
FACTORY
SYSTEM

147

labor was cheaper than that of building machinery. To a great extent, the truly exploited workers of the Industrial Revolution were those who worked in the cottages of the picturesque villages of the English countryside, not the laborers in the "dark satanic mills."

At the centre of most people's picture of Britain's industrial revolution in the nineteenth century stands the dark, satanic mill, where an exploited and dispirited army of men, women and children is engaged for starvation wages in a seemingly endless round of drudgery: the pace of their labour is determined by the persistent pulse of the steam engine and accompanied by the ceaseless clanking of machines; and the sole beneficiary of their efforts is the grasping, tyrannical, licentious factory master, pilloried by Charles Dickens in that loud-mouthed hypocrite and philistine, Mr. Bounderby. Crude and exaggerated though this image is, it depicts very clearly the main features of the pattern of production which became widespread in the manufacturing industries, not only of Britain, but also of the other advanced countries, by the end of the nineteenth century. For it highlights the emergence of the factory, where hundreds labour together under one roof and one direction, as the normal type of work-unit; it stresses the new importance of complex machine-technology in the process of production; and it emphasises that, because ownership of these machines, of the building which houses them and the engine which drives them, rests with the private capitalist, there exists an unbridgeable gulf between him and his property-less wage-earning employees.

This system of production, which is usually assumed to have been pioneered and rapidly adopted in Britain's textile industries around the end of the eighteenth century, did not, of course, emerge in a wholly non-industrial world. The popular picture suggests that it replaced—or rather, brutally displaced—an earlier type of organisation, variously referred to as 'the domestic system', the 'outwork system', or simply as 'cottage industry', which differed totally from the factory system. Whereas the latter concentrates workers under one roof in an increasingly urban environment, the former disperses employment into the homes of the workers, most of whom live in the countryside. Although the modern mill is filled with the factory master's costly machinery, the domestic workshop houses simple and traditional hand-tools—the spinner's wheel, the weaver's loom, the cordwainer's bench, the nail-maker's forge, and the seamstress' humble pins and needles—which actually belong to the worker. And whilst the factory system implies clear class division, with

COTTAGE INDUSTRY AND THE FACTORY SYSTEM   By Duncan Bythell, from *History Today*, April 1983, pp. 17–23.

the wage-earner firmly subordinated to, and perpetually at odds with, his employer, the domestic system gives the head of the household an independent, quasi-managerial status, which enables him to control his own time and to direct, in a 'natural' fatherly way, the efforts of his family team.

The unspoken assumption is that, in the undisciplined, fulfilling, and relatively classless world of cottage industry, the common man was certainly happier, even if he was materially worse off, than his grandson. Only in the last desperate phase, when the dwindling band of domestic handworkers found themselves competing hopelessly against the new generation of factory machine-minders, is the idyllic image tarnished; and the haunting picture of the doomed handloom weaver, striving in his cellar to match the output of his wife and children who have been forced into the factory, reinforces the notion that, between old and new systems, there is nothing but contrast, conflict, and competition.

Any concept of historical change based on snapshots taken on separate occasions tends to emphasise differences and discontinuities. In the caricature of the domestic and factory systems just presented, they appear to be completely antithetical. Yet on closer examination, the story of most industries which 'modernised' in the course of the nineteenth century is full of important elements of *continuity* and *complementarity* between the factory and the pre-factory stages of their development; and it is on these two dimensions, rather than on the stark contrasts suggested by the traditional stereotype, that I want to focus attention.

Let us consider continuity first. A number of historians have recently suggested that the existence of the domestic system of production in such industries as textiles was one of the main features distinguishing the pre-industrial economies of Europe from the Third World countries of today; and although they prefer the abstract concept of 'proto industrialisation' to the well-established and perfectly adequate term 'domestic system', they are essentially claiming that the industrial revolutions of the nineteenth century could not have taken place without the prior development of a form of production which, in their view, was to provide both the capital and the labour needed for modern industrial development.

In making this claim, proponents of the theory of 'proto industry' are drawing attention to one of the most important, but often misunderstood, features of the classic domestic system—the fact that it already showed a clear distinction between the capitalists who controlled it and the wage-earners who depended upon it for their livelihood. For the domestic system, no less than the factory system which replaced it, was a method of mass-production which enabled wealthy merchant-manufacturers to supply not only textile fabrics, but also items as diverse

COTTAGE
INDUSTRY
AND THE
FACTORY
SYSTEM

149

The weaver at his domestic hand loom (above) contrasts sharply with work on a factory power loom (at right).

as ready-made clothes, hosiery, boots and shoes, and hardware, to distant markets at home and abroad. In order to do so, they, like the factory masters who followed them, bought the appropriate raw materials and hired wage-labour to convert them into finished products. The pay roll of some of these merchant-manufacturers could run into many hundreds: in the late 1830s, for example, Dixons of Carlisle, cotton manufacturers, employed 3,500 handloom weavers scattered over the border counties of England and Scotland and in Ulster; a decade or so later, Wards of Belper, hosiers, provided work for some 4,000

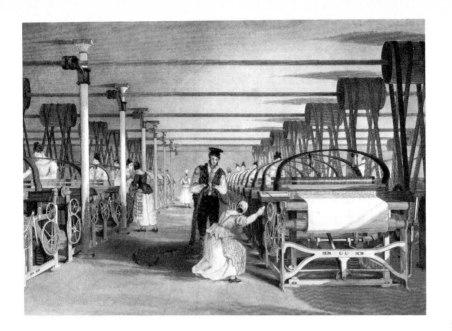

knitting frames in the counties of Derbyshire, Nottinghamshire, and Leicestershire; and as late as the 1870s, Eliza Tinsley and Co. put out work to 2,000 domestic nail- and chain-makers in the west Midlands.

To service and co-ordinate such large and scattered forces required an elaborate system of communication and control in which the key figures were the agents—variously known as 'putters-out', 'bagmen', and 'foggers'—who were the equivalents of the modern supervisor or shop-floor manager. Certainly, the workers whom these great men employed generally owned their own tools, although in the case of an elaborate piece of machinery like the knitting frame they often had to hire it; and most of them worked on their own premises—although, again, it was by no means rare for the individual weaver, knitter, or nail-maker to rent space and tools in another man's shop. But except in a few minor rural trades like straw-plaiting and lace-making in the south and east Midlands, they neither provided their own raw materials, nor had they any interest in marketing the goods they helped to make. They were, in short, wage-earners who happened to own some of the tools of their trade. But the trade in which they worked was organised by capitalists; and far from making goods to sell to local customers, they were often, all unknowing, supplying the wants of West Indian slaves and North American frontiersmen.

The crux of the argument about continuity between domestic and factory systems of mass-production turns on whether it was actually the case that the firms which set up the first modern factories in a particular industry were already active in it on a putting-out basis, and whether the last generation of domestic workers transformed themselves into the new race of factory hands. Of course, no one is maintaining that continuity was direct and complete in every single industry or region where such a transition occurred: indeed, there were areas such as East Anglia or the Cotswolds where the change-over simply did not take place, and where a once important industry gradually vanished as the old domestic system dwindled and died. But where 'modernisation' did happen in traditional outwork industries in the course of the nineteenth century, as it did in the textile industries of Lancashire and Yorkshire and in the hosiery trade of the east Midlands, historians seem to be agreed that it was existing firms which played a leading role, albeit cautiously and belatedly in some instances, in setting-up the factory system and in embodying some of their capital in buildings and machines; in other words the fortunes made, and the expertise in marketing and managing acquired, in the old system of production were important in enabling the new system to develop.

There is less agreement, however, as to how far the existing handworkers in any particular industry really did shift over to the factory. The theory of 'proto industry' suggests that the domestic system had created a country-dwelling but landless proletariat in many ways at odds with the traditional rural society around them: they had only a minimal involvement in the agrarian economy, and were therefore rootless and prone to migration; they possessed manual skills irrelevant to farming activities; and as wage-earners, they were obliged to respond to the pressures and opportunities of a market economy in which the price of survival was adaptability. In terms of both work-skills and mental outlook, that is to say, they were already well-equipped to form the first generation of the modern industrial labour force.

But did this actually happen? The traditional picture suggests not, because it depicts a stubborn refusal to come to terms with changed circumstances and, indeed, a downright hostility to 'machinery' which, in the Luddite movement of 1811–16 in the Midlands and the various outbreaks of loom-smashing in Lancashire and elsewhere, sometimes erupted in violence. Clearly, the worker's readiness to change with the times depended partly on age, and partly on opportunity. Case studies based on census returns for Lancashire weaving villages during the crucial phase of transition in the middle of the nineteenth century suggest that, once a powerloom shed had been started locally, the younger married men were ready enough to take work in it, but that the elderly were either reluctant to do so, or were debarred by the employer, and therefore stuck to the handloom. But until there was a mill virtually on the spot, most of these villagers believed they had little option but to stick to the handloom, and for want of other opportunity they continued to bring their children up to it. Probably the most important strand of continuity in the labour force was in fact provided by the children of the last generation of handworkers: by and large, a trade dies out because it stopped recruiting sometime before; and the demise of occupations like handloom weaving was finally assured when families were willing and able to put their offspring into something different, instead of forcing them to follow automatically in father's footsteps.

By highlighting the division between capital and labour which characterised the domestic no less than the factory system of production, and by considering the continuity which this engendered, the new theory of 'proto industry' has pinpointed certain popular misconceptions about the nature of cottage industry. First of all, it must be clear that when economic historians refer to 'outwork' or 'cottage industry' they are *not* talking about a world where each family simply makes manufactured goods for its own use—although in even the most advanced societies elements of the home-made and the do-it-yourself survive. Nor are they discussing the self-employed craftsman or genuine artisan—the village shoe-maker and tailor, or the more sophisticated urban wig-maker or cabinet-maker—who produced and sold 'one-off' goods directly to the order of their local customers, and whose successors are still to be found in some parts of the modern economy. Indeed—and this is a second error which needs to be corrected—in the strict sense they are not dealing with 'skill' or 'craft' at all. As a method of mass-production, the greater part of cottage industry involved the making of plain, simple, inexpensive goods by hands which, although they became more nimble and adept with experience, had neither needed nor received much initial training. Weaving heavy woollens and hammering nails and chains required a certain strength; but weaving plain calico, knitting coarse stockings, sewing buttons on shirts, plaiting straw, and sticking matchboxes together with glue called for neither brain nor brawn. A seven-year apprenticeship to learn the 'mysteries' of most domestic industries was unnecessary, when the work merely involved the monotonous repetition of a few simple movements of the fingers; and because the work was unskilled and undemanding it was considered particularly suitable for women and children. Domestic industry, like factory industry, involved the worker in much mindless drudgery; the chief difference was that, in working at home with hand-tools, the wage-earner could go at his or her own pace, instead of having to keep up with the steam engine.

Thirdly, just as we need to abandon the notion that the domestic system was all about skilled craftsmen, so we must reject the idea that it was predominantly about 'men' at all. One of the advantages which the old terms 'domestic system' and 'cottage industry' have over 'proto industry' is that they suggest an important feature which old-style mass-production shared with the early textile mills: a domestic or cottage workshop called on the efforts of housewife, grandparents, and children of both sexes, as well as those of the household's head. Thus the average weaving or knitting family would run two or three looms or frames, and in addition would operate any ancillary machinery needed to prepare or finish the work. Because it worked as a team, the domestic work unit could also practice division of labour, so that each member could specialise on just one stage in the sequence of production. Like any other family business, a workshop involved in the domestic system was a collective enterprise to which all contributed who could: and only when the household included no children old enough to do even the simplest tasks did it depend for its income on what a man could earn by his own unaided efforts. Because the capitalist-controlled outwork industries made particular use of women's and children's labour in this way, female workers were generally in a clear majority in the work force; and in the mass-production section of the needlework trades, where outwork remained particularly important until late in the nineteenth century, and which included men's tailoring and shirt-making as well as dress-making and lace stitching, the preponderance of women was especially striking.

Fourthly, we must not imagine that, in a capitalist controlled industrial system such as outwork was, relations between masters and operatives were marked by much sweetness and light. Since the main tie between them was the cash nexus, disputes about wages could be frequent and bitter. Most employers in the industries which used the domestic system operated in a tough competitive environment, and their likely reaction to a spell of bad trading conditions would be to cut the piece-rates they paid their workers. Most of the scattered rural outworkers were disorganised and docile, and could offer little, if any, resistance; and in any case, for women and children a pittance was deemed better than no work at all. But the adult men—especially those who lived in the towns, and did the better-class work which needed more strength or skill—were another matter. They had a clear conception of the work and wages proper for a man, and they were better able to take collective action against underpaying masters and weak-willed blacklegs who broke the conventional rules.

As a result, at different times in the late eighteenth and early nineteenth centuries, fierce strikes broke out in such towns as Manchester, Coventry, Barnsley and Norwich, major centres of handloom weaving; among the urban framework knitters of Nottingham and Leicester; and among the nail-makers of the Black Country. At a time when formal trade unionism was a shadowy affair, and in difficult political and economic circumstances, some at least of Britain's industrial outworkers played their part in sustaining patterns of collective bargaining which, *faute de mieux,* sometimes involved great violence; whilst the support these disgruntled men gave to the various campaigns for parliamentary reform between the 1790s and the 1850s has been frequently noted by historians.

Once we have abandoned such misconceptions about the nature of the domestic system as it had come to exist by the end of the eighteenth century, it is easier to see the similarities and the points of continuity between it and the factory system which was eventually and gradually to supersede it. And when we realise that the domestic system, far from being some prehistoric monster which expired when the first cotton factory was built, actually expanded and persisted in many industries and regions until well into the second half of the nineteenth century, we become aware, not only that the two types of mass-production overlapped in time, but also that they complemented each other, rather than competed. The textile industries usually occupy the forefront of any discussion of the domestic and factory systems; and in view of their wide geographic dispersal, their rapid expansion, and the hundreds of thousands they had come to employ by the late eighteenth century, this is entirely appropriate. But because, starting with the spinning branch of the British cotton industry in the 1770s, it was in these industries that the complete triumph of the factory system was achieved earliest, attention has been deflected from the many other trades—particularly shoe-making, clothing, and some branches of hardware—where the domestic system actually became more, rather than less, important. For although the first half of the nineteenth century saw the disappearance into the factory first of spinning and then of weaving in Lancashire and Yorkshire, it also witnessed the expansion of mass-production by outwork methods in the ready-made clothing trades and in the boot and shoe industries. And apart from the fact that these growing industries increased output by traditional rather than modern methods, there were other, less expansionary trades—such as Midlands hosiery and Black Country nail-making—which remained fossilised at the 'domestic' stage of development until well after 1850. In addition, the latter part of the nineteenth century actually saw a number of new, small-scale manufacturers, such as paperbag and cardboard-box making, establish themselves as cottage industries. Thus, if outwork had more or less disappeared from the staple textile industries by the 1850s, it was more firmly entrenched than ever in and around many of the industrial towns of the Midlands and the south of England, and, above all, in what were to become known as the 'sweated trades' of London. Why was this?

The pioneering experience of the textile industries suggests some of the answers. Contrary to popular belief, even in the cotton industry, the transition from the domestic to the factory system was a slow, piecemeal affair, which took three generations; and in wool, linen and silk, the process was even more protracted. The reason was simple: the first power-driven machines of the 1770s revolutionised *spinning* only; and by making it possible to produce thread on a scale and at a price which would have been inconceivable in the days of the spinning wheel, they simply created a good deal more work for a great many more workers—in this case, the weavers—at the next stage in the production process. And so long as enough extra weavers could be found at wages the employers were prepared to pay, there was no need to think of replacing the handloom with some labour-saving device, as yet uninvented. Thus between 1780 and 1820, the growth of spinning factories marched *pari passu* with a vast increase in the number of handloom weavers' shops; and technical progress in one section of the industry merely led to the multiplication of traditional handwork in associated sections.

The same thing was to happen in other industries later: when lace-making was mechanised in Nottingham from the 1820s, there was a consequent increase in the amount of stitching, finishing and mending for hand-sewers in their homes; when machines were first used to cut out the components of a stock-sized shoe or coat, they made more unskilled assembly work for domestic workers; and even when the sewing machine had transformed the traditional needlework trades, it did not necessarily drive them out of the home into the factory, because, as a compact, hand-powered, and relatively inexpensive tool, it could be used in a domestic workshop as effectively as in a large factory. In all these ways, factory and domestic systems often co-existed and complemented each other in a given industry. Since it was rarely either possible or necessary for new techniques to be introduced simultaneously at every stage in the process of manufacture, flexible combinations of centralised factory work at one stage, and cottage industry at the next, were perfectly practicable.

There was often a regional dimension to the co-existence of these two types of mass-production, and it was here that elements of competition emerged between them. In the classic case of cotton weaving, for example, the handloom survived as the dominant machine in some parts of Lancashire for almost a generation after it had largely given way to the powerloom in others: in large towns such as Stockport, Oldham and Blackburn, factory production was taken up in the 1820s by manufacturers who already operated spinning mills; but it made little progress in the small towns and villages of north-east Lancashire, such as Padiham, Colne and Haggate before the 1840s. In part, this reflected local differences in the availability of labour and capital, for the more remote rural areas were richer in the former than in the latter. But independent of such regional differences, there was also a qualitative side to this 'staggered' adoption of the powerloom, because the early, clumsy factory looms could cope better with the plain types of cloth than with fancy or patterned goods. Other industries were later to show similar disparities in the rate at which different districts and sections adopted new techniques: for example, the boot and shoe industry of Leicester seems to have relied more on factory production and less on outwork than did that of Northampton in the second half of the nineteenth century; whilst in the 1890s, cottage industry was more apparent in the ready-made clothing trade of London than in that of Leeds.

In short, the domestic system of mass-production in British industry took a long time a-dying during the nineteenth century. It might expand in one trade at the very time that it was contracting in another; in some industries, it could enjoy a harmonious co-existence with factory production for many years, whilst elsewhere it might struggle on in arduous competition for a generation or more. Why was this? How could this technically primitive form of large-scale production remain viable for so long in important parts of the world's first industrial economy?

To find the answer, we must try to fathom the minds of the entrepreneurs in the different industries, as they calculated how best, in a complex and competitive world, to get their goods to market with least cost and least trouble to themselves. A manufacturer who had grown up with the domestic system as the dominant mode of production in his trade would need strong inducements to abandon it, because under normal circumstances it offered him many advantages. If his employees provided their own tools and workrooms, he himself was spared the need to tie up his own capital in bricks and mortar and in machinery; and in times of periodic trade depression or slack seasonal demand—and most of these industries were subject to one or other of these risks, if not, indeed, to both of them—it was the worker, not his employer, who suffered when plant and equipment were standing idle. It was not that these great merchant-manufacturers lacked capital—indeed it required remarkably little fixed capital in most of these industries to build or rent a small factory and fill it with new or second-hand machinery; nor was it generally the case that appropriate new techniques were not available—the time-lag between invention and adoption of a new machine is a recurrent feature in many of these trades; it was rather the case that their capital under the domestic system was embodied in unused raw materials, goods 'in the make', and stocks in the warehouse.

Nevertheless, because it involved more sophisticated machinery, the application of power, and the construction of large, purpose-built work premises, the factory system of production was capital-intensive, rather than labour-intensive. By contrast, what an employer had to rely on to keep cottage industry viable was an abundance of cheap, unskilled, and unorganised labour. So long as he could find enough workers who had no choice but to take his work at the wages he was prepared to offer—no matter how low these might be—he could meet his production targets and reap his expected profits. From the late eighteenth to the late nineteenth centuries, there were many regions of Britain which could provide just such supplies of labour: a high and sustained

COTTAGE
INDUSTRY
AND THE
FACTORY
SYSTEM

157

rate of population increase, together with the greater commercialisation of agriculture, tended to create pools of unemployed or under-employed workers in many rural areas; and in so far as these impoverished country people moved off to the towns in search of more work and better wages, they often merely added to the chaos and confusion in the unskilled urban labour markets.

But what kept the domestic system alive after the mid-nineteenth century more than anything else was the continued availability—long after most adult men had deserted these low paid, dead-end jobs—of female and child labour: incapable of collective self-defence, and often deliberately ignored by their better organised menfolk; accustomed to regarding any earnings, however minute, as a worthwhile contribution to family income; and often only able to work on a part-time or casual basis—they were ideal for many employers' purposes. And in a perverse way, because it thrived on family labour, the domestic system actually helped to perpetuate its own labour force: because cottage industry, by enabling the whole household to earn, acted as a great inducement to early marriages and large families, and thus contributed to the 'population explosion' which was so important a feature of Britain's industrial revolution.

Because labour could be much cheaper in one part of the country than in another, an old-fashioned employer who stuck to outwork could still hope to compete with his more ambitious and enterprising fellows elsewhere who had switched over to factory production. Only in the last quarter of the nineteenth century did a combination of new circumstances—including rural depopulation, compulsory schooling (which both kept young children out of the labour market and widened their horizons), rising real incomes (which made small supplementary earnings less essential to a family), and more 'chivalrous' male attitudes towards women as workers—help gradually to eliminate some of the sources of cheap labour and thus undermine one of the domestic system's chief props.

Changes in market conditions, as well as the increasing difficulty of finding suitable labour, could also be instrumental in persuading entrepreneurs to abandon old-style mass-production in favour of the factory. When, for example, attractive new export markets opened up for the English cotton industry in Latin America in the early 1820s, Lancashire manufacturers knew that they would be better able to increase output by introducing powerlooms than by seeking out more handloom weavers at higher wages; and when, more than two generations later, British boot and shoe manufacturers were faced with an 'invasion' of their own home market by cheap mass-produced, factory-made American imports, they recognised that they could only stay in business if they themselves adopted American methods of production. Both the cotton manufacturers of the 1820s and the boot and shoe manufacturers of the 1890s had to overcome strong opposition from workers still suspicious of machinery and still attached (in spite of the precarious economic position in which it left them) to the domestic system: but once the entrepreneurs in any industry had concluded, for whatever reasons, that the disadvantages of cottage industry outweighed the benefits, its days were numbered.

From the worker's point of view, even if we forget the caricature, the dark satanic mill offered an uninviting prospect; but it is hard to escape the conclusion that the domestic system was in many ways even less agreeable. Even where cottage workers were not directly competing with factory workers—and I have suggested that it would be wrong to put too much emphasis on this side of the story—most of them were poorly paid, and likely to be alternately over-worked and under-employed. Worst of all, they were subject to all kinds of abuses, not only from employers and their agents, but often from heads of households and fathers of families who connived, however reluctantly, in the exploitation of their own wives and children. Men may have been unwilling to accept the separation of home and workplace which the gradual replacement of the domestic system by the factory system involved: but in its long-term implications for family life, it was probably one of the most beneficial, as well as one of the most fundamental, of all the changes brought about by the industrial revolution.

Suggested Readings

The social transformations occasioned by the Industrial Revolution are considered in E. P. Thompson, *The Making of the English Working Class* (London: Gollancz, 1965). The early stages of the process are discussed in P. Kriedte et al., *Industrialization Before Industrialization* (Cambridge: Cambridge University Press, 1981). Duncan Bythell, the author of this selection, treats cottage industry in greater detail in *The Sweated Trades: Outwork in Nineteenth Century Britain* (London: Batsford Academic Press, 1978). A workers' revolt against mechanization forms the subject of Charlotte Brontë's novel *Shirley*.

COTTAGE
INDUSTRY
AND THE
FACTORY
SYSTEM

159

Protestant Evangelists and Christian Samurai

Irwin Scheiner

Japan was opened up to foreign influences in 1853, after more than 200 years of virtual isolation. American Protestant missionaries were among the first foreigners to enter the country and to take advantage of Japan's new receptivity to Western ideas. Their evangelical efforts were unusually successful, attracting converts primarily from the aristocratic samurai class, and led to the establishment of Christian churches in Japan that were staffed by natives and were self-sustaining, neither needing nor wanting financial support from Western missionary societies. This reading selection investigates the reasons for this success.

It appears that the majority of converts were samurai from the clans that had lost out in the civil war just preceding the opening up of Japan. Barred by their defeat from immediate access to political power and influence, these men were attracted to the Western schools operated by the missionaries. While acquiring Western knowledge as a means of personal advancement, they also absorbed Western values. Conversions were facilitated by the character and policies of the missionaries, who presented Christianity as a way of life compatible with the samurai moral code and the concern for national integrity that animated most Japanese at the time. Native Christianity became an important element in the sweeping transformation of Japanese society during the latter half of the nineteenth century, and Christian converts played a significant role in the modernization of their country.

merican and English Protestant missionaries entered Japan under the provisions of treaties signed in the late eighteen fifties. Entry was restricted to a few ports, and proselytizing was prohibited. Japanese were forbidden by laws in existence for more than two hundred years to join or even take part in services conducted by Christian clergy. Missionaries were thus legally restricted from extending their influence over the countryside and incapable of presenting their message to any Japanese within the treaty ports. Even after 1873, when the proscription had formally ended, Christianity was merely tolerated by the government, held in severe opprobrium by a good part of the intellectual and political elite, and superstitiously feared by the great mass of people. Still, within ten years of the missionaries' arrival, small bands of samurai in search of Western knowledge and language began to gather about the missions. Later many of them joined or founded congregations in the ports of Yokohama, Kobe, and Nagasaki. As private mission schools drew samurai to the ports and then into the church, requests by domain leaders for Western teachers served as the fulcrum to bring Christianity into some of the interior domain.

Partly because of this initial pattern of proselytizing, Christianization in Japan developed an interesting social pattern. In Meiji Japan, 30 percent of the converts to Protestant Christianity were of samurai origin. Almost all converts in the first decade of the era came from this stratum. Throughout the first three decades of the period a high percentage of the converts were young men, usually students at high schools or universities. Although the religion during most of these three decades was proscribed, it was not difficult to recruit from the universities. Also, because of the same pattern of proselytizing, a vigorous Christian movement, even if small in numbers nationally, appeared in some domains and urban centers. Thus in spite of many difficulties, after the first thirty years the missionaries were happy at the success of their proselytizing and the promise of future evangelical success. By 1889 there were 34,000 converts, 300 churches, numerous lower schools, and a number of important Christian universities. Most important, Japanese Christians were publishing one of the major journals of the time as well as providing intellectual stimulus and inspiration to a number of other political and critical magazines and newspapers of the period.

Compared with China, where missionaries had been working for many decades, these were astonishing results. Few peasants in China had been converted, and the literati-gentry rejected Christianity and

PROTESTANT EVANGELISTS AND CHRISTIAN SAMURAI   From Irwin Scheiner, *Christian Converts and Social Protest in Meiji Japan* (Berkeley: University of California Press, 1970), pp. 7–40.

became its implacable enemy. Whereas Chinese Christian churches were starved for native intellectual leadership, Japanese converts became evangelists upon conversion and quickly spread the Word in lectures, journals, and books. Scarcely a Chinese church had a native preacher. On the other hand, from the very outset of the Christian mission in Japan three principles were established: a native church, a native clergy, and a national self-supporting church.

The key to these differences lies in the character of the convert himself. Where Christian leaders of both the West and Japan might in later years decry the highly intellectual, middle class, and urban character of Protestantism in Japan, it appeared in Meiji Japan to both the missionary and the convert that the fortuitous evangelization of the samurai held promise for the successful evangelization of Japan. The samurai formed a literate stratum as well as being a group traditionally oriented toward the acceptance of leadership. Both characteristics were important for the development of a strong, independent Japanese Christianity.

The conversion of Japanese, especially of the samurai, is related directly to the Meiji Restoration. The treaties that allowed the entry of the missionaries hastened the breakdown of the *bakufu* (shogunate) system. It was the Meiji government that lifted the prohibition against Christianity. The periods just preceding and following the Restoration were vibrant with political conflict and doctrinal dispute. There was no consensus among the samurai leadership on either the intellectual or political form that a Japanese national sovereignty should take. Converts to all ideologies were present everywhere, and the subsequent and often rapid apostasy of the same converts seemed to be just as prevalent. Among the samurai a simple division appeared: Westernizers or non-Westernizers. During the eighteen seventies the activity of the Westernizers increased and spread; by the eighties this group provided the most important intellectual leaders of the period. The conversion experience can be treated as a part of the intellectual Westernization of Japan. But in spite of this intellectual tendency, both the anti-Westernizers of the period and the Westernizers who did not join the church interpreted the convert's baptism as an indication of his subtle estrangement from Japanese values. Even when government censure of the Christians was replaced by friendly interest in the eighties, there was no overwhelming feeling of good fellowship. Why was Christianity opposed by so many in spite of the hospitality to Western ideas? In spite of constant opposition, why did a hard core of the traditional leadership—the samurai—become Christians? Who were they; how did they understand Christianity; what assumptions about society and politics appeared as a result of their Christian experience? Simply, how far can their acceptance of Christian values be regarded in fact as an estrangement from Japanese values and society? The answers to these questions must be sought in the activities of the earliest Protestant missionaries.

Protestant Missions to the Japanese

Several decades before Perry's arrival in Japan, American Protestant evangelists became interested in Japan. In Boston the ladies' auxiliary to a men's Bible Society discovered a delightful Japanese-made basket. Aware of the fact that no missionaries had yet gone to Japan, they began to solicit funds for the establishment of a missionary society in Japan. At the same time, missionaries stationed on the coast of China attempted to enter Japan by returning castaway Japanese sailors or by seeking provisions for their ships; but their entry was forcibly rejected. The Japanese sailors returned to China with their missionary benefactors where they aided the missionaries in learning Japanese and in preparing translations that could be used when eventually the missionaries could land. And in Boston collections continued to be made for the day when Japan would finally be opened to the West.

Perry's Black Armada broke Japan's seclusion in 1853. In 1858 the United States, represented by Consul-General Townsend Harris, concluded a treaty with the shogun, and similar treaties by other Western nations followed shortly thereafter, opening four new ports to Westerners, Western trade, and the practice of Christianity. Foreigners were still forbidden entry to the interior of the country; the treaties confined Christianity to the ports, and Christian worship was limited to the Westerners.

Within four years of Harris' treaty, eleven Protestants from the China mission were sent to Japan. First, Dr. S. W. Williams and E. W. Syles of the Episcopal Church entered Nagasaki. Thomas Liggins of the same church entered in 1859, and J. C. Hepburn of the Presbyterian Church arrived in Kanagawa in the same year. He was soon followed by Samuel R. Brown and D. B. Simmons of the Reformed Church. Before the end of the year, G. F. Verbeck of the Reformed Church had landed in Nagasaki. Jonathan Goble of the Baptists arrived in Kanagawa in April 1860, and a year later James Ballagh of the Reformed Church landed in the same port. Two years later D. Thompson of the Presbyterian Church arrived in Kanagawa. One year after the Restoration the American Board of Commissioners for Foreign Missions for the first time specifically assigned a missionary, Dr. D. C. Green, to the mission of converting the Japanese. He and his work were supported by funds that had been collected initially by the Boston Women's Auxiliary.

All these missionaries were Americans and all were to become influential. In the eighteen sixties and seventies, European mission societies were less interested in Japan. It was American Protestantism that dominated Christian activities and contributed the most influential missionaries to Japan. This dominance even led *The Church at Home and Abroad,* a Boston monthly devoted to mission activities, to assert that if Japan was to be Christianized it must be done by Americans. Japan was seen as a cultural protégé of the United States, and the missionaries turned toward it with a sense not merely of Christian duty but with a feeling of cultural pride.

Christian evangelism in Japan had a dual character. First, the missionaries devoted most of their energies to the task of proselytizing. Although they represented different denominations, their common beliefs so outweighed their minor theological differences that they were able to achieve the united efforts which so characterized American Protestantism in early Meiji Japan. Secondly, the missionaries were both conscious and unconscious carriers of the American cultural, political, and social traditions. Ever since 1786, with the founding of the first American Missionary societies to evangelize American Indians, most American missionaries and their organizations had agreed that proselytization must be accompanied, if not preceded, by education, and for many this also meant the introduction of American social institutions and political ideas. As one missionary wrote in 1823, he hoped that soon "the red man and the white man shall everywhere be found, mingling in the same benevolent and friendly feelings, fellow citizens of the same civil and religious community, and fellow heirs to a glorious inheritence." Most American missionaries to Japan shared the same assumptions. Secular and religious aspects of the West were so indivisible to them that Christianization assumed the character of Westernization, and Westernization implied the necessity of conversion to Christianity. Since to the American missionaries many of the Western social and political developments of the nineteenth century had to accompany or even precede successful evangelization, they felt that the utility of the West's culture and society could not be considered independent of its normative system. They linked Western science to Western norms, which were directly attributable to Christianity, and they identified American and English institutional progress with Christian beliefs. An obvious strategy of evangelization was to present Christianity in terms of its position in Western intellectual development. This was a convenient strategy, for although Christian doctrine was suspect, other Western ideas were beginning to be eagerly sought. The adoption of Western cultural attributes by the Japanese provided a logical entree to religious conversion. The missionaries, impatient with Japan, believed that they could use Western knowledge to expose tradition to ridicule at the same time as they led the students of Westernism to the logical conclusion that Protestant Christianity stood at the base of Western development.

None of the missionaries expected immediate success. They realized that their work would be difficult so long as the treaties restricted their activities and the shogunate banned Christianity. They were well aware that they were constantly watched by a suspicious government that threatened imprisonment or even death to any Japanese who came in touch with them.

Necessity thus forced the missionaries to forgo direct preaching, but happily an alternative consistent with their attitudes toward the essential meaning of evangelism was found in teaching Western culture and science. Most opportunities for teaching came after the Restoration, but preparation for this task began during their earliest years in Japan. The missionary first turned to his study and prepared language texts for other missionaries and then translated the Scriptures. For example, Liggins, who felt that the basic aim for the missionary was to remove Japanese prejudices and misunderstandings about Christianity, hoped to do this by using textbooks that relied heavily on Christian doctrine. To accomplish his aim, he procured such works as Schurner's *History of England* and E. C. Bridgeman's *History of the United States* from China and translated them into Japanese.

Samurai Students and Missionary Teachers

The Restoration brought a new government into power, but its immediate policies did not greatly aid the missionaries. Anti-Christian placards were renewed; Japanese who acted as language teachers to the missionaries were kept under close police surveillance, and some were arrested. The Japanese translation of the Bible was confiscated from Williams' home by the government.

Although Christianity was still proscribed in 1869, missionaries had begun to preach in Yokohama. Schools were founded in Tokyo, Yokohama, Kobe, Nagasaki, and Osaka. By 1871 Christian activity in Tokyo caused worried government officials to break up Bible classes. In the same year, private prayer meetings held for foreign residents in Yokohama were being attended surreptitiously by Japanese studying under missionaries. As a result of these meetings nine Japanese asked to be baptized, and by 1872 they and two earlier converts joined Ballagh in founding in Yokohama the first Japanese Christian Church. At the end of the year most missionaries attended a convention in Yokohama to establish a policy of proselytizing and to prepare and discuss translations of the Bible. Before the convention they tried to persuade Japanese officials to cease their persecution of Christians and for the first time appealed to their own governments for assistance in getting the anti-Christian edicts repealed.

In spite of its continued opposition to Christianity, the policy of the government was beginning to change. The Meiji emperor had declared in his Charter Oath of 1868 that "knowledge was to be sought all over the world." In 1873 a pioneer Westernizing association of intellectuals, called the Meirokusha, was founded for the purpose of studying all aspects of Western knowledge and their applicability to Japan. One leading member of this group was Nakamura Masanao, who had become a Protestant in 1871 in spite of the proscription against Christianity. In the same year the Roman Catholic descendants of a group of sixteenth- and seventeenth-century converts, newly discovered in Nagasaki, were punished by dispersion throughout the country. In protest against the punishment of Roman Catholics and the continued proscription of Protestant Christianity, Nakamura sent a petition to the emperor declaring that to persecute Christianity was inconsistent with the emperor's declared aim of a liberal spirit of education and knowledge. He declared that to seek only the arts, inventions, and machines of the West was meaningless, and that "in general, we may say that the condition of Western Countries is but the outward leaf and bloom of their religion, and religion the root and foundation on which their prosperity depends." Nakamura believed that unless persecutions ceased, Western nations would hate Japan. By 1873, the Iwakura mission discovered the truth of these assertions when it sought revisions of the extraterritorial treaties. Western nations refused to consider revisions while Christianity was proscribed. Iwakura telegraphed to Japan describing his difficulties, and the proscription was withdrawn.

Christianity was no longer forbidden but neither was it sanctioned. The government took no legal measures against it for the next sixteen years, but educational policies and job opportunities often discriminated against the missionary and the Christian convert. Beyond that, as a result of its cultural identification with the West, Christianity was sought or disdained as national feeling toward things Western either rose or fell. When Christianity was identified with Western governmental policy toward Japan—even some of the more pro-Western ideologues saw it as an instrument of Western policy—it was dealt with at best as useful in encouraging concessions from the West; and when Japan was at odds with the West it was regarded with distaste. Under these circumstances conversion was tantamount to political ostracism.

The period of intense missionary persecution was over by 1873, and events seemed to be fulfilling missionary aspirations. For example, missionary-led schools were often founded by native initiative rather than by missionary exertions. The elders of the old Kuwano domain recruited Reverend Brown in 1873 to teach several of the youngsters of the clan. Brown accepted this post only shortly after he had left his teaching post at a central government-sponsored school in Niigata. The leaders of Kumamoto requested Verbeck to seek an American who could establish and lead a school of Western learning in their domain. Verbeck himself was asked to teach in Nagasaki as was W. B. Griffis in Fukui. E. B. Clark was called to Shizuoka. When the central government itself founded an agricultural school in Hokkaido, it asked the president of the University of Massachusetts, W. B. Clark, to set the guidelines. Each man, whether sponsored by missionary societies or not, insisted that in teaching Western learning he had to teach Western ethics. Most Japanese involved with these schools were primarily interested in obtaining the techniques and learning of the West. In most cases lack of funds made the missionary schools the only available source of such knowledge. As it became increasingly evident that Western knowledge was a major means for samurai to retain their status or to move upward, the missionary schools came to have great appeal for members of this stratum. Although a few domains had begun to educate their own elite in Western subjects, samurai from most domains had to go to Yokohama, Tokyo, Kobe, Nagasaki, and Osaka for this purpose. Edo, the political center of Tokugawa Japan, had throughout the latter portion of the period been the congregating point of the earnest, politically questioning samurai. Even more attention was focused on Tokyo after the Restoration, when the imperial seat was shifted there from Kyoto. At the same time domain life was uncertain. Former allies of the shogunate worried about the future as leadership passed into new hands and a new oligarchic alliance became evident. Domains which had been undecided during the latter part of Tokugawa and had hedged during the war that ended the shogunate became increasingly undesirable places for the politically ambitious. These fears were confirmed when in 1869 the domain leaders turned their registers over to the central government and again in 1873 when the samurai lost their legally privileged status.

Uemura Masahisa, who later became the leading figure of the Presbyterian Church in Japan, was one of the former samurai who flocked to Yokohama. His family, high-ranking direct retainers (*hatamoto*) of the shogun, found life in changing Edo unendurable. He wrote years later:

> In Keio [last years of the *Shogunate*] and in Meiji many people lost their houses . . . they roamed about the city like boats which had lost their oars in the sea. . . . When we reflect upon the situation and the spirit of our parents, we can only feel as if our hearts were breaking. Our house in Tokyo was not pleasant, and my parents thought it foolish to spend many days in Tokyo with empty hands. We moved to Yokohama in 1868.

If life in Tokyo was unendurable for Uemura's family, life in Kumamoto, the capital of one of the largest and most important domains of the Tokugawa period, was even more frustrating for domain leaders who felt that the Satsuma-Chōshū accession to power eclipsed their own aims. Because of internal conflicts at the time of the Restoration, they were unable to participate in the great change but still retained their political ambitions. In domain conclaves the questions of how to act and what to do in the new situation were thrashed out. For a number of years before the Restoration, Western knowledge had been sought under the influence of Yokoi Shōnan. Now, in 1871, one of his nephews high in the councils of the *daimyō* (feudal lord of the domain) suggested that if a select group of highly capable samurai were educated in Western knowledge, the domain could jump to the forefront in leading Japan. Domain ambitions could thus be realized by a quick preemption of the advantages of Western knowledge and teaching. For this reason domain spokesmen asked Verbeck to find an American teacher to lead such a school. Further evidence indicates that, in about 1873, missionaries began to be beseiged by Japanese seeking Western education and training. In Kobe, Green and Gulich found at various times forty to eighty men seeking to enter their schools. Ballagh and Brown in Yokohama saw their tutorial sessions grow into schools attended by many samurai. In Tokyo the demands for Western knowledge led Hepburn and four others to found the Tsukiji college.

Most students attending these schools came from samurai families. Like members of the Kumamoto and Kuwano domains, they sought Western knowledge as a means of recapturing status in the changing world. Robert Bellah has suggested in another context that samurai norms were achievement-oriented. But, as Bellah also argues, samurai achievement (or "performance," to use Bellah's term) was sanctioned and rewarded by promotion (thus legitimatized) by the domain which he served. During the early Meiji period a samurai remaining in the old domain would have to give up any hope of a political future, which was the most acceptable career in terms of these norms. If he were ambitious enough to leave home and family to go to Tokyo, he would almost surely become interested in Western knowledge and techniques and would enter by necessity one of these schools, where Western learning was easily and cheaply available. Uemura, for example, was constantly reminded by his mother "that I was a son of a samurai and had to become gallant and great. . . . I had to revive our family and distinguish myself in the world." How was this to be done? He records in his notebooks: "My father learned of the benefits of Western learning from some person and told my mother that Western learning was the best way to rise in the world. Therefore my mother began to look for a teacher of Western learning and wanted to give me a Western education." In Uemura's case, his mother first found a Western school headed by a Japanese named Ishikawa. After attending this school for a few months Uemura was distressed by the incompetence as well as the dissipation of his teacher. He left and soon after drifted into Mr. Ballagh's school. Notes and memoirs of others attending this school suggest the same motivation.

The backgrounds of those samurai who became leading Christians reveal one other striking fact: most of them came from domains on the losing side of the Restoration battle. Yamaji Aizan, a perceptive social historian and reporter of the time, commented: "Who converted to the new faith? . . . Uemura Masahisa, a son of a shogunate samurai. He experienced all the suffering of a defeated member of the shogunate. . . . Honda Yoichi, a son of a samurai family of defeated Tsugaru domain." He continued to list other converts, all of whom came from domains on the wrong side at the time of the Restoration. Yamaji, who himself was drawn to Christianity at an early period in his career, concludes that conversion was a direct result of the declassé mental state of the samurai after the Restoration.

> The government of the Restoration knew that it needed new, capable men for the management of the new household. It was generous in gathering new talent and actively recruited any person with talents to respond to demands of the new age. . . . However, even though the victors showed their generosity they could not cast off their pride, and although the defeated were received warmly they could not be free of the feeling that they were hurt. Although the war was an old story, the wounded heart of the defeated was not completely healed. Therefore it is natural that the realistic young men who enjoyed the new age and who advanced with it appeared mostly among the victors, and those young men who criticized the age and harbored new beliefs to fight against it came mostly from the defeated. . . . they did not hope to be included in the glory of the secular world. They had little hope that they could occupy good positions in the secular world. . . . [This is] without exception the situation in which Christianity was transplanted into Japan.

With two or three exceptions, the entire leadership of the early Christian Church shared this background. Some came from the *Sabaku* [Support-the-shogunate] group, which wanted to open the country to the West. Many had believed that reform of the Tokugawa system was inevitable, but they had hoped that change would be accomplished under the shogunate's leadership. Honda Yoichi and many others had joined shogunate irregulars in order to fight the Satsuma-Chōshū-domain forces which dominated the Restoration movement; Okumo Masatsuna had even joined one of the imperial princes to fight the Restoration armies.

If conversion was the result of defeated samurai's estrangement from power, an explanation is required of how and why Christianity resolved that estrangement. This is possible only by a more comprehensive understanding of samurai ideals and ideas. But to speak of estrangement as the sole reason for conversion is to oversimplify the complex ideals, ambitions, political comprehension, and motivation of the samurai. Even if the estrangement was the dominant malaise of the defeated samurai, it was political—a result, at least in part, of frustrated ambitions—and social and psychological, since status was synonymous with political power. Samurai status had inevitably been coupled with domain political legitimacy. After the Restoration, many samurai could no longer believe that their past social position would ensure their success in the present or that their past beliefs could secure them rewards in the future. Because their ambitions remained alive, the samurai in early Meiji sought Western knowledge to assert themselves in the world. When they accepted Christianity, however, they adopted more than the mere utilitarian value of Western knowledge and techniques; they accepted a large segment of Western social and political norms. Seen in this light, estrangement gave the impetus that caused some samurai to redefine their social and political situation in terms of a new normative synthesis and, eventually, to find in that synthesis an alternative path to power. In order to demonstrate this process, it is necessary first to establish the relationship between the preaching of the missionaries and the desires of the samurai; the missionaries' social principles and the converts' norms; and the missionary personality and the samurai psychology. As a start, we may ask what was taught, why, and how it became a convincing argument to some of this declassé stratum.

The Evangelists

Converts in the period 1871–1881 were for the most part students or graduates of the missionary-led schools. Not all students at these schools became Christians, but in some cases, such as the Kumamoto *han* school led by Captain Janes and the Hokkaido agricultural school directed by Clark, virtually the entire senior class was converted. Attendance at these schools was very high, in comparison with missionary schools in China where after many years of evangelical effort it was still low. When we realize that government schools and numerous academies sponsored by local governments were also headed by missionaries, we can see that the Christian missionary effort must have had considerable impact on the samurai stratum.

The zeal of the students was reciprocated with similar vigor by a highly committed, well qualified, and intensely evangelical missionary group. To them Christianity as a social creed carried with it the responsibility of social action, so that they could not be content with a narrow-minded policy of conversion. Within the limits of Japanese law, missionary doctors proceeded to the interior of the country where they cared for the sick, and aided Japanese medical men without insisting on preaching the creed. Eventually joined by the full force of the missionary groups and converts, they led in the formation of orphanages, homes for the blind, and hospitals. Personal action by the missionary in its best sense revealed the social vocation of the doctrine to the Japanese, and provides us with a sense of the totality of the missionary's commitment to Western culture and its humane obligations that impressed the converts.

The missionaries' decisiveness and commitment to their ideals, especially in the face of adversity and difficulty, was particularly convincing since, as Uemura Masahisa pointed out, the samurai held these qualities in great esteem. Since low student-faculty ratios in most schools fostered personal relations, the impact of the missionaries' personal commitment was forcefully and easily made. Letters, notes, and memoirs of the converts reveal their awe at the missionaries' spirit and indicate the intensity of the feelings held by students in these schools for their teachers. "Even if he was a foreigner," Kanamori Tsurin writes of Janes, "he was like a teacher and parent who loved us. Without a word our hearts responded to his, we loved him and he taught us with an increasing affection." Yoshida Kanetaro in Niigata, where the Reverend Palm's fame was renowned, notes that it was said that "Confucius might have been a person like Mr. Palm." Verbeck was regarded as "a sincere gentleman . . . generous and he taught kindly and generously." To these may be added the encomiums to Brown, Hepburn, Ballagh, and others by their students.

The Japanese students felt that the missionaries were truly concerned with the secular as well as the religious development of Japan. Uemura said of Verbeck that "his life was spent for the development of Japan and he emotionally enjoyed her development." Brown is quoted as saying: "If I had a hundred years to live I should give them all to Japan." The intensity of Ballagh's preaching impressed the Japanese with his devotion not only to Christianity but to Japan and the Japanese. Missionaries such as Ballagh treated the samurai with respect; he "treated us as *bushi*," they said. Although the dangers of conversion were great, and a number of disciples of Ballagh were even arrested, Ballagh did not allow them to seek solace in castigating the state. When his disciples were later released, Ballagh told them: " 'Although you are in danger, you should not be displeased with your position. Christian disciples should follow the law of the state.' [Although] we could flee to America, he further told us [the disciples], this would not be in the Christian spirit. He told us to prepare to be exiled anywhere by the law. These teachings convinced me that he came to this country for the country's sake." Brown in 1872 told his disciples precisely the same thing:

> His instructions on this point [i.e., arrest] were as follows: even we were sentenced to death, to accept this judgment is not at all to hurt the name of the Christian. It is an easy matter to ask the American diplomatic representative at the legation to protect us. However, it is not necessarily wise to plan our safety by avoiding

difficulties. It is the duty of gentlemen to follow the state law. He told us that we should behave bravely as gentlemen. When I heard this, I realized that the noblemindedness of Christian ethics was finer than the Way of the bushi in Japan.

The same spirit moved the samurai attending Janes' school in Kumamoto. *Bushi* loyalties were appealed to and hastened conversion when the samurai recognized many of their ideals in Christianity. It was further aided by their conviction that the missionaries were devoting themselves and Christianity to the betterment of Japan.

This concern for the progress of Japan reflected the missionaries' assumptions about historical process. It was this concern that served to direct their attitudes concerning Japan and the Japanese and their missionary activities, so that the samurai converts always self-consciously thought of themselves as *Japanese* Christians and missionaries always spoke to them as Christians who were citizens of a Japanese state. Niijima Jō, founder of the Christian Dōshisha University in Kyoto, stated the Japanese converts' feeling best when he said that he sought to serve God and nation, both missions motivated by the same principles. Williams made apparent the missionaries' great concern for the direction of Japan's development when, in the early days of his mission and surrounded by only a small band of converts, he spoke of the future success of the mission in these terms:

> There is popular opinion to some extent. Unceasingly year by year the power of popular opinion has grown. . . . The merchant class has . . . learned of the position of the merchant class in other countries; they have awakened to the rights of the merchant class; by and by they will claim these rights. . . . Our age is sure to come and it is sure to come surprisingly earlier than people think it will. We can expect the time when the bourgeoisie will grow and their voice will have its proper power in parliament.

The accuracy of Williams' prophecy is secondary to his view that a particular pattern of historical development must precede or accompany successful Christianization. He made the point more clearly when he said: "In these early days of sowing the seed in Japan we can preach to samurai and meanwhile watch for the fomentation of a 'modern civil society' and development of a bourgeoisie (third estate) who can be evangelized as well as form the base of the new civil society." Apparently the ethics that stimulated these missionaries to evangelize Japan embodied a particular synthesis of nineteenth-century English and American ideas about modern society. Williams states that Christianity's success in Japan was dependent upon social change and the rise of a modern society. Christianity was the religion of a society governed by the concepts of a third estate. Modern society was a civil society; in effect, a society of free and equal citizens. To realize such a society "the commercial and industrial class joined with patriots [samurai] will engage in an anti-feudal struggle." Thus, this new society will be antithetical to the structures and beliefs of feudalism. Evangelization for the missionary was not an isolated task but a part of the entire process of modernization. From this assumption emerged the missionaries' concern not only with religious development but with political, economic, and social development as well. Many samurai, imbued with deep loyalties to their society, found this view attractive. The deep concern of both missionary and former samurai with Japan's development created a strong and sympathetic bond.

The National Church

At the level of practical application, the Protestant missionaries declared at their second conference in 1883 at Osaka that they would encourage the establishment of native churches with a native clergy and native funds. The convention proclaimed missionary unanimity on a policy that ministers like Green, Brown, and Ballagh had been advocating since their arrival in Japan. Green, in fact, had arrived in 1869 with explicit instructions from his board to encourage a self-supporting autonomous church in Japan. J. B. Davis, who collaborated with Niijima in the founding of Dōshisha, had already suggested in 1875 that at the earliest possible moment proselytizing in Japan should be turned over to the Japanese and that self-supporting churches should be established. Japanese converts attending the Osaka conference were in unanimous agreement with the missionaries. Kanamori Tsurin, a representative of the Japanese clergy at the meeting, discussed with the missionaries what everyone saw as the primary issues: how fast these goals could be accomplished, and what should be done with overseas funds. There was some discussion and division on the question of independence, with some members of the American Board of Commissioners for Foreign Missions arguing that independence should only be encouraged after individual churches became self-supporting. However, by 1883 the increasing pace of conversion suggested to everyone that this standard could easily be met.

Political circumstances had initially forced the missionaries to limit their proselytizing to the city and to former samurai. In order to guarantee the development of a self-supporting church, they continued to concentrate their efforts in the city where the resources of a large population could be drawn upon and among classes who were literate and curious as well as sufficiently wealthy to maintain the church. It is difficult to know whether in any specific instance missionaries consciously projected Williams' vision of social progress and Christian conversion into their everyday evangelizing. But in most cases they did feel, as Green wrote in 1874:

God has seen fit to make the influence of missionary work in Japan felt first and most strongly by the intelligent classes [in effect, the samurai]. Whatever may be right elsewhere, those who have become Christians hitherto are of this class, both here [Kobe] and in Yokohama and Yedo [Tokyo]. . . . Whatever might be right elsewhere there ought to be no question about having the Japanese support their own party and build their own churches from almost the first, if not the very first.

These missionaries saw the future of Christianity in Japan as dependent upon the leadership of this early group of samurai converts. The fervor with which the declassé samurai became Christians convinced the missionary that they were the agents who could bring about the rapid conversion of all Japan. The same intensity that awed the missionary led the samurai to sacrifice, scrimp, and save to establish self-supporting independent churches.

Indeed, independence was a vital issue to the Japanese converts. Samurai concern with a church led and supported by Japanese had preceded the formal discussion and proclamations of the Osaka conference on the same matter. It was also a matter of principle for many samurai students at the missionary academies to refuse offers of financial aid. For example, Oshikawa Masayoshi, a leading Christian convert, rejected offers of aid and determinedly badgered any students who accepted a missionary stipend. A number of returned students like Paul Sawayama chose to take poorly paying pastorates after refusing well-paying government jobs and then at the same time refused to allow the churches to receive any endowments from the missionaries.

Missionaries undoubtedly welcomed development of an independent church as evidence of genuine conversion. Sawayama, among the Japanese, best expressed this conviction:

It is said that it is obstinate or ambitious for our church to undertake to supply all the money and undertake self-support without the help of any foreign mission society. This is not true. Once we have received help we will relax and lose our diligent spirit.

The spirit of self-support makes Christians think that the church is their own and it cultivates an independent and diligent spirit toward our duties. Once we have received money from others we may feel that the church belongs to others and thus neglect our duties. Pastor and church members must endure together and from this mutual love is born.

Statements by most Japanese converts, however, suggest that they extended this interpretation of the character of a self-supporting, independent church to a more extreme position. Tamura Naoomi, an early Meiji convert and an important Christian social critic of the era, in his autobiography gave the reasons for the establishment of an Independent Presbyterian Church in 1876.

> The Christian Church in Japan was full of the spirit of independence from its beginning. . . . Christian churches in Japan should exist for the Japanese and sovereignty should lie with the Japanese. He who holds financial power is certainly sovereign. If we were under the power of the missions and favored it, we would have no right to insist that sovereignty lie in our own hands.

A year before this, an elder and ten members of the Tokyo Presbyterian Church withdrew and formed an independent body called the Nippon Kyōkai (Japan Church). According to a historian of the Presbyterian Church in Japan, "the motive of organizing this new church consisted in enforcing an extreme anti-foreign principle of independence because all the churches at those times were under the assistance of foreign churches and missionaries."

These quotations and events suggest that three principles dominated the establishment of an independent church: 1) that Christianity's growth and sustenance in Japan were dependent upon development of a community of native believers engaged in a campaign to work within the church; 2) that they sought to establish a Japanese church controlled by Japanese with Japanese interests always present; 3) that antimissionary spirit was always prevalent among Japanese Christians, since even to the convert the missionary sometimes represented varying interests. In simple terms, the converts were nationalists obsessed with a fear of domination by the West.

The act of conversion to Christianity must be seen as a gesture that engaged the samurai convert in the great debate of the time: how can Japan retain its national sovereignty and how can she become strong enough to resist Western incursions? In general, Western studies in Japan were begun with all these aims in mind and, as was demonstrated throughout the period, Western thought was accepted consciously or in many cases unconsciously with objectives stated in the Tokugawa period by Hashimoto Sanai, a late Tokugawa Confucian thinker: "Acquire mechanical aids from others, retain righteousness, sympathy, and filial piety as our own," or even more bluntly summarized by Sakuma Shōzan, an outstanding student of Western science in late Tokugawa Japan, as "Eastern morality, Western arts [i.e., technology]."

It is difficult to summarize the intellectual assumptions of Japanese nationalism. All Japanese thinkers of the first three decades of Meiji Japan were obsessed with the problems of national sovereignty, and this obsession was ably summarized by the slogan "fukoku kyōhei" (wealthy country, strong defense). Even radical liberals like Nakae

Chōmin were willing to put the extension of liberal rights as second to the establishment of a strong sovereign nation. Yet to draw out of this any clear ideas about the nation is difficult, perhaps impossible. However, Maruyama Masao has tried to abstract from Japanese behavior of the period a sense that traditional ideas of ruler-subject relations were transferred to the sphere of international relations.

> When the premises of the national hierarchy were transferred horizontally into the international sphere, international problems were reduced to a single alternative: conquer or be conquered. In the absence of any higher normative standards with which to gauge international relations, power politics is bound to be the rule.

International relations were seen primarily as a question of hierarchy based on the supremacy of superiors over inferiors.

Though this is an oversimplified statement, it is plausible to think that traditional ideas of social order acted as guidelines for Japanese political behavior. Norms of political behavior were thus dominated by social tradition. Also indisputably clear throughout the period is the political nature of almost all thinking. Questions of morality and ethics as found in traditional Confucianism were always questions of attitude toward authority rather than simply behavioral norms for the individual *qua* individual. For example, the government's most conscious effort to institute and legislate its ideas of proper political behavior appeared in the Educational Rescript of 1890. In effect, attitudes on political behavior were expressed via educational and moral scriptures. The Rescript itself is less important than the famous apologetic, which in effect defined the Rescript's role, written on it in 1891 and 1893 by the leading conservative philosopher of the time, Inoue Tetsujirō. In his first treatise, *The Interpretation of the Imperial Rescript,* Inoue defined the Japanese state ideology in sociomoral terms. "By cultivating the moral action of loyalty [to one's lord] and filial piety the foundation of nations can be made firm and by cultivating the true spirit of collective patriotism, preparation can be made for unexpected accidents." The establishment of patriotism, loyalty, and filial piety were the major objects of the Rescript. Moreover, Inoue equated loyalty and filial piety with patriotism. After extended argument, he concluded that everything was dependent on relationships of loyalty and filial piety in household and village and that cultivation of these virtues of the individual led to loyalty to the country. A consciousness that one must sacrifice, indeed die, for his lord and country emerged.

Inoue dealt directly with Christianity in his second treatise, *The Conflict of the Church with Education,* where he identified it as the major enemy of his national ideology. He emphasized the irreconcilability of Christianity with the national principles of the Rescript. Christians neglected their obligations as subjects, disturbed peace and order, lacked respect for the emperor, and hoisted a foreign nation's flag. He concluded: "The main point of the Rescript is nationalism, but Christianity [not only] lacks the nationalistic spirit, it is opposed to it. Thus, it must be irreconcilable with nationalistic principles."

Inoue's criticisms of Christianity were not new; he merely summarized two decades of anti-Christian criticism. Probably spurred on by the cancellation of the proscription on Christianity in 1873, Yasui Sakuken had established the major tenets of criticism: Christianity fostered disloyal and unfilial behavior. Yasui expressed Confucian strictures; a conservative but Western-oriented critic like Kato Hiroyuki assailed Christianity in the same terms: Christianity was opposed to Japanese *kokutai,* the belief that Japan had an incomparable moral and political heritage based on the rule of a divine imperial line unbroken for ages eternal. Fukuzawa Yukichi, a leading figure of the mentioned pioneer Westernizing association, the Meirokusha, bitterly attacked Christianity in his daily newspaper, *Jiji Shimpo.* In 1882 in successive issues of the journal he wrote: "Christianity is baneful to our national power"; "we do not care to discuss the truth or falsity of religious systems; but looking at the matter from a statesman's point of view we hold that in self-defense the foreign religion should be banished from these shores."

Whatever the personal rapport of missionary and convert might be, dependence upon missionary tutelage or financial support led anti-Christian critics to call the converts "rice Christians," "satellites of a foreign power," "beggar students" who have lost their independence. Tamura Naoomi implied in his autobiography that being called rice Christians led Japanese converts to emphasize their independence; as we have seen Tamura emphasized the need for Japanese Christians to assert their independence and sovereignty in a manner similar to Japan's attempt to assert its own sovereignty. Niijima in becoming a Christian sought to serve both God and nation; Uchimura stated he sought to serve Jesus and Japan. Samurai converted to Christianity because they believed Christian principles could help in the establishment of a new strong Japan. The converts were nationalistic Christians eager to emulate, but not be subordinate to, the West. Missionary concern with the development of Japan was happily noted, but when the missionary was assailed as a foreign agent and the convert called his lackey, the new convert sought to express his independence and the nationalism of the Christian Church through a self-supporting autonomous church.

Evidence of the importance of the independent church in proselytizing is easily found. The Congregational Church took the lead in establishing itself as self-supporting and independent. The Congregational Church became the largest single denomination in Japan. Out of its congregation came Christians who entered into political affairs and party politics, as Christianity propelled a number of men into the heart of political struggle. Kozaki Hiromichi and Uemura Masahisa and a number of others, for example, attacked traditional concepts of loyalty and filial piety, and they did so apparently in the attempt to establish an alternative political tradition and means to modernize Japan. Both men were also leaders of an independent antimissionary church. Thus the political character of conversion and the problems of Japanese nationalism must be taken into account in discussing the rise of the independent church. In extending an alternative view of the character of modern Japan the Christians had to confirm their own independence and thus establish their nationalism. In later years their failure to influence the character of the new state led some of their membership to either flee the movements into radical parties, to move away from any social or political standard, or in the most extreme cases to redefine, compromise, and bend their own principles to the prevailing ideas of the national polity. But for many Christian converts their success in establishing an independent, self-supporting church permitted them to argue convincingly that they were Japanese Christian nationalists, with a new vision, however, of what patriotism entailed.

Suggested Readings

The recent history of Japan is presented in Hugh Borton, *Japan's Modern Century: From Perry to 1970*, 2nd ed. (New York: Ronald Press Co., 1970), and the turmoil of Westernization is discussed in Thomas Huber, *The Revolutionary Origins of Modern Japan* (Stanford: Stanford University Press, 1981). Christianity in Japan is the subject of Richard H. Drummond, *A History of Christianity in Japan* (Grand Rapids: W. B. Eerdmans Publishing Co., 1971), and Winburn T. Thomas, *Protestant Beginnings in Japan: The First Three Decades, 1859–1889* (Rutland, Vt.: C. E. Tuttle Co., 1959).

The Business World of Jamsetjee Jejeebhoy

Asiya Siddiqi

Normally we think of imperialism as simply European domination of native peoples, either to exploit or to "civilize" them. The inner workings of the great empires were, in fact, much more complex, as this business biography of an Indian merchant, Jamsetjee Jejeebhoy, illustrates. In the early nineteenth century, British power in India still was largely confined to the coast. In Bombay, as in other coastal trading cities, British businessmen worked closely with a colony of Indian merchants. The Indians operated manufacturing concerns, provided capital, and, through their contacts with the interior, traded British wares for export goods. Chief among those export goods were cotton and opium, which the Indians traded in China—primarily for tea—for transshipment to Europe.

Although the maze of monopolies and regulations that governed imperial trade caused Jejeebhoy difficulties, he and his fellow Bombay merchants were able to work profitably within the system. They were an important element in British imperial trade in India, and they were valued as such. During the 1830s and 1840s, however, the old colonial system was replaced by a Liberal-inspired policy of "free trade." Under the new policy, Indian merchants faced unrestricted competition from European firms, and the position of native businessmen steadily deteriorated. Seen from the viewpoint of an Indian historian, the apparently enlightened policy of free trade seems only to have provided the Europeans with the opportunity to wrest profitable business from the native merchants.

Jamsetjee Jejeebhoy: The Main Features of His Business

Among the merchants of western India who came to have a large share in the opium trade was the well-known Parsi, Jamsetjee Jejeebhoy, whose firm a contemporary described as "the best managed business this side of the Cape." It was a mark, perhaps, of Jamsetjee's efficiency that copies were kept of the private and business letters written by him and by his firm. Fortunately, many of these letter books have survived. They provide an almost continuous and remarkably detailed account of the inner workings of the Jejeebhoy business. Not the least value of these letters lies in the fact that they are personal testimony: they record, often with impassioned candour, the strivings, problems, successes and failures of an extraordinarily dynamic Indian entrepreneur. In doing this, the letters throw light on the wider parameters of Jamsetjee's economic environment.

We shall briefly review the main features of Jamsetjee Jejeebhoy's business, especially his opium trade, and focus on one of his most perplexing problems, that of remitting the firm's funds back to India. At the end, we shall try to outline the circumstances in which India's "country" shipping declined.

The son of a poor weaver of Navsari, Jamsetjee lost his parents at an early age, and came to Bombay at the turn of the century to live with his maternal uncle, a seller of bottles. Ties of kinship and community certainly helped him in the early stages of his career although, as we shall see, before long he developed intimate business connections with persons belonging to almost every community and religious group. The details of his earliest activities are obscure. But we know that, in the first decade of the century, he made four voyages to China as an agent of various Parsi merchants including his cousin, Merwanjee Maneckjee Taback. During the Napoleonic wars, he amassed a fortune, estimated at two crores, exporting cotton to England. Jamsetjee's biographers have given vivid descriptions of his misadventure when the *Brunswick*, on which he was a passenger, was captured by a French warship in the Indian Ocean. They have not mentioned an event of far greater moment to his future career. On the *Brunswick*, Jamsetjee made the acquaintance of the ship's assistant surgeon, the young William Jardine. The friendship blossomed, some years later, into a business arrangement. Along with James Matheson, Jardine established the most

THE BUSINESS WORLD OF JAMSETJEE JEJEEBHOY   By Asiya Siddiqi, from *The Indian Economic and Social History Review*, 19 (1982), pp. 307–25.

successful opium business at Canton, and Jamsetjee became their principal collaborator in Bombay.

It may have been his association with Jardine and Matheson which induced Jamsetjee to alter the structure of his business in a number of ways. In his earlier years, he appears to have exported goods, mainly cotton, to Forbes Forbes and Company of London on which the latter earned a commission. He had, besides, similar relations with his friend, the Chinese Hong merchant, Howqua. We find him selling cassia and silk for Howqua in Bombay, and procuring pearls for him and shipping them to Canton. In the early 1830's, he seems to have given up commission business, and the exclusion of this category of business, namely, buying and selling on commission, became an accepted principle of his firm. So also, Jamsetjee declared he had "laid it down as a rule to which I have ever adhered, never to advance money to any private individual . . ." Besides, there was another category of business of which we find no evidence in Jamsetjee's correspondence, namely, guarantee brokerage, the staple business of so many of his contemporaries, especially Parsis. Consequently, he did not suffer as many of them did, when they had to pay the debts of bankrupt European firms. Nor did he, being an exceedingly careful man of business, invest in the kind of reckless speculation which brought ruin to many of his generation. Jamsetjee put large scale trade and shipping at the centre of his activities, and stood out apart from those businessmen who were occupied mainly in money lending and various forms of brokerage. Perhaps the stakes he set were influenced by his experience of freedom and success in trade during the period when the Navigation Laws had been temporarily suspended. His career enables us to identify the wider historical constraints under which he functioned.

Jamsetjee's Opium Trade

In the first quarter of the century, shipments of western India, or Malwa opium, had outstripped those of cotton. They had increased from 1,346 chests in 1800–01 to 21,988 chests in 1838–39. A considerable quantity of Malwa opium was finding its way out through the Portuguese port of Daman, as well as through Karachi. The Government of Bombay at first tried to control the outflow of Malwa opium by buying up the entire crop and conducting monopoly sales at Bombay as was the practice at Calcutta. We first catch sight of Jamsetjee Jejeebhoy in 1826, at one such sale of which he wrote a vivid account to Jardine.

The experiment with monopoly sales of Malwa opium was given up, and was replaced, in 1831, by a system of passes whereby opium could be exported from Bombay on payment of a duty. At first fixed at Rs. 175 per chest, the duty was revised several times afterwards. By 1845 it had been increased to Rs. 300 per chest. In 1848–49 the revenue of the Bombay Government from this duty amounted to Rs. 8,870,000.

The Government's failure to create an official monopoly of opium in western India reflected the power and influence of the network of opium dealers and merchants in this part of the country. This also made it difficult for Europeans to penetrate the opium market in the interior. When Forbes and Co., sent their agent, Mcleod, to Indore, an important centre of the opium trade, Jamsetjee commented, "Mr. Mcleod doing nothing but visiting the country and it would not answer to Europeans to establish as agent because that country belonging to native Prince and great objectionable to them to allow Europeans . . ." Again and again we catch glimpses, whether at Surat, or at Ahmedabad or at Indore, of well entrenched merchants and bankers confronting and often defying foreign penetration.

The earliest accounts of Jamsetjee's opium trade reveal a part of his network of connections. One of his oldest friends was a Goan resident of Bombay, Sir Roger de Faria, owner of several ships including the *Don Manoel,* and a large exporter of opium. Perhaps the ship *Castro* too was his. It sailed for Macao from Daman on the 29th of April, 1823, with 1,103 chests of opium on board, of which 537 belonged to de Faria. Through de Faria's influence, Jamsetjee and his friends obtained permission from the Portuguese authorities at Daman, to ship opium from that port. From the veiled references in one of his letters to de Faria we are introduced to the other participants in this trade. Perhaps the most important of them was Motichund Amichund who was for some time Jamsetjee's partner. ". . . the Marwaddies and Ahmedabad merchants," declared Jamsetjee, "would always willingly follow Motichund's advice, you are perfectly aware of Motichund's influence over them." We find Motichund ordering opium from Malwa and exporting it from Daman and Karachi.

Another close associate of Jamsetjee, one who remained his partner all his life was the Konkani Nakhuda, Mohammad Ali Rogay. Among the European firms of Bombay, he has a particularly close association with Remington and Co., the successor to the old firm of Bruce Fawcett & Co.

With the introduction of the pass system in 1831, nine tenths of Malwa opium began to be exported from Bombay while earlier one third had passed through Bombay and two thirds through Daman. Jamsetjee Jejeebhoy now endeavoured to have as much of the supply as possible consigned to Jardine Matheson and Co., at Canton. He was participating in a massive combination for monopolising the Malwa opium trade.

In the lists of consignments, we find the names of those who were shipping opium through Jamsetjee. Among them were some of the leading Jain merchants of Ahmedabad: Hutheesing Kessreesing, Vakatchund Khooshalchund and Currumchund Premchund. Hutheesing was the son of a well-known banker, Kessreesing Khooshalchund. Vakatchund, the *nagar seth* of Ahmedabad, was the descendant of the famous Shantidas Jhaveri of Akbar's time, and the ancestor of the present Nagarsett family of Ahmedabad. Currumchund was the great grandfather of Ambalal Sarabhai. With Jamsetjee acting as go-between, vast quantities of wealth accumulated in old time trade and banking were poured into the colonial mercantile network.

So successful was the combination that, at its height, something like one third of the entire quantity of opium to leave the shores of Bombay was going to the warehouses of Jardine Matheson and Co., at Canton. The combination was perhaps not altogether rigid for, in 1838 we find Jamsetjee shipping opium from Calcutta to Russel and Co., at Canton. Nevertheless, the bulk of the firm's shipments went to Jardine's. This was not only because of long standing connections and exemption from commission charges, but perhaps also because Jardine Matheson and Company came to handle the largest stocks of Chinese tea exports to Britain, after the East India Company's monopoly of the China trade ended in 1834. This enhanced their effectiveness as a clearing house for Indian produce: they were in a unique position to barter opium and cotton for tea when other mediums of exchange were not easily available.

Apart from opium, the other major item of Jamsetjee's exports from Bombay was cotton. Besides, he regularly exported opium and cotton from Calcutta, as well as cotton from Madras. His income was derived from five interlinked items: the profit of trade on his own account, the income from hiring freight on his ships, interest on loans to shippers, dividends on shares in marine insurance companies, and commission on the sale of his own bills. Perhaps, though we do not find explicit references, the Malwa opium syndicate may have been something like a limited joint-stock venture in which resources were pooled and profits distributed among the partners. Jamsetjee seemed to be acting more as a partner than as an agent. While he negotiated with the shippers to consign opium to Jardine Matheson and Co., the latter waived their commission on Jamsetjee's own consignments, and often also on those made in the name of "Jamsetjee Jejeebhoy's friends." From the guarded reference in one of his letters, it appears that Jamsetjee often himself enjoyed the benefit of this latter indulgence. But on certain occasions, as for instance when he was anxious to provide for the needy family of Sir Roger de Faria, he used the concession to help his friends.

The items we have enumerated exclude Jamsetjee's income from non-mercantile assets. These, consisting mainly of Bank of Bengal shares, Company's paper, shares in the G.I.P. Railway Company, and real estate, were very considerable. In 1854, his property in Bombay had a monthly rental value of ten and a half thousand rupees.

The Profit on Opium

When we consider the reputed profitability of the China opium trade, it comes as a surprise that the figures for calculating the return on opium indicate a relatively modest rate of return. Frequent fluctuations in cost price and sale price make it difficult for us to calculate the actual return. Nevertheless, it is possible to cite some figures picked at random. A number of shipments made in 1838, consisting of 247½ chests cost spanish $641 per chest, at Rs. 206 per $100, inclusive of all costs in India and China. This opium had been bought at a high price, with an eye to the sale price in China which had been $720 per chest. At the latter price, for a total investment period of somewhat less than a year, the return would be about 12 per cent. It is true that, some time earlier, the cost price had been lower, and the sale price higher. The decline in price had been the result of a great expansion in supply. A prominent feature of the mode of trade, was the use of fast moving ships, such as the clippers, which could make as many as three trips in one season. A number of sales made in 1838, ranged from $615 to $640 per chest. At this sale price, the profit would of course be much less.

Though not altogether spectacular, the return from opium was perhaps higher than that to be expected from other areas of investment. The rate of interest on loans on good security was 9 per cent. In 1814, the return on the eight largest properties on Bombay Island ranged from 4½ per cent to 10 per cent. The total return on opium, moreover, could be fairly sumptuous for those who could corner the supply and be the first to deliver it in China to their agents so as to monopolize the market there.

On an over-all view, it may be conjectured, that in a period when Indian textile production was rapidly declining there was probably a surplus of capital which, in western India, found an outlet in the China trade, especially opium. Further research is required in order to enable us to determine more clearly the process of the decline of the textile trade and of its foremost centre in western India, Surat. An integral part of this process, very probably, was the flight of capital from Surat to Bombay and the shift to investment in opium.

It was against this background that the opium trade expanded so enormously, even though it involved a number of serious hazards. There were, first of all, the political risks of a contraband trade. In 1839, the cargoes of opium surrendered to the Chinese, belonged mainly to Indian merchants of Bombay, who were only partially compensated several years later.

Further, as in all of consignment trade, the risk of a fall in sale price was borne by the shippers and was all the greater in distant markets with which they could not easily communicate. In fact, the shippers were at the mercy of the agency houses to whom they had consigned their goods and had no way of questioning the price at which their cargoes had been sold. The agency houses, on the other hand, operating on the capital of the shippers, happily collected their commissions and ran no risk. They liked "pure commission business," in which, "income comes to you without asking in the snug way of the China trade."

In short, for the East India Company, and British agency houses, there was a threefold advantage in drawing Indian merchants into the opium trade. It saved them from the political embarrassments of directly participating in a trade that was illegal in China, it effortlessly channelled Indian financial resources into this trade, and it placed the burden of price fluctuations and exchange difficulties on the shoulders of the Indian merchants.

The Payments Arrangements and the Remittance Problem

The most difficult problem which Indian merchants such as Jamsetjee Jejeebhoy encountered, and one which became increasingly acute with the abolition of the Company's monopoly of the China trade, and the subsequent commercial expansion, was that of routing their funds back from China to India. Two interconnected developments in the history of the payments arrangements associated with the China trade were important. One was that Indian merchants tended to be excluded from the market for bills of exchange. In the second place, India's China trade came to be balanced increasingly by means of the import of silver from China. Of these, the second is well-known, but its economic significance does not appear to have been acknowledged. For the first development, namely, the mounting pressures against Indian merchants in the bills market, we find ample evidence in the letters of Jamsetjee Jejeebhoy.

In common with other merchants, Jamsetjee preferred to have his China funds remitted through bills. The advantage of bills, over bullion, was that it involved less risk in shipment because of the system of sending triplicate copies of each bill. Besides, good bills were almost as good as paper money; they were simple to negotiate and had a known value reckoned in terms of the actual return in bullion. Jamsetjee found bills on the Court of Directors most convenient. These bills could be sold in India to persons wishing to make remittances to England. In July, 1826, for instance, he sold bills on the Court of Directors from China, amounting to £20,000, "to my friends". His next preference was good private bills on London. One method of transfer he was able to employ was to sell the bills of his own firm to Europeans in Bombay and Calcutta, to be discounted by his agents in London who, received funds for the purpose from his account with Jardine Matheson and Co.

On these bills, Jamsetjee probably earned a commission, and his extensive contacts with Europeans facilitated these operations. We find among his papers many lists of such bills.

The difficulty of buying bills on the Court of Directors at Canton arose from the fact that the requirements of the Company's Treasury at Canton were relatively limited. The sums it required for its export cargo, over and above the value of its imports, could generally be obtained by bills on the Bengal treasury. The China traders vied with each other to obtain Court of Directors' bills. We find Jamsetjee urging Jardine to use his good offices with the chief of the Canton factory to obtain these bills for him.

The expansion of trade and of British banking in the 1830s greatly aggravated Jamsetjee's difficulties. For, he now had to face competition from the Liverpool merchants, and this made it extremely difficult for him to get his funds back at a favourable rate of exchange. The competition was felt both in China and in India. In China, the brisk demand for bills and *sycee,* Chinese ingots of silver bullion, made the rate of exchange unfavourable for remitters; in India, the Liverpool merchants undercut the bills of Indian merchants.

At the root of these difficulties, was the development in these years, of those interlocking credit networks, with their nerve centres in Britain and America, which sustained the international economies of these countries.

American traders had been in the habit of bringing South American silver to Canton in order to purchase tea and silk. The expansion of trade, and with it, of the demand for means of remittance, led the American to offer at Canton, bills of exchange on London. What took shape was another triangular traffic whereby American traders at Canton began to purchase tea and silk by means of bills on London banks and mercantile houses, to be balanced by the shipment of American cotton to England.

This exchange network was ill-suited to the purposes of Indian merchants who wished to get their funds back home. While European remitters eagerly sought American bills, Jamsetjee found these bills difficult to sell in Bombay, and poor in exchange value. In 1835, for lack of good bills to India, a very large part of his funds had been sent from Canton to London. He was particularly anxious to avoid this expedient and urged Jardine to send him bills on the Supreme Government at Calcutta, and sycee. Repatriating funds via London not only involved delay but was becoming increasingly difficult because it was no longer easy to sell bills on London in India. Jamsetjee wrote:

> The sale of Bills on England is now a days very precarious, as you will perceive from the fact that since we commenced drawing on new account for 1835–36, we have hardly realized £1000 since September last. The practice of the Liverpool merchants of drawing

against shipments of cotton and ca. is very much against us—as they care but little for the rate of exchange, provided they can get purchasers of their bills, trusting that the loss on the Exchange will be made up by the profit on the venture, but for ourselves, we are differently situated, and cannot consistently increase our drawing rate. I therefore apprehend that we shall not be able to draw nearly so fast during the coming year, as we have hitherto done.

The fact that Jamsetjee operated on short term credit made matters that much worse when he was unable to get his funds back to India promptly. He said, ". . . we have always pursued the practice of never keeping any individual fixed Balance in our Books, but merely open accounts with different merchants, which we have closed and paid off as our outstandings came in . . . ."

In 1837, the American bills system collapsed. The unrestricted manner in which these bills had been accepted led to overspeculation and, in August of that year, a number of American houses stopped payment. It now became even more difficult to procure good bills on London in Canton. In order ". . . to avoid the highly disadvantageous expedient of Shipping Treasure . . .", Jardine resorted to a novel method for remitting Jamsetjee's funds, that of exporting Chinese produce, mainly tea and silk to Jamsetjee's agents in London. Although, Jardine declared, this remittance at 4s/7d to the dollar was advantageous as compared with the rate for American bills, 4s/6d, this move proved disastrous. Stocks of silk and tea on Jamsetjee's account began to accumulate with his London agents, Forbes Forbes and Co., who, despite desperate reminders, would not sell and remit the funds to India. In one instance, a cargo of Chinese silk remained unsold for over two years. In many cases, when accounts were eventually rendered, the exchange rate at which the remittances were made turned out to be miserable. When accounts were closed for the year 1837–38 it was found there had been a debit balance. Jamsetjee had already informed Jardine he was not interested in shipping China produce. Once again, he sought good bills and good exchange and once again he faced fierce competition especially from Liverpool merchants.

We notice that other merchants besides Jamsetjee encountered similar problems. When Forbes Forbes and Co., delayed selling his goods, he complained bitterly, ". . . the late Hormasjee Bomanjee's misfortunes arose from the same cause."

Even more significant, perhaps, than the export of Chinese goods to England as a means of remittance, was Jamsetjee's move to import British goods in order to reroute his funds back to India from England. In September 1838, he ordered from Forbes Forbes and Co., as an experiment, a variety of cotton textiles. In the following months, he placed a much larger order, not only for several kinds of cotton fabrics, but also for iron bars and copper. He wrote, ". . . we give you full authority to buy such goods as you think will pay us best . . . You are of course aware that it never was our intention to have our funds returned to us in produce, and we merely now resort to this mode in consequence of the rate of Exchange being so much to our disadvantage."

These arrangements reveal the critical features of an unequal economic relationship. For although we have been concerned with the experiences of an individual merchant, his problems reflect wider developments in the structure of Indo-British trade. The expansion of British commerce facilitated, and was in turn the consequence of Britain's growing command of international credit resources. With a worldwide field of operations, British mercantile and banking houses were able to buy and sell bills of exchange at rates which Indian merchants, with a much narrower area of activity, could not afford. Such were the altered terms of trade that Indian merchants were having to import British textiles and metals as a means of remittance. We are led to conclude that the import of British goods into India was developed not only by means of direct control of the market which political hegemony made possible, but also fostered indirectly through the rates of exchange which in turn influenced the form of remittance.

Meanwhile, as far as remittances from China were concerned, the difficulty of obtaining bills at favourable rates continued well into the 1840's. Although on occasion Jardine Matheson and Co., did procure good bills on London for Jamsetjee Jejeebhoy, a large part of his funds had to be repatriated in silver to India and to England where, because of its high gold content, *sycee* had a good market.

India's trade with China as a whole, we know, was balanced by very large imports of silver. To sum up, we must emphasize three facts. First, Indian merchants would have preferred to receive their remittances in bills rather than in bullion but, as we have seen, bills were either not available, or were too expensive. Second, the predominance of the British and the Americans in the bills market helped to amplify the range of their transactions and buttressed their international credit and trade networks. Third, in India, the value of the silver rupee as against gold had been declining since 1793, a trend which may be taken as an indication of the simultaneous decline of silver in terms of gold. In effect, therefore, India's trade balance was being realized in a depreciating medium. This must have had an adverse effect upon India's terms of trade.

British domination of India's trade and finance was exercised through a combination of direct and indirect means. Prominent among the institutions which embodied this domination was the consignment trade.

The Consignment Trade

At the core of the system of colonial commerce was the consignment trade as it had developed into the period of Britain's triumph as the world's prime maritime and commercial power. Certain structural features of this trade were carry-overs from older times. In the altered political and economic environment of the early nineteenth century, they ensured optimum benefit to the metropolitan centre.

It is well known that much of medieval and early modern European and Asian trade had been financed by means of respondentia bonds, whereby the shippers provided the capital, whether borrowed or their own, and bore the financial risk of the venture. The traders, adventurers or supercargoes, as they are variously called, ran the physical risk of the voyage and, if the venture was successful, earned a proportion of the profit. Being based on high interest, short term credit, the supreme objective in such enterprises was for the supercargo to sell the goods as quickly as possible and return with his ship.

As far as British trade was concerned, in the late eighteenth and early nineteenth centuries, the institution of supercargoes had been partly replaced, at Indian and Chinese ports, by resident agent, or agency houses, manifestations of Britain's growing commercial and maritime strength, and harbingers of her territorial ambitions. The role of the agency houses in providing long term activity and wider scope to British enterprise is well known. It needs to be stressed that the credit resources and commercial structures of India were important constituents of their economic base. Jamsetjee Jeejeebhoy's letters show that the cargoes consigned, through his firm, of opium to China and of tea, silk and cotton to London, were financed by Indian shippers on short term credit characteristic of their operations. The consignment trade, simply because the shipper bore the entire risk, in effect provided the agency houses both with working capital free of interest, and with stocks, the property of the shippers, which they could sell as they pleased. The consequences for the shippers were doubly disadvantageous. They bore the brunt both of price fluctuations and, as Jamsetjee and his clients discovered, of manipulation on the part of their agents in the accounting of sales.

It may be noticed that these arrangements were a sharp contrast to those of the East India Company as they stood on the eve of the cessation of its commercial activities. The Company's cargoes of cotton from Bombay to China were sent not on consignment, but were under the charge of the captains of ships who acted as supercargoes. In letter after letter of instructions, the captains of ships sailing out of Bombay with the Company's merchandise, were ordered not to sell below the market price. Being its servants they were answerable to the Company.

The position of the Indian merchants was altogether weaker, almost wholly dependent as they were upon the goodwill of their agents in China. Jamsetjee's letters to Jardine Matheson and Co., invariably ended with a declaration of confidence that their friends would dispose of their cargoes as they would their own. The breathless frequency of these declarations tells its own tale of the anxiety which Jamsetjee felt. With time, the grounds for confidence were eroded. Jamsetjee particularly regretted William Jardine's departure from China in 1839, and his untimely death four years later.

The bickerings and ill-feeling which marred the relations of the two firms in the years that followed were the result partly of the snapping of a personal link, and partly of altered circumstances. From the modest position they had occupied at the time when Jamsetjee first became associated with them, Jardine Matheson and Co., had become the wealthiest and most powerful European commercial house in China, having accumulated vast profits and having acquired the major share of the tea trade with Europe. They were far less dependent now upon their Indian friends for capital and for supplies. In the attainment of this happy situation they had been helped, in no small measure by the consignment trade with India.

For the shippers, by contrast, the consignment trade involved yet another hazard. When goods on their account were consigned to England as remittance and not in response to an actual demand, the disadvantages were compounded. This happened, as we have seen, to some of Jamsetjee's shipments of tea and silk. In these years, it had been noticed tea became the common man's drink in Britain. It is worth suggesting this happened not only, as is argued, because incomes went up, but perhaps also because it became cheaper as a consequence of the stocks that were poured in as remittance.

To recapitulate, the over-all function of the consignment system was to provide Britain with cheap credit and cheap produce from India and China. By so doing it helped to build the capital stocks of British banking and trading houses, the cumulative consequence of which was the strengthening of the London money market.

The consignment trade, together with official monetary controls, and the pressure of India's obligatory payments to Great Britain, appears to have exercised a sustained depressive influence on the prices of Indian produce during this period.

The Decline of Country Shipping

In the early 1840's Jamsetjee appeared anxious to sell off his ships. A decade later, his impressive fleet had been reduced to two, the *Charlotte* and the *Good Success*. When the *Charlotte* was wrecked in the Bay of Bengal in 1855, he had only one ship left, the *Good Success,* the first ship to have come into his possession.

The fact that the eclipse of country shipping almost coincided with the advent of steam ships would perhaps lead us to assume this was the result of the technological superiority of the latter. This assumption is not quite borne out by the evidence. For, it seems, country ships were losing out, in the initial stages, not to steam ships, but to sailing ships owned by "free traders."

Jamsetjee was amazed to find free traders could sail their ships to England at £3 or £4 per ton whereas he could barely sail his own for £7 to £9. In a composite business, shipping costs, of course, were not unconnected with successful trade and with access to convenient payments arrangements. We have noted some of the difficulties under which Jamsetjee laboured. But shipping had its own special problems besides. In order to operate efficiently, it was important to widen the scope of activity so that losses might be counterbalanced. Country ships carrying opium and cotton to China encountered an acute lack of return freight. In the early 1830's, it was observed, imports from China had greatly diminished and ships were often obliged to return empty to Bombay. One reason for this may have been a falling demand in India for commodities, such as alum, used in the manufacture of textiles. Meanwhile, the need for economy became all the greater because of increased competition and because of the new duties introduced in 1834. Ships to China were now required to pay a tonnage duty as well as import and export duties on goods. In Bombay, it had become increasingly difficult to procure cotton cargoes for export. The agency houses from Liverpool and Glasgow were bartering piece goods and other European staples at throw-away prices for cotton, and in this way cornering cotton supplies.

To a man of business as efficient and perceptive as Jamsetjee, it was obvious the way to combat these difficulties was to extend the range of his trading activities and, among other moves, to sail his ships with freight from China to England. So, in April, 1834, he resolved to send the *Fort William* with tea on freight from Canton to London. On this occasion, the plan was given up for fear the ship would lose its passage to China in the coming season. Later on, the bitter experience of sending some of his ships to England induced Jamsetjee to remark, "The result that always attends our country ships going to England would almost lead one to think that some evil destiny was attached to them, as we find the Free Traders can sail very cheap while our ships are burthened with immense expense." There was a widespread prejudice, he declared, ". . . against our country ships and the surveyors will purposely make all sorts of objections." No sooner did a country ship arrive in London, than clerks, brokers and tradesmen set themselves to make money by running up bills at the expense of the owners. Jamsetjee had hoped this could be avoided through the vigilance of the captain and of his agents in London, and that a country ship making a round voyage from China to London and back to Bombay, would do as well as other ships. But these hopes were belied when a voyage of his ship, the *Earl of Balcarras* to London cost him £5000 instead of the estimated £2000. In the face of such high expenses he was forced to the conclusion that it was not advisable to send country ships to England.

In Bombay, ships were no longer easy to maintain. There were so many ships now, that crew were difficult to get. In 1841, Jamsetjee had to send the *Fort William* to England at "very very heavy expense", in order to procure European seamen which a ship was required to have under the law. Indian crew too were not easily available because of the large number of ships competing for their services.

The big country ships, such as the *Fort William* of 1200 tons, had been bought for the transport of cotton, a bulky commodity. The cotton trade was no longer profitable, and the maintenance of these large ships was costly and difficult. Jamsetjee confided to an associate he had been refused docking facilities to repair the *Fort William*. He wrote to a former captain of the ship of "the great difficulty of ever obtaining the use of the Docks. Since the steam communication our Docks have been constantly occupied by Government. . . . We are now very badly off in this respect."

Clearly, the favoured treatment at the hands of a friendly Bombay Government, which had enabled country shipping to flourish, was no longer available under the new dispensation.

The smaller ships were more economical. And so, for a while, a fine small country ship like the *Good Success* could do "as well as neighbours notwithstanding all the disadvantages under which she labours." Nevertheless, country ships as a whole, faced unrelenting competition. Jamsetjee wrote to a friend in London.

". . . we have now in Bombay harbour an immense fleet of free traders, who are willing to take cotton on to China for the very lowest freights, at which it is impossible to sail a country ship. Last year many of our fine teak ships were laid up, and this season have gone at miserably low freight."

People, complained Jamsetjee, would not give them China freight; they were "afraid to come near us." With the abolition of the Navigation Acts, the situation became difficult for now the port was freely accessible to American as well as to European ships. Jamsetjee's son wrote of "the utter inability of our Indian shipping to compete with the Free Traders and Yankees which flock here." Freight to China had fallen to Rs. 5 per candy for cotton and $2½ per chest for opium, less than a half and a quarter, respectively of the lowest rates which country ships could offer.

Meanwhile, as if to confirm Jamsetjee's premonition that an evil destiny threatened country ships, a new menace made its appearance. In June, 1842, the crew set fire to two ships in Bombay harbour and attempted to burn a third. Exactly a year later, the *Thomas Grenville,* about to set sail for China with a full cargo was destroyed by fire. "There is not a doubt," declared Jamsetjee, "that it was by design, but nothing can be proved." Two years later, the crew of Jamsetjee's ship, the *Charlotte* loaded with cotton for China tried to set fire to it, but the act was checked. Desperate arrangements had to be adopted in order to guard against "incendiarism", Jamsetjee began to employ hired porters, rather than the regular crew, to load his ships. But within a short while the malady had spread to Calcutta where, in 1846, his ship the *Bombay Castle,* was burnt. In the decade between 1841 and 1851, seven ships had been burnt in Calcutta and eight in Bombay by "lascar incendiaries". The total estimated loss was over half a million sterling.

What was the motive that prompted the burning of so many fine vessels? When the first incident took place, Jamsetjee remarked the crew had burnt the ships, just when they were about to sail, in order to save the two months' wages that had been advanced to them. With an abundance of ships in the harbours, sailors perhaps reckoned it would not be difficult to find employment and better wages. But the large number of burnings that took place for several years raises the question whether there may have been a design to destroy country shipping and ruin the insurance companies in which many owners of country ships had shares. A third possibility must also be considered. There had been a precedent going as far back as the seventeenth century, for owners of old ships to arrange to have them burnt and claim insurance. We know the owners of country ships were finding it extremely difficult to sell their ships. Whatever the real motives, insurance offices were no longer willing to underwrite "lascar manned vessels."

By the middle of the century, there was no "country service" left "almost all the old Bombay vessels having been burnt, wrecked or sold in England." English vessels now had "almost all the Trade to themselves."

The striking feature of the picture of shipping in Bombay that emerges from Jamsetjee Jejeebhoy's letters is that before steamships fully established their dominance, country ships had been ousted by English sailing ships. The victory of English shipping, in other words, was not simply a technological one. Just as their links with the dominant international networks, of commerce and banking, centred in Britain, enabled the Liverpool trading houses to sell bills of exchange at rates which Indian merchants could not afford, so also were English ships able to offer freight far cheaper than what Indian ships could do. For those who enjoyed patronage and protection in their home base in Britain, and at the imperial outposts in India and China, it was feasible to practice economies of scale and unleash cut-throat competition.

The other side of the picture seems equally clear. Jamsetjee Jejeebhoy's career shows that in western India, at this time, neither financial resources for business enterprise, nor entrepreneurial initiative and skill were wanting. He and his friends attempted to build a business of shipping and long distance trade. Their endeavours were stifled because they came into conflict with British shipping interests which, increasingly from the 1830's onwards, came to have official backing. On this count, and on others, the "age of reform" was, for India, one not simply of hiatus but of regression.

Before the middle of the century, the fortunes of some of the older merchants had declined. Framjee Cawasjee and Dadabhoy Pestonjee had lost heavily, the former in speculation, the latter in his obligations as a guarantee broker. For certain reasons, which space does not permit us to discuss here, in the 1840s and 50s there was a marked trend towards speculative trade. Some of the prominent speculators of these years were Jamsetjee's former friends and associates, among them, Hutheesing and the sons of Motichund.

Besides, other alignments seemed to be taking shape. Frequent references in Jamsetjee's letters to Marwaris holding up stocks of opium suggest they had strengthened their position through control of the produce at its source. Although hampered by the Taipeh disturbances, the opium trade continued to be profitable. New groups were moving into it, often operating in Bengal opium in order to keep up the price of Malwa. In 1854, some of the principal shippers were Marwaris, Khojas and Baghdadi Jews. Fifty years later, just before the opium trade came to an end, the drug importers at Shanghai included the Sassoons and other Jewish firms, as well as a number of prominent Parsi firms, Cawasjee Pallonjee and Co., Tata and Co., and P. B. Petit and Co. It is not clear to what extent the financial and commercial arrangements of these traders differed from those of Jamsetjee Jejeebhoy. It is true that, unlike him, many of them sent their own agents and relatives to China. How did they overcome the remittance problems of which we find extensive evidence in Jamsetjee's letters? His difficulties, we have argued, arose in part from the fact that the trade he managed was based on high-interest credit characteristic of medieval commerce. Did the opium traders of later times have access to easier credit associated with more modern forms of banking? It would perhaps be possible to answer these questions if detailed records of their business, such as those we have for Jamsetjee Jejeebhoy, were available for study.

One feature of change in the opium trade is nevertheless noticeable. It was no longer a monopoly trade dependent on the delivery of cargoes by an independent shipping service. From mid-century onwards, Malwa opium was shipped by the "regular monthly steamers" and the bulk of the earnings from freight went to the coffers of the P. and O. Company, the largest shipping company in eastern waters.

Suggested Readings

Pamela Nightingale, *Trade and Empire in Western India, 1748–1806* (Cambridge: Cambridge University Press, 1970), provides a detailed description of the commercial system established in the area. David E. Owen, *British Opium Policy in China and India, 1748–1806* (Hamden, Conn.: Archon Books, 1968), is a scholarly discussion of an important element of British imperial trade; although written in 1927, it is a classic on the subject. An example of the interaction between the British East Indian Company and the native peoples may be found in Pratul Chandra Gupta, *Baji Rao II and the East India Company, 1796–1818,* 2nd rev. ed. (Bombay: Allied Publishers Private, 1964).

University Students in Nineteenth Century Russia

Abbott Gleason

Student movements have sometimes been instrumental in effecting significant social changes, and in some parts of the world, particularly in emerging nations, university students constitute a potent political force. This selection examines the evolution of university students into a radical force in pre-Revolutionary Russia. Soviet historians regard student activism as having been critical in ending the feudal phase of Russia's development and ushering in the short-lived capitalist stage of its history.

Universities were a relatively recent phenomenon in Russia, and there were few traditions of student life, much less of student activism. The author attempts to uncover the factors that created a sense of identity among university students and led them to espouse reformist or even revolutionary positions. He finds that the causes varied from school to school, but that some common features included the leadership of a few liberal and student-oriented faculty, student access to dissident literature, and the failure of the authorities to develop a consistent and effective policy against student activism. Underlying those factors, however, the author sees certain aspects of adolescent psychology as predisposing the students toward the attitudes and paths of action they adopted.

"Oh Lord! Gracious goodness! Here they are, here they are!" screams Lyuba with her face glued to the window.

Sure enough, there is Volodya sitting in the phaeton with St. Jérome but no longer in his dark blue coat and grey cap but in the uniform of a University student with its blue-embroidered collar, three-cornered hat and short gilt sword at his side.

"Oh, if only *she* were alive!" cries grandmamma, seeing Volodya in his uniform, and falls into a swoon.

—*Leo Tolstoy,* Boyhood

I n a country that is being "modernized," however poorly this painful process may be understood by all concerned, the university, and higher education generally, is in a central but deeply ambiguous position. On the one hand, institutions of higher education are necessary in molding and training the personnel necessary to run a modern state. On the other, the university is almost certain to produce a variety of criticism, ranging from the purely technical sort to the radical moralism of the intelligentsia point of view.

Student political activists are drawn naturally, if far from exclusively, to intelligentsia attitudes. Even upper-class students, who have a definite stake in the existing order, may not, at that early stage of their lives, perceive their interests rationally, clearly, or selfishly. Nor are they likely to understand the duration, difficulty, and social cost of political change. As Donald K. Emmerson, a perceptive recent commentator, has written:

> Righteous in tone, symbolic in content, student politics tend to differ from "adult" politics in the sense that it is more often the art of the impossible. This emphasis on style over program and commitment over compromise is at once the weakness of student movements and their strength. Student political leaders cannot always escape criticism for the irrelevance of their conceits, for dissipating their energies in proclaiming and protecting ideal images of self and society while ignoring the complex, mundane, "low-payoff" tasks of incremental reform. Yet in those very images—in the credibility of the myth of student innocence, in the purity of their rage against evil—lies the fragile chance to effect basic change, albeit not singly or directly but by triggering or accompanying larger forces into action.

The student movement was of fundamental importance in Russian politics, from the late 1850s on—precisely the period in which the situation in the universities became of major and practical concern to the Russian government. Both Alexander I (in his late years) and Nicholas I had

UNIVERSITY STUDENTS IN NINETEENTH CENTURY RUSSIA   From Abbott Gleason, *Young Russia: The Genesis of Russian Radicalism in the 1860s* (Chicago: University of Chicago Press, 1983), pp. 114–36.

worried about subversive ideas in the universities. But under Alexander II, the old prophecy of Joseph de Maistre seemed to be taking on flesh: what Russia had to fear was not the specter of peasant insurrection, not Pugachëv, but "a Pugachëv of the university."

The Russian universities in the mid-nineteenth century were of comparatively recent origin. The oldest, in Moscow, had been founded only in 1755. Kharkov and Kazan' received universities in 1804, St. Petersburg in 1819, and Kiev only in 1834. (The two non-Russian universities of the Russian Empire, Dorpat and Vilna, are somewhat peripheral to our concern with social ferment in Russia, as is the University of Odessa, which came into existence only in 1865.

The relationship between the Russian gentry and the universities had always been uncomfortable. In fact, until after 1825, the gentry never took to the educational institutions the state had created, in large part for them. The student body in Moscow remained very small throughout the eighteenth century. (In 1764 there were only forty-eight students in residence, of whom eight were members of the gentry. At the end of the century, there were still no more than a hundred.) Tutors and foreign universities were the rule for most gentry who cared about ideas and culture; those who cared less, but wanted a service career, often attended military academies, which gave them a high rank upon graduation. Despite the fact the university was heavily plebeian in social composition (its students being largely the sons of lower officers, priests, free peasants, and even serfs), it failed to democratize the ruling elite because of its small size.

Under Alexander I and Nicholas, the situation grew more complex. Alexander was determined to reconcile the gentry to the universities, three of which were founded under his reforming auspices, and Nicholas showed signs of wanting to restrict university education to them, despite his fears of a gentry *Fronde*. Alexander's reforming minister, Mikhail Speransky, changed the situation with his Education Act, which became law in August 1809. This decree made the achievement of the eighth rank in the service hierarchy (which conferred nobility) dependent upon a certificate from a university "testifying to the successful study of sciences appropriate to his branch of civil service." If the candidate could not produce such a certificate, he had to go to the university and pass an examination to the same effect. The Education Act thus went some distance toward restoring "the Petrine bond between education and state service." Despite this blow to aristocratic dilettantism, however, it was not until after 1825 that the thinking members of the gentry, at any rate, really embraced the university. With the increasing mistrust between the monarchy and the more cultivated and speculative members of *obshchestvo* ((particularly those who approached an intelligentsia mentality), the university became the refuge of the latter and thereby took on a respectability and prestige it had never before enjoyed in gentry circles—as evinced, for instance, in the quotation from Leo Tolstoy's memoirs that heads this chapter.

Despite Nicholas's distrust of the gentry, an attitude that was permanently exacerbated by the Decembrist Revolt, he was even less inclined to the idea of raising up substantial numbers of the lower classes through the educational process. Although in theory the universities were open to all the free estates of the realm (in 1827 serfs had been forbidden by statute to attend), the talented plebeians who had previously used the university to advance their fortunes now found new obstacles placed in their path. Secret ministerial directives sharply qualified open admission to the university in practice. The gentry-dominated gymnasia, with their classicized curriculum, became, if not the only means of entrance, by far the easiest way into the university, not least because they were in part given over to direct preparation of the student for university entrance examinations. Tuition fees had been introduced in the last years of Alexander I. In 1845, they were raised, not so much out of financial need as for reasons of social control.

Nicholas also divested the universities of a great deal of their internal autonomy. All educational levels came under direct bureaucratic supervision and control; the universities were placed under the administrative authority of the curators of the educational districts in which they were located. The governance rights of the university councils were sharply curtailed, and the curator might dismiss "unreliable" professors. A substantial number of inspectors, often of military background, kept tabs on the intellectual, political, and moral situation in both schools and universities, including student church attendance and reception of the sacraments. The total number of gymnasium and university students remained small, and the rate of growth modest. By 1848, university enrollment had reached only 4,566, and gymnasium enrollment 18,911. In the immediate aftermath of the upheavals of that year, the number of university students dropped by one fourth.

The year 1848 had other negative consequences. The University of Moscow was the only Russian university that had begun to develop the kind of tradition and *esprit de corps* so characteristic of the ancient universities of Western Europe. And although the center of the Slavophile-Westerner confrontation had been the Moscow salons, the university had been a forum, too. But in the fear and then torpor that prevailed in intellectual circles after 1848, the university lost much of this intellectual vitality. Philosophy, under perennial suspicion in the nineteenth-century Russian university, disappeared again from the curriculum, as did the public law of the states of Western Europe. The remaining rights of the university councils were further curtailed; rectors and deans were no longer elected but were made agents of the Ministry of Education, and their functions were conceived by the government as identical with those of the detested inspectors. As the reign of Nicholas drew to a close, both faculties and students were passive, demoralized, and opportunistic. Apathy and careerism seemed totally predominant.

As in so many other areas of Russian life, the Crimean defeat quickly convinced the government that "improvements" were necessary: the quality of education had to be improved and the quantity of educated men increased. So the new era began quickly in the universities, and a stream of decrees and administrative changes were launched after 1855. The universities were opened up to all those who could pass the qualifying examinations, and a dramatic increase in enrollment resulted. Between 1854 and 1859, the population of the universities increased by more than half. St. Petersburg almost tripled in size. Formerly proscribed subjects were reintroduced. Travel restrictions and the ban on the importation of scholarly materials were relaxed. Many of the military bully boys who had occupied the crucial posts of curators and inspectors were replaced by milder men with civilian backgrounds, and even more important was a general relaxation of "supervision." After 1858, student inspectors were relieved of their supervisory responsibilities except within the walls of the university.

The response of the rapidly growing student body to these changes—and to the feeling of liberal drift that accompanied them—was rapid and pronounced. Students seem to be particularly sensitive to the inner strength and self-confidence of the authorities whom they "confront." So it is no wonder more and more Russian students sensed that neither Alexander nor his subordinates had a clear sense of what they wanted to achieve, beyond the broadest possible commitment to "improvement." Indecision at the top translated itself down the chain of command. Curators, inspectors, rectors, and the older professors lost their sense of the situation and some of their self-confidence. And the students were not slow to take advantage of this development. Beards, mustaches, and long hair—formerly strictly forbidden—made their appearance, then as now symbols of liberation.

The situation in which the students found themselves fostered the dramatization of certain adolescent behavior patterns—specifically what Jean Piaget has called the "constant mixture of devotion to humanity and acute egocentricity." The adolescent, writes Piaget,

> thanks to his budding personality, sees himself as equal to his elders, yet different from them, different because of the new life stirring within him. He wants to surpass and astound them by transforming the world. That is why the adolescent's systems or life plans are at the same time filled with generous sentiments and altruistic or mystically fervent projects and with disquieting megalomania and conscious egocentricity. . . . The adolescent in all modesty attributes to himself an essential role in the salvation of humanity and organizes his life accordingly.

If a propensity for messianic elitism is characteristic of able young people, a number of factors in the Russian situation contributed to its luxuriant development. One was that there were so few students—still fewer than five thousand in 1860–61. Then there was the importance the new Tsar clearly ascribed to the university and its personnel. To be a student was to be in the vanguard of progress, to be the hope of the nation; to the students from lower-class backgrounds, there was the additional feeling that they were joining this new elite, rather than merely assuming their natural place within it. And around them they perceived an inchoate or articulated sympathy; *obshchestvo* wanted to "believe in youth," especially in university youth, especially at the dawn of the new era.

No other social forces could contest the students for their self-assumed role as the nation's hope. The government had been disastrously defeated in war, and Nicholas was dead. A substantial modern middle class was still decades away; the Great Reforms had yet to do their work. And the students were geographically concentrated; their developing *esprit de corps* could easily assume tangible and organized forms.

Until very recently, it has been customary to rely heavily on social factors to explain the growing radicalism of Russian students in the latter 1850s and 1860s. Alexander's measures to democratize the universities, so the argument runs, brought plebeian elements into *obshchestvo* (or at least into its vicinity), resulting in quite substantial changes in the quality and texture of Russian culture within a surprisingly brief period. These people—the children of priests, doctors and medical functionaries, marginal landowners, and lower bureaucrats—received the now-famous label of *raznochintsy* (literally, "the people of various ranks"), those who could not or did not fit into Russia's disintegrating caste system. Soviet historians, analyzing the alleged replacement of "feudalism" by "capitalism" on the historical stage, often periodize the history of the intelligentsia similarly, indicating that at some point around 1861 the gentry ceased to be the dominant social element in the intelligentsia and were replaced by the *raznochintsy*. Many Western historians have endorsed this general view, without claiming a comparable sociological precision: "From Gentry to *Raznochintsy*" or some similar phrase indicates that Chernyshevsky is about to be introduced in textbook or lecture.

That much of the intellectual leadership in Russian radicalism in the 1850s and 1860s was in the hands of *raznochintsy* cannot be denied. In such an aristocratic culture as Russia was, the appearance of so many sons of priests on the social and intellectual scene could not fail to make a deep impression, and it is perhaps not surprising that historians often characterize the entire period as *raznochintsy*. To the most obvious names of Chernyshevsky and Dobroliubov one could add a score of others. Certain of the seminarians pioneered a militant and uncompromising style and image that proved deeply attractive to several generations of Russian radicals. With the broadening of the social base of the universities, upper-class students came to be more immediately aware of the poverty of their lower-class confreres, and in the atmosphere of the period diluted their snobbery with a volatile mixture of compassion and admiration. This opening up of the university, despite periodic attempts by the government to limit or even reverse the policy, proved irresistible, and it undoubtedly hastened the demise of the educated gentry's virtual monopoly over Russian intellectual life.

Still, despite the leadership provided by Dobroliubov and Chernyshevsky and the prominence of seminarians at both the *Contemporary* and the *Russian Word*, there is little evidence to suggest that *razno-chintsy* students as a group were decisive in the growth of student dissatisfaction and radicalism. Nor does the figure of Chernyshevsky seem to have been more attractive to the sons of priests or poor army doctors than to the children of gentry landowners. Indeed, the reverse may be true. To an upper-class student, tormented about his privileged position and exploitative social role, and determined to repudiate them, the persona of Chernyshevsky could have a special appeal—based on militant moralism and cultural strangeness. Despite the appearance of a number of *raznochintsy* in prominent positions, the evidence suggests that most lower-class students were simply trying to "make it" in the upper world of Russian society, whose doors were now at least ajar.

The two great Russian novels about the radical politics of the 1860s, Turgenev's *Fathers and Children* and Dostoevsky's *The Possessed*, suggest opposite answers to the question: Were the young radicals of the 1860s rebelling *against* the values of their "parents" (the gentry liberals of the 1840s) or simply acting out those values in a more vigorous, extreme, and uncompromising fashion? Turgenev stressed rebelliousness, and his version of the generation gap has been more generally accepted. It is certainly true that in any period of impending social change or upheaval, generational conflicts are exacerbated, which is one reason why Turgenev's vivid portrayal of those differences has always seemed so compelling.

But it might be argued that Dostoevsky's view of the situation was more profound, however idiosyncratic his demonic portrayal of 1860s radicalism. Stepan Trofimovich Verkhovensky, the 1840s Westerner (and a caricature of Granovsky), is the father of Pëtr Verkhovensky, the radical of the 1860s. Their values are ultimately identical; the younger Verkhovensky is merely more thoroughgoing and consistent, less timid and sentimental. What Dostoevsky saw less clearly is that the Slavophile ideas that affected him so powerfully had themselves contributed to the satanic social doctrines against which he fought so hard.

The fact is that we do not know enough about the backgrounds of individual radicals to generalize as to whether they were rebelling against the personal values of their families or putting those values into practice in a more consequent and militant fashion, a question that has often been raised with respect to more recent "young radicals." A comparison of Chernyshevsky and Dobroliubov suggests the difficulties of the question. Up to a point, the backgrounds of the two were remarkably similar. They were both the sons of priests, both had demonstrated piety and intellectual precocity as children, and both were from provincial backwaters. But Chernyshevsky's biography suggests a substantial carryover in basic values from childhood to maturity, from the bright, ascetic, repressed child of the provinces to the radical of St. Petersburg. One has the sense that Chernyshevsky's rejected Christianity gave him the emotional basis for his radicalism and guided him in his first intellectual formulation of moral principle. Nor does Chernyshevsky seem to have regarded his intellectual break with the values of Russian society as a repudiation of his parents. "More and more," Chernyshevsky wrote in his diary at the age of twenty, "I recognize a similarity between [my father] and me in the best moments of my life, or, in any case, between him and what I consider to be the best in man."

Dobroliubov's case was very different. If Chernyshevsky's childhood was idyllic, Dobroliubov's was grim. Dobroliubov's father, far from being generally respected, beloved, and permissive, seems to have been an irritable tyrant with a penchant for bootlicking. Chernyshevsky was sent by his family to the University of St. Petersburg, but Dobroliubov broke with his father when he left the seminary for an intellectual career in the capital. The stages in Chernyshevsky's biography flow into each other, while Dobroliubov's brief career speaks of tremendous repression, followed by a frenzy of revolt and permanent instability.

An unquestionable precondition of the growing student radicalism of the late 1850s was the mood of "liberal" reformism unleashed by Alexander II's educational reforms and most of all by the coming of Emancipation. In general, this link between student attitudes and broader and more diffuse social moods seems characteristic. A determined radical minority can pursue its activities for some time without broad social sympathy, but a large-scale student movement depends on its participants feeling that they have substantial—if halting or inarticulate—support outside the walls. When the social mood changes drastically, as Americans have recently had occasion to observe, student attitudes are likely to alter correspondingly. Perhaps it is best of all to be able to feel that you are doing the right thing, that most people know you are, and that they admire you and wish you well, although they are too timid or socially encumbered to join you, despite the belief, shared by all thoughtful parties, that the future is on your side. For a time in the late 1850s, Russian students—or at least an activist minority—were in that happy position.

Student movements also need non-student figures with whom they can identify—members of the faculty or other individuals within the university, or figures from the larger world of journalism or politics. Russian students, in fact, had both. There were the remote but glamorous figures of Herzen and Ogarëv in London, and the increasingly influential group around the *Contemporary*—above all, Chernyshevsky. Nearer at hand were sympathetic and popular "liberal" professors, like Konstantin Dmitrievich Kavelin, professor of law at the University of St. Petersburg. L. F. Panteleev, whose memoirs illuminate the period vividly, recalled Kavelin in the following striking terms:

> He tried to become close friends with his students; all those of any talent could count on being received at Kavelin's Sunday morning receptions, which were specially arranged for students. He always expressed his opinion without the least hesitation, without nervous or sidelong glances—whether it was agreeable or not—while at the same time he knew how to listen attentively to any objection, without ever attempting to intimidate a young opponent with his authority. At the receptions, scholarly questions were discussed, as well as the latest in literature, but primarily the phenomena of our contemporary domestic politics. Principally, of course, this meant the liberation of the peasants. Being very well informed as to the course of the reform, K.D. informed us of its most trifling details and the difficulties which it was encountering. . . . It was first from K.D. that we learned of the initial preparations of N. A. Miliutin for the creation of the zemstvo institutions,* and it was also K.D. who explained to us the full significance of the transformation which was being prepared, not only from the economic point of view, but the social. . . . Through his broad contacts, K.D. was *au courant* with everything which then had social significance, and he gladly shared it all with his interlocutors. There was only one boundary which K.D. never crossed: even I, a student enjoying his particular favor (when he left for the country in the summer, he entrusted me with arranging the juridical chronicle in [the journal] *The Century,* one of whose editors he was)—even I never saw *The Bell* at his place, although he undoubtedly received it. He did, however, often tell us interesting things from it.

* The zemstvos were organs of local government that were introduced after the Emancipation.

Kavelin was probably the most influential of the activist, reform-minded professors of the late 1850s, but at the climax of student unrest and disorders in 1861–62 he ran into trouble. His was the basic dilemma of all moderate progressives in periods of acute disorder. He did not provide the kind of uncompromising support the most militant students demanded, while the more moderate and conservative authorities held him responsible for the breakdown of order. Kavelin always prided himself on being able to communicate with people of radically different persuasions: the Slavophiles, conservative bureaucrats, Herzen, Dobroliubov. In that respect he belonged to the 1840s, not the 1860s. And when the political situation polarized beyond a certain point, he ended by being acceptable to no one.

The relationship between what one might call "campus issues" and the dramatic development of reform at the national level was complex. Undoubtedly, most student activists focused on local rather than national concerns, although the excitement of the Emancipation drama had a catalytic effect. What people seem to have noticed first was that students seemed to be thinking and feeling more as a group, that class and regional differences seemed to be diminishing, and that the students who arrived at the universities in 1858 seemed to be distinctly more interested in politics than their predecessors had been.

Soon the greater cohesion of the students began to create "we-they" situations. Since the attitude of the university authorities—the curators and rectors—was now uncertain or even sympathetic, student organizations began to spring up: libraries, scholarship funds (financed by the richer students for their poorer colleagues), social clubs, and a spectrum of periodicals—ranging from quite acceptable scholarly journals to badly printed imitations of the *Bell*. As student corporatism developed, clashes with the police began to be more serious, if not actually more frequent. In the old days, these clashes seldom had had serious consequences. Increasingly, after 1856, students viewed the beating or maltreatment of one of them as an offense against the entire body, and they met, often in large numbers, to seek redress. Sometimes they succeeded, particularly at first, as neither the university nor the civil authorities were accustomed to dealing with crowds of determined students. Under Nicholas the educational bureaucracy would automatically have had recourse to Draconian measures. Now its officials hesitated—either because they simply had lost their bearings, or because the signals they received from above were confusing, or because elements among them were touched with the sympathy toward reform, so common to *obshchestvo* in general. As Anthony Graham Netting, a perceptive student of Russian public opinion, wrote a few years ago, "political and cultural revolutions depend less on their dedicated partisans than on the apparent enemies who in crucial moments partly give way. It was this involuntary reserve army that liberal *obshchestvo* [had assembled] under the very guns of Nicholas I."

Sometimes the animus of the students was directed at university officials, particularly the prying and officious student inspectors. After a rather nasty case at Kazan' in 1857, which began with a parietal violation, a number of students were expelled, but the inspector resigned and so, eventually, did the curator. A rather similar case occurred at Kharkov in the same year, when one of the curator's minions struck a student in the course of "arresting" him for appearing on the street in an improper uniform. A series of tumultuous student meetings ensued, in the course of which the curator felt himself forced to resign. Both of these incidents, and others like them, were regarded by the students as victories and whetted their appetites for more.

Incompetent, indifferent, or authoritarian professors (some were all three), who were regarded as holdovers from the bad old days of Nicholas, were frequent targets. To achieve their removal was not merely educationally desirable but took on a political coloring as well: it was part of the task of reforming Russia. Students answered back to these professors in class, petitioned against them, boycotted their lectures, or resorted to systematic harassment (clapping, whistling, and so on). These incidents, too, were likely to escalate, and the administration frequently found itself in the middle, between an outraged and defensive faculty majority and an aroused student body. In the spring of 1859, Prince Viazemsky, the son of the great poet who was Pushkin's friend, became curator of the educational district of Kazan.' He replaced a man who had been driven out by just such an episode—an attack on a professor, which had led to a series of boycotts, expulsions, and general chaos.

For better than two years, Viazemsky managed to keep matters under control. He was cognizant of the relationship between "student unrest" and social reforms being carried out elsewhere, and he did his best to be reasonable, accessible, and not to overreact and make things worse. Conservative officials tended to feel that he was not reacting at all.

But even an intelligent and tactful conservative like Viazemsky was not immune from the pressures of the day. The Kazan' students had tangled with an Italian professor of geography in 1859; although he was an eminent scholar, his Russian was so bad no one could understand his lectures. In the tumultuous fall of 1861, the students began to work on him again. This time, Viazemsky and his hitherto tactful and discreet inspector let the matter get completely out of hand. The university was closed for several months in the late fall and winter, and the buildings were briefly occupied by troops. Several scores of students were expelled, and after two separate investigations, one of them involving an elaborate government commission, Viazemsky was replaced in June 1862.

The principal means of mobilizing student support in one of the frequent *istorii* ("histories") was the so-called *skhodka*. The term was of peasant origin, significantly; it meant the meeting of the village assembly and was taken over by the students to designate their own meetings. As the 1850s wore on, *skhodki* became ever more common and often unruly. In most instances, they were unauthorized, although rules governing *skhodki* were at least hazy; in some instances (St. Petersburg), the curators and rectors had initially encouraged them, thinking to draw the students into orderly and practical cooperation in their own governance. But the *skhodki*, like other forms of student assemblies, came to be regarded by the authorities as dangerous in the extreme, and they were forbidden by law in May 1861, unless specifically authorized, as was "all bargaining with them through deputies or mobs."

Although the primary focus of the students' discontent was on their own position in a university badly in need of reform, a few were getting more interested in radical solutions to national problems; after 1858, the loose congeries of ideas that would become known as Populism was more and more attractive to a minority of the students, although not necessarily to the most militant. Everyone had something to say about Herzen's *Bell*. Newssheets and "journals," some printed and some handwritten, began to make their appearance in the universities during and after 1858. In St. Petersburg there was the *Herald of Free Opinion* (*Vestnik svobodnogo mneniia*) and the more radical *Little Bell* (*Kolokol'chik*). Venturi notes that in Moscow alone at least four manuscript newspapers were circulating in 1858: the *Spark*, the *Living Voice*, the *Echo*, the *Unmasker*. Kharkov had its *Free Word*. Finally, at Kazan', St. Petersburg, and elsewhere, the corporate, student-run libraries became centers for the accumulation and distribution of the *Bell* and other illegal literature. Most of the students' own newspapers were largely oriented toward what was taking place on campus, but there was a distinct subcurrent of interest in national politics, and the hostility toward local figures spilled over into criticisms of the government and Alexander himself.

Toward 1860, on most university campuses, groups were forming who cared only about the national arena and who utilized campus issues primarily to radicalize the student body. Also at Moscow was the so-called Library of Kazan' Students, from whose ranks were drawn some of the most dedicated and extreme radicals of the 1860s, among them P. E. Argiropulo and P. G. Zaichnevsky, the principal author of the extremist Jacobin manifesto *Young Russia*. The Library of Kazan' Students undertook a considerable venture in clandestine publishing, beginning in 1859; extensive selections from Herzen appeared, followed by Ludwig Feuerbach's *Essence of Christianity* and Friedrich Karl Büchner's materialist tract *Force and Matter*. Only Zaichnevsky's arrest in 1861 prevented the publication of P. J. Proudhon's *What is Property?*

The University of Kazan' gave rise to the so-called Kazan' Circle in 1860, whose membership included the radical ethnographer I. A. Khudiakov. The ultimate goal of the group was to induce a peasant insurrection; in the short run, the circle tried to keep the student body "aroused and alert to attempts to deprive it of its 'rights.'" There was a "secret society" at the University of Kharkov that as early as 1856 was vaguely discussing extremely radical ideas: how to make a political revolution, the revolutionary potential of the cossacks, and even the question of regicide. A decision was grandly taken to extirpate the imperial family, although no one actually did anything.

What is the best way to get at the relationship between student discontent within the university, spilling over into national politics, and the larger question of the development of Russian radicalism? Was the radical literature, to which the students had access in the late 1850s, actually important in their development? An even harder question to answer: What was the nature of the radicalizing experience that many of the Russian students underwent in the five-year period following the death of Nicholas?

To the first question, Soviet scholarship has given a fairly simple and unequivocal answer: student discontent was an important part of the larger upheaval that brought about Emancipation in 1861 and inaugurated the "capitalist period" of Russian historical development. Like the ideas of Herzen and Chernyshevsky, student unrest was in the final analysis a "reflection" or "echo" of the so-called crisis of serf agriculture and the rising curve of peasant disorder. But this "explanation" is quite inadequate. Perhaps the notion of "reflection" is never adequate to explain the relationship between ideas and an economic substructure. Still, it is true that peasant unrest helped generate the excitement of the late 1850s. The Kazan' Circle believed that a peasant insurrection was a distinct possibility, and the expectation of an "inevitable" peasant insurrection was a recurrent motif in radical thinking into the 1860s. Still, this belief was basically a fantasy of the disenchanted portion of the Russian elite, and it often was more a function of their own powerlessness than anything else. The largely self-generated excitement that animated *obshchestvo,* and the students in particular, had more to do with their own altered situation than with any frightening or challenging upheaval from below. The government and many of the landowners certainly worried, among other things, about a peasant uprising, but the students saw themselves bestowing a full humanity on the peasants; their attitude was generous and rather patronizing.

The significance of literature and ideas as radicalizing agents has been much discussed, both by Soviet and particularly by Western historians. Certainly the cluster of ideas, feelings, beliefs, and prejudices that eventually became known as Populism has a genuine intellectual content, and as the 1860s went along, people spoke and wrote in this vocabulary. But one should not exaggerate the direct, unmediated role of books and ideas. The ground must be prepared and the times right. Büchner's *Force and Matter,* which seems to have shattered so many Russians' faith in revealed religion, now seems to educated readers, even to radicals, not only a cramped and pedestrian tract but a new form of metaphysics. Even in Russia its vogue was brief, if powerful. The books that "influence" us this year may fail to move us two years hence. Intellectuals, and students in particular, are notably susceptible to fashion or, to employ a more complimentary term, to "the intellectual currents of the day." To say this is not to deny the sincerity of the commitment of the radical minority, but merely to stress their vanguard role; the commitment of most students to the "intellectual currents of the day" was "broad, rather than deep," as Panteleev remarked of the influence of the *Contemporary.*

Very rapid and at least superficially "extreme" shifts in political allegiance were common in the late 1850s. Many students who had never really had any political views at all became "radical" quite quickly. But this characteristic of the period, attested to both by contemporaries and historians, should not be exaggerated. The movement of some students to the left was gradual and rather hard fought. Such moderate, vaguely "liberal," and Westernizing journals as the *Russian Herald (Russkii vestnik)* and the *Annals of the Fatherland* also had student adherents. The *Annals,* in particular, appealed to students who retained a pronounced bureaucratic mentality, who wanted orderly reform from above, and who continued to dream of brilliant careers within the limits of *obshchestvo* Russia as it then seemed to be evolving.* Such students, who were likely to regard Chernyshevsky and Dobroliubov as rabble-rousers, were in a real sense not "typical" of the times, but they, too, applauded the Emancipation and, from time to time, looked into Herzen's *Bell.*

Nor is it anachronistic to discuss the matter of "image," so important in American politics today, not least in student and radical politics, in the Russian radicalism of the 1850s and 1860s. Men like P. N. Rybnikov and especially P. I. Iakushkin helped by their lives and examples to create the figure of a Populist-ethnographer, wandering among the people and becoming part of them. That this image is not an adequate rendering of these men does not matter to the student of the 1860s. What matters is to understand how an influential minority of their contemporaries regarded them.

Part of the declining appeal of Herzen to Russian youth and his replacement by Chernyshevsky has more to do with the two men's

* Dmitry Pisarev was such a student in 1858. See A. M. Skabichevsky, *Literaturnye vospominaniia* (Moscow-Leningrad, 1928), pp. 107–17. Panteleev remained an adherent of Katkov's *Russian Herald* until the very end of the 1850s. See his *Vospominaniia* (Moscow, 1958), p. 145.

images than with the ideas they put forward. The "younger generation" of Russian radicals in the late 1850s and 1860s was powerfully attracted to Chernyshevsky's puritanism, asceticism, deliberate lack of charm, and social ease. His whole bearing was an affront to the existing order, and he conveyed the impression that he would not make the slightest social concession: to smile and murmur a few ceremonial words to put an interlocutor at his ease would be, somehow, to betray his whole position. Sincerity was everything. He insisted on being accepted exactly as he was. Herzen, on the other hand, was a "gentleman," even an aristocrat. He loved good food, good wine, and brilliant conversation. He was charming—or could be—and however much he might criticize the existing order, he was clearly a product of it and was bound to it by a myriad tangible and intangible ties—not least the substantial sum of money he arranged to have brought out of Russia when he emigrated. Chernyshevsky conveyed none of this sense of attachment to the old. Both he and Dobroliubov embodied the most militant rejection of the old and the determination to create something new.

Much of this collision of images emerged in an open letter to Herzen, which was written by a young radical in France in 1866. I quote it at length, not because it is fair or accurate—probably very few of even the most extreme and embittered Russian radicals would have endorsed its rhetoric except in the heat of battle—but because it conveys so well the way in which Herzen's image, persona, and style, rather than his ideas, were being rejected.

> I have long since ceased [wrote Alexander Serno-Solovëvich] to read, or at any rate to be interested in your sheet [the *Bell*]. Hackneyed, long familiar sounds; rhetorical phrases and appeals, ancient variations on an ancient theme; witticisms, sometimes fairly clever, but more often flat; commonplaces about "Land and Liberty"—all this has become too tedious, too boring, too repulsive. . . .
>
> Yes, the young generation has understood you. Having understood you, it has turned away from you in disgust; and you still dream that you are its guide, that you are "a power and a force in the Russian state," that you are a leader and representative of youth. You our leader? Ha! Ha! Ha! The young generation has long outstripped you by a whole head in its understanding of facts and events. Failing to perceive that you have been left behind by events, you flap your enfeebled wings with all your might; and then, when you see that people are only laughing at you, you go off in a rage and reproach the younger generation with ingratitude to their teacher, to the founder of their school, the first high priest of Russian socialism! You are a poet, a painter, an artist, a storyteller—anything you please, but *not* a political leader and still less a political thinker, the founder of a school and a doctrine. . . .

So you were the complement of Chernyshevsky! You marched shoulder to shoulder with Chernyshevsky! Such an idea I never expected even from you, and I have studied you closely. . . . You the complement of Chernyshevsky! No, Mr. Herzen. It is too late now to take refuge behind Chernyshevsky. . . . Between you and Chernyshevsky there was not, and could not be, anything in common. You are two opposite elements which cannot exist side by side or near one another. You are the representatives of two hostile natures, which do not complement, but exterminate each other—so completely do you differ in everything, not only in your philosophy of life, but in your attitude toward yourself and to other people, not only in general questions but in the minutest details of your private life.

Conceit is your great misfortune, it completely blinds you. . . . Come down to earth; forget that you are a great man; remember that the medals with your effigy were struck not by a grateful posterity, but by yourself, out of your blood-stained wealth. Look more closely at what is going on around you, and you will then perhaps understand that dry leaves and paper snakes interest nobody . . . that you, Mr. Herzen, are a dead man.

Few, if any, students of the late 1850s and early 1860s consciously modeled themselves any longer on Herzen, while Chernyshevsky was personally fascinating to many. Leo Tolstoy thought that "a bilious, spiteful man is not normal," but increasing numbers of radical students did not agree. In an aristocratic society like that of Russia, smelling of bugs was an excellent way of proclaiming one's disaffection. Good manners and reasonableness not only bound one indirectly to the established order, they were among the essential guarantors of liberal impotence.

Many contemporaries and historians noticed the intellectual shallowness of the radicalism of students (and some older people) in the late 1850s. In one sense they were correct. Very few of the students had really mastered Büchner, Moleschott, Proudhon, or Fourier, and their radical impulses most often found expression in sloganizing. (The arguments of their opponents, one might add, were not ordinarily on a higher level.) But intellectual influences are a secondary consideration here. Most people do not become radicals because of the books they read—although they may appeal to books and draw sustenance from them. To understand the radicalizing experience that students underwent in the late 1850s, one must look instead to the sharp break with the past that occurred in 1855–56 and the *consciousness* it helped induce, a consciousness that men were not wholly impotent with respect to their environment, that things might be changed, ought to be changed—and were about to be changed. One must look to the special qualities of youth and adolescence, and to the privileged and isolated position of

Russian university students. Various Western intellectual currents helped to provide a language for expressing these feelings of mission: German materialism; the utilitarianism of Bentham and Mill; the socialism of Saint-Simon and Fourier. And many of the ideas and preoccupations that had animated both the Slavophiles and the Westerners in the 1840s were reappearing now as guiding motifs of the new radicalism, although not in a form that was intelligible to the older generation.

Some students understood these ideas, made a deep commitment to them, and contributed in turn to their development. For others they remained satisfyingly shocking slogans that corresponded to the emotional needs of the moment and gave them an important but fleeting sense of themselves and their generation. Some students went on to a deeper involvement with radicalism and the revolutionary movement; for others, radicalism was merely their kind of wild oats. But those whose radicalism could survive the withdrawal of the inchoate, "liberal" support of the late 1850s were a minority.

The view that institutions of higher education became, from here on out, the nursery of Russian radicalism is a theme of recent Western scholarship on this period. But which students were likely to be radicalized at the university? Behind this question of university radicalism lies the larger general question of secondary education in Russia. The seminaries, the gymnasia, and the military schools were all harsh in their discipline, primitive in their pedagogical methods, and notably lacking in creature comforts. Most memoir literature that tells about these schools in the time of Nicholas is bloodcurdling, even to the reader who has cut his teeth on *Tom Brown's Schooldays.** But until much more systematic study has been made of secondary education under Nicholas, no serious discussion will be possible.

In fact, no background discussion of causal factors and circumstances can take us very far in analyzing what went on in Russian universities in the late 1850s and early 1860s. What happened there had a rhythm of chronological development that was determined in part by national politics and in part by the logic of events within each university. These patterns were similar in a rough kind of way, but there

---

* In an admittedly impressionistic survey, Alain Besançon has taken note of the bitter memories that many Russian radicals had of their secondary education, and contrasted it with the warm nest from which most of them had emerged. More concretely, he stresses the Manichaean attitudes that were nurtured in the gymnasium: the hatred of authority, the vague democratic tendency, the beginnings of a culture of student solidarity. The harsh conditions in these schools must also have contributed to the popularity of the small number of "liberal" or "modern" secondary-school teachers who managed to survive under Nicholas. Their concern for the students and/or their hostility to the prevalent scholastic teaching methods appears to have won them a sympathy that no intellectual radicalism could then have achieved. See *Education et société en Russie dans le second tiers du XIXe siècle* (Paris and The Hague, 1974), pp. 16–49.

were many local variants. The "student movement" at the University of St. Petersburg was the most tumultuous, in part because the excitements of national politics were greater in the capital than elsewhere, in part because there was greater support for student attitudes and activities, both within the university and in its immediate surroundings, in *obshchestvo*.

The situation at Kharkov was complicated by the many Polish students there—better organized than the Russian students, but rather suspicious, even separatist, in their attitudes. Their complex relationship sometimes reminds a contemporary American professor of the difficulties that black and white student radicals encountered in the late 1960s in working out a concerted campaign against that "common enemy," the university administration. In fact, Polish nationalism sometimes made the Russian and Ukrainian students more moderate in their actions and demands.

Another variant is provided by the University of Kazan', the most remote and, in a sense, isolated of the Russian universities. There the faculty was considerably less competent than at the other universities.* Kazan' students, furthermore, had a tradition of rowdyism and indiscipline, so it is not surprising that many disorders at Kazan' developed around bitter encounters between professors and students over the intellectual qualifications and performance of the former.

Soviet historians generally employ the term "student movement" as if there had been some kind of coordinated leadership and formally agreed-upon program—as if the students' encounters with the authorities were an organized political movement. But despite a good deal of interuniversity contact, the ferment and the disturbances developed autonomously. One crucial difference between the Russian student movement of the 1850s and 1860s and the student radicalism in America a hundred years later has to do with the means of communication. Geographical mobility and in particular the electronic media gave American student politics of the 1960s a national and even supranational unity that was far removed from anything possible in the nineteenth century. The spread of radical politics on American campuses was often abetted by the gnawing feeling of inferiority that many students began to feel if their campus had remained relatively tranquil, while nightly news programs showed building seizures at Stanford and Columbia and a bombing at Wisconsin. Russian students simply could not be anything like so aware of what their confreres elsewhere were up to.

But one should not treat each university as a separate and unrelated story: the drama was far too similar. The national excitement and

---

* An exception might be made for the discipline of chemistry, and of course the great mathematician Nikolai Lobachevsky had spent his life at Kazan' as professor and rector. But his brilliant work on non-Euclidean geometry was recognized in Russia (and Europe) only subsequently.

the government's attitude were unifying factors; and students moving from one university to another did help push the movement along. Fundamentally, however, structural similarities, rather than "influence" of one institution upon another, made for similarities in their histories during this period.

Suggested Readings

The author provides an account of the student movement at a particular institution in "The University of St. Petersburg," in his *Young Russia: The Genesis of Russian Radicalism in the 1860's* (Chicago: University of Chicago Press, 1983), pp. 137–59. The Russian educational system is discussed more generally in Patrick Alston, *Education and the State in Tsarist Russia* (Stanford: Stanford University Press, 1969), and student radicalism during the period is treated in Daniel Brower, *Training the Nihilists: Education and Radicalism in Tsarist Russia* (Ithaca: Cornell University Press, 1975). The issue of student political activism in a wider context is the subject of *Students and Politics in Developing Nations*, ed. Donald K. Emmerson (New York: Praeger, 1968).

Irish Servant Women: The Irish "Biddy"

Faye E. Dudden

It is hard for most of us to realize that the servantless household is a relatively recent development in the West. Before the advances of the twentieth century, the labors of food preparation and preservation, child care, the making and maintaining of clothing, cleaning and polishing, and the host of other household tasks to be done in even a small family were beyond the powers of one woman. Household help was a necessity, not a luxury or a status symbol. Yet, necessary or not, servants were subservient to their mistresses, generally were poorly paid, and, except in the most elaborate of establishments, were without any hope of real advancement. Thus, it was always difficult to secure and keep good household help. That was particularly true in the United States, where an expanding economy and free land in the West created opportunities for servants to marry and establish their own households. The problem was met in the South by the use of slaves (or, after Emancipation, former slaves), and in the North by hiring immigrants. Even the latter expedient was not without problems of its own, however.

This selection examines some aspects of the entry of Irish women into the field of domestic service during the great Irish immigration of 1820–1860. Although dependent on the Irish for household help, their employers regarded them with suspicion and were dissatisfied with them. Much of the bad feeling was caused by the fact that they were foreign, Catholic, and often ignorant and uneducated. The real problem, however, was that the Irish were entering domestic service only as a means of making money and bettering themselves; they were not content with the role of "faithful family retainer." Relations between employer and employee were often strained, but domestic service proved the avenue by which tens of thousands of Irish made their way into American society.

When the famine immigration poured into the United States from Ireland in the late 1840s and early 1850s, it began to look as though every servant was Irish, at least in the major seaboard cities. The Irish "Biddy" became the stereotype of the servant, and Biddy jokes celebrated her inadequacies. Biddy answered the door by yelling through the keyhole; Biddy, accustomed to descend by a ladder, went down stairs backward. In fact, Irish immigration in significant numbers had begun earlier, in the 1820s, and the early stream helped to encourage and finance the later flood. The Irish immediately altered servant recruitment patterns. When the Society for the Encouragement of Faithful Domestic Servants began to run its placement service in New York City in 1825, 60 percent of the applicants were Irish-born.

The prominence of Irish women in American domestic service reflected the operation of an international labor market. In entering it, Irish women brought expectations and commitments that led them into service. More young single women were included in the Irish migrant population than among migrants leaving other European countries. Facing no language barrier, they could find ready acceptance as servants, and entering service solved the problem of finding housing in a strange city where tenement landlords practiced price gouging. Irish women left behind family economies in ruins; their labor market choices seem to have reflected a desire to send money home to pay their rent or to pay for the passage to the United States of another family member. Domestic service, unlike needle or factory work, could yield a cash surplus that need not be depleted during frequent layoffs.

Irish servant girls who sent money home helped to account for remittances in staggering amounts. The British Colonial Land and Emigration Commissioners calculated that remittances from America transmitted through shipping and banking firms totaled at least 1,730,000 pounds in the single year 1845. The relatively steady demand for domestic servants actually gave female immigrants an advantage over their male counterparts in finding employment. Addressing advice to prospective immigrants, John Francis Maguire warned in 1868 that girls and women could come at any season of the year, but men, for whom the counterpart in unskilled work was outdoor day labor, should not

---

IRISH SERVANT WOMEN: THE IRISH "BIDDY"   From Faye E. Dudden, *Serving Women: Household Service in Nineteenth Century America* (Middletown, Conn.: Wesleyan University Press, 1983), pp. 60–71.

come in the fall or winter. When Wilson Benson and his wife Jemima arrived in Canada in 1841, their need for employment led them to separate. She immediately found work as a servant, while he tried one job after another, plagued by a lack of saleable skill. Carol Groneman speculates that Irish families may have chosen to send daughters rather than sons to the New World precisely because daughters were more assured of finding employment and more faithful in sending remittances home.

So powerful was this combination of pushing and pulling factors drawing Irish women into service that it often seemed that service was their only occupation. A volume called *Advice to Irish Girls in America, by the Nun of Kenmare* simply assumed that all its readers would work as servants. The Nun of Kenmare never mentioned any other kind of work but devoted much of her advice to detailed explanations of proper conduct within service.

Recent community studies document the heavy concentration of Irish-born girls and women in domestic service. Stuart Blumin found that in Kingston, New York in 1860, of the 254 Irishwomen of all ages for whom occupations were listed, 240 were domestic servants. In Hamilton, Ontario, Katz found that in 1851, 47 percent of Irish Catholic girls aged fourteen to sixteen and 61 percent of those aged seventeen to nineteen were servants. Laurence Glasco reported that in Buffalo, New York between half and two-thirds of Irish-born women aged eighteen to twenty-one were servants. Given the high turnover in domestic service, such high proportions in cross-sectional data imply that almost every young Irish woman who came to America spent some time in domestic service.

Had other immigrant women gone to work as domestics as often as the Irish, perhaps employers like Caroline Barrett White would not have been so quick to blame their servant problems on the "Irish race." But other immigrant women did not do so, at least not in large enough numbers to outweigh the Irish. Some recent research suggests that young single German-born women entered service as readily as did their Irish-born counterparts. But because Germans were a much smaller group in most cities and evidently because German servants tended to work for German-speaking employers, such as boarding-house-keepers in working-class neighborhoods, German servants were both too few and too confined to ethnic ghettos to affect the stereotypic view of the Irish as the source of servant problems. Scandinavian women also exhibited a marked propensity for service, but they too were a smaller group and concentrated in particular geographical areas.

Differences in the availability of the different groups helped to make ethnicity the medium through which employers expressed dissatisfaction. As David Katzman has pointed out, employers in Maine claimed to prefer Scandinavian servants, who were scarce, while in Minnesota, where many Scandinavians worked in service, employers considered them inept and untidy. Direct comparison of the factors that propelled some immigrant women into service and kept others out is difficult because data on the composition of the immigrant stream—age, sex and marital status—were not collected as immigrants entered this country. But it does seem clear that different ethnic groups responded differently to the market for women's work, the largest element of which was domestic service. The differing composition of the immigrant stream from different countries itself reflected different judgments about who should come to the New World in order to undertake jobs available here. Labor-market behavior seems to have reflected differences in traditional family roles and culture as well as in attitudes toward or strategies for the process of migration itself.

Whatever the differences between ethnic groups, immigrants in general were often, by the very fact of their migrating, demonstrating severe economic need, need that made them willing to put up with the harsh lot of the domestic. Contemporaries recognized that the immigrants' willingness to enter service in numbers made them indispensable. In her *Treatise on Domestic Economy,* Catharine Beecher noted, "There is such a disproportion between those who wish to hire, and those who are willing to go to domestic service that in the nonslave-holding states were it not for the supply of poverty-stricken foreigners there would not be a domestic for each family who demands one." This steady demand took on institutional forms. When New York State authorities belatedly organized a reception center at Castle Garden in 1855 to protect immigrants from the abuses of "runners," they included a labor bureau where virtually every woman who wanted work was placed as a servant. In 1869, for example, a total of 12,111 women were placed in jobs, 11,673 of whom went to work as domestics.

Race also made a difference in the emerging market for domestics. The flood of immigrants dwarfed free blacks in the ranks of service, so that, even though female black employment was heavily concentrated in domestic service, blacks constituted only a small segment of domestics as a whole. In New York City in 1855, the entire Negro labor force was concentrated in just four occupations—laborers, waiters, laundresses, and domestic servants. Yet blacks constituted only one thousand of the thirty-one thousand domestics in the city. Competition from immigrants may have contributed to or confirmed a distinct pattern among black domestics of living out—that is, living away from their employers' homes. Katzman suggests that this characteristic pattern was southern in origin, dating from the exodus of the freedmen from their former owners' homes upon emancipation. However, a propensity for live-out service had already appeared among free blacks in antebellum Philadelphia. Probably living out did stem in part from the dynamics of emancipation and manumission, as ex-slaves sought to establish their independence in their own homes but found employment opportunities severely restricted. Blacks' tendency to live out may also reflect reaction to the competition of immigrants, especially the Irish.

Historians have noted that immigrants tended to drive blacks out of the skilled trades and much unskilled work during the 1830s and 1840s, thus contributing to a pattern of socioeconomic decline among free blacks in the antebellum North. Some evidence suggests that a similar displacement occurred in service, where it may have been particularly pronounced because co-workers had to eat together and often sleep in the same room, as well as work together. European travelers noted the difficulty or outright impossibility of having black and white servants together on the same staff. As white immigrants put blacks in a distinct minority, the employer who wished to take the line of least resistance would simply hire an all-white staff. Thomas Hamilton observed that in New York in 1833 many families had recently replaced their colored servants with "natives of the Emerald Isle." William Chambers referred to the Irish as having "dispossessed in a great degree the colored race" in service. One Philadelphian witnessed a direct and ugly example of this process when a neighbor discharged an Irish servant and in his place employed a Negro: "Shortly after, his garden was trespassed on, plants and shrubbery destroyed and a paper stuck on one of the trees threatening further injury if he did not sent away the Negro." In Louisa May Alcott's novel *Work*, the heroine shows her character when, reduced to taking a job in service, she does not object to working with a black cook, who had been "an insurmountable obstacle to all the Irish ladies who had applied." Since service lay at the bottom of the occupational scale, there was nowhere else for blacks to go, and many of them seem to have turned to live-out service. So long as blacks remained a small minority of servants, this pattern would be easily overlooked. After emancipation and increased migration to the North, black patterns of service would begin to have a significant effect on service as a whole.

The Irish "Biddy"

The Irish domestic, stereotypically referred to as "Biddy," who dominated the labor market at mid-century and therefore drew the blame for servant problems, tended to make an unsatisfactory servant. She carried to extremes what were, in the eyes of employers, the characteristic faults of domestics. Among "faithless strangers" the immigrant woman was most faithless, because so greatly in need of money, and most strange, not just personally but culturally. Like most migrant workers, she tended to think of work instrumentally, and her attitude reinforced her employer's propensity to treat her in the same spirit. The immigrants' motives and qualifications provided a grain of truth for nativist sneers such as that voiced by the editors of *Harper's Weekly* in 1857. They reported that the immigrant women waiting for places at the offices of the New York commissioners of emigration demanded top wages, refusing any offers of less than seven dollars a month, as their relatives in America had written them that they might earn this much. Yet, the editors declared, they were "unwashed and totally ignorant of housewifery." The editors noted with satisfaction that the officials quashed such pretensions, dismissing the women from their offices if they refused to work for whatever wage was offered.

The immigrant woman's heroic struggle to send remittances home, so admirable in the abstract, resulted in the strenuous effort to maximize earnings that employers resented in practice. The author of *Plain Talk and Friendly Advice to Domestics* considered this ruthless concern a common problem among Irish domestics. She told the story of "Bridget," aged sixteen and just off the boat, who expects to receive six dollars a month because her cousin Margaret gets that, although Margaret has been in America twelve years and is quite expert. "They are ever striving to 'better themselves,' or, in other words, obtain higher wages," one commentator noted. "I believe nothing will bind them but dollars and cents," wrote Elizabeth Sullivan Stuart of her Irish servants.

Most Irish immigrant women had not grown up in households that provided them with useful experience in housework. The very terminology of household equipment was foreign to them. In 1850 Elizabeth Sullivan Stuart took on a "raw" Irish girl who had arrived in Detroit only four days before and who "did not understand the name of an article in the house." Dr. D. W. Cahill explained the situation in a letter to the *Metropolitan Record* in 1860: "Being the daughters of laborers, or needy tradesmen, or persecuted, rack-rented cotters, they are ignorant of the common duties of servants in respectable positions. They can neither wash nor iron clothes. They don't understand the cleaning of glass or silverplate. They cannot make fires expeditiously, or dust carpets, or polish the furniture. Many of them never saw a leg of mutton boiled or roasted. Several of them cannot even prepare their own dinner bacon or pork." Another writer pictured Bridget as wreaking household havoc in a thousand ways, washing her feet in the soup tureen and stirring the fire with the silver gravy ladle.

Such ignorance was more troublesome than it would have been for women accustomed to hiring help. Training a girl was a major disruption for a woman who did not regularly spend her days at housework, since she had to drop her other concerns and descend to the kitchen. Elizabeth Sullivan Stuart explained her method with her raw Irish girl: "By being with her (and I give up the whole of my time to her) I have a servant, and . . . if I succeed in breaking her in, in a little while I shall have some time to *myself*." A writer in *Lippincott's* in 1879 pictured her sacrifices: "Never a pleasant party could I join, because of my pupil—no friendly visitor receive with prompt welcome, because I was a captive below with Biddy. I am to hear the merry voices of my dear ones in the distance and cannot mingle my own with theirs." Caroline Barrett White noted the difficult days she passed instructing new domestics, when the calls and rides of ordinary times had to be suspended. She called it a *tough business.* Once she wrote that the day held "nothing pleasant while *testing* new domestics—except the evening with Frank." Of course women who did not regularly spend the whole of their days at housework were apt to make poor instructors, either from outright ignorance of the work or of realistic work standards, or simply from a desire to get the girl "broken in" as quickly as possible.

Even the charge that immigrant women were "unwashed" may have contained a grain of truth. Certainly the conditions on immigrant ships may have resulted in just such a state among the newly arrived. More to the point, immigrant women probably brought with them standards of cleanliness that were unacceptable to their employers. Individuals raised in dirt-floored cottages might not have found it easy to adopt standards appropriate for Brussels carpets. Elizabeth Sullivan Stuart, admittedly a martinet on these matters, claimed she had encountered one servant who ordinarily kept her hands so greasy that she found it difficult to turn a doorknob.

The editors of *Harper's* failed to mention one other drawback of hiring Irish immigrant domestics, probably because it seemed so obvious. For many employers, Irish girls made less satisfactory servants because of their religion. Increasing religious differences converted a potential source of reconciliation into grounds for profound conflict between servant and employer. This had been true even when the differences were those between Protestant denominations or between evangelicals and nonevangelicals. In 1837 William Ellery Channing, the Boston Unitarian minister, addressed a letter to the editor of an evangelical newspaper to complain of the objectionable aspects of evangelical religion, including the irregular habits spawned by religious enthusiasm among Boston domestics. "In this city," he wrote, "I have heard complaints of your female members, who are domestics in families, as neglecting the duties and the interests of their employers in their anxiety to attend church meetings." Rather than provoking disagreement, Channing felt, religion should bind servant and employer together with Christian love, "a holier tie than self-interest." While common religious beliefs could provide a salve for the frictions of self-interest, a spirit of denominational competition between servant and employer might prove all the more sharp-edged because honed in the close knowledge each party had of the other's daily lapses in spiritual life. Susan Huntington, a prominent member of the Episcopal church and its benevolent organizations in Boston, found this to be so. On

August 20, 1812, she wrote, "One of my domestics treated me in an unbecoming manner, and when I expostulated with her, only continued to justify herself and persist in her rudeness. This circumstance led me to realize, how infinitely important it is that I should ever tread in the precise path of duty, and never turn to the right hand or to the left, lest it should bring a reproach on religion." In hiring Catholic domestics, employers confronted an increasingly heterogeneous society, one in which threatening foreigners could not even be excluded from "sacred" home circles. Some employers simply made servant girls the butt of their nativist hatreds. Mary Grey Duncan asked, "Is Popery having no influence, when, in accordance with its usual treachery, it insinuates female Jesuits—lay sisters—now into this family now into that, in the guise of domestics, to learn family secrets and discover vulnerable characters?" Fretting about Popish treachery when domestics attended mass, employers worried about irreligion when they did not. No wonder some Irish Catholics found it useful to claim they were Protestants in order to be hired.

The idea that Catholic domestics had been dispatched to spy for the Pope was urged in tracts such as *The Female Jesuit, or, The Spy in the Family* (New York, 1851). "Wherever Catholic domestics are, the views of the family are known to the priest or confessor," declared one nativist editorial. When in 1855 a rumor swept over New England that Irish servants had been instructed to poison the food of their Protestant employers, many domestics lost their places. Even employers who could resist these sensational claims found some reasons to entertain suspicions, especially since servants so often cared for their children. The readers of *The Mother's Magazine and Family Monitor* learned that William Hogan, ex-priest and author of lurid anti-Catholic propaganda, had declared that priests routinely encouraged Catholic servants to carry the small children of the family to them for secret baptism. Hannah Wright Gould of Hudson, New York was no fool, but she allowed such suspicions to cross her mind. In November 1851 she went out to attend a funeral, leaving her infant daughter Lizzie with her Irish nursemaid. Mrs. Gould sat in the Catholic church waiting for the service to begin.

I was wondering if Lizzie was hungry and how long it would be ere the corpse came, when from the other end of the Church where the font is I heard a baby's cry the perfect echo of Lizzie's and Mr. Lamson's voice repeating "renounce the Devil and all his works, all the pomps and vanities of this wicked world?" Then the responses but above loud and clear rose a cry as if Lizzie's own—a staunch denial of the promises given. . . . I was really fidgety—what if it should be Lizzie thought I—what if Winny in her holy Catholic zeal had run down while I was away with Lizzie to the font—that her fond Irish heart may henceforth hope the blessings of the Almighty are with the child.

Mrs. Gould strained her neck in vain, finally relaxing only when the child's screams became too furious to be Lizzie's.

Fears like this led many employers to stipulate "No Irish" when they advertised for domestics. A typical ad declared, "Wanted—at 95 Montgomery Street, A GIRL, to take care of children and do plain sewing. None but Protestants need apply." "Irish" and "Catholic" seemed to be synonymous in common usage.

While the existence of secret baptisms remains questionable, perhaps mothers did have some reason for caution. The Nun of Kenmare in her *Advice to Irish Girls* counseled those who had charge of children to teach them to say "Jesus and Mary" and "short prayers." She held out the hope that Catholic servant girls could convert the Protestant families for whom they worked by their exemplary piety. "I have heard of several families who have been converted to the Catholic faith by the good example of their servants, and the good explanation which they gave of their religion." Mothers who found their children reciting a "Hail Mary" might well prefer Protestant servants.

Fear could be tempered by competition. The editors of one Protestant missionary magazine prodded their readers with the story of "Bridget's Comment." Bridget, a domestic employed by an officer of the denominational foreign missionary board, scoffed at the small sum of money raised by the board: in the same period of time she and her fellow servants had contributed more than twice as much to clear the Catholic church debt. "Give me the Catholics yet!" she was supposed to have exclaimed.

Some advice to employers suggested that they make the best of religious differences by considering their servants as handy objects for missionary work. Such a suggestion was logical enough: the foreign missionary crusade had become a popular preoccupation among middle-class Protestant women, who supported large missionary organizations and read a vast amount of evangelical literature that routinely focused upon the plight of "heathen" women. Yet missionary hopes, like those suggested by the Nun of Kenmare for servants, could only have exacerbated the friction in employer-domestic relations, for Irish Catholics were well accustomed to withstanding efforts to convert them. The advice-givers who urged missionary efforts among servants could seldom cite examples of success. The sensation surrounding the supposed "abduction" of Hannah Corcoran probably testifies to the rareness of her case as well as to nativist fears. Elizabeth Sullivan Stuart, who may have been especially vehement on the subject because her family was, although Irish, staunchly Protestant, assessed the limitations of a missionary policy toward servants in a letter to her daughter. "I think with you that 'Protestant Mistresses have a work to do among the Catholics,' but who is sufficient for these things? Our holiest, wisest Missionaries say tis easier to go to the Heathen than to the Catholics." If, as Ray Allen Billington asserted, "The women of America embraced the No-

Popery cause with more enthusiasm than the men," this may in part account for the sense, prevalent by mid-century, that the servant was not merely a stranger but an alien and threatening stranger.

Blaming the Irish "Biddy" for servant problems reflected her exemplification of the characteristic shortcomings of domestics, for she was forthrightly oriented to cash, and strange not just personally but culturally. In fact the servant problem arose not from Biddy's ethnicity but from a new kind of relationship between employer and employee. Blaming "Biddy" acknowledged the change in patterns of service but obscured many of the determinants of change.

Suggested Readings

Two excellent studies of domestic service in America are David Katzman, *Seven Days a Week: Women and Domestic Service in Industrializing America* (New York: Oxford University Press, 1978), and Daniel E. Sutherland, *Americans and Their Servants: Domestic Service in the United States from 1800 to 1920* (Baton Rouge: Louisiana State University Press, 1981). Irish immigration to the United States is discussed in Carl F. Wittke, *The Irish in America* (Baton Rouge: Louisiana State University Press, 1956).

Quinine and the European Conquest of Africa

Daniel R. Headrick

    The American historian Walter Prescott Webb claimed that the settlement of America's Great Plains was made possible by three essential technological innovations: the six-shooter, the windmill, and barbed wire. Certainly, appropriate technologies are necessary to the penetration of inhospitable territories, and in this reading Daniel R. Headrick points out that Africa was inhospitable in the extreme to white men. Although the Portuguese had established footholds along the African coast in the late 1400s, it was not until the mid-1800s that Europeans were able to penetrate the interior effectively. The Europeans' great enemy was not terrain, climate, or hostile tribes, but the microorganism that carried the deadly African strain of malaria.

    Headrick discusses the attempts in the early eighteenth century to extend European control inland and upriver, and he notes the appalling death toll among the white explorers, who lacked any immunity to the disease. Although the effectiveness of quinine against malaria was already known in the 1830s, the drug was not put into regular use in West Africa for another 25 years. Once the great powers regularized the use of quinine, however, they were able to ascend the great rivers of Africa by steamship and begin the subjugation of the continent and its native peoples. Headrick's article serves to remind us that technology is not always mechanical; biological innovations have also played a great role in shaping world history.

By the time Columbus first sighted the Americas, the Portuguese were well acquainted with the west coast of Africa, for they had been exploring it for sixty years. Yet, during the next three and a half centuries, Africa remained in the eyes of Europeans the "dark continent," its interior a blank on their maps, as they chose instead to explore, conquer, and settle parts of the Americas, Asia, and Australia.

How can we explain this paradox? For one thing, there was little motivation for Europeans to penetrate Africa before the nineteenth century. The slave traders—Africans and Europeans alike—who met along the coasts to conduct their business wanted no outsiders with prying eyes disrupting their operations. Furthermore, despite legends of fabulous wealth, there was little concrete evidence that the profits to be derived from the penetration of Africa would even approximate those resulting from the slave trade or from trade with Asia and the Americas. Thus, the penetration of Africa that occurred in the nineteenth century was tied closely to missionary and abolitionist movements reacting against the slave trade.

But even more significantly, the means of penetration were also lacking. Much of Africa is a plateau. Rivers cascade from the highlands to the sea in a series of cataracts. The coasts are lined with mangrove swamps and sandbars. And throughout the tropical regions, pack animals could not survive the nagana or animal trypanosomiasis. Those who wished to enter Africa would have to do so on foot or in dugout canoes.

These deterrents were by no means absolute prohibitions. After all, Europeans had explored the Americas with primitive means of transportation, despite difficult climates and topographies. It was disease that kept Europeans out of the interior of Africa. Although steamboats came to Africa and Asia at the same time, in Asia they wrought a revolution in the power of Europeans, whereas in Africa their effect was postponed for several decades. Before Europeans could break into the African interior successfully, they required another technological advance, a triumph over disease.

In his novel *War of the Worlds,* H. G. Wells described a group of extraterrestrial creatures who invade the earth in strange futuristic vehicles. As they are about to take over the globe, they are decimated by invisible microbes and are forced to flee. Wells could just as well have been writing about the various European attempts to penetrate Africa before the middle of the nineteenth century. In 1485 the Portuguese captain Diogo Cão sent a party of men to explore the Congo River; within a few days so many had died that the mission had to be called off. In 1569, Francisco Barreto led an expedition up the Zambezi valley

INDUSTRIALISM
AND
DEMOCRACY

226

QUININE AND THE EUROPEAN CONQUEST OF AFRICA   From Daniel R. Headrick, *The Tools of Empire: Technology and European Imperialism in the Nineteenth Century* (New York: Oxford University Press, 1981), pp. 58–76.

to establish contact with the kingdom of Monomotapa; 120 miles upriver, the horses and cattle fell victim to trypanosomiasis and the men succumbed to malaria. Henceforth until 1835, Portuguese communications with the Zambezi interior were carried on through African or part-African agents.

Similarly, in 1777–79, during William Bolts' expedition at Delagoa Bay, 132 out of 152 Europeans on the journey died. Mungo Park's 1805 venture to the upper Niger resulted in the death of all the Europeans present. In 1816–17, Captain James Tuckey led an exploring party up the Congo River, in which 19 out of 54 Europeans perished.

These setbacks in no way curtailed European attempts to explore Africa. Each generation spawned a fresh crop of adventurers willing to risk their lives to investigate the unknown continent. With the nineteenth century appeared new motives to do so: a revival of the Christian proselytizing spirit, the abolition of the Atlantic slave trade and a curiosity elevated to the rank of scientific research and funded by a newly wealthy bourgeoisie. Among the enterprising explorers of this era was Macgregor Laird, the younger son of the shipbuilder William Laird, who was to play a pioneering role in opening up Nigeria to British influence. In the early 1830s, his father's firm had just begun to build iron steamboats. Macgregor Laird, then twenty-three years of age, was not content to remain the junior partner in a struggling new business. He was imbued with that restless spirit—part missionary fervor, part scientific curiosity, part commercial hope—which inspired so many nineteenth-century Britons to venture out and remake the world. In 1832 he saw opportunity beckon along the Niger River. Three decades earlier Mungo Park had explored the upper reaches of this river down to the Bussa Rapids. Then in 1830 the brothers Richard and John Lander traveled north from Lagos to the rapids and sailed downriver in a canoe, thus proving that the Niger and the Oil rivers, which flowed into the Bight of Benin through a mangrove swamp, were one and the same. When the Landers returned to England with the tale of their discovery, Laird realized that a boat capable of sailing up the river with a cargo of trade goods—in other words, a steamer—would open up an immense part of Africa to the commerce and influence of Great Britain. To do so, he later wrote, would please

> . . . those who look upon the opening of Central Africa to the enterprise and capital of British merchants as likely to create new and extensive markets for our manufactured goods, and fresh sources whence to draw our supplies; and those who, viewing mankind as one great family, consider it their duty to raise their fellow creatures from their present degraded, denationalized, and demoralized state, nearer to Him in whose image they were created.

In 1832, therefore, Macgregor Laird and several Liverpool merchants founded the African Inland Commercial Company "for the commercial development of the recent discoveries of the brothers Lander on the River Niger." The directors sought a charter and a subsidy from the treasury but were refused. They went ahead with their venture anyway and hired Richard Lander to lead their expedition. They bought the brig *Columbine* as a storeship and ordered two steamers in which to ascend the Niger. The larger of the two, the *Quorra,* was built of wood by Seddon and Langley. She measured 112 by 16 feet, drew 7 feet at sea and 5½ feet on the river; she was powered by a 40-horse-power engine and carried a 26-man crew. Macgregor Laird himself built the smaller one, the *Alburkah.* She was 70 feet long by 13 feet wide with a draft of 4 feet 9 inches. Except for the deck, she was made entirely of iron. She had a 15-horsepower Fawcett and Preston engine and carried a crew of 14. Both boats were heavily armed. In addition to handguns, the *Quorra* had a 24-pound swivel gun, eight 4-pound carriage guns, and an 18-pound carronade. The *Alburkah* carried a 9-pounder and six 1-pounder swivel guns.

Under Laird's command, the little fleet reached the Niger delta without incident. Leaving the *Columbine* in the Bight of Benin, the steamers then went upriver, past the trading towns of the delta to the confluence of the Niger and the Benue. There Laird hoped to found a trading post and to buy palm oil at low prices.

Laird's steamers succeeded admirably in their assigned task, and for this Laird deserves his reputation as an innovator and an explorer. As a cultural and commercial mission, however, the expedition was a failure and his expectations were shattered. Of the forty-eight Europeans present on the trip, only nine returned, the rest having died of disease. Laird himself returned ill to England in January 1834 and never quite recovered his health. Despite the power of steam, the African environment had once again defeated the European attempt at penetration.

Though very few Europeans ventured into the interior of Africa before the mid-nineteenth century, a substantial number had for centuries been trading along the coasts. After 1807, in an attempt to end the slave trade, the British government stationed a fleet along the West African coast to intercept slaving ships. Small army units were also placed at intervals along the shores to lend weight to the abolition campaign. Here and there the first Christian missions were founded. These various groups of whites were subject to the diseases prevailing in the region.

We know much more about the death rates among British military personnel in West Africa than among the slave traders, their predecessors, for this was the time when the keeping of statistical records became a vital part of Western culture. The Royal African Corps, stationed from the Gambia to the Gold Coast, was composed of military criminals and offenders allowed to exchange their sentences for service in Africa. In most cases this meant substituting death for prison. In 1840 the *United Service Journal and Naval and Military Magazine* devoted an article to the health of these troops. It gave the following figures. Of the 1,843 European soldiers who served in Sierra Leone between 1819 and 1836, 890, or 48.3 percent, died. The worst year was 1825, in which 447 out of 571 (78.3 percent) succumbed to disease. Despite a constant influx of European arrivals, the size of the garrison declined by over a hundred each year. The Gold Coast was just as deadly: Two-thirds of the Europeans who landed there in the years 1823–27 never lived to return home; in the year 1824 alone, 221 out of 224 lost their lives. On the whole, 77 percent of the white soldiers sent to West Africa perished, 21 percent became invalids, and only 2 percent were ultimately found fit for future service.

Among West Indian soldiers stationed in the same region, the death rate was only one tenth that for whites, though still twice that prevailing in their native lands. During the 1825–26 epidemic in the Gambia which killed 276 out of 399 whites, only one out of 40 or 50 West Indians fell victim to the illness. It is likely that the epidemic in question was yellow fever, a disease endemic to the West Indies against which many West Indians had developed a resistance. In 1830 the British government recognized the significance of the death rates and stopped sending white troops to West Africa, except for half a dozen sergeants to command the West Indian soldiers.

The authors of the article, of course, did not understand the exact causes of this horrendous situation. At least they did not blame the men themselves, for they noted that robust, teetotalling English missionaries living on the same coast were as likely to suffer the effects of the disease; of 89 who went to West Africa between 1804 and 1825, 54 died and another 14 returned in bad health. Nor was the climate to blame, for dry and windy stations were as dangerous as those adjoining fetid marshes. The cause of the problem, they concluded, was fevers, either yellow or remittent. A scientific approach was beginning to replace the moralistic judgments of former times.

Philip Curtin, in his writings on the question, gives equally appalling death rates. Among British military personnel recruited in the United Kingdom who served during the years 1817 to 1836, the death rates per thousand were:

on the eastern frontier of South Africa (1817–36)	12.0
in the United Kingdom (1830–36)	15.3
in Tenasserim, Burma (1827–36)	44.7
in Ceylon (1817–36)	75.0
in Sierra Leone (1817–36) (deaths from diseases only)	483.0
in Cape Coast Command, Gold Coast (1817–36)	668.3

Among Europeans serving with the African Squadron of the Royal Navy off the coast of West Africa, the death rate in 1825–45 was 65 per thousand; among British troops in West Africa in 1819–36 it was 483 per thousand for enlisted men and 209 for officers. Meanwhile, West African soldiers serving in the British army in the same area suffered a death rate of only 2.5 per thousand. It is for this reason that Africa became known as the "white man's grave."

Though dysentery, yellow fever, typhoid, and other ills contributed to the high death rates, the principal killer of Europeans in Africa was malaria. Throughout history malaria has probably caused more human deaths than any other disease. It exists in several varieties. Tertian malaria, endemic throughout much of the world, is caused by the protozoan *Plasmodium vivax* and produces intermittent fevers and a general weakening of the body. Another variety, brought on by the *Plasmodium falciparum,* is endemic only to tropical Africa and is far deadlier. It is found not only in swamplands and rainforests, but also in the drier savannas. The body's resistance, gained from a successful bout with the disease, is temporary at best, and many Africans suffer repeated low-level attacks throughout their lives. To adult newcomers to Africa, who have not had the opportunity to build up a resistance, the disease is most often fatal.

Early nineteenth-century European medical opinion, influenced by the age-old association of malaria with swamps, blamed humid air and putrid smells for the disease; hence the French word *paludisme* (from the Latin word for swamp) and the Italian *mal'aria,* or bad air. The strangest theory of all was put forth by Macgregor Laird. In trying to explain the epidemic that had decimated his Niger expedition, he wrote Thomas Peacock in 1837:

> Captain Grant mentioned the possibility of getting firewood at Fernando Po, nothing can be more injurious both to the Vessel and the Crew . . . to the Crew, as the miasmatic exhalations from it will infallibly produce fever and disease. I have had melancholy experience of the effects of wood taken on board & used as Firewood for the Engines on the Coast of Africa.

Not until 1880 did a French scientist, Alphonse Laveran, discover the *Plasmodium* that invades the bloodstream; and only in 1897 was the vector of malaria, the *Anopheles* mosquito, identified by the British physician Ronald Ross and the Italian scientists Giovanni Batista Grassi and Amico Bignami.

That the cause of malaria was not known to science until the end of the century did not prevent a remedy from emerging much earlier out of a long process of trial and error. Before our own century, technological advances often preceded a scientific explanation of the underlying natural phenomena; technological advances arising out of scientific discoveries were the exception. We should not think of technology as "applied science" before the end of the nineteenth century, but rather of science as "theoretical technology."

For centuries, people had sought relief from the dreaded disease. In the seventeenth century, Jesuits had introduced the bark of the cinchona tree as a cure for *vivax* malaria and disseminated it in Europe. Cinchona bark, though effective, had a number of drawbacks. Because it came from trees that grew only in the Andes, the supply in Europe was often limited. Making matters worse, what did reach the consumers was not only expensive but often adulterated or deteriorated. Moreover, its Jesuit connection made it suspect among Protestants; Oliver Cromwell, dying of malaria, is said to have refused the "popish" remedy. It also was useless against yellow fever and a number of other fevers that were then confused in medical theory. And finally, it had an awful taste.

Yet up through the eighteenth century, medical authorities regularly prescribed the bark. By the turn of the following century, though, physicians favored treating fevers with doses of mercury for salivation and calomel for its purgative qualities. Frequent bleedings and blisters were other common treatments. These "remedies" undoubtedly killed more patients than they saved and must have contributed to the extraordinary death rates among British military personnel in West Africa.

The dawn of a breakthrough in treating malaria dates from the year 1820, when two French chemists, Pierre Joseph Pelletier and Joseph Bienaimé Caventou, succeeded in extracting the alkaloid of quinine from cinchona bark. Commercial production of quinine began in 1827, and by 1830 the drug was being manufactured in large enough quantities for general use.

From the late 1820s on, doctors in malarial areas conducted experiments with quinine and published the results of their investigations. The first important experiments were carried out in Algeria, following the French invasion of 1830. Serious health problems plagued the French troops stationed there, with typhoid and cholera outbreaks common occurrences. The most severe problem, however, was malaria. Bône, which was surrounded by swamps, had the highest incidence of disease in Algeria, and epidemics broke out every summer. In 1832, of the 2,788 French soldiers stationed in that town, 1,626 were hospitalized. The next year, 4,000 out of 5,500 were similarly affected, and out of every 7 hospitalized soldiers, 2 died. The cause of these deaths was not disease alone, but also the treatment the patients received. French army doctors at the time were influenced by Dr. J. Broussais, head of the army medical school of Val-de-Grâce, who taught that fevers should be treated with purgatives, bleedings, leeches, and a starvation diet.

Quinine, he believed, should be administered in tiny doses only after the seventh or eighth attack; among other reasons, the new drug was too expensive, at twenty-five francs an ounce, for military use.

Two army physicians, Jean André Antonini and François Clément Maillot, rebelled against the accepted practices of their colleagues. Antonini noted that intermittent fevers responded to quinine, and this permitted him to distinguish malaria from typhoid fever. He moderated the bleedings and gave his patients more food. Maillot, posted to Bône at the height of the malaria epidemic of 1834, went further. At the first sign of fever, he prescribed twenty-four to forty grains of quinine immediately, instead of four to eight several days later as Broussais had taught. He also fed his patients a nutritious diet. The results were most impressive. Only one out of every twenty patients died, compared to two out of seven the year before. Consequently, sick soldiers began fleeing other hospitals to come to Maillot's. In 1835 he described his methods to the Académie de Médecine in Paris, and a year later he published his findings under the title *Traité des fièvres ou irritations cérébro-spinales intermittentes.* Yet it was many years before his methods were accepted by the French military medical service. Finally, toward the end of his life, Maillot was idolized as a hero of French science, and in 1881 the Scientific Congress of Algiers honored him with the phrase: "It is thanks to Maillot that Algeria has become a French land; it is he who closed and sealed forever this tomb of Christians."

In West Africa, too, the use of quinine became more common, while purgings and bleedings gradually fell into disfavor. By the mid-1840s, Europeans in the Gold Coast regularly kept a jar of quinine pills by their bedside, to be taken at the first sign of chills or fever. Yet this treatment, although beneficial against the *vivax* form of malaria prevalent in Algeria, was generally insufficient against *falciparum* malaria. To defeat the *Plasmodium falciparum,* the human bloodstream had to be saturated with quinine before the onset of the first infection; in other words, throughout one's stay in *falciparum* areas, quinine had to be taken regularly as a prophylactic.

Two chance events led to this discovery. The first occurred in 1839, on board the *North Star* stationed off Sierra Leone. While serving on the ship, twenty crew members took cinchona bark daily and one officer did not; he alone died of malaria. The second incident took place two years later, when the British government sponsored the largest of all the Niger expeditions up to that time. With three new steamers—the 457-ton *Albert* and *Wilberforce* and the 249-ton *Soudan*—Capt. H. D. Trotter led 159 Europeans up the Niger to the confluence of the Benue. To avoid the health problems of previous missions every known precaution was taken. The crew was specially selected from among athletic young men of good breeding, the ships were equipped with fans to dispel bad air, and the expedition raced at top speed through the miasmic delta to reach the drier climate of the upper river as soon as possible. Nonetheless the first cases of fever appeared within three weeks, forcing the *Wilberforce* and the *Soudan* to return to the Atlantic as floating hospitals. Within two months, forty-eight of the Europeans had died, and by the end of the expedition another seven fell victim to the disease. Africa had regained its terrible reputation among the British.

Despite this disappointment, the Niger expedition of 1841 represents a major step toward a solution to the problem of malaria, for the physician on board one of the ships, Dr. T. R. H. Thomson, used the opportunity to experiment with various drugs. Some crew members received cinchona bark with wine, others got quinine; Dr. Thomson himself took quinine regularly and stayed healthy. He later wrote his observations on the matter in an article entitled "On the Value of Quinine in African Remittent Fever" which appeared in the British medical journal *The Lancet* on February 28, 1846. A year later, Dr. Alexander Bryson, an experienced naval physician, published his *Report on the Climate and Principal Diseases of the African Station* (London, 1847), in which he advocated quinine prophylaxis to Europeans in Africa. In 1848 the director-general of the Medical Department of the British Army sent a circular to all British governors in West Africa, recommending quinine prophylaxis.

Yet quinine prophylaxis was not immediately adopted. It took a spectacular demonstration to achieve this end. In 1854, Macgregor Laird, never cured of his fascination with Africa, proposed still another expedition to that continent. Under contract with the Admiralty, he had a ship called the *Pleiad* specially built. She was a 220-ton iron propeller-steamer rigged as a schooner, designed to pull two or three barges behind her on her way up the Niger. As was usually the case, she was armed with a 12-pounder pivot gun, four smaller swivel cannons, rifles, and muskets. The crew consisted of twelve Europeans and fifty-four Africans.

Before the ship sailed, Dr. Alexander Bryson wrote a set of instructions in which he described the clothing, diet, activities, and moral influences best suited to protect the health of the crew. To prevent fevers he recommended that each crew member take six to eight grains of quinine a day from the time the ship crossed the bar until fourteen days after she returned to the ocean. The captain of the ship, Dr. William Baikie, was himself a physician and saw to it that the crew followed this advice. The *Pleiad* stayed 112 days on the Niger and Benue rivers, and returned with all the European crew members alive. Thomas Hutchinson, a member of the expedition, attributed this to Dr. Bryson's suggestions; as he put it,

> Since my first visit to Africa in 1850, I have felt firmly convinced—
> and that conviction urges me to impress my faith on all who read
> this work—that the climate would not be so fatal as it has hitherto

QUININE AND THE CONQUEST OF AFRICA

233

proved to Europeans, if a different mode of daily living, a proper method of prophylactic hygiene, and another line of therapeutic practice in the treatment of fevers, were adopted. Before, and beyond all others, is the preventive influence of quinine as it was used in the "Pleiad," in the mode here described. . . .

As the prophylactic use of quinine spread, and as purgings and bleedings vanished, the death rates fell significantly. Philip Curtin gives some statistics: In the Royal Navy's Africa Squadron, the mortality rate fell from 65 per 1,000 in 1825–45 to 22 per 1,000 in 1858–67; in 1874, during the two-month military expedition against Kumasi, only 50 of the 2,500 European soldiers died of disease; in 1881–97, among British officials in the Gold Coast, the rate was 76 per 1,000, and in Lagos it was 53 per 1,000. On the whole, the first-year death rates among Europeans in West Africa dropped from 250–750 per 1,000 to 50–100 per 1,000. To be sure, this was still five to ten times higher than the death rates for people in the same age bracket in Europe. Africa remained hostile to the health of Europeans. Yet psychologically the improvement was significant. No longer was tropical Africa the "white man's grave," fit for only the most ardent visionaries and the unluckiest recruits. It was now a place from which Europeans could reasonably hope to return alive. In Curtin's words, ". . . the improvement over the recent past was understood well enough in official and missionary circles to reduce sharply the most serious impediment to any African activity."

One immediate consequence of quinine prophylaxis was a great increase in the number and success of European explorers in Africa after the mid-century. Exploration, of course, remained a dangerous business, but no longer was it quasi-suicidal. With the prospect before them of fruitful discoveries, perhaps even glory and wealth, many more adventurous souls volunteered in the service of knowledge. David Livingstone, the most lionized of all the explorers, first heard of quinine prophylaxis while he was in Bechuanaland in 1843. During his march across southern Africa in 1850–56 he took quinine daily. By 1857 he was convinced that quinine was a preventive. In preparation for his Zambezi expedition of 1858 he made his European crew take two grains of quinine in sherry every day. Throughout the expedition, many suffered from malaria, but only three out of twenty-five died. Later he came to doubt the efficacy of quinine as a preventive, for it only lessened the impact of the disease. His favorite remedy for malaria was a concoction of quinine, calomel, rhubarb, and resin of julep which he called "Livingstone Pills."

In the footsteps of the explorers, lesser protagonists of European imperialism penetrated the African interior: missionaries, soldiers, traders, administrators, engineers, planters and their wives and children, and finally tourists. All of them needed their daily quinine. In India and other tropical areas, the influx of Europeans added to the growing demand for the drug.

Until the 1850s all the world's cinchona bark came from the forests of Peru, Bolivia, Ecuador, and Colombia, where the trees grew wild. As world demand increased, the bark exports of the Andean republics rose from two million pounds in 1860 to twenty million in 1881. At that point the Andean bark was swept from the world market by the competition of Indian and Indonesian bark, the result of deliberate efforts by Dutch and British interests.

The idea of growing cinchona in Asia had been discussed many times, but with little effect as long as demand was small. In the early 1850s, as demand grew, Dutch botanists and horticulturists in Java urged the Netherlands East Indies government to import cinchona seedlings. In 1853–54, Justus Charles Hasskarl, superintendent of the Buitenzorg Botanical Gardens in Java, traveled to the Andes under an assumed name and secretly collected seeds; most of them perished, however. In 1858–60, Clements Markham, a clerk at the India Office, aided by a gardener from the British Royal Botanic Gardens at Kew named Weir, traveled to Bolivia and Peru, again secretly, to collect seeds of the *Cinchona calisaya* tree. Simultaneously, the English botanist Richard Spruce and another Kew gardener, Robert Cross, collected 100,000 *C. succirubra* seeds and 637 young plants in Ecuador; of these, 463 seedlings reached India, forming the nucleus of the cinchona plantations at Ootacamund in the Nilgiri Hills near Madras.

There followed a period of intensive experimentation. At botanical gardens in Bengal, Ceylon, Madras, and Java, horticulturists and quinologists exchanged seeds and information, and provided cheap seedlings and free advice to planters. A hybrid species, *C. calisaya Ledgeriana,* grafted onto the stem of a *C. succirubra* tree, formed the basis of the Javanese cinchona plantations after 1874. Techniques such as mossing (cutting strips of bark and wrapping the trees in moss) and coppicing (cutting trees to the ground every six or seven years) greatly increased the yield of alkaloids. While Peruvian bark had a two percent sulphate of quinine content, scientific breeding in Java raised the content to six percent by 1900, and later to eight or nine percent.

In the late nineteenth century, after the demise of the Andean bark industry, a compromise was worked out between the British and the Dutch. Plantations in India produced a cheaper, less potent bark from which chemists extracted totaquine, a mixture of antimalarial alkaloids. Almost the entire Indian production was destined to British military and administrative personnel in the tropics, and the excess was sold in India. The Javanese industry, which produced the more potent and expensive pure quinine, captured over nine tenths of the world market by the early twentieth century. This world monopoly of cinchona resulted not only from scientific methods of cultivation, but also from a marketing cartel, the Kina Bureau of Amsterdam, which coordinated the purchase of bark and the price and quantity of quinine sold. Not until the Japanese conquest of Indonesia in World War Two and the development of synthetic malaria suppressants did this Dutch control over one of the world's most vital drugs come to an end.

Scientific cinchona production was an imperial technology par excellence. Without it European colonialism would have been almost impossible in Africa, and much costlier elsewhere in the tropics. At the same time, the development of this technology, combining the scientific expertise of several botanical gardens, the encouragement of the British and Dutch colonial governments, and the land and labor of the peoples of India and Indonesia, was clearly a consequence as well as a cause of the new imperialism.

River steamers had overcome the obstacle of poor transportation, and quinine that of malaria. Together, they opened much of Africa to colonialism, that is, to the systematic intercourse with Europe on European terms. The scramble for Africa has often been explained as a consequence of French political psychology after the Franco-Prussian War, or of the ambitions of King Leopold II of Belgium, or as a by-product of the Suez Canal. No doubt. But it was also the result of the combination of steamers, quinine prophylaxis, and, as we shall see, the quick-firing rifle. From among the myriad events of the scramble, let us consider only a few that illustrate the arrival of steamers on the rivers of Africa, their European crews now protected from a certain death by quinine prophylaxis.

Macgregor Laird had not sent expeditions up the Niger River out of curiosity or philanthropy alone. They were, in his eyes, investments that must surely pay off, for the Niger trade was both lucrative and necessary to Britain. Palm oil, which had replaced slaves as the principal export of southern Nigeria, was essential as the raw material for soap and as a lubricant for industrial machinery. But the price of palm oil was kept unreasonably high by the Niger delta middlemen who brought it to the coast, and by the small European traders who shipped it to Europe. The instrument that would break through these bottle-necks, Laird believed, was the steam engine. In 1851 he wrote Earl Grey that steam "will convert a most uncertain and precarious trade into a regular and steady one, diminish the risk of life, and free a large portion of the capital at present engaged in it. . . ."

What was needed was a double application of steam. One was to be a steamship line between Britain and West Africa. . . . The other was a regular steamboat service along the Niger in order to bypass the Nigerian middlemen. Laird's first appeals were rejected. After the *Pleiad* expedition in 1854 had vindicated his faith, however, the Royal Geographical Society convinced the British government to support his projects. In 1857 the Foreign Office agreed to send Dr. Baikie to open relations with the Caliphate of Sokoto on the middle Niger. The Admiralty contracted with Laird to send three steamers up the Niger annually for five years.

The *Dayspring,* the *Rainbow,* and the *Sunbeam* were built by John Laird's Birkenhead shipyard for this service. In the course of their voyages they naturally aroused the resentment of the delta traders whose business they were ruining. In 1859, after traders attacked the *Rainbow* and killed two of her crew members, Laird appealed to the government for a warship to accompany his steamers. Two years later H.M.S. *Espoir* entered the Niger and destroyed the villages that had been responsible for the assault on the *Rainbow.* By the 1870s several British companies were trading on the Niger with armed steamers, and every year a military expedition steamed up the river to destroy any towns that resisted the British intrusion. By the 1880s, Sir George Goldie's United African Company, uniting all the trading interests in the area, kept a fleet of light gunboats patrolling the river year round. In 1885 the British government declared the Niger delta a protectorate. Despite sporadic resistance, no African town along the rivers and no war-canoe could withstand for long the power of British gunboats.

The Niger River was the scene of the earliest and most active use of steamers by the invading Europeans, because it was the easiest to navigate in all of tropical Africa. The other major rivers—the Congo, the Zambezi, the upper Nile, and their tributaries—were broken by cataracts which barred access to them by seagoing steamers. Boats had to be brought in pieces, portaged around the rapids, and reassembled before they could be used to explore the upper reaches of these rivers. To portage the steamers and equipment for an entire expedition required labor, technology, organization, and financing on a scale that the Niger explorers had never faced.

Livingstone used a series of small steamers: the *Ma Roberts,* the first steel steamboat, on which he explored the Zambezi River up to the Kebrabasa Rapids in 1858; the *Pioneer,* in 1861; and the *Lady Nyassa,* which was carried in pieces around the falls to Lake Nyassa. Samuel White Baker had the steamer *Khedive* transported to the upper Nile. To open up the Congo river basin, Henry Stanley had a steamer, the nine-ton *En Avant,* carried in pieces from the Atlantic to Stanley Pool. Shortly thereafter Savorgnan de Brazza's *Ballay* also appeared on the Congo.

After that the number of steamers multiplied quickly, for exploration, conquest, trade, and missionary work. They were transported to the most remote regions of the continent. In 1895–97 the French lieutenant Gentil conquered the area of the Ubangi and Shari rivers and Lake Chad using the first aluminum steamer, the *Léon Blot.* And in 1898 on his cross-Africa expedition, Commandant Marchand had two steamers and three rowboats carried from the Ubangi to the Nile, on which he then steamed to his celebrated confrontation with Kitchener at Fashoda.

Given the harsh topography of much of Africa, and the lack of pack animals, it is doubtful whether Europeans could have penetrated so fast or dominated so thoroughly if they had had to go on foot. Regions lacking good water transportation—for example the Central Sudan, the Sahara, Ethiopia, and the Kalahari—were among the last to be colonized. The contrast between the ease of water transport and the difficulty of land transport in nineteenth-century Africa accounts in large part for the European patterns of penetration and control.

Suggested Readings

Philip D. Curtin, *The Image of Africa: British Ideas and Actions, 1780–1850* (Madison: University of Wisconsin Press, 1964), provides a good background to the British role in opening up Africa in the later nineteenth century. A good introduction to the general subject of disease in history is found in Frederick F. Cartwright, *Disease and History* (London: Hart-Davis, 1972), while malaria in particular is discussed in Paul F. Russell, *Man's Mastery of Malaria* (London: Oxford University Press, 1955). One may compare biological factors in the opening up of Africa to those encountered in the settlement of America by reading Percy M. Ashburn, *The Ranks of Death: A Medical History of the Conquest of America* (New York: Coward-McCann, 1947).

The Emergence of Team Sports: Baseball's Early Years

William J. Baker

One feature of the late nineteenth and early twentieth centuries was the phenomenal rise in popularity of team sports—not only among the participants, but, more particularly, among spectators. Many factors contributed to the development, which must be counted as one of the more dramatic social consequences of the Industrial Revolution. Increased population, more leisure time, better transportation, greater amounts of individual disposable income, technical improvements in equipment, the development of mass audiences through radio and television, and governmental support and encouragement all have played a role in the rise of sports in the Western world. The result is that sports have become a dominant passion of our time. It is a truism that a people will not allow their prejudices to interfere with the things they consider really important. It is also true that virtually the only two occupations in which race, creed, and nationality are considered irrelevant are those of scientist and athlete.

This reading selection traces the origin and development of American baseball through the nineteenth century. Americans tend to romanticize their sports, preferring to consider them as something other than primarily business ventures. William J. Baker's account proves the contrary, showing that financial considerations shaped the development of baseball from the time it first gained substantial spectator support. From that point of view, the most important single event during the period was the consolidation of control over professional baseball by the owners, rather than by clubs or the players themselves.

The French painter Eugène Delacroix captured the spirit of the nineteenth century in his romantic *Liberty Leading the People*. Liberty is a woman of goddess proportions. The People range from affluent middle class to the laboring poor, from the young to the very old. All appear confident but determined. All are militantly moving forward to claim the rights of full citizenship. They are people for whom the combined effects of industrialization and the French Revolution have broken the grip long held on European society by priests, kings, and aristocrats. For the first time ever, the masses began to concern themselves with politics, economic and social policies, education, and recreational activities of their own choosing.

In sheer numbers the ranks of common folk enlarged dramatically—from about 193 million Europeans in 1800 to 423 million by 1900. Over the course of the century the population of England and Wales alone leaped from 9 million to 32 million. The greatest numerical growth occurred during the second half of the century, when diets and sanitation improved and fewer wars claimed civilian lives. Despite even the frightful losses of the American Civil War, the population of the United States grew from 32 million in 1860 to 75 million in 1900.

Many of those new Americans were immigrants from Europe, people literally on the move seeking better lives for themselves. An average of 400,000 Europeans annually emigrated during the second half of the nineteenth century. More than half took cheap steamship passage to North America; others went mostly to South America and Australia. Yet emigration was only one aspect of the mass movement of people. Exodus from the countryside into the cities, begun early in the Industrial Revolution, accelerated. By 1900 city dwellers accounted for about three-quarters of all British citizens, more than half of the German population, and just under half of traditionally rural France. Even the United States, with a western frontier still largely unsettled, doubled its urban population within the three decades following the Civil War.

Economic opportunity was by no means the sole magnet drawing people from the countryside. Cities offered variety, excitement, and anonymity. But freedom from the restrictions of rural family and village life soon proved to be a mixed blessing. The cost of urban independence was a loss of ties that came from shared assumptions and common experience. City schools, churches, social and civic groups, and labor unions satisfied some of the need to be part of a well-defined community. Sports clubs and teams served similar functions. Sponsored

THE EMERGENCE OF TEAM SPORTS: BASEBALL'S EARLY YEARS   From William J. Baker, *Sports in the Western World* (Totowa, N.J.: Rowman and Littlefield, 1982), pp. 115–17, 138–50.

by clubs, schools, and universities, numerous new team sports became organized as antidotes to the individualistic tendencies of modern city life.

Team sports also reflected the nationalistic, patriotic tendencies of the age. Individuals found a sense of self-importance as parts of a larger whole—a nation, club, or team. As one youngster in the novel *Tom Brown's Schooldays* (1857) said of the team game of cricket, "The discipline and reliance in one another which it teaches is so valuable, I think. It ought to be an unselfish game. It merges the individual in the eleven; he doesn't play that he may win, but that his side may." Tom Brown heartily agreed: "That's very true and that's why football and cricket, now one comes to think of it, are such much better games than fives or hare and hounds, or any others where the object is to come in first or to win for oneself and not that one's side may win." Although individual sports also became highly organized in the second half of the nineteenth century, team sports peculiarly suited the temper of the times.

Moreover, team sports appealed to city spectators repelled by the brutalities of the prize ring, and bored by the lack of variety offered by footraces, boat races, and horse races. The fast, intricate movements of soccer, rugby, and American football presented a kind of coordinated complexity akin to the character of city life. Spacious cricket and baseball fields, on the other hand, evoked pleasant pastoral images reminiscent of the recent rural past. Seldom absent from the history of sports, spectators in the nineteenth century became a central feature of the sporting scene.

Most modern organized team and individual sports originated in Victorian England, just at the time when the British Empire stretched to the four corners of the earth. Sport as well as commerce followed the flag to distant places such as South Africa, India, New Zealand, and Canada. In a less orderly fashion, British industrial advisers, merchants, sailors, and tourists enthusiastically introduced their sports around the world—to Hungarians as well as Frenchmen, in Russia as well as the United States. Britain's imperial involvement in world affairs facilitated the rapid geographical spread of sports in the late nineteenth century.

In industrialized Britain and the United States, especially, several factors coalesced to encourage sports participation and spectatorship. Rising wages and a shortened workweek (half-day Saturdays at first) allowed laborers to make their way to new parks, playgrounds, and sports fields. City tram systems, first drawn by horses and later by electricity, provided transportation. Cheap train service carried both players and spectators to games in other cities. Newspapers exploited innovative print technology to publicize forthcoming events, and then they gave instant reportage by means of new telegraph and telephone systems. Editors soon discovered that more sports coverage meant higher circulation figures, particularly with the arrival of yet another nineteenth-century invention, photography. By 1900 some sportswriters were pecking away at a new contraption called a typewriter.

Technological advances also played a major role in sports equipment. Tougher iron and steel went into the making of goals for soccer, rugby and American football, ice hockey, and basketball, and for golf clubs, ice skates, bicycle frames, gymnastic equipment, spiked shoes, and face masks, not to mention the construction of sturdy stadiums. Vulcanized rubber provided resilient, air-filled balls of all shapes and sizes and pneumatic tires for bicycles and harness-racing rigs. Mechanical sewing machines turned out uniforms at a pace and low cost never before possible; new synthetic dyes added touches of color to the fabrics. Most important of all, perhaps, was the invention of the incandescent light bulb. By the mid-1880s indoor gymnasiums and sports arenas began scheduling evening prizefights, gymnastic classes, wrestling matches, and pedestrian contests under electric lights rather than by the earlier inadequate, foul-smelling gas lamps and torches. Outdoor night games lay several decades in the future, but by 1900 electric lights had revolutionized the social life of the cities. Amid all the strategic factors affecting sports in the nineteenth century, technology stood tall.

On the eve of the Civil War, cricket was the most popular of all organized team sports in the United States. English immigrants brought the game with them, especially to large cities such as Boston, New York, and Philadelphia. In 1857 twelve representatives from cricket clubs as far away as Albany and Philadelphia convened at the Astor House in New York City to form the United States Central Club, an American equivalent of the Marylebone Cricket Club in London. According to one commentator, cricket was "the leading game played out of doors" in the United States in 1858, "the favorite game of the country village and the country town, as well as the larger commercial cities." In the following year a cricket match between a visiting English team and a local team at the Elysian Fields in Hoboken, New Jersey, drew a crowd of 25,000, requiring extra ferries to carry people over from Manhattan.

Yet the enthusiasm surrounding that cricket match was misleading. Scattered throughout the American past was another, simpler kind of bat-and-ball game. A derivation of the old English games of stoolball and "old-cat," the game of rounders was traditionally played by children on a field with four stones or posts set on a square, which runners traversed clockwise. As far back as 1700, in both England and colonial America, it was sometimes known as "base," "base ball," or "goal ball." The batter was "out" when he missed three swings, hit the ball foul, had a batted ball caught before it hit the ground, or was struck by the ball while he was running the bases. Rounders was a far more active game than cricket. Batters and fielders ran more; a batter quickly relinquished his place to another; teams frequently changed from offense to defense and back again. Compared to cricket, rounders was also a relatively brief game. It was ideally suited for active children.

And for active Americans. According to diarists of the day, soldiers played "base" on 7 April 1778 at Valley Forge, and in 1786 Princeton undergraduates played "baste ball" on the campus. Throughout the Northeast, boys played on village greens while their elders attended town meetings. Not surprisingly, the name "town ball" became common. Yet the forms and rules of town ball, or base ball, varied according to local customs. By the early nineteenth century, two dominant versions had emerged. The older "Massachusetts game" featured bases (usually poles) on an oblong pattern; after the batter hit the ball, fielders scrambled to retrieve it and threw it at the runner to "plug" or "soak" him before he safely reached a base. The "New York game," on the other hand, set the bases on a square and required fielders to touch the base or runner with the ball rather than throwing it at him.

Beginning in 1842, a group of affluent merchants, professional men, and white-collar clerks began playing the New York game regularly on a vacant lot at 27th Street and Fourth Avenue in Manhattan. In 1845 a member of the group, Alexander Cartwright, suggested that they form a baseball club. Restricting their membership to forty, they charged annual dues of $5.00 each, held a banquet after each game, and levied strict fines against any ungentlemanly conduct, such as swearing, disobeying the captain, or disputing an umpire's decision. They were an elite social clique as well as a sports club. Common laborers, poor immigrants, or black Americans need not have applied for membership. America's first organized baseball team, the Knickerbockers, prided themselves on being exclusively "gentlemen."

To keep order on the field of play, Alexander Cartwright drew up a rudimentary set of rules. He set flat bases (not poles) at ninety feet apart in a diamond-shaped layout, with a pitching "box" forty-five feet from "home plate"; he limited teams to nine players, forbade throwing the ball at a runner, and designated twenty-one "aces" (runs) as the number necessary to win a game. Alexander Cartwright, not Abner Doubleday, is the "father" of American baseball. Unfortunately, the father did not stay around to see his child develop into manhood. In 1850 Cartwright left for Hawaii and never returned.

Decked out in blue woolen pantaloons, white flannel shirts, and straw hats, the Knickerbockers spawned imitators who soon began issuing challenges for games. On 19 June 1846 the Knicks played their first game against another club, the New Yorkers, to whom they curiously lost, 23–1. Baseball clubs quickly became the rage. By the mid-1850s the Knickerbockers, Gothams, Eagles, Empires, Mutuals, and Metropolitans in Manhattan, and the Excelsiors, Putnams, Eckfords, and Atlantics in Brooklyn engaged in spirited competition. By 1858 about fifty clubs regularly played in the metropolitan area of New York City, and already clubs were being formed in upper New York State, in major cities such as Cleveland, Detroit, and Chicago, and in Maryland, Delaware, and Pennsylvania.

In New England, too, baseball clubs first took shape in the 1850s. The Boston Olympics, founded in 1854, led the way, and in 1857 representatives of ten clubs met in Dedham, Massachusetts, to form the Massachusetts Association of Base Ball Players. Predictably, they agreed to compete according to the "Massachusetts rules" to which they were accustomed. The first intercollegiate baseball game, on 1 July 1859 between Amherst and Williams, was played under the Massachusetts rules; Amherst won, 73–32, in twenty-six innings. Not until after the Civil War did the New York rules become established in New England's urban centers. In rural areas, features of the Massachusetts game survived well into the twentieth century.

Organization proceeded apace in New York City. In 1858 delegates from twenty-two clubs convened to form the National Association of Base Ball Players; it elected six officers and a committee to draft a constitution. Quickly the group became national in authority as well as in name. Within its first year membership more than doubled as five new clubs from upstate New York and four from New Jersey joined. For thirteen years delegates and officers met annually to revise rules, settle disputes, and generally to govern the game of baseball.

Except for a new provision of a nine-inning game to replace the traditional twenty-one "aces," the game itself largely remained faithful to the rules established by Alexander Cartwright in 1845. Foul balls caught on the first bounce still put a man out; pitchers continued tossing the ball in a stiff-armed underhand motion; batters stilled called for their favorite high or low pitch and swung only at pitches they liked. In time, of course, all these rules and styles would be altered, largely for the purpose of crowd appeal. But from the beginning baseball was a conservative game, slow to change.

Beyond the rules and style of play, however, the founding of the National Association signaled a profound change that had already occurred. Not one of the original six officers of the National Association came from the old Knickerbocker club. The brief day of gentlemanly dominance was past. As New York and Brooklyn shipwrights, mechanics, firemen, policemen, teachers, and bartenders organized their own baseball clubs, the "Base Ball Fever" celebrated in a popular song of 1857 was a popular, democratic fever:

> Our merchants have to close their stores
> The clerks away are staying,
> Contractors too, can do no work,
> Their hands are all out playing.

Simple and inexpensive, the old English game of rounders lent itself to the playful impulses of clerks and laborers no less than to merchants and contractors.

Yet baseball was not solely derived from rounders: it was a hybrid of rounders and cricket. From rounders baseball took its rudimentary "diamond" design and the practice of running around bases, but from the more highly organized game of cricket it borrowed the idea of a fixed number of players on each team, a vocabulary ("batsman," "playing the field," and the like), and an umpire to whose authority players deferred. More important, from cricket baseball took its spirit, its code of sportsmanship. Despite baseball's subsequent history of seedy characters, petty power struggles, and numerous scandals, it retained the indelible stamp of its gentlemanly cricket origins: the ideal, if not always the reality, of fair play.

Baseball became a distinctive Yankee game in part because of the innovative efforts of English immigrants in the United States. One, Henry Chadwick, became baseball's first notable journalist, author, and editor. He invented the box score, and for the first half-century of organized baseball he constantly demanded "gentlemanly demeanor" on the field. Another English immigrant, a man named Wright, left England in 1835 and for years played for the St. George Cricket Club on State Island. Three of his sons became outstanding baseball players. The eldest, Harry Wright, at first bowled (pitched) for New York cricket clubs, then launched a baseball career in which he played, managed, and promoted the game into the national limelight. Sometimes called "the father of professional baseball," Wright nevertheless retained his English cricketer's sense of amateur delight in the game.

A National Game

Because of its widespread popularity, baseball could scarcely remain amateur for very long. The constitution of the National Association sternly forbade pay for play, gambling on games, and players jumping from one team to another. Yet in the same year that organization was formed, some New York teams began charging admission to games, with the players dividing the gate receipts. Winning teams drew the largest crowds, so teams competed for the services of the better players by offering money under the table. Outstanding pitchers, especially, were in great demand. Thomas Wentworth Higginson, a Boston preacher and essayist, said more than he knew when he suggested in 1858 that baseball was "our indigenous American game . . . whose briskness and unceasing activity are perhaps more congenial . . . to our national character, than the comparative deliberations of cricket." Baseball satisfied not only America's love of brisk activity, but also its acquisitive tendencies. On the eve of the Civil War, increasing crowds and players' willingness to turn a fast buck all pointed to professionalism.

The Civil War momentarily retarded the growth of baseball. As men took up arms, they laid down their bats and balls. Yet Yankee soldiers took their game with them, played it in army camps, and taught it to friends and foes alike. Imprisoned Union soldiers occasionally challenged their Confederate captors to baseball contests. A painting immortalizes such an event in Salisbury, North Carolina, in 1862. According to a documentary source, a game on Christmas Day, 1862, at Hilton Head, South Carolina, attracted the attention of an entire army base of 40,000 men. Before the war eccentric versions of town ball were played in places such as Charleston and New Orleans; after the war the "New York rules" uniformly governed play in much of the South as well as the North, in the West as well as the East. The Civil War contributed mightily to the geographical diffusion of baseball.

On a more subtle level, the Civil War caused Americans to recognize baseball as their "national game" in contrast to cricket, the Englishman's game. Sport reflected diplomacy. When the war began, support for the Confederacy was strong in Britain, especially among the ruling aristocracy. The English government declared itself neutral and allowed Confederate representatives to borrow money, buy arms, and build ships in Britain. Throughout the war the influential London *Times* editorially backed the Confederate cause, infuriating Union politicians and newspapermen. The northern press was rabidly anti-British. American sport got caught up in that patriotic fervor. In 1862 a Brooklyn newspaper shrewdly observed that cricket would never again be "in much vogue with the Americans," not only because cricket was too slow a game but also because it was "not an *American* game, but purely an *English* game." Sour Anglo-American relations during the Civil War helped to spoil cricket's chances for popularity in the United States.

As the war ground to an end in the spring of 1865, some Philadelphians met to reorganize their Old Olympian Cricket Club, which had been disbanded during the war. "At first, it was hard work," wrote one member of the club, "[because] the baseball mania was just beginning to spread, and no one would join a cricket club." Most of the older, socially prominent members returned to their cricket club, but younger men turned to baseball. The generation gap was significant. Baseball appealed both to youthful patriotism and to youthful energy.

In the wake of the Civil War a baseball mania swept the nation. A game between the New York Mutuals and the Brooklyn Atlantics in the late summer of 1865 attracted about 20,000 spectators, a record for that era. More important, baseball quickly became the dominant summer pastime in small towns, villages, and rural crossroads throughout the United States, and the favorite topic of winter conversation around hot stoves in country stores. During the decade following the Civil War, baseball became a rural and small-town game as well as a city pastime, a national rather than a regional mania.

In 1865 a convention of the National Association of Base Ball Players attracted representatives of ninety-one clubs, nearly double the highest prewar figure. In the following year the number more than doubled again, to 202 clubs from seventeen different states. By 1867 the annual convention was so large and unwieldy that the officers of the Association changed the constitution to allow only representatives from state associations to attend the annual conference.

The professional question quickly reasserted itself. In 1866 the Philadelphia Athletics openly paid three players $20 each per week, but for most teams the payments remained secret or disguised. In a fashion that has come to be known as semiprofessional, players were supposedly paid to work, but actually they were paid to play baseball. Large industries and affluent merchants carried baseball players on their payrolls; politicians paid them at public expense. William Marcy Tweed, the notorious boss of Tammany Hall, was also the president of the New York Mutuals (1860–71). He placed virtually all his Mutuals on the New York City payroll as clerks and streetsweepers. According to one estimate, Tweedism in baseball cost New York City taxpayers $30,000 annually. Baseballers in Washington, D.C., similarly enjoyed an easy ride during the corrupt first term (1869–72) of President Ulysses S. Grant. As one critic noted, the United States Treasury Department was "the real birthplace of professional base ball in Washington."

In that postwar society, where public scruples were at a premium, enterprising baseball players often cooperated with gamblers in fixing ("hippodroming") games. They also frequently "revolved" from one team to another in response to the highest bidder. William Fischer, for example, agreed to play for the Philadelphia Athletics, who gave him a suit of clothes, paid for his room and board, got him a job, and gave him $115 as a bonus for signing. Yet Fischer remained in Philadelphia for only a few days. Wearing his new clothes and keeping his bonus, he left to take a better offer from the Chicago Cubs.

The first admittedly all-professional club was the Cincinnati Red Stockings of 1869. Their manager, Harry Wright, raided clubs in Washington, New York, and Brooklyn to obtain the best players, and he ended up with only one Cincinnati native on his ten-man squad. Salaries ranged from $800 to $1,400 for the starting team, with the one substitute drawing $600 for the season. The total payroll was $9,300. The Red Stockings traveled throughout the Northeast, then returned home briefly before launching a trip to the West Coast. In all, they won fifty-six games and tied one in 1869. They were Cincinnati's darlings. "Glory, they've advertised the city," exclaimed one proud and grateful resident, "advertised us, sir, and helped our business."

Their season in the sun was brief. Throughout the next season, fans stayed home and the club lost money. As the owners drastically cut salaries, Harry Wright took his best players with him to Boston, where he established another dynasty. Having robbed Cincinnati's roster, he even stole their nickname. The modern Boston Red Sox and Cincinnati Reds take their nicknames from an age of chicanery and ruthless competition.

Wright's move to Boston coincided with a crisis in the old National Association. Irritated with rampant professionalism, amateurs withdrew to form their own organization, and in March 1871 ten professional clubs formed the new National Association of Professional Base Ball Players. From the outset, the organization was unstable. Gambling, hippodroming, and revolving continued unchecked. Each club arranged its own schedule, but toward the end of each season the clubs that were losing money simply refused to travel afar to fulfill their commitments. Clubs rose and fell rapidly. Within the five years of the Association's existence, twenty-five different clubs came and went as members; eleven teams survived only one year.

A nationwide economic depression, beginning in 1873, added to the problem. Few clubs made money. The most successful of all, Boston, lost $3,000 in 1872, netted less than $1,000 in 1873 and 1874, and finally netted only $3,000 in 1875 despite an outstanding record of 71–8. While indirect investment nearly doubled between 1865 and 1878, a narrow profit margin and a high risk of loss cooled the ardor of potential investors in the baseball enterprise. As the season of 1875 came to a close, negotiations were underway to restructure the professional game, taking control away from the players and putting it in the hands of owners.

Yet professional teams represented only one aspect of the national game. Years later Clarence Darrow recalled growing up in a small Ohio town in the 1870s, playing baseball as if it were the "one unalloyed joy in life." Darrow and his schoolmates were shocked when they heard that professionals moved from team to team playing the game for money rather than for local pride. In young Darrow's Ohio, fierce rivalry between neighboring towns was played out on the diamond. Ohio was a microcosm of small-town America. "The game is truly a national one," observed the popular *Spirit of the Times* in 1873: "In every little town and hamlet throughout the country we find a ball club, generally two, bitter rivals, at it with hammer and tongs, ding-dong the entire summer, as though all creation depended on the defeat of the other crowd, and then away goes a challenge—to the next town, and from there to the next, and so on."

On college campuses, too, baseball flourished. For a decade or so before football became established as the autumn sport, baseball dominated the autumn as well as the spring portion of the academic year. In 1873 the son of a future president of the United States, Rutherford B. Hayes, wrote to his father that he dreaded leaving college because he might not then be able to play baseball. "The love of other boys for smoking, chewing, drinking, skating, and swimming," he concluded, "in my case is all concentrated on ballplaying." From its earliest years, the national game meant wholesome, popular activity as well as professional spectacle.

In 1876 the first of the two present major leagues, the National League, was founded. Replacing the short-lived National Association of Professional Base Ball Players, the full name of the new organization was the National League of Professional Base Ball Clubs. The new title accurately conveyed the essence of the change. For the first time club owners, directors, and administrative staffs separated the management of the game from the playing of it. In the age of Rockefeller, Carnegie, Vanderbilt, Gould, Pillsbury, Armour, and Swift, baseball also spawned its investment barons.

Foremost was William A. Hulbert, a Chicago businessman. Representing a new breed of baseball magnate, Hulbert never played the game; financial and civic interests rather than sporting enthusiasm attracted him to baseball. In 1870 he became a charter stockholder of the newly founded Chicago White Stockings, and soon he became president of the club. At the end of the season of 1875, he collaborated with a Chicago journalist, Lewis Meacham, in outlining the inadequacies of the player-controlled Association. Player control of the game, he insisted, produced inflated salaries, team jumping, gambling scandals, team imbalance, and uncompleted schedules, all resulting in tepid spectator interest and subsequent losses at the gate. Hulbert's remedy was simple. He proposed that a "closed corporation" of baseball owners impose discipline and order on the game.

Before he made his move, Hulbert covered his own base. In 1875 he raided the championship Boston Red Stockings team of its four best players, and the Philadelphia Athletics of one. From Boston he got a gem of a young pitcher, Albert G. Spalding, whom he immediately installed as playing manager and team captain. Like Hulbert, Spalding was an astute businessman. Upon arriving in Chicago, he opened a sporting-goods store primarily to sell "all kinds of base ball goods." He equipped his own team, of course, and shortly after the founding of the National League gained a monopoly for the furnishing of the league's official balls, as well as the exclusive rights to publish the league's first informational and statistical record, the *Base Ball Guide*. Spalding's sporting-goods investment quickly outweighed his commitment to playing the game. A millionaire by his early thirties, he was living proof of the profitable marriage of sport and business. He fully supported Hulbert's efforts to establish baseball on a firm business basis.

Spalding applauded the formation of the National League as a means of giving management the upper hand in "the irrepressible conflict between Labor and Capital." Yet regional as well as financial interests lay in the background of the new organization. Recovering quickly from its great fire of 1872, Chicago mushroomed both in size and importance as the commercial center of the Midwest. Civic leaders such as William A. Hulbert resented the political and cultural dominance of Philadelphia, New York, and Boston, a dominance symbolized in the control of professional baseball by eastern clubs. Acting on his resentment of those "Eastern cusses," Hulbert late in 1875 secretly invited baseball owners from Louisville, Cincinnati, and St. Louis to meet with Chicago officials to devise a new professional baseball league. The group convened in Louisville, drafted a constitution, and then (in early February 1876) presented their plan to four eastern clubs. The charter members of the National League represented Boston, Hartford, New York, and Philadelphia in the East; Chicago, Cincinnati, Louisville, and St. Louis in the West.

They agreed to protect their "territorial rights" by having only one club per city and forbidding league members from playing any nonleague teams. Each club paid annual dues of $100, ten times the amount levied by the old National Association. The constitution provided for a central office, and for governance of league affairs by a five-man board of directors selected by the owners, one of whom served as president of the league. Predictably, no player representatives were allowed on the board.

According to the preamble of the constitution, the purpose of the National League was to "encourage, foster, and elevate" the game by making it "respectable and honorable." As a first move in that direction, league officials constructed a seventy-game schedule for each club, and they dealt severely with an old problem that had long plagued professional baseball: the reluctance of losing teams to finish their schedules at the end of the season. In 1876 the Philadelphia Athletics and New York Mutuals were expelled from the league for refusing to make a final western tour. Then the owners turned to more visible signs of respectability. In order to attract a higher class of spectators, they banned gambling and the selling of beer at the ball park; to raise the image of the game, they forbade Sunday contests. For better discipline on the field, they created a paid corps of umpires (a departure from the traditional use of local amateur arbiters) and ruled that only the captain of a team could dispute the umpire's decision.

Like their counterparts in American industry, National League owners imposed a stern discipline on their workers, the players. Ruthlessly they cut salaries, required players to pay for their own uniforms, and charged fifty cents a day for expenses on road trips. In 1877 they banned four Louisville players for life for throwing a game. Nor was their control of players limited to public affairs. In 1880 they announced that players would be barred "from play and from pay" for "insubordination or misconduct of any kind." Albert Spalding, who took over the presidency of the Chicago club following the death of Hulbert in 1882, required his players to sign a pledge of total abstinence from beer, wine, and whiskey, then hired a private detective to trail suspected offenders. Threats of fines and suspensions were written into contracts. Players who protested were blacklisted. At one point in the early 1880s, thirty-four players and one umpire were blacklisted.

Of all the measures taken by owners to discipline their players, the creation of a "reserve clause" was the most important in its long-term effect on professional baseball. Determined to prevent players from moving freely from one team to another in quest of higher salaries, owners in 1879 secretly agreed among themselves that each owner would designate his best five players as "reserved property," off limits to other owners. Soon the arrangement became public knowledge. In 1883 the number of reserved players per club was extended to eleven and in 1887 to fourteen. In that day of small squads, fourteen players included virtually the entire team.

Written into every player's contract, the reserve clause meant that only the club owner could terminate the contract. A player could no longer bargain annually with other clubs. His owner might sell his contract or release him outright, but if a player refused to come to terms with his own club, he simply had to quit baseball altogether. From the owner's point of view, the reserve clause was deemed a necessity. As William A. Hulbert candidly admitted, it was a "business coalition . . . , a perfectly just and proper stroke of business." Certainly it was consistent with the practice of big business in late nineteenth-century America.

As in the industrial sphere, however, the abuse of managerial authority provoked worker resistance. Rules governing personal conduct were irritants to rough and boisterous youths. Fines, suspensions, blacklisting, and the reserve clause were barely tolerable. But the imposition, in 1885, of a salary ceiling of $2,000 proved to be the final straw. In the autumn of 1885 a kind of players' union, the Brotherhood of Professional Base Ball Players, was formed to work for the abolition of the salary ceiling, a modification of the reserve clause, and generally for a more active voice in determining the terms of employment as professional athletes.

John Montgomery Ward, a most unusual baseballer, led the rebellion. In a day when most players were barely literate, Ward held a bachelor's degree from Pennsylvania State College and a law degree from Columbia University, earning the latter as a part-time student while playing for the New York Giants. He had begun his baseball career as an outstanding pitcher for Providence, where in 1879 he achieved a phenomenal 44–18 record. Shortly thereafter he injured his arm, switched to the infield, mastered switch-hitting, and became the captain of the Giants. Handsome and dashing, he also became a prominent figure on the New York social scene, marrying a beautiful, well-known actress. In terms of money and status, Ward had little to gain from leading his baseball teammates in their stand against the owners. But lead them he did. Within a year of its formation, the Brotherhood numbered more than a hundred members, well over half of all major league players.

Adamantly refusing to enter into serious negotiations with their players, the owners intimidated newspaper editors into discrediting the Brotherhood, bribed hesitant players, and threatened to fire the "hot-headed anarchists" who led the rebellion. Ward and his comrades refused to be intimidated. For four years they pushed their points, and in several states they took the reserve clause to court. Legal decisions went consistently in their favor, against the reserve clause, but were not enforced. Finally, in 1890 the players faced a fateful decision: to strike or to form a league of their own in competition with the National League. They chose the latter course. They were not even union-minded men, much less anarchists.

A throwback to the earlier days of player-controlled baseball, the Players League was a grand but brief experiment in owner-player co-operation, featuring shared profits as well as governance. Unlike the old National Association, however, the Players League had to compete with an established, better-financed rival. The season of 1890 was a catastrophe for all concerned. Although the Players League lost only half as much money as did the National League, the latter had sufficient capital to survive and to buy off both investors and players from the rebel organization. The folding of the Players League prompted John Montgomery Ward to utter one of his few truisms: "Baseball is a business, not simply a sport."

Yet despite the big-business orientation of major league owners, baseball remained a shaky business right up to the end of the nineteenth century. The Players League was only one of several new leagues that rose to challenge the monopoly of major-league owners. The most successful of all those rivals, the American Association, lasted for nine seasons (1883–91). It charged a lower admission price, sold beer at games, and allowed games on Sundays. With those Association clubs, the League owners reached an accommodation. In exchange for major-league status, Association officials agreed not to raid National League teams of their players. More important, they provided opposition for a series of postseason playoff games, forerunners of the modern World Series. Yet even that early version of the World Series reflected the experimental, fumbling character of the baseball business in the late nineteenth century. At first League and Association champions played for the best of five games, then several times for the best of seven, and once scheduled fifteen games scattered in most all the cities represented by the two bodies. Not surprisingly, spectator interest dwindled to a ridiculously low level.

Amid all the organizational and personnel strife, several players emerged as popular American heroes. Adrian "Cap" Anson, a burly, boisterous farmboy from Iowa, enjoyed a long and illustrious career (1871–98) as a player and manager with the Chicago White Stockings. One of his players, Mike "King" Kelly, was as spectacular on the base paths as he was in the batter's box, and in 1887 he was sold to the Boston club for the record price of $10,000. William 'Buck" Ewing was a fiery catcher for the New York Giants, drawing the top salary of the day, $5000. In the 1890s William "Wee Willie" Keeler ignited the fans in Baltimore, especially in 1897 when he hit safely in forty-four consecutive games. The first famous spray hitter, Keeler had a simple formula: "Keep your eye clear and hit'em where they ain't."

Free spirits all, each of these superstars had a nickname, a sure sign of notoriety. They were also all white. Shortly after the Civil War the amateur National Association of Base Ball Players banned blacks. For a time the new professional leagues put more stock on winning games than on the color of players' skin, opening the door in the 1870s and early 1880s for several blacks to compete on northern major and minor league clubs. In the late 1880s, however, the color line was drawn in baseball as in all American society, more by a tacit, unwritten agreement of white owners and players than by explicit legislation. The infamous separate-but-equal clause in the *Plessy v. Ferguson* decision of 1896 simply put a legal stamp of approval on Jim Crow reality. Segregated baseball was no worse, though no better, than the society of which it was a part.

Except for its lily-white personnel, baseball at the close of the nineteenth century bore a striking resemblance to the modern game. The ball was not as lively as the one now used, requiring more scientific hitting and strategic maneuvers on the base paths. But by 1900 the pitcher threw overhand, sixty feet and six inches from the batter. Catchers stationed themselves immediately behind the plate, used a heavy mitt, and wore a mask and protective armor. Most defensive men wore gloves, admittedly small and frail by today's standards. Then, as now, journalists wrote colorful accounts of games, filled with jargon and usually partial to the home team. Setting American sport on its way toward the modern statistical fetish, journalists also dutifully recorded and daily publicized each player's batting, fielding, and pitching statistics. Yet baseball at the end of the nineteenth century was in a bad way. In 1900 the *New York Times* observed that "rowdyism by the players on the field, syndicalism among the club owners, poor umpiring, and talk of rival organizations . . . are the principal causes accountable for baseball's decline." As Americans entered the twentieth century, the future of their national game hung in the balance.

Suggested Readings

A popular history of baseball is Arthur C. Bartlett, *Baseball and Mr. Spaulding: The History and Romance of Baseball* (New York: Farrar, Straus & Young, 1951); David Q. Voight, *American Baseball: From Gentleman's Sport to the Commissioner System* (Norman: University of Oklahoma Press, 1966), provides a more scholarly account. The role of sports in American life is studied in its more general aspects in Richard Lipsky, *How We Play the Game: Why Sports Dominate American Life* (Boston: Beacon Press, 1981). John Underwood, *Spoiled Sports: A Fan's Notes on the Troubles of Spectator Sports* (Boston: Little, Brown, 1984), presents a provocative commentary on recent developments in sports.

DISCUSSION QUESTIONS:
INDUSTRIALISM AND DEMOCRACY

1. The author of "University Students in Nineteenth Century Russia" characterizes Russian universities after 1848 as dominated by "apathy and careerism." The inference is that a university loses its intellectual vitality when its students concentrate on preparing themselves for jobs and careers. To what extent does that appear to be true? If it is true, why should it be the case? If the intellectual vitality of a university does not lie in its professional training, where does it lie? The reading shows that some things can stultify university intellectual life. What things can preserve and enhance it?

2. The author of "Two Parsons" clearly prefers her idea of pre-industrial eighteenth-century life to what she thinks life in the industrial nineteenth century was like. What was so attractive to her about the eighteenth century? What features of the period does she ignore? After reading "Cottage Industry and the Factory System," how accurate do you think her idea of the period was? What does this tell us about the value of "anecdotal history," making general judgments about the past on the basis of a specific event? Do the same problems arise with a work such as "The Death of Woman Wang" in Part I?

3. The employers in "Irish Servant Women: The Irish 'Biddy' " saw their Irish servants' "orientation towards cash" as an undesirable characteristic and would have preferred their servants to regard their positions as personal relationships rather than jobs. Why did employers feel that way? Was it simply a selfish desire to have "loyal" servants willing to work for little pay, or were there other motives?

4. One of the converts quoted in "Protestant Evangelists and Christian Samurai" claimed that Christianity was an integral part of the "Western way." The Protestant evangelists certainly would have agreed—that was the way they taught—but how true is the statement? Evangelism was an important part of the expansion of Western influence, but was it a necessary one?

5. What were the factors that allowed the development of the radical student movement described in "University Students in Nineteenth Century Russia"? Which of them are integral and desirable features of university life in general? What measures should the Russian authorities have adopted if they had wanted both productive universities and a docile student body—or is that even possible?

6. In an industrial society, workers perform clearly defined and limited duties in exchange for an adequate and predetermined wage, and it is expected that they will change jobs if they can find better terms. Not all members of society are supposed to behave this way, however. In "Irish Servant Women: The Irish 'Biddy' " employers wanted their domestic employees to be loyal and not overly concerned about wages, and in "The Emergence of Team Sports: Baseball's Early Years" professional

baseball players' contracts had a legally recognized "reserve clause" that denied them the right to switch teams. Teachers, nurses, and others are supposed to be willing to neglect their economic self-interest in deference to "a higher commitment." Why are some individuals expected to act contrary to market forces, and why do we feel that they should do so?

7. Although Western power ultimately was based on technological superiority, the devices by which the Western powers imposed their will and expanded their influence were, more often than not, economic and organizational in nature. From reading "The Business World of Jamsetjee Jejeebhoy" and "Protestant Evangelists and Christian Samurai," what do you think were the most effective tools of imperial control?

8. "The Emergence of Team Sports: Baseball's Early Years" discusses the growth of one spectator sport up to the close of the nineteenth century. What reasons do you see for the phenomenal increase in popularity of spectator sports during that period? Why has the popularity of spectator sports continued to grow in industrial nations? How important are they in modern society, and what needs do you think they fill?

9. During the period covered by this group of readings, the Industrial Revolution and technological advancement were pervasive influences. Consider each of the readings and determine what role technological progress played in the subject it discusses. Was the movement of benefit to all during the period? If not, who won and who lost?

10. The word "exploitation" is used often, but the phenomenon it represents takes so many forms that the word can be somewhat difficult to define adequately. Using "The African Slave Trade" and "The Death of Woman Wang" in the previous section and "Cottage Industry and the Factory System," "The Business World of Jamsetjee Jejeebhoy," "Irish Servant Women," and "The Emergence of Team Sports" from this section, try to identify the various forms of exploitation discussed. Can you develop a simple definition of exploitation that covers all these cases?

PART
III

THE
TWENTIETH
CENTURY

1914 TO THE PRESENT

	1914	1920	1930	1940
EUROPE	**1914–1918** World War I **1917** Bolshevik Revolution **1919** Paris Peace Conference	**1922** Mussolini's March on Rome **1923** French occupation of Ruhr **1924** Death of Lenin, rise of Stalin **1924–1925** Adolf Hitler, *Mein Kampf*	**1933** Hitler becomes chancellor **1935** Nuremberg Laws against Jews **1936–1939** Spanish Civil War	**1939–1945** World War II **1940** Fall of France **1941–1945** Mass murder of Jews **1945** Yalta Conference **1947** Marshall Plan **1949** Germany divided **1949** NATO alliance
SOUTHWEST ASIA AND AFRICA		**1923** Kemal Attatürk, president of Turkish Republic		**1948** *Apartheid* in South Africa **ca. 1948–1987** APARTHEID: ITS ORIGINS AND NATURE **1948** Founding of Israel, first Arab-Israeli war
SOUTH AND SOUTHEAST ASIA		**1920–1922** Gandhi's first Civil Disobedience Movement **1927** Indonesian Nationalist party founded by Sukarno	**1930** Gandhi's March to the Sea	**1947** Independence of India and Pakistan **1948** Mahatma Gandhi assassinated **1949** Independence of Indonesia
EAST ASIA		**1927–1937** Nationalist regime in Nanjing	**1931** Japan seizes Manchuria **1934** Long March of Chinese Communists **1937–1945** Sino-Japanese War	**1941** Japan attacks Pearl Harbor **1945** Atomic bombing of Hiroshima and Nagasaki **1946–1949** Civil war in China **1949** People's Republic of China
THE AMERICAS AND THE PACIFIC	**1917** U.S. enters World War I	**1929** The Great Depression begins	**ca. 1933** DEPRESSION AMERICA AND ITS FILMS **1933** Franklin D. Roosevelt's New Deal	**1941** U.S. enters World War II **1941–1945** DEMOCRACY AND HYPOCRISY ON THE HOMEFRONT **1945** United Nations organized **1946** First electronic computer **1948** Transistor invented

PART III: 1914 TO THE PRESENT

1950	1960	1970	1980
1953 Death of Stalin **1955** West Germany joins NATO **1955** Warsaw Pact **1957** First earth satellite, USSR **1957** European Economic Community	**1960** Yuri Gagarin, first man in space		**1980** Solidarity movement in Poland **ca. 1980–1987** LEISURE TIME IN RUSSIA
1954 Nasser takes control in Egypt **1956** Second Arab-Israeli war	**1960–1975** Independence movement sweeps Africa **1967** Third Arab-Israeli (Six-Day) war	**1971** Indo-Pakistani war **1973** Fourth Arab-Israeli war **1978** Camp David Accords **1979** USSR invades Afghanistan **1979** Revolution in Iran	**1980–** Iran-Iraq war **1980** Black majority rule in Zimbabwe (Rhodesia) **1981** President Sadat assassinated
1955 Bandung Conference, Indonesia	**1961** Increasing U.S. involvement in Vietnam	**1973** U.S. forces withdraw from South Vietnam **1975** Communists take over Vietnam, Laos, Cambodia	
1949–1976 Mao Zedong's Chinese revolution **1950–1953** Korean War **1951** U.S. peace treaty with Japan	**ca. 1965–1969** LIHUA: A YOUNG WOMAN IN CHINA'S CULTURAL REVOLUTION	**1971** People's Republic of China joins UN **1972** Nixon visits Beijing **1976** Death of Mao Zedong **1977** China begins liberalizing under Deng Xiaoping	**1980–1987** ROBOTS AND JAPAN
1959 Fidel Castro's victory in Cuba	**1962** Cuban missile crisis **1963** President Kennedy assassinated **1968** Martin Luther King, Jr., assassinated **1969** Neil Armstrong, first man on moon	**1974** President Nixon resigns **1975** Helsinki Accords **1977** Panama Canal Treaty **1979** Civil wars begin in Nicaragua and El Salvador	**1982** Falkland Islands war **1980–** HIGH TECH/HIGH TOUCH **1980–** HUMAN WAVES

Western confidence and apparent superiority over the rest of the world reached their height in the early years of the twentieth century. A century of relative peace had allowed advances in the general standard of living and quality of life that persuaded many that a golden age had arrived. Democratic advances had been slow and had not disturbed prevailing social and political institutions. Although many were preaching revolution, most Europeans believed that the human condition would continue to improve through peaceful, evolutionary processes. With the development of international organizations of all kinds—the World Court, Red Cross, Postal and Telegraph Union, Boy Scouts, Rotary, and many others—there was room to believe that the age of international competition was being replaced by a new era of international cooperation. The result was the confident—in many ways, complacent—society of 1914 that the historian Barbara Tuchman has characterized as "the proud tower."

That confidence was shattered by the First World War. The European governments led their people into a war that their industrial and scientific establishments ensured would be the most destructive and expensive ever known. Once having got their nations into the conflict, political leaders seemed incapable of extricating them. When the war ended, many pre-existing political institutions, such as the Romanoff, Hapsburg, and Hohenzollern empires, were in ruins, and others were discredited. The nations that had suffered the most began to search for radical means of obtaining security and prosperity, and fascism and communism arose to compete with traditional European political values and institutions. On the international scene, subject peoples began to lose their awe of Western ways and to question European dominance. Local independence movements were starting to trouble the Western empires.

Before the damages of war had been fully repaired, the Westerners' confidence suffered another blow with the Great Depression of the 1930s. If the Great War had challenged the validity of European political institutions, the Great Depression brought Western economic institutions into question. "Depression America and Its Films: The Marx Brothers and W. C. Fields" illustrates the bitter and critical spirit of the times.

Yet a third blow, the Second World War, fell before the Western nations had really come to grips with the Great Depression. During that struggle, the Westerners had to relinquish a large measure of their claim to moral superiority in the world. "Democracy and Hypocrisy: The American Homefront During World War II" shows the extent to which racism was prevalent in the United States and how easily the American people took to the concept of the concentration camp. The great shock that came with the discovery of the Nazi death camps at the end of the war was partially due to the realization that such a horror was in many ways only a logical extension of certain values and attitudes that were prevalent thoughout the Western nations.

The years following the war saw the dismantling of the Western empires. Virtually everywhere, native peoples were given a greater or lesser degree of political freedom. "Apartheid: Its Origins and Nature" discusses one area in which that did *not* occur. China during this period can be seen as an example of the Soviet Union's failure to establish an empire in the East. "Lihua: A Young Woman's Experience with China's Cultural Revolution" provides an insight into the turmoil China underwent as it attempted to establish a communist society independent of Russian tutelage.

Despite the Cold War between the United States and the Soviet Union, the unrest created by various liberation movements throughout the world, and the rise of terrorism as a political tool, the years since the Second World War have been a period of relative peace. In "Leisure Time in Russia: The Timeless Approach to Life" we see the degree to which Soviet society has abandoned its ideal of revolutionary struggle in favor of consumer goals not unlike those prevailing in many capitalist nations.

During this period of peace, the pace of technological innovation has again increased, and the effects of progress are being felt more widely and deeply than ever before. But the confidence that Western political and social institutions are capable of controlling events—a confidence shaken early in the century—has never been restored, and there is widespread concern that the direction, the extent, and the nature of change in the world today may be out of control. "Human Waves," "Robots and Japan: The New Breed," and "Forced Technology: Hi Tech/Hi Touch" all confront aspects of that problem, without offering any clear solution. The present era is a questioning one, but perhaps the dominant issue is whether or not we can, in fact, control the forces presently at work in our world and, by so doing, shape our future.

Depression America
and Its Films:
The Marx Brothers
and W. C. Fields

Andrew Bergman

America's spectacular stock market crash of 1929 brought a swift end to the great economic boom that had followed World War I. The crash marked the beginning of the Great Depression, a long and bitter experience for the millions of Americans who suffered through it. The effects of the economic crisis permeated nearly all facets of American society from the crash until the nation's entry into World War II. Millions were thrown out of work, families were disrupted, and people's faith in the economic, political, and social institutions that had formed the core of American life was severely damaged.

The Great Depression was an era of extreme stress, and in such periods of stress there exist certain tensions that affect all aspects of society. The movie industry, like most American institutions, felt the impact of a dying economy. American films came to reflect the social and intellectual mentality of a disillusioned people. The nation needed its movies. Films had ceased to be a luxury and had come to play a significant role in ordinary people's lives. Americans needed to see films they could relate to, and during the depression such films generally depicted things lost or desired. The movies became, in many respects, a reflection of the nation's consciousness.

This first selection in Part III, from a book by Andrew Bergman, traces the changing attitudes of Americans during the depression through a study of one of Hollywood's greatest art forms, the comedy. He cites the comedies of the early 1930s as the film motif most reflective of the despair and bitterness of the early depression years. The Marx Brothers' Duck Soup

THE TWENTIETH CENTURY

and W. C. Fields' The Fatal Glass of Beer *are used as examples of the comedic films that best depicted the irreverence Americans held for their economic, political, and social institutions during the early 1930s. Bergman's explanation of why* Duck Soup, *arguably the Marx Brothers' greatest film, failed to attain the popularity of their earlier movies is an enlightening look into America's changing mentality as it began its slow recovery from the economic crisis.*

In 1929, Hollywood was riding the high crest of profits: the intro-duction of sound had resulted in approximately one hundred million moviegoers per week, a virtual nation. Profits soared: Warner Brothers to seventeen million, Loews, Inc. to nearly twelve million, Fox and RKO to one and a half million. But from 1930 to 1933, the industry saw those profits turn into hefty debits.

That the movie industry suffered during the economic slide should be self-evident, yet Lewis Jacobs' respected history of American film insisted that "for two full years after the stock market crash, the box office had been unaffected, still thriving on the wonder aroused by sound . . . The dangerous year for Hollywood . . . was not 1929 but 1933." Nineteen thirty-three was certainly dangerous, but for Holly-wood, as for the entire nation, 1930 through 1932 were hardly less threatening years. And those close to the industry knew it. Hollywood did not dream peacefully through the early thirties, only to be rudely awakened in 1933. If one is to trace any relationship between Depres-sion America and the movies it produced and watched, it seems nec-essary to point out that, almost from the start, Hollywood observed the economic disaster with great apprehension.

The initial assurances should not be surprising. Carl Laemmle, President of Universal Films, stated in November of 1929 that movie theatres "are the last to feel the pinch and the first to get over it," and Harry Warner and E. W. Hammons avowed the utter necessity of movie-going. Paramount's Adolph Zukor, recollecting in tranquility, remembered that the crash "at first did not affect the motion picture industry" but was aware of the "hazardous nature" of the picture busi-ness and did not expect "complete escape from the ills besetting oth-ers."

1930 saw worries begin to nag. John W. Ailcoate, publisher of the trade paper *Film Daily,* summed up the year as "trying and irritating" and underscored "the fact that the survival of this business rests on a

DEPRESSION AMERICA AND ITS FILMS   From Andrew Bergman, *We're in the Money: Depression America and Its Films* (New York: New York University Press, 1971), pp. xix–xxiii, 30–41.

continued flow of good products." Cecil B. DeMille clung to Herbert Spencer and saw "uninterrupted prosperity" as a "national disaster":

> The year 1931 in the film industry, as was the case with latter months of 1930, will continue to be a test of courage. . . . Artists who can only stand pleasant times and pleasant words are not of lasting value. This year will be a splendid year for the industry, for during it we will see much of the purging effect of that greatest of all natural laws: the survival of the fittest.

The weakest started wilting in the jungle as 1931 opened. Studio jobs which normally opened up after Christmas remained vacant in January, 1931, as New York-based studio executives ordered a "rigid economy wave." Movie theatres began cutting admission prices, by up to twenty-five cents, in an attempt to bolster sagging patronage. By year's end, *The Film Daily Year Book* called the twelve-month period "the most trying year in the short history of screen entertainment." Innovations like increased use of color and wide screen techniques were put aside, and "the last half of 1931 was filled with rumor, uncertainty and turmoil."

And red ink. RKO saw a 1930 surplus of 3.3 million turn into a 5.6 million deficit in 1931; Fox suffered a loss of 5.5 million after a 9.2 million profit the year before; Warner Brothers went from profits of 17.2 million in 1929 and 7.0 million in 1930 to a loss of 7.9 million. Nineteen thirty-one, not 1933, represented Hollywood's first deeply jolting confrontation with the hard facts of America's dying economy; the dream factory was stricken along with the steel factory. Paramount told *Saturday Evening Post* readers to stop worrying: "There's a Paramount Picture probably around the corner. See it and you'll be out of yourself, living someone else's life. . . . You'll find a new viewpoint. And tomorrow you'll work . . . not merely worry."

Paramount's Jesse Lasky summed up 1931 by recognizing that Americans were "weary and depression-ridden." Only "new ideas" could get people back to the movie habit. Yet Hollywood would suffer badly until mid-1933, and 1932 would be the worst.

The industry's financial downfall could be traced, in part, to its wild and overoptimistic expansion in the mid and late 1920s. The five major film companies of the period (Loews, Inc., Fox, Paramount, RKO, and Warners) fought for control of the country's movie theatres. As their frantic buying accelerated, their "fixed-charge obligations" (the hard cash committed to the operation of the theatres) more than tripled, to 410 million dollars. When the movie public began to stay home, the direct financial impact on movie companies owning theatres was immediate and immense. The movie companies tried to return movie houses to local ownership in 1932, but receipts tumbled further.

John Alicoate's Introduction to the 1933 edition of *The Film Daily Year Book* was free of the conditional optimism of earlier depression prognoses. It reflected the culmination of two years of suffering for Hollywood:

> 1932 was a trying year for the industry and its close found the fortunes of the business at their lowest ebb. The year marked the end of the so-called era of extravagance. . . . It saw the start of a movement of disintegration culminating in the receivership of Paramount and RKO. . . . Unless the general economic situation takes a decided change for the better, the industry can hope for little in the way of progress and genuine prosperity.

(Adolph Zukor, however, foresaw only that if "general conditions improve or stay at the present level, we will take care of ourselves.") But if they deteriorated? As Roosevelt took office in March of 1933, receipts hit rock bottom: they were forty percent of what they had been in January of 1931.

But by the fall of 1933, the bank scare was over and the industry began slowly to recover. The *Motion Picture Herald* reported that "abandonment of the industry's emergency salary order got underway this week and grosses at motion picture theatres continued improving." Attendance increased and spokesmen felt it "not unlikely that most major companies will show a profit for the first six months of 1934." By the end of 1933, all the big studios reported improvement. Yet the automatic movie-going of the late 1920s was no more; theatre managers had to work for their patronage. And so it was that Bank Night spread across the land. Cutting ticket prices was not sufficient; gimmickry was called for. Charles Urban Yeagar, an official of Fox Theatres in the West, first introduced Bank Night to Colorado. Simplicity itself, Bank Night involved drawing lucky numbers with cash rewards to the chosen few. In a year when people were grateful for the most trifling windfall, it proved an immense success. (Yeagar quit his job with Fox, placed a copyright on the idea, and formed Affiliated Enterprises, Inc. Anyone who wanted to run a Bank Night thereafter would have to purchase a franchise from Yeagar. The depression made him a wealthy man.)

Other gimmicks were devised: Screeno was introduced, and crockery was distributed in lobbies on given nights. Generations of children broke bread over Rialto chinaware. A Brooklyn theatre owner seriously proposed dropping movies from the program: "All we need is [sic] Bank Nights." The gimmicks did help, and during the partial recovery of 1935 and 1936 attendance rose to weekly averages of seventy-five and ninety million. The 1935 edition of *The Film Daily Year Book* saw an "about face on prosperity road" and noted that "competition was never more keen." In the summer of 1936, it was reported that all major companies were running in the black for the first time since 1931. Warner Brothers and RKO were recovering, and the Frank Capra films *(It Happened One Night, Mr. Deeds Goes To Town)* were starting to elevate Columbia Pictures to the class of a major studio.

The recession of 1937 also hurt Hollywood, but the industry was on a sounder footing by that time. Calamity had been avoided, theatre ownership cut back, and employment in the industry was nearing normal.

But Hollywood had been hurt and deeply frightened during 1930–1933. And the most compelling evidence of its fears lies not in financial reports or the statements of industry leaders; it lies in the films themselves. The preliminaries completed, we proceed to the black and white footage itself.

Perhaps it was his experience as a member of Warren Harding's Cabinet that made Will Hays think he was an authority on comedy. For whatever reason, he was able to prophecy, in his 1934 *Annual Report* to the MPPDA, that "historians of the future will note the . . . fact that the movies literally laughed the big bad wolf of the depression out of the public mind." It was a reassuring thought. After a long day on the soupline or after being thrown off his farm, the citizen could gather his family and amble down to the Strand, to relax in the plush and chuckle away disaster. But there was a stream of film comedy in the early thirties that had little to do with chasing away bad wolves: an anarchic stream in which meaning and meaninglessness fused, in which the pun routed rational dialogue. Spiritual forerunners of those who would create the theatre of the absurd in the 1950s, The Marx Brothers and W. C. Fields exhibited little of the good-natured horseplay implied by Will Hays. Much of Hollywood's highest art had been comic: it should not be so surprising that in the early thirties the movies most related to the bitterness and despair in America be comedies.

The Marx Brothers

They were Chico, Groucho, Harpo, and Zeppo. The Depression did not create their comedy; that craft had been mastered by years on the road, playing vaudeville stages and Broadway. But the Depression endorsed it and made it a national pastime.

Chico, his stagy Italian accent a heritage from the great days of dialect comedy, mangled English usage, arranged malapropisms, and made conversation completely impossible. Harpo came on as an impulsive lunatic—grabbing chambermaids and dancing with them suddenly and frantically, the music in his head. From his pockets appeared scis-

(From left) Zeppo, Harpo, Chico, and Groucho Marx, the most popular and influential comedy team in the history of American film.

sors, blowtorches, table service, cups of coffee, and the horn with which he communicated. Zeppo, the straight man where none was needed, mainly stood around and was dropped after *Duck Soup*. And Groucho, the very raise of whose eyebrows was a statement, was a man who had erased the boundaries between logic and illogic, for whom disorder was an assumption rather than a problem. He was in some ways the traditional American "wiseacre," the town prankster.

The prank in Marx films became a system unto itself and was all-inclusive. Language became a prank. Every dialogue between Chico and Groucho became conversational feedback and fuzz. In *The Cocoanuts*, Groucho tries to explain the location of a viaduct. "Why a duck," asks Chico again and again. Groucho finally admits he doesn't know why a duck. In *Animal Crackers*, the two discuss the search for a stolen painting:

G: Suppose nobody in the house took the painting?
C: Go to the house next door.
G: Suppose there isn't any house next door?
C: Then we gotta build one.

While the games played with language stemmed from old burlesque traditions of the malapropism, dialect confusion, and the verbal pratfall, the brothers made word play an art. Misunderstanding and understanding were identical.

From 1929 to 1933, the Marxes made five films for Paramount—*The Cocoanuts* (1929), *Animal Crackers* (1930), *Monkey Business* (1931), *Horsefeathers* (1932), and *Duck Soup* (1933)—and gave new life to the words "chaos" and "shambles." They had reached great heights on Broadway in the revues, *The Cocoanuts* and *Animal Crackers,* when their agent, William Morris, convinced Paramount's Jesse Lasky that the brothers were naturals for the screen. In those early days of talkies, many of Chico's dialect mumblings and Groucho's rapid-fire snappers were unintelligible on the sound track. After they were shown the final cut of *The Cocoanuts,* the Marxes were so appalled that they attempted to buy the negative back. Paramount resisted, and the film made a profit of close to two million dollars.

Animal Crackers was Parmount's biggest moneymaker in 1930, and people began to perceive that the Marxes represented a kind of gloriously American liberation from convention. The French critic and playwright, Antonin Artaud, pronounced *Animal Crackers* an "extraordinary thing" and saw in it

> the liberation through the medium of the screen of a particular magic which the ordinary relation of words and images does not customarily reveal, and if there is a definite characteristic, a distinct poetic state of mind that can be called *surrealism, Animal Crackers* participated in that state altogether.

Yet Artaud doubted of Americans would see the metaphysical implications of the Marxes' horseplay. Being literal-minded people, the chances were they would "take these films in a merely humorous sense." Yet it was clear that the brothers were producing a "hymn to anarchy and whole-hearted revolt." The terms of the revolt were not clear, and the raise of Groucho's giant eyebrows not the exact equivalent to the unfurling of a red flag, but the wild reception of the Marxes' chaos between 1930 and 1933 seems no accident.

Artaud perhaps had good reason to be skeptical of American movie audiences. The review of *Animal Crackers* in the *Motion Picture Herald* was not encouraging: "It is all nonsense, of course, but nobody cares. It is all silly but everybody laughs." It was all silly. Yet no matter how dim the surface reaction, the films were produced and wildly received in a specific context, for from 1930 to 1934, a number of "silly" films, with next to no plot, appeared in our movie theatres as the economy sank out of sight.

Will Hays had surely not meant that Americans were escaping into pure Dada. Yet the success of disjunctive, chaotic efforts that mocked intelligibility seems to reveal a nation not so much searching for silliness as one capable of sensing the absurdity of the verities and relations that had been treasured before. Obviously, this might be an overgeneralization, and one does not suggest a nation of fledgling Ionescos, but the fact remains that absurdity has never had it so good in American film since that time.

Million Dollar Legs (1932) is a plotless pastiche of ancient slapstick and sight gags that utilized nationhood and the Olympic Games for manic purposes. The *Motion Picture Herald* accurately observed that Paramount had "gone back into the dark ages of motion pictures" in resurrecting the aesthetics of the Keystone comedies. The ludicrous national setting was Klopstockia, a land subsisting on the export of goats and nuts. Its president, W. C. Fields, holds office via an electoral process that requires him to win at Indian wrestling each morning. An uneasy head of state, he sits at cabinet meetings with a gun and brass knuckles, as totally incomprehensible intrigues are plotted against him. The film is a string of *non sequiturs*. Jack Oakie portrays a travelling brush salesman considered subversive by Fields' opponents. He croons the Klopstockian love song, "Wolf-boogle-gik" and learns that all Klopstockian men are named George and all women, Angela. The nation goes to the Olympics. Fields appears in gym togs, constantly spied upon by the great cross-eyed silent comedian, Ben Turpin. Government is reduced to a kind of vaudeville. In *Million Dollar Legs,* the sight humor and verbal gags seem to run independently of each other, creating an effect both unsettling and very funny. The film manages to reduce everything it considers (like spying and statehood) to a kind of accident.

Million Dollar Legs was a box office success in the late summer of 1932. Its success, together with the huge success of the early Marx pictures, indicates that its form was attractive. It was not merely the personality of the Marxes which brought people to their films, but rather, the kind of action the brothers loosed.

Groucho's position changed during the course of the Depression. In the early films, he had been an outsider. In *The Cocoanuts,* he ran a fading Florida hotel and auctioned off swampy real estate; *Animal Crackers* presented him as Jeffrey Spaulding, the fortune-hunting and cowardly African explorer (rhymed with 'schnorrer"); in *Monkey Business,* he was merely a stowaway on a boat.

Yet in 1932 and 1933, of all times, Groucho achieved a dizzying rise in position, if not stature. In 1932, Paramount released *Horsefeathers* and placed him, as Quincy Adams Wagstaff, at the head of Huxley College. At his inaugural, Groucho sat on stage shaving. So much for education; he and his brothers stage some early campus disruptions. The ascension of Groucho to this position of authority was only a dry run for *Duck Soup,* when as prime minister he would attempt to run the land of Freedonia into the ground. More confined in *Horsefeathers,* he could only dismember a university. But in 1933, Groucho, as Rufus T. Firefly, assumed effective non-leadership of Freedonia. Not since Woodrow Wilson had the step from university leadership to national power been made with such consummate ease.

WAR IS SWELL

. . . when the Marx Brothers are in it.
They'll be out of the trenches by Christmas . . . if the food doesn't improve

THE 4 MARX
BROTHERS
IN
"DUCK SOUP"

A Paramount Picture   Directed by Leo McCarey

Movie poster for the Marx Brothers' 1933 film Duck Soup.

Duck Soup was the most fully orchestrated attack upon the sanct-
ity of the state ever to reach the American screen. But the public that
had flocked to *Animal Crackers* and would fill theatres for *A Night At
The Opera* in 1935, just would not support *Duck Soup,* the Marx Brothers' most audacious film.

It was not just the general populace. American critics also failed to grasp what the application of the Marxes to a political situation ultimately implied. The New York *Herald-Tribune*'s Richard Watts, Jr., at this time a fairly outspoken leftist critic of film, claimed that "American experts at satirical farce are not at their best when mocking the frailties of dictatorship" and concluded that the brothers were not concerned with "providing a significant social comment." *The New York Times* found *Duck Soup* "almost impossible to follow." But the most symptomatic critique came from William Troy, writing in *The Nation*:

> The present story might have been shaped into a hilarious burlesque of dictatorship; but this would have amounted to humor with a point, and the essence of Marxian humor is its pointlessness. . . . It consists of a disassociation of the faculties rather than a concentrated direction of them toward a particular object in the body social or politic.

The middle thirties were not the time for abstract mockings of statehood. What *The Nation* wanted was an attack upon dictatorship, a satiric crusade against political evil. But *Duck Soup* was an attack against political anything; it came out of the deepest cynicism about all government. What is perfectly clear after ten minutes of the film is that the whole idea of statehood and national loyalty is preposterous. The very idea of political action becomes a bad joke. (While *The Nation* felt *Duck Soup* had missed its chance to burlesque dictatorship, Benito Mussolini felt it had done quite well. The film was banned in Italy.)

In *Duck Soup*, Prime Minister Firefly ("A fearless, progressive leader") has been handpicked by the dowager Mrs. Teasedale (Margaret Dumont—the butt of a thousand gags) to run Freedonia. He does not hesitate to demean both his office and his duties immediately. He slides down a fire pole into his inaugural ceremony, where he does pointless card tricks and asks the ambassador from neighboring Sylvania for a personal loan of twelve dollars. Presiding over the Chamber of Deputies, Rufus plays jacks. He reluctantly stops in order to begin the meeting, during which he refuses to consider either old or new business, declares himself unable to read a treasury report and bullies a minister into quitting. He convinces Chico to give up his peanut stand for a "soft government job." When Chico insults him, he is made Secretary of War. Riddles are substituted for civil service exams. The apparatus of government is gleefully dismantled.

The most important game is the war game, and the great part of this short film is taken up with the degenerating relationship between Freedonia and Sylvania, a deterioration accelerated by Firefly's outrageous defense of personal honor. When Mrs. Teasedale announces that the Sylvanian ambassador is coming to apologize for an earlier "insult," Rufus works himself into a rage, arriving at the conclusion that he "is coming to make a sap out of me." Firefly stakes the prestige of Free-donia upon the totally fabricated assumption that the ambassador is coming *not* to shake hands with him. When the ambassador arrives, Rufus cries, "So you refuse to shake hands with me," and slaps his face. And the war came.

The handshake issue was a beautiful parody of the kind of pro-tocol lapses, flag incidents, and so on, that have been maneuvered into pretexts for carnage. By such trifles do nations define their honor. Free-donia gaily plunges into war as the massed populace sings "We're Going To War," led by the Marxes. They put the patriotic anthem through a series of changes, nasally twanging "Comin' Round the Mountain," phasing into minstrel style and clapping their hands and waving them to "All God's Chillun Got Guns." The citizens follow their leader's every move. When Rufus stands on his hands, they stand on theirs. Patriotism becomes a game of Simon Says.

Having made loyalty a grotesque pose, the Marxes dispose of war in a series of sequences which are nothing so much as a vaudeville *All Quiet On The Western Front*. The cutting edge was very sharp, the brothers' attitude being expressed when Harpo is sent across "enemy lines" (Harpo and Chico keep switching sides) in the heat of the battle. As he heads out, Rufus declares, "While you're out there risking life and limb . . . we'll be in here thinking what a sucker you are." Having made the war pointless politically, he makes it pointless personally. One is fighting neither for a cause nor for personal glory. One is fighting because one is fighting.

And one fights because that's what countries are supposed to do. The war sequences are "historical." The Marxes emerge in different costumes: as revolutionaries, redcoats, rebels, union men, frontier coon-skinners, Allied Expeditionary Forces. Sides are irrelevant: the uni-forms are obviously costumes, get-ups, rather than symbols of side or cause. The tragicomedy of it all is summed up by Rufus when he is informed he is firing on his own men: "Here's five dollars, keep it under your hat. Never mind, I'll keep it under my hat." And when Freedonia has "won" the war, Mrs. Teasedale bursts into "Hail, Hail Freedonia" and the brothers bombard her with fruit. It is a perfect finale: nationhood supreme in victory beaten down by a hail of oranges.

When *Duck Soup* was distributed to local theatres early in 1934, it was generally met with hostility. The manager of a Nebraska movie house complained "Even a small town knows when there is a flop. This was sure it." Joe Hewitt, who ran the Lincoln Theatre in Robin-son, Illinois, saw it as "a lot of gags and chatter that did not appeal to the masses. Draw was much less than previous Marx release." "Silly, disgusting," was one reaction from Anadarko, Oklahoma, and a theatre manager in Ellinwood, Iowa, was "afraid these boys are washed up."

At least three managers were unhappy over Harpo's failure to play the harp and the absence of Chico's piano routines.

Yet surely *Duck Soup* did not fare poorly just because it lacked musical interludes. Were people getting tired of the Marxes? The great box office success of their next two films, *A Night At The Opera* (MGM, 1935) and *A Day At The Races* (MGM, 1937) seems to rule that out. Was it that the moviegoing public was loathe to see political institutions mocked? *Million Dollar Legs, The Dark Horse* and *The Phantom President,* as well as shyster politico films, demonstrated that the government was a fit target in 1931 and 1932.

The seemingly anomalous failure of what is perhaps the Marx Brothers' finest film is most likely explained by its timing. After a year of Roosevelt's energy and activism, government, no matter what else it might be, was no absurdity. The New Deal would breed its own myths in film, but in 1934 it seems to have utterly cut the ground from under Groucho as prime minister. Furthermore, as the Watts and Troy critiques make clear, the social consciousness that was permeating Eastern intellectual life could not abide the absolute destructiveness of the Marxes.

A new kind of comedy became popular in 1934, with the unexpected and gigantic success of Frank Capra's *It Happened One Night.* Labelled "screwball" comedy, it stressed a breezy nuttiness that worked to pull things (marriages, social classes) together, rather than break them apart. It dominated film comedy for the rest of the decade. At another time, maybe the Grouchos could assume power, but for the time being they were relegated to more limited spheres. The public still loved the Marxes, so long as they knew their place. They did. In *A Night At The Opera,* Groucho plays a jobless opera impresario; in *A Day At The Races,* a seedy horse doctor; in *Room Service,* a penniless Broadway producer.

W. C. Fields and *The Fatal Glass of Beer*

No look at the anarcho-nihilist films of the early thirties can ignore the W. C. Fields short, *The Fatal Glass Of Beer.* A comic masterpiece, it was filled with cynicism about two treasured American institutions: the family and the frontier. The family is a sham; the frontier is a place nitwits get stuck in.

Fields was such a genius that he could bring it all off in twenty minutes. A study of absurdist drama called this runaway from a Philadelphia home a "brilliant Surrealist comedian," and James Agee saw Fields as "the one great comedian of the talkie era." His ability to sense the crippling pettiness of daily life was nothing less than magical and his art was never purer than in the four shorts he made for Mack Sennett in 1933. In *The Pharmacist, The Dentist* and *The Barbershop,* Fields painted the funniest and saddest portraits of small town life imaginable. His druggist wrapped stamps in paper bags and freely distributed huge vases; his barber, the local sadist, was a badgered man who strapped patrons into their chairs before dropping blazing towels on their faces. His bogus dignity was unshakable; his view of the hounded head of the family shattering.

In *The Fatal Glass Of Beer,* Fields the frontiersman is forced to cope with a series of strange disorders. His only son Chester has run off to the city, had some beer and then embezzled bonds. We learn this in the form of a ballad sung by Fields to a weeping Canadian mountie. Fields accompanies himself on a zither, wearing gloves. Chester suddenly comes home and his father runs around the cabin in joy, his foot caught in a bucket. The pathos attendant upon Chester's return is quick-frozen into a ghastly bedtime ritual. The members of the family address each other as if speaking from separate mountaintops. The good-night ceremony involves:

Good night, Pa.
Good night, Chester.
Good night, Ma.
Good night, Chester.
Sleep well, Pa.
I will. You too, Chester.
Sleep well, Ma.
Thank you. You sleep well, Chester.
Don't forget to keep your window open, Chester.
I won't. You remember too, Pa.
I will, Chester. Good night.
Good night, Pa.
Good night.

The constant use of their names, as if to remind themselves who the others are, is a macabre and hysterically funny parody of the family relation. (Fields' childhood was not a happy one and all his films treated family life as a cruel sham.) The *coup de grace* to family ties comes about when Chester admits to having stolen the bonds. His parents thoughtfully forgive him. When he adds that he "threw away all that tainted money," Ma and Pa beat him senseless and toss him into the freezing night. The myth of the home as the last refuge for the beleaguered is thus ruined. If in time of stress one could not lean back upon home and family, what did one have. An obvious answer being inner steadfastness and determination. Fields succeeded in making a travesty of both.

Fields the pioneer is faced with a totally hostile environment. Coping with it is impossible. Snow comes in through the windows of his cabin, cascades from his pockets and falls from his hat into his soup. It is inescapable. Most importantly, the snow flies directly into his face whenever he observes that "It ain't a fit night out for man or beast." Fields stands stock still when he says this, in a kind of madman pioneer tableau. Determined, stoic and wooden, the frontiersman peers straight ahead and appears oblivious to the hale of snowflakes that lands on his head. This occurs perhaps a half-dozen times in the movie, and it grows funnier as it grows more inevitable. Fields obliterates the legend of the pioneer and the qualities that composed the legend. What could be seen as steadfastness in the face of hardship becomes obtuseness in the face of the unavoidable. The tough, silent pioneer is transformed into a sucker, a dunce. Fields' frontiersman does not cleverly adapt to his environment: he botches his elk call, maintains a dachshund on his dog team and still can get nothing better than ice cubes from the town pump. When he gets hungry out on the trail, he eats his lead dog: "He was mighty good with mustard." Fields the frontiersman exists in spite of, rather than because of, his personal qualities. For, what did personal qualities have to do with a world in which the snow kept flying in one's face? A comedian like Charles Chaplin, working contemporaneously with Fields, worked his comic character against tangible enemies: the rich and the powerful. Chaplin's world contained great reserves of decency and innocence which he drew upon with unabashed sentimentality.

Fields saw decency and innocence as at best irrelevant, at worst positive obstacles. What made his comic intelligence the sharpest of any American funnyman was his intuition that the "enemy" was not so easy to find: it appeared to be the whole vague universe. In the final moment of *Fatal Glass,* Ma and Pa, having deposited Chester on a snowbank, stare into the distance, as Pa declares, "Ain't a fit night out. . . ." This time Fields tempts fate and recoils ever so slightly to avoid the snow. It doesn't come. Man is a sucker, helpless to do anything about the fact.

The film appeared in the spring of 1933 and got less than an enthusiastic reception. As Fields admirer William K. Everson describes it:

> "The Fatal Glass Of Beer" was almost universally disliked at the time. Exhibitors complained that it had no story and no slapstick; audiences were puzzled, waiting for it to "take off" and go somewhere, which it never did. All it had was Fields, which in those days was hardly enough. Even confirmed Fields fanciers felt let down by it. Actually, it was another case of a brilliant little film being offered at the wrong time, before the public was attuned to such bizarre and even black comedy.

The most desperate years of our national experience produced our most desperate comedy, one that rang some hilarious and savage changes on a hundred conventions. The freewheeling nihilism of the early Marx and Fields films has not been approached since; the "screwball" comedy of the mid-thirties would stress goodheartedness and social unity. The screen anarchists entertained a bleak and heartsick civilization that expected the worst from everyone. What has been called "zaniness" was really the dark side of American irreverence, a wild response to an unprecedented shattering of confidence.

Suggested Readings

Other readings about the relationship between society and film are I. C. Jarvie, *Towards a Sociology of the Cinema* (London: Routledge and Kegan Paul, 1970); Richard D. MacCann, *Film and Society* (New York: Scribner's, 1964); John D. Rimberg, *The Motion Picture in the Soviet Union: A Sociological Analysis* (New York: Arno Press, 1973). Siegfried Kracauer, *From Caligari to Hitler* (Princeton: Princeton University Press, 1966), presents an often controversial examination of film as a serious reflection of Weimar Germany.

For further readings on the Great Depression in America, see Robert S. McElvaine, *The Great Depression: America, 1929–1941* (New York: Time Books, 1984), and Albert U. Romasco, *The Poverty of Abundance* (New York: Oxford University Press, 1965). A. J. H. Latham, *The Depression and the Developing World, 1914–1939* (New York: Barnes & Noble, 1981); Joseph S. Davis, *The World Between the Wars, 1919–1939: An Economist's View* (Baltimore: Johns Hopkins University Press, 1975); and Charles P. Kindleberger, *The World in Depression, 1929–1939* (Berkeley: University of California Press, 1973), offer a world view of the economic crisis.

Democracy and Hypocrisy: The American Homefront During World War II

Mark Jonathan Harris, Franklin Mitchell, and Steven Schechter

The Great Depression and World War II represent two of the most traumatic periods America has seen in the twentieth century. Both events left an indelible impression on the country, and, indeed, on most of the world. The outbreak of World War II found America unprepared. Isolation and pacifism were dominant in a country still trying to recover from a decade of social and economic devastation. America's mobilization for war, however, effected profound changes in the character of life in the United States. A new era began with World War II. While most of the world emerged from the war poorer and weaker than when it began, the United States ascended to a position of economic, political, and military dominance.

DEMOCRACY
AND
HYPOCRISY
ON THE
HOMEFRONT

277

America's defense of democracy against the threat of fascism and racism abroad was not without its contradictions on the homefront. Minority groups in the United States were subjected to treatment vastly at variance with America's democratic ideals. Two of the minority groups that suffered the degradation of racial discrimination were blacks and Japanese Americans. Although each group endured both official and unofficial discrimination, the war was to have a differing impact on the two minorities.

The status of blacks was significantly changed by the lowering of social and economic barriers to their advancement. Blacks made up approximately 10 percent of America's wartime population, and their participation was essential in a war requiring a total effort. For the black population, therefore, the economic necessities of war brought slow but significant gains.

For Japanese Americans, World War II held an entirely different fate. Between 1942 and 1945, approximately 110,000 persons of Japanese ancestry living on the West Coast were forcibly uprooted from their homes and resettled in internment camps in remote and desolate regions of the country. This Japanese American relocation program, justified on grounds of national security and public safety, was a violation of the fundamental tenets of democracy. This breach of human rights, caused largely by prejudice and fear, represents one of the most disgraceful moments in America's history.

The racial discrimination experienced by both blacks and Japanese Americans during World War II is vividly portrayed in the following article. Through the wartime recollections of three blacks and two Japanese Americans, the authors show the contradictions that often existed between the beliefs for which America fought overseas and the values it practiced at home.

I'm for catching every Japanese in America, Alaska, and Hawaii now and putting them in concentration camps. . . . Damn them! Let's get rid of them now.

—*Congressman John Rankin*, Congressional Record,
December 15, 1941

Hitler jammed our white people into their logically untenable position. Forced to oppose him for the sake of the life of the nation, they were jockeyed into declaiming against his racial theories, publicly.

—*Roy Wilkins, Executive Secretary, National Association for the
Advancement of Colored People*

World War II severely tested America's commitment to its democratic ideals, especially in its treatment of blacks and persons of Japanese ancestry on the West Coast. Both groups felt the sting of official and unofficial discrimination, and both sought in its own way, and with varying degrees of success, to make democratic beliefs conform closer to reality.

DEMOCRACY AND HYPOCRISY   From Mark Jonathan Harris, Franklin Mitchell, and Steven Schechter, *The Homefront: America During World War II* (New York: G. P. Putnam's Sons, 1984), pp. 92–113.

Blacks were struck with the nation's hypocrisy in waging a war against fascism and racism abroad while practicing racial discrimination at home. At the outbreak of the war American Negroes were, for the most part, desperately poor and hardly any closer to equality than they were before World War I. In May 1941, A. Philip Randolph, president of the Brotherhood of Sleeping Car Porters, and other black leaders called for "a thundering march" on Washington to "shake up white America" and protest the lack of job opportunities for blacks in defense industries. The march was canceled five days ahead of time, only after President Franklin D. Roosevelt issued an executive order banning discrimination in defense industries and government based on "race, creed, color, or national origin." Roosevelt's executive order, the first presidential intercession on behalf of equal rights for blacks since Lincoln's Emancipation Proclamation, also created a Fair Employment Practices Committee to enforce the ban. Although the FEPC had the authority to investigate complaints, it had little power to compel compliance. Still, noted black historian John Hope Franklin has concluded that "its existence had a salutary effect on the employment status of Negroes."

The FEPC scored a major triumph in 1944 in Philadelphia, the country's second-largest war production center. When the local transit company hired eight black trolley-car drivers, a wildcat strike by protesting white drivers shut down the city's entire public-transportation system. Roosevelt responded by calling in eight thousand soldiers to break the strike and keep the buses and trolleys running. The strike was broken, and the black drivers retained their jobs.

Blacks found the military services no more willing to promote equality of opportunity than society at large. President Roosevelt condoned the segregation of white and black soldiers and allowed the Navy, the Marines and the Coast Guard to limit the number of blacks admitted to these services. Black sailors, marines and coast guardsmen were generally excluded from the officer ranks and assigned to menial duties. Nevertheless, many blacks were exposed to positive aspects of American society during their tour of duty and returned to civilian life with new—if not always attainable—expectations.

The most serious breach of civil liberties during wartime involved the relocation and internment of more than 110,000 persons of Japanese ancestry living on the West Coast. President Roosevelt ordered the forcible evacuation in February 1942 of anyone who had at least one Japanese great-grandparent. The internees, two thirds of them American citizens, were then imprisoned in ten relocation camps in remote and desolate parts of the country. The government justified its action on grounds of national security and public safety. In fact not a single case of sabotage by Japanese in the Untied States had occurred. In the court of public opinion, however, where racial antagonism against the Japanese ran high, the West Coast Japanese were convicted of real or potential disloyalty. When the evacuation order finally came under review by the United States Supreme Court in December 1944, the High Court upheld the validity of exclusion, but in another related case the justices held that while the government could temporarily detain a citizen, it lost that right after a citizen's loyalty was proven.

Alexander J. Allen

When the war began, there were a number of blacks who were not enthusiastic about fighting it. They were sensitive to the inconsistency of a country that professed to be fighting for democracy and yet was not practicing it at home. But I felt then, and still feel, that the future of American blacks is in this country, and that our destiny is bound up with the destiny of the rest of the U.S.

Joe Louis, I think, spoke for most blacks and for most Americans when he said, "We'll win because we're on God's side." There were those who noted that he did not say, "God is on our side." That's an interesting distinction, and he made a point of it.

Certainly the blacks, as well as anybody else, and perhaps better than most, understood the negative side of fascism and racism. I was in Cleveland in school with Jesse Owens, and I remember when Hitler left the stadium at the 1936 Olympics because Jesse had defeated the best that Aryan society had been able to produce. So blacks were aware of what was wrong with Hitler and what was wrong with Mussolini and understood the reason for opposing the Nazi war machine as it began to take one country after another in Europe. But at the same time, blacks were extremely concerned over the fact that racism and bigotry and discrimination were a continuing practice in this country. Fascism was not a monopoly of Hitler, or of Mussolini, or the Japanese. It was something that we saw every day on the streets of Baltimore and in other places. We did not see much sense in the war unless it was tied to a commitment for change on the domestic scene. It made a mockery of wartime goals to fight overseas against fascism only to come back to the same kind of discrimination and racism here in this country.

So black leaders decided to fight a two-front war—one against the Axis and the other against bigotry at home. Both of them had to be defeated if this country was to live out its ideals. That was the philosophy of the Double V Campaign, which stood for victory at home and victory abroad. We felt it was an absolute necessity to take advantage of every opportunity to achieve change during this period of ferment, when people were perhaps more sensitive than they might otherwise be to the way the United States was viewed by its allies and by other people in the world.

In January of 1942 I went to work in Baltimore as the industrial-relations director of the Baltimore Urban League. It was an impressive title for a one-man operation. There was no department except myself and the secretary. But we worked trying to open up jobs for blacks in the building trades and the defense industries. In the beginning it was slow going. All the problems of racism and racial discrimination that were part of peacetime carried over to the war industries.

The Maryland State Employment Service, which became a branch of the U.S. Employment Service during the war, was part of the problem rather than part of the solution. Even though President Roosevelt had signed an executive order that said all defense workers should be given equal consideration for job vacancies, that was just so much verbiage. Actual practice in Baltimore was that black workers were denied entrance to 39 Hopkins Place, where the best jobs were. Blacks were sent around the corner to the annex on Lombard Street, where they handled common labor and unskilled work. Even if you had a graduate degree in electronics, you would still be sent to the black entrance. And there were police to enforce it. If you resisted you might very well be arrested, as a number of people were. So many of the blacks would come to the Urban League offices to look for jobs, because they knew we were trying to place people in war industries. We'd go to work at the Urban League in the morning and the lines of people waiting to be interviewed would be two or three blocks long.

Trying to persuade the employers to hire black workers, you met with a lot of ignorance, and a lot of resistance. Many employers didn't have the courage to step out in a way that could conceivably subject them to criticism or abuse from their colleagues. To some degree there was a feeling that "I can't afford to be the first one. If somebody else would do it first, then I'll go along." That's not the kind of thing anybody likes to say about himself, though, so instead you'd get "Well, the time isn't right," or "Black workers don't perform," or "We're afraid that our white workers will walk out." Under Baltimore city law at that time, you not only had to have separate toilet facilities on the basis of sex, but you had to have separate toilet facilities on the basis of race. So they'd say, "Well, we'd like to do it, but we can't afford to set up a whole new set of toilet facilities." So one of the campaigns that the Baltimore Urban League undertook was to change the municipal ordinance. Eventually, we succeeded in doing that.

For me the war period was a very compelling, very exhilarating era. There was a feeling that you had hold of something that was big and urgent and was not going to be here forever. There were opportunities for change which would not exist after the war was over.

And we did begin to see changes. In some places employers got a little religion. They began to realize the inconsistency and inequity of discrimination. Sometimes it was pressure from the government. A lot

DEMOCRACY
AND
HYPOCRISY
ON THE
HOMEFRONT

281

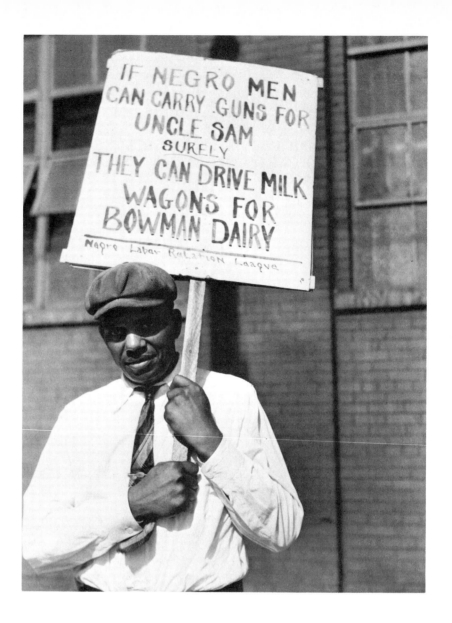

of times it was pressure from local citizens, black and white, who felt a commitment, sometimes through the Urban League, sometimes through other organizations. But mainly what contributed to the change was the economics of the situation. Some companies just ran out of white workers to hire.

The pressure of labor-market shortages simply forced many employers to change their attitudes toward what they might call marginal workers—blacks, other minorities, women—in nontraditional capacities. The denial of opportunity to people who were competent and desirous of work just didn't make sense economically. War orders were pressing, they had jobs that needed to be done, so employers began to tap this long-neglected part of the labor market.

In 1942 the number of blacks in manufacturing industry in Baltimore was nine thousand. By 1944 they had increased to thirty-six thousand, which was a jump not only numerically but also percentagewise, from six percent of the work force to fifteen percent. After VJ Day the number dropped back to twenty thousand blacks, but they were twelve and a half percent of the work force. So the retention rate was far beyond the original expectation. Even though the peak had been passed, the employment picture for blacks was far better at the end of the war than it had been at the beginning of the war.

Henry Fiering

As the Depression receded, you had a large influx of blacks into industry, although they were mainly relegated to menial jobs. My union, the United Electrical Workers, and a few others made it a policy to place special emphasis on the advancement of blacks on the basis of equality of opportunity, but the weight of the mores of the times militated against it.

You have to realize that the people who came into these industries came off the farms; they came out of the hills of Kentucky and Tennessee, and out of the South. Just because they came to work in the cities didn't mean they had changed their social beliefs. They had the same biases and prejudices that they always had. They had to be educated.

There was a union I organized during the war at the Hoover Vacuum Cleaner plant in North Canton, Ohio. I succeeded in negotiating their contract for them and it was a very good contract, so I came out of it in good shape in terms of my relationship with the workers. One day I got a call from their leadership that the plant was shutting down because the company had hired some black women and there was a violent reaction by the white workers, both male and female, in the plant.

This was a lily-white community; they wouldn't even permit a black into town. But with the need for labor and the issuance by Roosevelt of his Fair Employment Practices order, the company had hired a few black employees. But as soon as a black worker entered the shop, the three thousand other white employees shut down the plant.

When I got the call that there was trouble, I went down and walked into a storm. There wasn't much problem with the management. They were following the governmental directive, which was why they had hired the blacks in the first place, but they were frightened. Of course, my committee was frightened, too. I hate to say it, but it was so. I convinced them as to what was right, but I couldn't get them

DEMOCRACY
AND
HYPOCRISY
ON THE
HOMEFRONT

283

to go out and confront their members, and they were leaders of the workers.

There was a mass meeting during working hours, and I took them on. I remember to this day a screaming, hysterical audience of three thousand people calling me everything under the sun and threatening me, but I knew I had the kind of standing that would make them stop there. They would not attack, It took a couple of hours, and although I did not convince the workers that it was right, I did persuade them to go back to work, that there was no alternative. When I look back at the hysteria that took place, I'm amazed that they accepted it, but they did. And it wasn't long after that there were more black women hired into that plant. Blacks and whites worked together, and there was never any other major problem. The people learned to work together very quickly.

You had that same kind of experience in lesser form in many other plants. During the war you began to see a bold change in the relationship between blacks and whites inside the shop. Compared to what it is today, you might say it really wasn't that significant; but for the time it was.

William Barber

I was born in Columbia, South Carolina. There wasn't much work in Columbia, so when I was nineteen I decided to try my luck someplace else. I had a couple of aunts and uncles in Philadelphia, so in '37 I went there.

My first job was as a butler in Chestnut Hill. My second job was as a short-order cook and a bartender at St. Anthony's Club on Twenty-second and Chestnut. I stayed there until June of '41. St. Anthony's Club was a fraternity house and so many of their members were drafted into the service that they had to let someone go, and since I was last hired I was the one to go. But the steward of the club got me a job with the Philadelphia Rapid Transit Company (PRT).

When I first went with PRT, I was a laborer. I worked on the tracks with a pick and shovel and a jackhammer. I was one of the smallest guys on the job, and my foreman made a water boy out of me; plus, I had to put coal oil in the lamps and set the lamps out for night work. I worked there for about a year, but I felt I could do better. At that time you could go to Second and Wyoming after work and take up welding and grinding, which I did, so I worked my way up to welder and grinder.

Of the jobs that were actually available for blacks, that was about the best you could do. At the time, I was not able to become a bus driver, a trolley operator, a supervisor, a dispatcher, a clerk or a receiver or anything in other departments. But during the war things began to change.

The first black transit car drivers in Philadelphia. William Barber is fifth from the left.

There were a couple of write-ups in the paper about different places that didn't have any blacks, such as the cab and transit companies. They also had announcements in the paper of different meetings of civil-rights groups. I attended a couple of the meetings and they persuaded us to put in applications for trolley drivers. The biggest reason the company claimed there wasn't any black trolley operators is that it never had any blacks actually file an application. So forty or fifty of us went up there one morning and filed applications. We all went through an examination, and out of that number only eight of us passed.

About two weeks later we were notified to come to different locations throughout the city. The night before my first day it was announced over the news that they had accepted eight blacks to be trolley operators, and it was in all the newspapers. The following morning I got up to catch a trolley car to report to my location. There were ten or twelve people on the corner, and there wasn't any vehicle running in the city. I went back home, turned on the radio and I heard that all the trolley operators and the bus drivers had gone on strike on account of eight black drivers. So I walked down to the depot.

Once I arrived the whole area was blocked off by whites. Myself and two more gentlemen who were appointed to that location made an attempt to go into the building. At first we thought there was going to be some violence, but the guys moved aside. We three knocked on the door—it was actually locked—and the superintendent unlocked it and

DEMOCRACY
AND
HYPOCRISY
ON THE
HOMEFRONT

285

let us in. He explained the situation and said, "We want you all to sign this paper and you'll get paid for eight hours' work." So we did and every morning of the strike we had to go in to sign this particular paper in order to get paid.

The strike was not sanctioned by the union heads. The union tried to get members to accept us, but they were against the union and had a wildcat strike. The white drivers said they definitely did not want blacks on the trolley cars or buses because they were inferior, they smelled, they carried a certain amount of disease, and just about anything they could possibly say about a black. As far as they were concerned, it was perfectly all right for blacks to clean the toilets, but they did not want us operating the buses or the trolleys.

So there it was until Roosevelt sent the troops in. They tacked signs up on the bus doors: "AS OF NOW, THIS IS GOVERNMENT PROPERTY." They gave the drivers twenty-four hours' notice, "Either you go back to work or you go to war." So naturally, they decided to go back to work. For the next seven or eight days, every trolley car and every bus that left the depot or garage had two soldiers on it. One in the front, one in the back, with fully loaded carbine rifles with clips on the belt. And they were on those trolley cars twenty-four hours a day. The biggest reason they had those troops on there was that those white fellows were afraid that the black people were going to jump them. A lot of those routes went through black neighborhoods, and the white drivers refused to take a trolley car unless they had protection. They figured once they got out there they would be bodily harmed unless they had soldiers to protect them. I feel that was a big reason for the troops. It wasn't for our protection. It was for the white trolley operators. The troops stayed on for about a week, until things cooled down.

At first, I must admit, I had a pretty rough time of it. On a lot of those routes the people were very nice, but on some routes it was like you went into a different country. I had people get on and attempt to pay their fare and see that I was a black man, then they'd step back and say, "I don't ride with no niggers," just like that. Then they'd step back off the trolley car and wait on the next one. I'd have others get on and pay the fare and throw it right on the floor. I even had people spit on me. I'd pull up to a corner and open the doors and they'd spit inside and say, "Go on down the street, nigger." I'd just close my door and go on down the street. I thought, "Well, I'll just take that as long as they don't hit me."

Once, though, I got very angry. This woman said she wanted to get off at Broad Street. I was a conductor, and I rang the bell at Broad Street. We let out about four or five people, but she was sitting in the back and didn't get up. By the time we pulled up to the next stop she was up, and she said, "Didn't I tell you I wanted to get off at Broad Street?"

I said, "Well, miss, I called Broad Street. I let off about four or five people."

And she said, "You know what, you black so and so, I'll spit in your face."

So I stood up out of the booth and I said, "Miss, I'll tell you what, and I want all these people on the car to hear this. Now, if you spit in my face this morning, the way I feel, one of us is going to heaven or to hell." So I opened the door and she got off and everybody said, "You told her right."

After a while, though, people got used to having a black driver and they just took it as it went. I stayed on the job almost forty years, so the way I look at it, anytime a man is on a job that long, he must have been doing something right. As it went along I think I had more white friends than I did blacks.

At one time after I had passed the examination for trolley driver, I almost decided not to go through with it. To be truthful, I was losing money accepting the job. As a welder and grinder I was making ninety-two cents an hour, and at that time they were only paying sixty-four cents an hour on trolleys. So I was actually taking almost a thirty-cents-an-hour cut. The biggest reason I continued was the principle of it. I figured that by doing that I would become somewhat like a pioneer and would prove to people that I actually could do the job. And by breaking the ice it would make a better opportunity for the blacks to continue to be hired. At the time they hired the first eight, they refused to accept another black application for the job for at least six months, because they wanted to see just how we would make out. But we made out all right.

I give a lot of the credit to Roosevelt. If it wasn't for him sending the troops in, ordering those men to go back to work, I figure nine times out of ten, I would never have become a driver. The strike would have continued and they probably would have said, "Well, the whites don't want you. You just got to go back to your old job."

Roosevelt was tops. And Mrs. Roosevelt. I was crazy about her. When both of them passed away, I shed tears, especially when he did. I was operating a trolley car when I heard that he passed away. And I teared. I wasn't the only one. We'd pull up to the corner and people would get on the trolley with tears in their eyes and they knew I had heard the news because I had a handkerchief to my face. I figured he was one of the greatest presidents we ever had.

Margaret Takahashi

When the war started I was married and had two children and was expecting a third. My husband, Jimmy, was gardening and going to school studying landscape architecture, and we had started a nursery

DEMOCRACY
AND
HYPOCRISY
ON THE
HOMEFRONT

in Los Angeles. We had been working on it day and night for about a year, and we were just starting to sell. Then everything went up in the air.

I was born in Japan. My mother was from Ireland and my father was from Japan. They met when my father came to the United States to go to college and my mother came from Ireland to work. They met on a train, fell in love and got married. They had three children; then they went on a visit to Japan and had me. They thought if they stayed and I was a boy I'd inherit, but since I was a girl, forget it. Plus we were mixed, and they don't like mixed people in Japan. So they came back to the United States.

Jimmy's parents were both Japanese, but he was an American citizen, for he was born in Covina, California. Anyone born here was a citizen. Since I was born in Japan, I wasn't, and Japanese were not allowed to become naturalized at that time. But we didn't feel Japanese. We felt American. That was the way we were raised.

After Pearl Harbor we started to get worried because the newspapers were agitating and printing all those stories all the time. And people were getting angrier. You kept hearing awful rumors. You heard that people were getting their houses burned down and we were afraid that those things might happen to us. My husband worried because he didn't know if people would kick him out of his jobs. You didn't know when the blow was going to fall, or what was going to happen. You didn't quite feel that you could settle down to anything. Your whole future seemed in question. The longer the war dragged on, the worse the feeling got.

When the evacuation order finally came I was relieved. Lots of people were relieved, because you were taken care of. You wouldn't have all this worry.

People would come to the door and ask if the house was for rent. I got so mad once I hollered at them and the lady said to me, "No wonder they're kicking you out."

We had the baby on Easter Sunday, and it was a boy, and I was really happy about having a son. I had two daughters first, and I had always wanted a boy. Then three weeks later we were evacuated.

You could only take one suitcase apiece, but people who had gone to camp before us were able to tell us what to bring, so we were a little better off than others. My husband bought foot lockers, so our luggage was pretty big and we took sheets and things that the other people hadn't taken.

We sold our nursery stock to a different nursery, and all the lath houses we'd built, but we didn't get much for them. The rest of the stuff we stored with a friend who was reliable. A lot of people I knew gave things to friends to keep and they never saw the friends again, but ours was a good one.

INSTRUCTIONS
TO ALL PERSONS OF
JAPANESE
ANCESTRY
Living in the Following Area:

All of that portion of the City of Los Angeles, State of California, within that boundary beginning at the point at which North Figueroa Street meets a line following the middle of the Los Angeles River; thence southerly and following the mid line to East First Street; thence westerly on East First Street to Alameda Street; thence southerly on Alameda Street to East Third Street; thence northwesterly on East Third Street to Main Street; thence northerly on Main Street to First Street; thence northwesterly on First Street to Figueroa Street; thence northeasterly on Figueroa Street to the point of beginning.

Pursuant to the provisions of Civilian Exclusion Order No. 33, this Headquarters, dated May 3, 1942, all persons of Japanese ancestry, both alien and non-alien, will be evacuated from the above area by 12 o'clock noon, P. W. T., Saturday, May 9, 1942.

No Japanese person living in the above area will be permitted to change residence after 12 o'clock noon, P. W. T., Sunday, May 3, 1942, without obtaining special permission from the representative of the Commanding General, Southern California Sector, at the Civil Control Station located at:

Japanese Union Church,
120 North San Pedro Street,
Los Angeles, California.

Such permits will only be granted for the purpose of uniting members of a family, or in cases of grave emergency.

The Civil Control Station is equipped to assist the Japanese population affected by this evacuation in the following ways:

1.   Give advice and instructions on the evacuation.
2.   Provide services with respect to the management, leasing, sale, storage or other disposition of most kinds of property, such as real estate, business and professional equipment, household goods, boats, automobiles and livestock.
3.   Provide temporary residence elsewhere for all Japanese in family groups.
4.   Transport persons and a limited amount of clothing and equipment to their new residence.

The Following Instructions Must Be Observed:

1.   A responsible member of each family, preferably the head of the family, or the person in whose name most of the property is held, and each individual living alone, will report to the Civil Control Station to receive further instructions. This must be done between 8:00 A. M. and 5:00 P. M. on Monday, May 4, 1942, or between 8:00 A. M. and 5:00 P. M. on Tuesday, May 5, 1942.
2.   Evacuees must carry with them on departure for the Assembly Center, the following property:
(a)   Bedding and linens (no mattress) for each member of the family;
(b)   Toilet articles for each member of the family;
(c)   Extra clothing for each member of the family;
(d)   Sufficient knives, forks, spoons, plates, bowls and cups for each member of the family;
(e)   Essential personal effects for each member of the family.
All items carried will be securely packaged, tied and plainly marked with the name of the owner and numbered in accordance with instructions obtained at the Civil Control Station. The size and number of packages is limited to that which can be carried by the individual or family group.
3.   No pets of any kind will be permitted.
4.   No personal items and no household goods will be shipped to the Assembly Center.
5.   The United States Government through its agencies will provide for the storage, at the sole risk of the owner, of the more substantial household items, such as iceboxes, washing machines, pianos and other heavy furniture. Cooking utensils and other small items will be accepted for storage if crated, packed and plainly marked with the name and address of the owner. Only one name and address will be used by a given family.
6.   Each family, and individual living alone, will be furnished transportation to the Assembly Center or will be authorized to travel by private automobile in a supervised group. All instructions pertaining to the movement will be obtained at the Civil Control Station.

Go to the Civil Control Station between the hours of 8:00 A.M. and 5:00 P.M., Monday, May 4, 1942, or between the hours of 8:00 A.M. and 5:00 P.M., Tuesday, May 5, 1942, to receive further instructions.

DEMOCRACY
AND
HYPOCRISY
ON THE
HOMEFRONT

289

The day we were taken to camp we had to go to a special designated place to get the bus. This friend of ours took me and the baby
so that we wouldn't have to walk. Most people just walked. We got on
the bus and everybody was sitting there, and I was thinking, Gee,
everybody's so brave, nobody's crying, and I wasn't going to cry either,
because Japanese frown on weakness, so I wouldn't look at anybody.
And then this colored lady came up and looked in the bus window
and she said, "Oh, look at the poor thing, she has a tiny baby." And
then I started to bawl, and I bawled the whole way to camp. I felt like
a fool, because nobody else cried. They didn't even cry when I cried.
They just sat zombielike. They could hold it in that much.

We were taken to Santa Anita Racetrack, and they had built barracks for us. The first people who were taken to Santa Anita had to
live in the stables. They had it bad, because the stables had a lot of
fleas, and they smelled. But they had showers. We had to walk there
to take showers and wash at first, and it was almost a mile from our
barracks.

When we first arrived, we were examined by doctors, and they
made you open your mouth and I didn't want to open my mouth, so
this doctor pulled it open, and I kicked him in the leg. I felt good
about that.

The first meal was spaghetti without meat, and yams. Plain boiled
yams. I'll always remember that. Nothing tasted good. The whole time
we were in camp, nothing tasted good.

We were in Santa Anita a few months, and my five-year-old,
Winkie, my oldest daughter, came up to me one day and said, "Momma,
I don't like this neighborhood. Can't we move?" And I just felt we
had to get out of there. We had heard a rumor that Father Flanagan
of Boys Town was hiring people. So, being a Catholic, I felt familiar
with him and I thought he would help us. I couldn't stay in camp any
longer. I just couldn't. So my husband wrote him a letter, and he wrote
back right away and told us to come. That was Father Flanagan's
mission in life—to take the rejected or unwanted. He had a home for
homeless boys near Omaha and he needed workers, for all of his workers were being called up to the Army.

We wrote back and forth for several months, and nothing happened. We just couldn't get permission to leave. We'd go up to the
office and say, "When are we going to get to leave?" and they'd say,
"No orders have come out." So finally we telegraphed to the head of
the camp. They were going to move the whole camp out in a few days.
Our group was to go to Amache, Colorado, and we said, "Oh, God,
we aren't going to get to go to Boys Town." It was very tense. I thought
they wouldn't let us go. But finally they sent a telegram and we got
permission. The telegram was signed by Herman P. Goebel, Jr., I'll
never forget that name.

So we went into town and got the train tickets. And my husband was given permission to go back to Los Angeles and get his truck, and he picked up a lot of our belongings and drove to Nebraska himself. We took the train. He thought it was safer. Everybody was warning, "Oh, they're going to massacre you." There was a lot of fear, but I didn't have any. And everybody on the train was very nice. I don't think anybody even paid any attention.

My husband went by way of Arizona, and he stopped at a motel and people started to gather around and talk and look at him, and he got worried. So he asked where he could get something to eat, and instead he just took off and drove straight through to Nebraska. He said he stopped once and slept by the side of the road, but he was worried because we had heard that in Arizona several people had had their cars burned.

We arrived in Boys Town at night, and Father Flanagan met us at the train. I expected him to look like Spencer Tracy, but he looked like Eddie Rickenbacker. He was a very tall, gentle, warm man. When you first met him, you could feel this warmth. I've never felt that from another human being. He was so full of love that it radiated out of him. It was startling.

Then my husband came three days later, and we settled in this farmhouse on Boys Town property and started right in to work. We lived on a real farm with a pump and cistern, and there was a place you could plant your garden. We had a victory garden with the Bishop of Omaha. We raised the vegetables and gave them to him. We learned to can, and to cook on a cook stove, and what a real winter was. I just loved it there. I didn't want to come back, but my husband wanted to be his own boss, so after the war, in 1947, we moved back to Los Angeles.

When I think back to the internment, I want to call it a concentration camp, but it wasn't. We have a neighbor who escaped from Auschwitz during the war, and there's no comparison. In our life it was only four months, and that's not long.

But the evacuation did change our philosophy. It made you feel that you knew what it was to die, to go somewhere you couldn't take anything but what you had inside you. And so it strengthened you. I think from then on we were very strong. I don't think anything could get us down now.

DEMOCRACY
AND
HYPOCRISY
ON THE
HOMEFRONT

291

Henry Murakami

After Pearl Harbor we were ordered not to go out fishing. We put away all the nets, tied the boats, and all you had to do was stay home and watch what was going on. It was worse than terrible. You could do nothing. Day after day you just had to stay around the house, and that's all.

On February 11, I was outside the house, holding my year-and-a-half daughter in my arms. And a big flock of tall American men came around. One of them had a piece of paper in his hand, and he started asking me who lives where, where is this man, and so on. So I said, "What is this?" and he said, "We're just asking a few questions." I asked, "Is my name on the list?" And he asked, "What's your name?" So I told him. He was checking the names, and he found it. So right there he said, "You come with us for just a little while and you'll come right back." I called my wife and she came on the porch and I asked the FBI man if I could go in and put my shoes on. I had no socks, just Japanese slippers. And the FBI man said, "No, you don't need to change. You'll come right back." I believed what they said. I couldn't argue. So I handed the baby to my wife and I went with them.

They took us to the immigration office in San Pedro. We were there two days and two nights, then they put us all in old trains. Two days and two nights more we traveled. No windows, all closed; you couldn't look outside. And suddenly the trains stopped and the guards said, "Get out." We came out, and all you could see was white, nothing but white. You couldn't even see houses or buildings. Just snow. They said eight feet high. And we found out it was Bismarck, North Dakota, and it was twenty-nine degrees below zero, and I was walking on the snow in my bare feet and slippers.

They took us to Fort Lincoln, and we had to go to the mess hall where hundreds of people were standing in line. You know how hard it is to stand only fifteen or twenty minutes in cold like that? Within a week I had frostbite. I couldn't walk anymore.

Why? We hadn't done anything wrong. We obeyed the laws. None of us were spies. We didn't know anything about those things. But we were all arrested because we carried fishermen's licenses.

After I was at Fort Lincoln a few weeks I received a letter from my wife that she had had forty-eight hours' notice to evacuate from the island. She was eight months pregnant and there was nothing she could do. So she abandoned everything. Pregnant and with four children, how much could she carry? So she took the children and one suitcase and they all went to the camp the government had built at the Santa Anita Racetrack.

They were there about sixty days, then they were sent to Manzanar. In July I was sent to Manzanar and joined my family, and my new son who was born in May. And we were really joyous.

Manzanar was easier than Fort Lincoln. You didn't feel so much like you were in a concentration camp, but when I came there in July it was hot and windy. You can't imagine how windy it was. It would blow the heck out of you.

The camp was divided into thirty-six blocks, all separated, and each block chose their own manager. Right away I was appointed manager of Block 9, where all the fishermen lived. This was about the

roughest block. They had a fight almost every day. I stayed at Manzanar for a year, but I just couldn't take it anymore.

I heard the United States was calling for help for work in Chicago. The government paid the bus fare to Chicago, and I decided to go.

The people at the camp called me all kinds of names because I volunteered for the United States government. They called me a dog, a crook, everything. When I left Manzanar, many of them didn't even say goodbye. But I took it because I had to think of the future too. What about after the war? I wasn't a citizen yet, but I had to think of my children. They were all future American citizens. So I thought I should do the best I could. That's why I worked for the government during the war.

I went to Chicago and started work at the Fort Bushnell Lumber Company on Summit Road. They were doing one hundred percent manufacturing for the government, building shipping crates for the B-29 engines and ammunition crates.

There is one incident I remember. The general manager wanted me to take the job of foreman of one of the departments. The trouble was, a lot of the Polish workers refused to work under me because I was an enemy alien. So the general manager said, "Okay, whoever can take Henry's job, come on out." But no one came out. So the general manager said, "Well, then I have to let Henry keep the job, because he knows how to do it." So we kept working that way until the war was

DEMOCRACY
AND
HYPOCRISY
ON THE
HOMEFRONT

293

over. One six-month period I worked almost twenty hours a day. The Army gave me an appreciation certificate for doing a good job. So you can imagine how hard I worked.

After the war I came back to California, but I couldn't fish anymore. I had no gear to start with. I had no money. How could I go back to fishing? None of the old Japanese fishermen ever went back.

My own loss I can say, was $55,000 or more. Minimum. In 1940 I bought three new sets of nets. One was for tuna, one for mackerel, and one for sardines. The mackerel and sardine nets each cost $15,000; the tuna net cost about $25,000, because it had all heavyweight webbings. I worked so hard to pay for them. I bought everything by cash. I didn't like that credit business.

Each of the nets we kept in a big flatbed truck on the street where we lived. The day I was arrested I saw with my own eyes my three sets of nets sitting on the flatbeds. I saw them. When we were sent to Fort Lincoln I asked the FBI men about my nets. They said, "Don't worry. Everything is going to be taken care of." But I never saw the nets again, nor my brand-new 1941 Plymouth, nor our furniture. It all just disappeared. I lost everything. But I don't blame anyone. It was a war. We had nothing to do with the war, but we were its victims.

Suggested Readings

A. Russell Buchanan, *Black Americans in World War II* (Santa Barbara, Calif.: Clio Press, 1977), examines the progress blacks made during World War II toward attaining equality of status. An informative study of the effects of World War II on blacks and of their role in American society in general is Neil A. Wynn, *The Afro-American and the Second World War* (London: Elek Books, 1976); the author also includes an extensive and helpful bibliography.

Morton Grodzin, *Americans Betrayed* (Chicago: University of Chicago Press, 1949), examines the Japanese American internment during World War II from the legal and constitutional point of view. Jacobus ten Broek, Edward N. Barnhart, and Floyd W. Matson, *Prejudice, War and the Constitution* (Berkeley: University of California Press, 1968), is a study of the historical origins, political characteristics, and constitutional consequences of the Japanese American detention of 1942–45; particularly interesting is the coverage of the attitudes and actions of anti-Japanese Americans. Joseph D. Harrington, *Yankee Samurai* (Detroit: Pettigrew Enterprises, Inc., 1979), is an account of the Japanese-American soldiers of World War II and their contributions to victory. Daisuke Kitagawa, *Issei and Nisei: The Internment Years* (New York: Seabury Press, 1967), offers a very personal look at the Japanese American internment, based on the author's own experiences. Two indispensable sociological studies of the Japanese American detention are available in Dorothy S. Thomas and Richard Nishimoto, *The Spoilage* (Berkeley: University of California Press, 1946), and Dorothy S. Thomas with Charles Kikuchi and James Sakoda, *The Salvage* (Berkeley: University of California Press, 1952). Carey McWilliams, *Prejudice; Japanese Americans: Symbol of Intolerance* (Boston: Little, Brown, 1949), focuses on the interracial tensions on the Pacific Coast that culminated in the mass evacuation of the Japanese Americans.

Apartheid: Its Origin and Nature

David Lamb

The conclusion of World War II marked the beginning of the end for the European colonial system, which had dominated and exploited Africa and a substantial part of Asia since the late nineteenth century. Liberation movements fueled by strong nationalistic convictions rapidly led to the political independence of the vast majority of Europe's African and Asian colonies. The nationalistic movements were, in part, a result of racial tensions between the European colonizers and the indigenous inhabitants. Western imperialism was characterized by the economic, political, and social oppression of native majorities by relatively small white minorities. The racial conflicts created by this exploitative system of minority rule often bred bitterness and hatred that have endured long after the period of colonization ended.

Africa was the last region to be swept by the tide of nationalism. Presently, only one of the former European colonies, the Republic of South Africa, remains under white rule. The white minority in South Africa, constituting only 18 percent of the population, dominates and oppresses the majority black population through a policy of strict racial separation, called apartheid, *which the government introduced in 1948. South Africa is one of the very few nations in the world that has a large officially unenfranchised population and a legal system to enforce racial and ethnic segregation. The roots of apartheid lie deep in South Africa's colonial experience. Today, it is a troubled and tense nation whose racial problems have become a central issue for the world.*

David Lamb, the author of this reading, spent four years in black Africa as the bureau chief for the Los Angeles Times. *During those years he traveled extensively throughout the continent, including South Africa. His firsthand observations of economic, political, and social conditions in South Africa are a valuable aid in understanding its contemporary history. Lamb views South Africa's current problems as much more than a racial clash. He clearly presents the irreconcilable differences that exist between the white minority and the black majority, and, while suggesting actions both South Africa and the United States could take, he foresees nothing but further racial unrest and political instability as long as the system of apartheid continues to exist.*

All other African black nations govern themselves. We have been in Africa three hundred years and have the same right to govern ourselves as they. This right we cannot and will not forfeit.

—*John Vorster, former South African prime minister*

Right from my days as a young military officer, I always felt that I would achieve a life ambition if I could fight for liberation in southern Africa.

—*Lieutenant General Olusegun Obasanjo, former Nigerian head of state*

South Africa is Africa's only developed First World nation. Were it not for its institutionalized racism, South Africa is what every African country would aspire to become. Built with cheap black labor, white ingenuity and a seemingly endless supply of gold and diamonds, South Africa is advanced enough to have the capability to make an atomic bomb, powerful enough to withstand the condemnation of the entire world, prosperous enough to make any government in Europe, not to mention Africa, full of envy. The great irony of all this is that South Africa's resources are no greater, its farmland no more fertile, its people no more inherently intelligent than those of other countries whose economic and social infrastructures have collapsed.

South Africa's economy is as solid as a cement foundation, its leadership united, its army disciplined and skilled. Even its physical characteristics often stand in contrast to the rest of equatorial Africa. There are little towns that seem to belong in England's Cotswolds, beach resorts along the 2,700-mile coastline that remind you of the Riviera, and perhaps the world's most magnificent city, Cape Town, overlooking the "Tavern of the Seas"—the confluence of the Indian

APARTHEID: ITS ORIGIN AND NATURE   From David Lamb, *The Africans* (New York: Vintage Books, 1984), pp. 313–37.

and Atlantic oceans. The moderate climate, with warm sunny days and cool nights, provides excellent growing conditions for everything from grapes to grain. On Table Mountain in Cape Town there are more varieties of wild flowers than can be found in all the British Isles.

If you asked an Afrikaner why his country had fared so much better than the rest of Africa, he would give you a simple explanation: South Africa is run by whites, the rest of sub-Sahara Africa by blacks. "Let a black man be trained as an airplane mechanic; let him overhaul a Boeing 747 from nose to tail and let [Prime Minister] P. W. Botha and his cabinet go for a ride in it," says Jaap Marais, a conservative former member of parliament.

Marais did not, of course, mention that black Africans pilot and provide maintenance for most national carriers on the continent (and I've never known one to crash with a load of government officials). But white South Africans look at the world—and their own country—with tainted glasses, and everything they have accomplished has been achieved at a terrible cost. The fact that what they have done to their black population is no worse than what some black governments have done to their own people is not a viable argument on the continent. To most Africans, the world's ultimate crime is the racism of whites toward blacks. In its shadow the threats posed by poverty, disease, warfare or Communism all pale. There is only one place left in Africa where that racism is both overt and legal, and until it ends, however violent that ending may be, Africa can never be at peace with itself.

Before we take a close look at this country, which is really the linchpin of the continent's future, let me recite two telling statistics: (1) With 125,400 people in jail, South Africa has the highest per capita prison population in the Western world.* The government provides no racial breakdown, but diplomatic sources estimate that less than 3 percent are white. (2) Ninety-five percent of the Western world's executions are carried out in South Africa. In 1980, the hangings totaled 130. Only one of the victims was white.

Today it seems impossible to think of South Africa without remembering a haunting phrase from Alan Paton's *Cry, the Beloved Country.* "I have one great fear in my heart," says a black minister, "that one day when they [the whites] turn to loving, they will find we are turned to hating."

Every evening at five-twenty a South African Railways passenger train pulls out of Maputo, the Mozambican capital, bound for Johannesburg, 376 miles away. It is a journey between two universes, be-

* The prison population figures were provided by the National Institute for Crime Prevention and Rehabilitation in Johannesburg. Although many people might not consider South Africa part of the "Western world," the term refers broadly to all non-Communist, industrialized countries.

tween two mutually dependent enemies separated by seventeen hours in travel and light-years in mentality.

All seven cars—like the toilets inside—are marked NONWHITES and in them are packed five or six hundred Mozambicans, men heading for the South African gold mines, women clutching chickens and vegetables to be sold at the markets along the way, everyone squeezed together like matchsticks, two and sometimes three people sharing the same seat. I checked my ticket again. Sure enough, it said "First Class." The coal-black Mozambicans around me, the only non-African on the train, chuckled good-naturedly as I sucked in my breath and wiggled my buttocks, hoping to salvage an extra inch or two on the wooden seat. For three hours our train poked along, its whistle clearing cows and errant children from the tracks, moving ever so slowly through the sleepy, primitive villages between Maputo and Ressano García on the border.

The town of Ressano García is all but invisible in the blackness of night. The train grinds to a halt there with squeals and hisses, and an amiable Mozambican soldier dressed in sandals and baggy old fatigues ambles onboard. While checking everyone's ticket he borrows a few cigarettes from the passengers and waves his rifle around casually as though it were only a plaything. Then we all file into the dark, dingy terminal. The kiosk is dust-covered and closed, apparently abandoned long ago. The overhead light fixtures are without bulbs and hang from frayed electrical cords. In the far corner an immigration official, holding a flashlight over the top of his little wooden table, riffles through the passports of the people queued in front of him, stamping an exit visa in each. One by one the travelers saunter back onto the train for the final leg of the journey, which will carry them into the strange land of South Africa.

Komatipoort, the South African border town, is only a few miles down the track, but its bright lights can be seen for quite a distance. The terminal is clean and freshly painted; the white-owned homes nearby have small tidy yards and windows ablaze with lights. The train stops briefly in Komatipoort so that a white crew can take over and two cars designated WHITE ONLY can be added. Now, I'm told, I will have my first-class seat. The black passengers file off the train again, standing this time silently and rigidly before an Afrikaner immigration officer in a crisply pressed uniform. They shuffle their feet uneasily. The white man eyes them wordlessly, as though seeing through them rather than looking at them. He examines each travel document with deliberate thoroughness. His rubber stamp falls with a thud. Permission to enter South Africa granted.

To cross that border is almost like landing on an alien planet, for no two countries in Africa represent greater extremes, ideologically and politically. Mozambique, a revolutionary Marxist state, which defeated the Portuguese colonials in a war of independence, is dedicated to the downfall of the white government in Pretoria; South Africa, a quasi-fascist state, which has borrowed philosophical elements from the Nazi doctrine, is committed to the supremacy of the white race. Understandably enough, black Africa is obsessed with the injustices of the racist giant at its southern doorstep, yet it needs South Africa economically, and its calls for boycotts and sanctions and wars amount to little more than idle threats it cannot back with action. When your grain silos are empty—and your enemy's are full—you do not have much bargaining power.

Indeed, black Africa depends on South Africa. Without it, national economies in the southern third of the continent would fall like dominoes. Because of its economic self-sufficiency and military strength, South Africa—governed by the continent's only white tribe, the Afrikaner—has managed to do pretty much as it pleases to its black majority while remaining immune to mild pressures exerted by the international community. As long as black Africa remains economically weak it can do nothing to influence change within its southern neighbor, and South Africa will continue to stand out like a millionaire general in a room of penniless privates. It is one of only eleven countries in the world that feeds itself and has food left over to export. It is the only industrialized country on a continent otherwise populated exclusively by Third World nations. It is the world's richest nation in terms of white-per-capita, non-petroleum wealth. And its military could take on any dozen black African armies in conventional warfare and still punch through to the northern Sahara in a month or so.

The government can afford to spend nearly 20 percent of its budget, or $3 billion a year, on defense. Its armed forces are comprised of 86,000 regulars and 260,000 reservists—blacks and whites, though 90 percent of the officers are white and military facilities at the camps are segregated. The South African army is one of the most mobile and self-sufficient in the world, needing only one man in the rear to support one soldier on the front lines. (In Vietnam the United States had seven support troops in the rear for each combat soldier.)

Only one black African nation, Malawi, has diplomatic relations with South Africa, and virtually none admits to doing business with South Africa. But what goes through back doors is another matter. Each year at least twenty African countries indirectly support apartheid by purchasing more than $1 billion worth of South African goods and services. Kenya buys South African maize, which it says comes from Mozambique. Zambia buys South African beef, which it says comes from Botswana. Gabon buys South African construction equipment, which it says comes from Europe. Zaire gets 50 percent of its food from South Africa; eighty percent of Zimbabwe's trade goes through South Africa; Malawi built its new capital at Lilongwe with the help of a

$12 million South African loan; Mozambique keeps its ports and railroads running with South African technicians and administrators; six neighboring countries supply 182,000 laborers for the South African mines; the Republic of Cape Verde gets 20 percent of its foreign earnings from landing fees and refueling charges at the South African-built airport on Ilha do Sal. (Denied landing rights at almost every other airport in Africa, South African Airways could not make its long-haul flights to New York and Europe unless its planes stopped at Ilha do Sal.)

Make no mistake, though. South Africa *is* the enemy. Fewer than 4.5 million whites there hold 24 million blacks, colored and Indians* in a form of bondage unique to the modern world, and if there is one thing that unites black Africa, it is a shared hatred of the Afrikaner and his system. But in business, pragmatism takes over where morality and ideology leave off. Apartheid in another country is one thing; economic suicide at home is quite another. As President Nyerere once said, "If I didn't have shoes and South Africa was the only place to get shoes, then I would do without them. But if I didn't have corn and South Africa was the only place to get corn, then I would go to South Africa."

I had been traveling throughout black Africa for nine months before I got to South Africa for the first time. By then I had grown used to hearing how beautiful cities such as Luanda and Maputo had once been. I had become accustomed to visiting dirty, understaffed hospitals, government offices full of broken typewriters and telephones, and schools without chalk for the blackboards or seats for the toilets. Nothing, I thought, could faze me anymore, but when I reached South Africa, I was dumbfounded. *It works.* You pick up the phone and get a dial tone. You summon a waiter and are handed a menu. You get on an airplane and it departs on schedule. Modern highways carry you through the country, which is twice the size of Texas, and the stores are stocked with goods (radios, cotton shirts, hardcover books, tennis rackets) that I hadn't seen since my last trip to Europe. Arriving in Johannesburg is like being back in Cleveland or St. Louis.

Johannesburg, built on a mile-high plateau, did not exist until gold was discovered there in 1886. The city is neither pretty nor exciting but it has a sense of vitality, a feeling of substance and permanence, unlike so many African cities that seem ready to blow away in a strong wind. It has high-rise office buildings, more than a hundred carefully

* The 20 million blacks are African descendants of the Sotho and Nguni people who migrated southward centuries ago. The 3 million "coloureds" are the progeny of the earliest white settlers and the indigenous people or Malay slaves from Dutch West India. The 1 million Asians, mostly from India, were first imported in 1860 as contract laborers for the sugar plantations. These three groups are officially lumped together and classified as "nonwhite."

tended parks, and Beverly Hills-like suburbs that contain more swimming pools and tennis courts than I've ever seen in one place. Johannesburg (population 1.5 million, about the same as Houston) is also the starting point for the world's most elegant passenger train, the Blue Train, which makes the twenty-four-hour trip to Cape Town three times a week, usually arriving within the appointed minute.

But the spooky thing about South Africa is that—if you are white—you don't sense initially that anything is wrong. You can't sense the tension or feel the oppression. There is, in fact, often no awareness that you are in a *black* country. In the heat of downtown Johannesburg, you don't even see many blacks around. You go through the department stores, which are staffed with white clerks and filled with white customers. You sit in a restaurant and find only white patrons. But where are the blacks? If this is their country, where is their world? Poking through Johannesburg after dark is like visiting Iowa and finding no farmers.

What you don't see—and what you can't see without government permission—is Soweto (short for South-West Township), thirty minutes from Johannesburg on the black-only commuter train. It is a teeming, clamorous township of 2 million blacks, an enclave where horse-drawn coal carts creak along the dirt roads between box-shaped houses with outhouses and no electricity, where men confront their defeats with half-jacks (half-quart bottles) of brandy in more than 1,400 illegal *shebeens* (speakeasies), where gangs of young toughs calling themselves "Wild Geese" or "Russians" roam the dark streets with pistols stolen from whites' homes, where on any given day there are three murders.

"If you take a million whites," says Shimane Kumalo, a black social worker in Soweto, "and you subject them to the same process of uninterrupted poverty, the same poor schooling facilities, the same school dropout rate, the lack of occupational skills and the unemployment rate, you will certainly have a murder rate just as high."

The irony of all that is sad and wrong in South Africa is that the South African black is, on the whole, the best educated, best dressed, most prosperous, most literate black on the African continent. He has access to the best medical care—the 2,700-bed Baragwanath Hospital in Soweto is the largest in Africa—and to the steadiest employment. But such superlatives are both relative and irrelevant. The South African black does not want to be compared with other blacks in Africa. He compares himself, and his opportunities, to white South Africa, and on that score he comes up miserably short. He is not a citizen of his land. He is its hostage. In Soweto and other townships adjoining white cities, he is not allowed to buy property. He cannot enter Johannesburg without a pass and cannot stay in the city after nightfall without permission. He has no vote for or say in the all-white parliament. If he is over sixteen years of age, he must carry a pass book listing his tribe, his employer and his tax payments. If he wants to use a restroom in Johannesburg, he has a choice of 161 public toilets. All the others are reserved for whites.

His is the only country in the world where racism is institutionalized—the government operates one television channel for whites, another for blacks—and every aspect of his life is dictated by South Africa's 300-plus discriminatory laws. They determine whom he can love, kiss, marry and have sex with, where he can live, eat, travel and go to school, what he can do for his vocation and avocation. South Africa's "Heartbreak Laws" maintain racial separateness at all significant levels of society. A 1949 act outlaws mixed marriages. "A marriage," it says, "between a European and a non-European may not be solemnized and any such marriage solemnized in contravention of the provisions of the section shall be void and of no effect . . ." A 1953 act bars interracial sex. Persons violating the sex law are arrested, tried and usually sentenced to six to nine months in prison. The sentence is frequently suspended if the couple agrees "not to carry on."

Although the government in recent years has made cosmetic changes to reduce petty discrimination—some public parks and sport teams, for instance, are now integrated, and about 650 blacks attend white universities—the bottom line of South African society is that a man's color establishes his identity. And the basis of that policy is fear, the whites' fear that without apartheid the Afrikaner culture and economic superiority would wither and die like the green grass of summer. "If the European loses his color sense, he can not remain a white man," former South African prime minister J. G. Strijdom once said. The Afrikaner believes that if the blacks gain, the whites lose. He views minor changes such as the integration of city parks as revolutionary. The black sees them as meaningless. Both groups have entirely different concepts of what constitutes change, and the blacks, at least the more militant ones, want nothing less than the same rights other Africans have won throughout the rest of the continent. They are not eager to destroy Africa's only technologically advanced country, but eventually they will if that is what it takes to win their political rights.

The ultimate authority in deciding to what caste a person belongs is the little-publicized Population Registration Board, a group of white social workers who meet privately and classify all South Africans according to race. The board is the final appeal for people who think they have been wrongly classified and for people who want to "pass" from colored to white or vice versa in order to legalize a relationship. (Whites and nonwhites cannot legally stay under the same roof overnight.) Deliberations take months, sometimes years, with the board paying careful attention to skin tint, facial features and hair texture. In one typical twelve-month period, 150 coloreds were reclassified as white; ten whites became colored, six Indians became Malay; two Malay became Indians; two coloreds became Chinese; ten Indians became coloreds; one Indian became white; one white became Malay; four blacks became Indians; three whites became Chinese.

The Chinese are officially classified as a white subgroup. The Japanese, most of whom are visiting businessmen, are given the status of "honorary whites." Absurd? Yes, if all this were part of an antiutopian novel. But in real life it is a chilling part of the most complex system of human control in the world (the Soviet Union notwithstanding). When Mymoena Salie became the first black woman to win a multiracial beauty contest in South Africa several years ago, she found herself unable to accept the prize—a two-week seaside vacation—because the hotel did not admit blacks. An American tourist at the hotel that offered the prize was gazing out one day at the beach and the sea beyond. "Is that the Indian Ocean?" he asked the waiter who brought him a drink. "Oh no, sir," the waiter replied. "That's the European ocean. The Indians use the next beach over."

Cape Town is the home of South Africa's oldest white settlement and a beautiful city it is, full of manicured gardens and sheltered bays, overlooking the Cape of Good Hope and the shipping routes for supertankers that make South Africa one of the continent's most strategically important countries. "This cape is a most stately thing and the fairest cape we saw in the whole circumference of the earth," Sir Francis Drake wrote after rounding the cape in 1580 on the *Golden Hind*.

On a clear night, which most nights are in Cape Town, you can see the lights of Robben Island a few miles off the coast. It is a low, flat, scrub-covered islet where the U.S. ambassador, John Heard, used to hunt birds in the early 1970s. But Robben Island is no more a recreation facility than Alcatraz was, for that is where the government keeps the blacks who would be the leaders of a South Africa ruled by the majority. The currents are treacherous there and no one has ever escaped, even though the mainland is so tantalizingly close.

The large picture windows of the seaside restaurants in Cape Town look directly out at the island, and one evening, over a dinner of fresh lobster and a bottle of local wine, the conversation turned, as almost every one eventually does in South Africa, to race. Sandy and I were with another couple we had met earlier in the day. Martha and George were both divorced and in their fifties. She worked as a secretary for a European embassy, he owned a small hotel.

"See that blinking light out there?" George volunteered, as though the subject could not be ignored. "That's Robben Island, where they've got the political prisoners. You've heard of Nelson Mandela? He's out there. Walter Sisulu? Govan Mbeke? They're there too. There are one hundred and sixteen of them."

"Only one hundred and sixteen?" said Martha. "If I had my way, there'd be two hundred and sixteen. I don't like subversives, and it's as simple as that. I'm conservative. I don't apologize for it."

"Well, I don't think it's right myself," George said. "I don't think they should be locked up for not going along with the government. And I don't think the government should tell a man where he can go. Like if I want to invite a black person into my house, I need a permit."

"That's rubbish," Martha said. "You don't need any permit. I've been to lots of parties with blacks, whites, coloreds. I've got black and colored friends, and I never needed any permit."

"Have you ever had one of them in your house?"

"Of course."

"When?"

"I have, that's all," said Martha, an Afrikaner, and the conversation quickly shifted to how tasty the lobster was.

The next morning as I was checking out of the hotel, I was paged for a telephone call. It was Martha. "You deserve an apology for the way George was talking," she said. "I really don't know him very well, and I didn't want you to think that all South Africans feel that way. He wasn't speaking for me, I can promise you."

Most impartial observers would refer to the prisoners on Robben Island as nationalists. The South African government calls them subversives, Communists and terrorists—which, indeed, they may well be if they ever get their freedom.* To deal with these dissidents South Africa, like most police states, has a myriad of laws to legalize its mistreatment. A 1950 act outlaws the South African Communist Party and any other organization that furthers the aims of Communism. A 1962 act makes sabotage a capital crime and presumes the accused guilty unless he can prove his innocence. A 1967 act provides for indefinite detention in solitary confinement without access to a lawyer for suspected terrorists. The most bizarre tool the government uses to silence dissent is called "banning," which in effect turns a person into a nonperson. The 150 or so banned people in South Africa are not allowed to leave the city where they live, to talk with more than two people (including relatives) at one time, to publish, teach or entertain visitors at home. The local press is not allowed to quote anything they say or

* The most significant antigovernment group is the outlawed African National Congress, founded in 1912 to seek peaceful change through reform. Its philosophy became revolutionary only when the whites' intransigence made reform impossible. The ANC's titular head is Nelson Mandela, who has been in prison on terrorist charges since 1964 (when he was 46 years old). The ANC, with 6,000 guerrillas based in neighboring black African countries and thousands of clandestine supporters inside South Africa, is credited with eighty acts of sabotage that killed eight persons between 1981 and mid-1983.

anything they have ever said or written. For all practical purposes, they cease to exist.

So when Martha called, I said she did not need to apologize and let the subject drop. Talking race with an Afrikaner is like discussing mathematics with a stone wall. Unlike other whites in Africa, the Afrikaner has no ties to Europe. He has no home other than Africa, no passport other than South Africa's. He is the descendant of the stern, hard-working Dutch, French and German pioneers who came to Cape Town in the seventeenth century and who stayed on to confront first the British, then the black Africans and now the world. His perspective is introverted and fiercely nationalistic, his society rigid and so puritanical that bars and movie theaters are closed on Sunday. He speaks a unique Dutch-based language called Afrikaans, follows a fundamentalist form of Calvinism and has a sense of special mission created by his own history of suffering. But the very history that gives him strength is also the source of his isolation and imprisonment, the burial ground into which the seeds of his own self-destruction have been sown.

Afrikaner history dates back to April 1652, when, after nearly four months at sea, the Dutch ship *Dommedaris* brought the first whites—Captain Jan van Riebeeck and a crew of 125 men—to Cape Town. They came to establish a station for the Dutch East India Company where vessels on the route to India could stop for provisions and medical facilities, and they met no resistance from the indigenous Hottentots and Bushmen who then inhabited the cape. The company had not intended to set up anything more than a way station, but gradually, almost imperceptibly, a colony of settlement began to emerge. In 1657 the company released some of its servants as free burghers to cultivate land and raise cattle. That same year slaves from Angola and the East Indies were imported as laborers. Dutch settlers began to arrive, along with French Protestant Huguenots seeking religious freedom. Later came German immigrants. Interracial marriage was common—and legal—and the Cape colored became a new ethnic group. The way station grew and became a regular port of call for European vessels. Cape Town was no longer a mere outpost. It was the birthplace of a nation—and of a new, white tribe.

Britain seized the cape in 1795 and soon missionaries, traders, administrators and settlers were arriving by the shipload. They considered the original white settlers inferior and obdurate and treated them with disdain. The Afrikaner was denied land rights and fined for such minor offenses as allowing his cattle to stray. He was excluded from jury duty because of his language and forced to accept English-speaking ministers for his churches. If his children spoke Afrikaans at school, they were punished by having to put a placard around their necks that read: "I am a donkey. I speak Afrikaans."

The British returned the cape to the Dutch in 1803, then took it back in 1806 because of the need to protect their sea routes to India during the renewed Napoleonic Wars. The Dutch settlers, who called themselves Boers (farmers), felt threatened. And in 1835, rifle and Bible in hand, they began moving north in small groups to escape the British and to secure a land of their own. Over the next eight years more than 12,000 *voortrekkers** rolled across the plains in ox wagons, headed on an uncharted course for the high veld of Natal and Transvaal provinces, firmly convinced that God had chosen them to implant a new nation in Africa. On their odyssey, which became known as the Great Trek, they carried with them much bitterness and a sense of purpose forged on the anvil of oppression.

The trek was a perilous one, and in times of danger the Boers took up positions in the *laager*—a protective circle of wagons with locked wheels. In the bloodiest battle of the trek, 12,000 Zulu warriors attacked a *laager* in 1838 along the banks of the Ncome River. The 500 Boer defenders annihilated them, and keeping the vow they had made to God during the fight, built a church to commemorate the victory. The day of that victory, December 16, is celebrated today as a national holiday, the Day of the Covenant, and the Ncome in Natal province is now known as Blood River. (The Zulus, however, remained a formidable force in northern Natal until 1879, when the British destroyed them militarily and occupied Zululand.)

In the early 1850s the Boers established two independent republics, one known as the South African Republic in the Transvaal, the other as the Orange Free State. They made alliances with the local chiefdoms, but the peace and isolation that they sought still eluded them. Britain was uneasy with this maverick white tribe and it annexed both the Transvaal and Natal. In 1886 one of the world's richest gold deposits was found in the Witwatersrand (the "Ridge of White Waters") region of the Transvaal, where Johannesburg is now located. English-speaking immigrants and British investment poured into South Africa. Again the Boers felt threatened. Only this time, instead of trekking north, they stood and fought. It was Africa's first war of independence and the only one that pitted whites against whites.

The two Anglo-Boer wars (1880–1881 and 1899–1902) were among the bloodiest Africa has ever witnessed, and they divided the British population much as the Vietnam war would divide the United States in the 1970s. Britain committed 500,000 troops to the Second War of Freedom, as the Afrikaners called it, against a force of 88,000 Boers. The campaign cost Britain 22,000 dead and 150,000 wounded. The Boers, using the same guerrilla tactics that black nationalists would rely on in

* *Voor* means "forward" in Afrikaans, thus *voortrekkers* translates as the forward trekkers, or pioneers. The trekkers and their descendants are known today as Boers.

liberation wars against colonial authorities nearly a century later, attacked on two fronts, into the northern Cape from the Orange Free State and into Natal from the Transvaal. Their commandos harried British supply lines and communications facilities, and for awhile the Boers held the British to a stand-off.

But Lord Herbert Kitchener, the British commander in chief, responded with a scorched-earth policy, protecting railway installations and government facilities with barbed wire and destroying the farms of both the Afrikaners and the black Africans. The wives and children of Boer farmers were rounded up and put in concentration camps, where more than 20,000 died because of neglect and unsanitary conditions. As brutal as they were, Kitchener's tactics paid off. In May 1902 the defeated Boers accepted the loss of their independence and signed the Peace of Vereeniging treaty. (Later, in 1910, the former Boer republics and the two British colonies, Natal and the Cape, were joined to form the Union of South Africa, a dominion of the British Empire. The union became a sovereign state within the empire in 1934. South Africa left the British Commonwealth in 1961 and became a republic.)

The Boer wars helped fashion a new sense of Afrikaner nationalism. His language, his culture, his claim to the African land made him unique, and everyone, white or black, was seen as a potential enemy. In defeat he had become a second-class citizen in what he considered his own country. New Dutch immigrants had long since stopped coming to South Africa and, isolated and alone, he knew that Afrikanerdom could survive only as a unified entity if it were uncorrupted by outside influence. He took a refuge in his church and his secret societies such as the Broederbond (literally, association of brothers), and he waited for the political power which would enable him to build a nation, where everyone was of the same mind, the same color, the same faith.

That opportunity came in 1948 when the Afrikaner-led National Party upset Jan Smut's United Party and began the longest uninterrupted reign of any political party still in power in the Western world. Believing that integration would lead to the ultimate destruction of the whites, the Afrikaner government moved quickly to enact a web of racial laws and to strengthen its system of self-preservation known as apartheid. It is worth noting here that apartheid did not create racial discrimination; it only institutionalized it. Back in 1909, for instance, the British withdrew the rights of nonwhites to sit in the South African parliament. The next year coloreds staged a nonviolent protest demonstration in Cape Town led by Mohandas Gandhi.

In Afrikaans, *apartheid* means "apartness" or "separateness," although the word has become so stigmatized internationally that South Africans no longer use it officially, preferring instead euphemisms such as "plural democracy" or "separate development." According to the doctrine, every race has a unique destiny and a unique cultural contribution to make; therefore the races must be kept separate to develop along their own lines. But however one rationalizes it, the real intent of the system is the retention of *baaskap* (white supremacy). Apartheid still means racial purity, the subjugation of the nonwhite majority for the benefit of the all-white minority. It is the instrument that officially transformed the oppressed into the oppressor.

Although there are some black lawyers and doctors and millionaire businessmen in South Africa (and, unlike anywhere else in Africa, even a few poor whites), it goes without saying that the whiter a person's skin, the better his fortunes. The government spends $677 a year to educate each white child, $277 for a colored, and $66 for a black. White miners earn $16,630 a year and get a house virtually rent-free; black miners average $2,546 and sleep in crowded dormitories. In the construction industry, a white makes twice the salary of an Asian, three times that of a colored, and five times that of a black. Ignoring the almost insurmountable barriers that these educational and monetary inequities create, the Afrikaner then dismisses the black as being incompetent, unmotivated and inarticulate. "It's the K factor," he will say with a shrug, meaning that blacks are inherently inferior. The *K* stands for "kaffir" (the Kaffirs being one of the South African aboriginals), a pejorative whose meaning and use is similar to the word "nigger."

The centerpiece of apartheid is the Land Resettlement Act of 1936, which, paradoxically, was the result of international pressure on South Africa, exerted by the League of Nations in an attempt to improve the blacks' lot. The plan called for resettling of the blacks, who comprise 67 percent of the population, into ten separate *Bantustans,* or "homelands," that represent 13.7 percent of the country's total area—and hold almost none of its natural wealth. Only four of the homelands are composed of a single piece of land—the others are broken into two or more parts surrounded by South Africa—and most are not even identified by any sign at their borders to inform a traveler that he is leaving South Africa and allegedly entering a new country. By 1982 four homelands, each representing a particular tribe, had been declared independent states by Pretoria.* Each has a president, a parliament and some political autonomy. But their "independence" is only a sham, an event staged by Pretoria, and no government in the world other than South Africa's extends them diplomatic recognition.

South Africa claims that the Bantustans are designed to give all peoples equal opportunities, but the obvious purpose is simply to seg-

* In 1976 Transkei became the first "independent" homeland. It was followed by Bophuthatswana in 1977, Venda in 1979 and Ciskei in 1981. The other six homelands are Kwa-Zulu (the eight splintered parts of the once powerful Zulu nation), Qwa Qwa, Lebowa, Gazankulu, Kangwane and South Ndebele.

regate the four main racial groups—white, colored, Asian and Bantu—into separate national communities, thus maintaining the whiteness of the Afrikaners without disturbing their access to cheap labor. The scheme is like a giant United States' school busing project in reverse. (No rural land is set aside for the coloreds and Asians; instead they are allocated residential areas in the urban centers.) The only ones who benefit are the whites.*

What apartheid does, then, is to sever the links of contact and communication that people have in a normal society. The whites meet only black garbage collectors and janitors, not their counterparts who are teachers, doctors and social workers. The blacks deal mostly with white Afrikaans-speaking policemen and civil servants. By day the black works in the shadow of the white preserve, in the clean, sparkling cities and the expansive suburbs. By night he returns to his smoky slum where, by law, he must remain until dawn. The discontent builds, and the envy and resentment take firm hold.

To be sure, there are some moderates in the white community who see what the inevitable result of apartheid has to be. But they can be found mainly among the people of English stock, who make up 40 percent of the white population. The Afrikaner remains intransigent. Contrary to what he believes, though, his intransigence is endangering the whites' long-range interests in South Africa. It will create the very conditions that the Soviet Union can best exploit—racial unrest and political instability. It will make Communism a far more real threat to South Africa than it is to the rest of the continent. For no matter how alien the tenets of Communism may be to Africa, there comes a point, when the unhappiness of the general population runs deep enough, that the propaganda of the left sounds like a hopeful panacea.

President Jimmy Carter recognized this and put some distance between his Administration and the Pretoria government. Not so with President Ronald Reagan. He moved quickly to repair the damaged relationship, asking: "Can we abandon this country that has stood by us in every war we've ever fought?" It is true that South Africa did fight with the Allies in the two world wars, took part in the Berlin Airlift, participated in the postwar United Nations' force in Korea and maintains a foreign policy that is staunchly anti-Communist. But Reagan's statement seriously distorted the historical record.

* Western entertainers and athletes had refused to perform in the homelands on the premise that to do so would give them—and South Africa's scheme—credibility. But in 1981 Frank Sinatra provided Bophuthatswana with a much needed sense of legitimacy by giving nine concerts at the Sun City, a Las Vegas-style gambling resort, for a reported fee of $1.6 million. The $85 top ticket price ascertained that the audience would be mostly white, though Sinatra insisted he was in no way supporting segregation. "I play to all—any color, any creed, drunk or sober," he said. President Lucas Mangope was so delighted that he awarded Sinatra the "nation's" highest decoration, the Order of the Leopard, and made him an honorary tribal chief.

The South Africans who twice stood by the Allies at the start of global hostilities were largely the English-speaking white minority. The Afrikaners argued against declaring war on Germany in 1914. They held demonstrations throughout South Africa to protest the United Party's decision to enter the war, and in 1939 the Nationalist leader, J. B. M. Hertzog, defended Hitler in the South African parliament and contended that Germany had annexed Czechoslovakia in self-defense. South Africa joined the Allies only after a close parliamentary vote, 80–67.

The end of World War II saw the political emergence of the Afrikäner and the introduction of apartheid. The international community gradually cut South Africa adrift. In 1974 the United Nations revoked its General Assembly seat. In 1977 an embargo on the shipment of weapons to South Africa, which the UN had made "voluntary" fourteen years earlier, became mandatory. South African sports teams were barred from the Olympics and most international competition. South African airplanes were banned from landing at almost every airport in Africa, and South African resident diplomats were welcome nowhere on the continent except in Malawi. Telephone operators in most black-run countries won't even connect a caller to a South African number. By 1982 South Africa had only one unquestioning friend left, Israel, another outcast of the world community. There are 120,000 Jews in South Africa, but the relationship seemed to be based more than anything on the premise that my enemy's enemy must be my friend.

South Africa has not only survived in the face of global condemnation, it has prospered. A century ago it exported little more than some wine from Cape province. Today it mines nearly three quarters of the West's gold, manufactures everything from refrigerators to automobiles, exports vast quantities of food, textiles and machinery, and is the tenth largest weapons producer in the world. Some of those armaments are both indigenous and innovative, notably the Ratel, a high-speed armored personnel carrier that has a range of 900 miles and is built for rugged conditions. The weapons and munitions are assembled by black laborers and are a major factor in the continuation of white rule.

Two aspects of South Africa seem abundantly clear: the country must make a dramatic change to transform itself into an integrated multiracial society; and if that change is initiated by violence, perhaps in the form of Africa's first race war, the effects on the continent and the world would be cataclysmic. What can the United States do to effect a peaceful change? One popular line of reasoning says that the 350 U.S. companies in South Africa should close down and the United States should divest itself of all investments there and should terminate its trade with the Pretoria government, which runs in excess of $5 billion a year.

The gesture would, I believe, be futile. First, embargoes and sanctions have never been effective because, whether the culprit is Communist Cuba or capitalistic Rhodesia, someone is always willing to break them. Second, if the South African economy deteriorates and jobs are lost, the first to suffer will be the blacks, not the whites. Third, if Washington ordered U.S. companies to pull their money out of South Africa, the Pretoria government would undoubtedly freeze the funds, and another country such as France or Japan would step in to pick up the United States' share of the trade market. Fourth, if the United States cut its commercial ties, it loses whatever leverage it has to pressure South Africa to make changes. Fifth, any action taken by the West is meaningless as long as black Africa demands that others do what it is unable or unwilling to do itself.

That leaves Washington with only one sensible policy to follow, other than the use of diplomatic pressure: make sure that American companies in South Africa provide equal pay for equal work to all races, formulate training programs to elevate blacks into positions of authority, end all segregation in their plants. The results will not topple the pillars of Afrikanerdom, but they will make them quiver, for anything that gives the South African black a fair share of wages and increased authority gives the South African white reason to worry that what he has created cannot last forever.

In the end, the apartheid that gave the Afrikaner his strength may be the very system that will destroy him. He has relentlessly denied the blacks opportunity, and now the white population is no longer large enough to supply all the skills and services an industrialized country of 28.5 million people needs. He has built a powerful military and developed nuclear capabilities to protect this system. But the threat is at home, not abroad, so what are his choices? To rain bombs on his own country in a frenzy of self-destruction? He has enjoyed one of the highest standards of living in the world while holding 85 percent of the people in a form of serfdom. The prison on Robben Island is already full. What does the Afrikaner do with the young, educated, unemployed blacks who surely will not be as tolerant as their parents were?

I can think of no single event that would bring more benefit to all of Africa than the peaceful advent of an integrated multiracial society in South Africa. If South Africa could trade freely with the rest of the continent, its political and economic influence would be gigantic. It would dominate Africa as no single country dominates Europe or South America. It could take the leadership role in the Organization of African Unity (of which it is not even a member now). Its technicians and experts could travel without restriction and help other governments develop their countries the way the Afrikaner has developed his own. They could make the ports and railroads and telephones of

Africa work again. The resultant economic stimulation to the continent would be nothing short of revolutionary. The Russians would have to pack their bags and go home, for without poverty, instability and discontent they have little hope of gaining the foothold they seek in southern Africa.

And what of the comfortable life style the white man in South Africa cherishes so dearly? It probably would not change much if the transition occurred before, as Alan Paton wrote, the blacks "are turned to hating." The Afrikaner would still control the commercial and professional world. He would still belong to the same country club (with, to be sure, a few black members). He would still live in a comfortable suburban home and have a domestic staff. He would learn, as others in Kenya and Zimbabwe already have, that there is no reason why blacks and whites cannot work together to build a nation and a continent, especially when both races are African.

But however shameful his system is, one cannot ignore the fact that the Afrikaner has built the most remarkable country in Africa. "Everyone knows that if you took away apartheid, South Africa would be the best place around," a black Kenyan friend told me. I suspect most Africans would agree, and perhaps it is time for other African governments to take a fresh look at their southern neighbor. They already know what South Africa has done wrong. Now they ought to start considering what it has done right. The farms, industries and mines that produce so bountifully, the cities that function so smoothly and efficiently, the government officials who work without the incentive of bribes and thievery—these are achievements that should be examined, not dismissed out of hand. If the Organization of African Unity spent as much time studying South Africa's agricultural sector as it did drafting resolutions to condemn apartheid, the fifty member states might eventually grow strong enough to pressure Pretoria into changing its internal policies.

In 1978 a poll taken at the University of Stellenbosch showed that 54 percent of the students "would die if necessary" to uphold white rule. They may have that chance unless meaningful reform starts dismantling the structures of apartheid. But the Afrikaner is not going to change voluntarily for the sake of being a humanitarian. Black urban terrorism will probably come first. The whites will respond with increased repression. Blood will be shed. The whites of English origin will start leaving South Africa (as, in fact, they already are in small numbers). The blacks' strength will grow, and so will their population, to a projected 35 million by the year 2000.

It is not a cheery scenario, and the sane world should pray that the inevitable violence can be kept limited and controlled until the South African whites come to understand—as did the Rhodesians—the futility of fighting. Given a choice between relenting or perishing, the white man in Africa has always relented. The Afrikaner is now confronted with the same choice. He must soon make his decision because for South Africa, time is running out.

Suggested Readings

Richard W. Hull, *Southern Africa: Civilizations in Turmoil* (New York: New York University Press, 1981), focuses on the Republic of South Africa in his examination of the origin and development of southern African civilizations from the fourteenth century to the present. Tom Lodge, *Black Politics in South Africa Since 1945* (New York: Longman, Inc., 1983), treats the history of resistance movements within the black population of South Africa from the end of the Second World War to the present. Sam C. Nolutshunger, *Changing South Africa: Political Considerations* (Manchester, England: Manchester University Press, 1982), stresses the role of politics in the general problem of change in South Africa. Peter Magubane, *Black Children* (New York: Knopf, 1982), is a brief portrait of the tragic living conditions under which black children grow up in South Africa. Bernard Magubane, *The Political Economy of Race and Class in South Africa* (New York and London: Monthly Review Press, 1979), is a sociohistorical account of the evolution of racial oppression in South Africa, with emphasis on African labor exploitation. Other readings dealing with apartheid are Peter Lambley, *The Psychology of Apartheid* (London: Secker and Warburg, 1980); George W. Shepherd, Jr., *Anti-Apartheid* (Westport, Conn.: Greenwood Press, 1977); Robert I. Rotberg, *Suffer the Future: Policy Choices in Southern Africa* (Cambridge: Harvard University Press, 1980); and Gwendolen M. Carter, *Which Way Is South Africa Going?* (Bloomington: Indiana University Press, 1980).

Lihua: A Young Woman's Experience with China's Cultural Revolution

Fox Butterfield

The creation in 1949 of the People's Republic of China brought an end to more than a century of political and social instability. Since then Communist China has gone through over three decades of change, often for the better, but frequently resulting in brutality and horrible human suffering. The transformation of contemporary China was marked by a series of political campaigns whose effects permeated all of Chinese society. Chief among them were the land reform of the early 1950s, the Hundred Flowers campaign, the Great Leap Forward in 1958, the Cultural Revolution of the 1960s, and the constant factional battles of the 1970s. Of all the programs China's government embarked upon, none had as tumultuous an impact as the Great Proletarian Cultural Revolution, from 1965 to 1969.

The Cultural Revolution was an attempt to restructure society entirely and to change the consciousness of the Chinese people. It was begun by Mao Zedong both as a purge of his political adversaries in the party hierarchy and as a way to prevent the country from drifting back to the traditional cultural values of pre-1949 China. The Cultural Revolution quickly broadened into a mass movement that virtually destroyed the existing establishment. It was marked by great brutality and waste. Many were persecuted, arrested, tortured, or killed because of their class backgrounds. Intellectual and cultural life was disrupted, families were uprooted, and property was confiscated or destroyed. The Cultural Revolution became a human tragedy on a grand scale.

The following selection by Fox Butterfield is a vivid portrait of the social upheaval caused by the Cultural Revolution. The author recounts the life of Lihua, who at six years of age was taken from her home and, along with her family, forcibly moved to a remote village in the countryside. The struggle of Lihua and her family to survive is a poignant example of the suffering experienced by countless Chinese during this era. Butterfield shows not only the brutality of the Cultural Revolution but also the accompanying fears, apathy, and cynicism of the millions of victims. A picture emerges of a disillusioned China in which necessities were scarce, living conditions cramped, and society strictly regimented.

Everyone is given a difficult sutra to read.

—*A Chinese proverb*

She was only six years old when it happened.

Until then, Lihua ("Strength for China") had lived in a spacious apartment in Peking with her three older brothers, a younger sister, her father, who was a scientist, and her mother, a nurse. They thought of themselves with pride as what the Chinese call intellectuals, the carriers of the great tradition. Her mother used to tell the children about her own grandfather, who had passed one of the imperial exams under the Qing dynasty before the turn of the century and had held a sinecure job in the court in Peking.

But they had a neighbor who was jealous of them. He was a worker and a Communist Party member, in Chinese terms a good class status. But he drank and smoked a lot, his wife was unemployed, and he had a hard time supporting their five children. In 1966, at the start of the Cultural Revolution, the neighbor moved quickly to organize a radical faction in their apartment building in support of Mao. His new position enabled him to examine Lihua's father's confidential dossier in the Party's files; in it he found her father had once been briefly a member of the Kuomintang before 1949 when he was a student. That was enough to convict him. A rally was held, Lihua's father was judged a "hidden counterrevolutionary," and he was stripped of his teaching post.

"Red Guards came to search our house, they confiscated everything," she recalled. "They took my father's books, my mother's jewelry, her college photo albums, our furniture. Then they built a bonfire in the yard outside and burned everything.

"That was the end of my childhood," Lihua said.

LIHUA: A YOUNG WOMAN'S EXPERIENCE   From Fox Butterfield, *China: Alive in a Bitter Sea* (New York: Bantam Books, 1982), pp. 113–28.

Afterward, the Public Security Bureau ordered her entire family to move to a village in a remote part of Hunan province, eight hundred miles south of Peking. It was punishment for her father's supposed past sins. Lihua's ancestors had come from the village, Gold Mountain, but neither her mother nor father had ever lived there, and no one in the family knew how to farm. Six teen-age Red Guards accompanied the family on the three-day train trip to make sure they got there.

"When we arrived, the local cadres took away the few things we had left, our clothes and our bedding. They left us only what we had on our backs." The family was put in the village schoolhouse, a small one-room building with holes in the walls where the windows should have been and a roof that leaked. There was no furniture. Lihua had to learn to sleep on the mud floor. The school had already been closed by the Cultural Revolution. The teacher had been arrested as a reactionary.

"The peasants and the cadres made my parents parade through the streets every day for several weeks," she related. "They hung a placard around my father's neck, they made him kneel down to confess his crimes, and they beat both my father and mother with iron bars.

"A person is made of flesh. If you beat them long enough, they will die." Within a month her mother was dead and her father was left deaf and unable to use his right arm.

"My mouth is very stupid because I didn't go to school, but these are a few of the facts."

Lihua recounted this story the first time we met in September 1979 on the steps of the Peking Municipal Party Committee Headquarters, a functional gray-concrete building. I had gone there when I heard there were a number of petitioners from the countryside standing outside the Party office trying to present their grievances to the city authorities. It was one of those periods when China's leaders temporarily relaxed their control. Some young factory workers and students took advantage of the slack to put up wall posters or print unofficial journals criticizing the regime, what we foreign correspondents came to call the "democracy movement." Thousands of other people materialized from the countryside asking to have their own personal cases reexamined. The Chinese referred to them as *shang-fang,* meaning they were "entreating a higher level for help." Lihua was one of these.

I didn't notice her at first. I was interviewing an eighteen-year-old man, dressed in a faded, soiled pair of loose blue trousers, who said he had been sold by his father for a pig after the family had been forced out of Peking during the Cultural Revolution. Lihua had come over and stood quietly by my side, waiting for me to finish asking the other man questions. She didn't look like a petitioner. She was wearing a neat tomato-red cotton jacket, with a blue- and white-striped shirt underneath. Her long hair, worn in braids to her waist, was carefully combed; her skin was creamy, unlike most peasants, who have been burned brown by years in the sun; and her teeth were straight and white. Above all, it was the easy smile on her broad face—she didn't look angry. She talked in a calm, dispassionate voice, almost as if all this had happened to someone else, but her story soon gathered a crowd.

After her mother died and her father became an invalid, she had to find a way to earn a living, for the cadres in charge of the village retroactively labeled her family "landlords" and at first wouldn't let her brothers take part in working in the collective fields or have their own small private plot for raising vegetables. The one thing she found she could do as a six-year-old was to go out to the mountains around the village to collect firewood to sell to a brick kiln nearby.

"I would walk thirty li [ten miles] up to the hills at sunrise every day, then back that evening. Sometimes I had to carry a hundred pounds, almost twice my weight. But I was inexperienced and often cut myself with the ax," she said. When I looked down at her hands, there were long scars on the backs of both hands and a gash down the middle finger of her left hand from the tip of the nail to the first joint. "We didn't have enough money to pay for a doctor to stitch it," she explained. The village, as part of a commune, had a cooperative medical program, but families of landlords were not eligible to join.

"In that first year, our clothes soon became like tattered pieces of paper. I had to teach myself how to sew for the family by taking apart our old clothes and then putting them back together.

"I was born into the new society," she went on, using a Chinese expression for the years after the Communists' victory in 1949. "I grew up under the Red flag and at first I didn't understand how such things could happen. But gradually I came to realize that I represent many thousands of people. It is just like in the old feudal society before Liberation. We Chinese must still *chi-ku,* 'eat bitterness.' Nothing has really changed.

"As humans, we should have rights, the right to a job, to get an education, but the cadres often treat us like dogs and pigs," she said, still speaking in her level, matter-of-fact tone, addressing both me and the crowd around her.

I broke off our talk here. It was as much as I could listen to that morning, and I was getting nervous about the size of the crowd, now over a hundred people. It was noontime, and a number of Party officials were coming out of their offices. A cadre in his fifties, gray-haired and dressed in a well-tailored Mao tunic, walked down the steps and into a chauffeur-driven black Mercedes that was waiting. He did not stop to talk to any of the petitioners. I was with Jan Wong, my assistant, who dressed and looked like a Peking college student, a useful disguise. Jan wrote out *The Times*'s office phone number, and Lihua agreed to meet us again.

I felt depressed by Lihua's story, but euphoric about meeting her. Confined to Peking, it was rare for me to encounter someone from the countryside. Most Chinese I knew were city people, and the Information Department had rebuffed all my requests to live even for a few days in a village. Yet four fifths of China's one billion people were peasants, and perhaps 200 million of them still lived in isolated areas in conditions that the government itself described as verging on poverty. By chance, Lihua's village was in one of the most remote and poorest regions, the Jinggangshan, a legendary belt of forested mountains on the border of Hunan and Jiangxi provinces. Mao had taken advantage of its isolation and backwardness to set up his first guerrilla base there in 1928. At our next meeting, I asked Lihua if she would describe life in Gold Mountain. I didn't have to put another question to her—she was a born raconteur, like one of the traditional storytellers who recited picaresque sagas of adventure and misfortune at rural fairs.

Evidently little had changed since Mao's Red Army days in the Jinggangshan in the 1930s, she indicated. From her village it was still a half day's walk to the nearest road. There was no electricity—most villages now do have electric power, the government claims—and no running water. The peasants used ponds and irrigation ditches to wash their clothes. Gold Mountain had seven hundred inhabitants, in one hundred families, larger than the average village because the government had formed it by consolidating four separate hamlets scattered across a mountain during the Great Leap Forward in 1958. Officially it was designated as a production team, the lowest of the three tiers that make up a commune, but in size it was more like a brigade, the middle level.

"Our village used to be in an area the people called the land of rice and fish," Lihua said. "The land was fertile, rainfall was plentiful, rice grew in the paddies, and the peasants had to work only half the year to survive."

But the Great Leap Forward in 1958, when Mao ordered the formation of the communes, altered all that, she asserted. Mao had calculated that China could be transformed almost overnight from a poor agricultural country to a modern industrial power if the peasants labored hard enough in the fields and began enough small-scale rural factories. In Gold Mountain, the cadres tried to produce Mao's miracle. Some officials in Peking believed there was coal in the area, so the peasants were told to dig tunnels in all their fields. The rice and sweet potato crops were left to rot in the rush, though no coal was found. Some other ministry determined that the peasants could increase their supply of fertilizer by cutting down all the trees around the village, and spreading the ashes on the fields. That left them without fuel for cooking and heating their homes.

When Lihua's family arrived in the village a few years later, it had still not recovered. They found themselves constantly short of food.

"We had to borrow or beg a few ounces of rice or sweet potatoes from the other peasants," she remembered. "My brothers didn't know how to cook, so I had to learn that also. I would put the rice in a pot, with too much water for it, to make a thin gruel, then add in whatever vegetables we could scavenge, maybe some cabbage, turnips, scallions, wild herbs, or mushrooms from the mountains. The peasants say, 'There are poor people, but no poor mountains,' You couldn't cut down the mountains."

Her hunts in the mountains were not always successful. "I was still very young, and I didn't know what I could pick and eat. One day I was poisoned by something I had gathered. My face turned purple, I vomited, and was delirious. An old woman saved me with some herbal medicine she had.

"Sometimes we were so short of food we had to eat the husks of the rice too. I would make them into pancakes. But they were so hard, I couldn't swallow them unless I was very hungry. I would carry one up to the mountains and eat it when I was cutting firewood.

"For years we couldn't get cooking oil," she said, meaning vegetable oils like peanut or rapeseed oil that the Chinese use for frying their food. "There was so little oil our cooking pot got rusty."

Lihua blamed this diet for her current health problems. Her hair was falling out in clumps when she brushed it, she said; her eyes hurt when she read, and she often felt weak or dizzy. I noticed that at lunch she ate only two or three mouthfuls of rice and some chicken soup. She had no appetite for more, she insisted. Over the next few months, as we met several dozen times, I never saw her eat a normal meal.

Lihua's family faced other shortages too. They couldn't buy soap or matches. Each peasant family was supposed to get a pack of 1,000 matches a year, but the cadres in Gold Mountain took that ration away from Lihua's brothers and sisters, as they had been labeled landlords. "We had to take a bundle of loose straw to a neighbor's house to borrow fire," she recalled. "They took pity on us." Soap simply wasn't available.

The peasants in Gold Mountain ate meat only five or six times a year, on the traditional festival days like the lunar New Year, she said. Before 1949 the peasants never had much meat either, but the problem had been compounded by the Communists' limits on the number of chickens and pigs each family could raise. Mao had been afraid that a family that grew more than a few animals would turn into capitalists. So each household in Gold Mountain, Lihua related, had been restricted to raising one pig and two chickens. They had to be sold to the state, at the state's low, fixed price.

"If you slaughtered them yourself, the cadres would ask for a piece," she said. "Once at New Year's, they asked us for a whole pig. If they were being polite, the cadres would say, 'Such and such a cadre is coming down for a visit from a higher level for a visit and we need some money for his food. It is your duty to give it.' Sometimes they would just get people to write a slip to the production team to borrow money from the collective account. Then they took the money for themselves. It was up to you to repay it." Lihua claimed her family had lost about $600 this way, counting chickens, pigs, and cash.

"We called the head of the production team the local emperor. He was master of all. They weren't any different from the landlords in the old society."

The man who was head of the production team when she first arrived in Gold Mountain was a veteran of the Red Army who had gained local prestige by fighting in the Korean war with China's troops. He had now retired and his son had taken over the post. Although China's official policy is that the heads of production teams are to be elected, Lihua said she had never heard of any vote in her village. As far as she knew, the cadres were all appointed by some higher authority.

The team leaders were faced with the problem of trying to make Gold Mountain's production figures look better. The average distribution to able-bodied male peasants at the end of the year in the village, when the harvest of all the crops was added up and state taxes were deducted, came out to 550 pounds of unhusked rice or its equivalent in sweet potatoes, Lihua recalled. That works out to about 380 pounds of edible rice. When she said that, Jan Wong, who was helping me interpret, was shocked. Jan calculated that she, herself, consumed 350 pounds of rice a year in Peking, but that was in addition to the generous amounts of meat, fish, and vegetables she ate every day. Published Chinese government figures suggest that 330 pounds of rice a year is semistarvation rations. Moreover, Lihua added, unlike better-off teams, Gold Mountain had no cash to divide at year's end because the village had no sideline occupations, like growing oranges or silkworms, and no local factories.

One year the cadres decided they could raise production by introducing a new high-yield variety of rice with short stalks they heard about. But it required extra amounts of fertilizer, which they didn't have, and, as the peasants soon discovered, it was susceptible to insects. To try to overcome the pest problem, the cadres bought new chemical sprays; the pesticides soon killed most of the fish in the village ponds. In the end the crop failed, and the peasants had to go for a year without rice, begging from a nearby village. Even the stalks left in the fields weren't as good for fuel as the old long-stemmed strain.

But the team leader reported an increase in output anyway, Lihua charged, and consequently had to deliver a larger amount to the state. "To cover up what had happened, he ordered us to put what good grain we had on the tops of the rice sacks, to put stalks at the bottom, and rocks in the middle.

"This was our education from the Cultural Revolution.

"Before, the peasants were very *lao shi,*" a Chinese virtue that translates as "honest and upright." "Afterward they became evil. People began to steal from each other's private plots. You had to watch out your neighbors didn't take your chickens or pig. People's philosophy became *guo yi tian, suan yi tian* [get through the day and forget it]. Everyone was very pessimistic."

Lihua herself was growing up in these years. At the early summer and fall harvests (they grew two crops a year), she made her way to a state farm fifteen miles away where they paid 50 cents for every bag of 110 pounds of husked rice she brought in. They also gave her eight pounds of rice to eat.

"That was my best chance of the year. I would work day and night till I couldn't bend from the waist. Then I would lie down and crawl to harvest the rice. In the war the soldiers used to sleep while they marched. I used to sleep while I worked, I was so tired."

Some of the other workers on the state farm were young people who had been sent to resettle in the countryside from their homes in Shanghai. They were part of the 18 million urban Chinese school graduates rusticated on Mao's order after the start of the Cultural Revolution. "When they first arrived, their heads were full of beautiful ideas about the villages," Lihua remembered. "They believed what they had heard, that the land was rich, that the peasants were revolutionary. " But once they found how hard life was, they changed. Many of the city youth couldn't work hard enough to support themselves and had to depend on money sent by their parents. Some of the men took to carrying knives and going around in gangs.

"When they showed up in Gold Mountain, it was just like a scene in a movie about bandits. The people all scattered and ran indoors. The chickens flew in the air."

One afternoon when she was thirteen, Lihua recalled, she set out for a small rural market with eggs from their chicken to sell. Her family didn't eat the eggs themselves, they were too valuable. She was walking through a sugar cane field, the maturing cane over her head, and had just crossed a small stream when she saw a man in his early twenties in front of her. He was wearing a watch and glasses, and his clothes were clean, not like a peasant. He asked her to sit down and talk with him.

"I was afraid, my heart was beating fast," Lihua told me. Then he produced a knife from under his shirt. He ordered her to take off her clothes.

"I don't know why I thought of it, but I said, 'You take off your clothes first.' "

The man agreed and, in a bout of modesty, turned his back before loosening his pants. He also put the knife down on the ground.

"When he did, I rushed forward and grabbed it and began stabbing him. Blood spurted all over the place. He fell to the ground, and I kept stabbing him until I thought he was dead. Then I fainted, I can't remember exactly."

When she awoke, it was dark, and she washed herself off in the stream. On her way home she came across the graveyard where her mother was buried. "I dug at her grave with my hands. I wanted to crawl inside." Then she passed out again. The next morning an old man on his way to the mountains to gather wood found her and notified one of her brothers, who came to get her.

"He thought I was overtired. I didn't tell him what had happened." After the incident, she went on, she didn't feel like living anymore. "But I had responsibilities. My little sister was four years younger than me, my father was weak. I decided I would never get married and just devote my life to taking care of them. Men are a bad thing."

There never was an investigation, she said. At the time, with the large number of discontent rusticated students in their area, violence was not uncommon and there had been a number of violent fights and murders in the village.

It was at this period in her life, in her early teens, that Lihua began to listen to the stories of other peasant women about spirits, demons, and ghosts. "I wondered how life could be so cruel. Sometimes at night, when I had gone out to wash our clothes after my day's work was done and hadn't had anything to eat, I would look up at the moon and wish some fairy would come down and save me. I began to burn incense, and I thought that I must have been a criminal in an earlier life. When I walked down the road, I imagined that every plant, every tree, was cursing me for my previous life."

There had been a Buddhist temple with a priest in the village before Red Guards destroyed it in the Cultural Revolution, she said. "Some of the peasants said that was the reason the era was so poor." But many of the villagers continued to practice their old rites at home. On the first and fifteenth day of each month they burned incense and put a bowl of rice in front of a picture of the kitchen god, which they kept on an altar. "You were supposed to put meat or fruit in front of the god, but they were too poor," she said.

Lihua's description was the first authentic account I had heard of continued folk religion in the countryside. In theory China's constitution guarantees freedom of religion; but in practice the Communists have tended to see religion as a rival claim to Marxism and have imposed tight restrictions on most religious rituals and beliefs. I was curious, therefore, if other traditional ideas that the Communists had derided as superstition and tried to eradicate had survived. Yes, she said.

"There was a witch in our village. The authorities couldn't do anything about her because she was protected by the *lao bai xing,*" literally, the "old hundred names," the Chinese word for common people. "She and the witches in some other villages were really mad, so they weren't treated as commune members by the cadres. They didn't work in the fields. But the people gave them food for their services, like curing illnesses. For example, they will place a bowl of clear water on the altar table in the former temple. That night, the person who was sick would drink it, believing that in the meantime the gods have added some medicine to it."

The peasants in Gold Mountain also practiced a Chinese form of voodoo, she said. "If someone you hate is very sick and you want them to die, to speed up the process you must find out the exact date of their birth. Then you learn some chants for that date, make a wooden doll, and stick it with seven pins. Finally, you burn it at night. The person is guaranteed to die by morning."

Somehow during all these years Lihua managed to educate herself. Her only formal schooling was part of a year in first grade before the family was forced out of Peking. "But I wanted so much to learn," she explained. "My language teacher was a dictionary. Everyone I met was a teacher to me, I could ask them questions. I got a copy of the *Three Character Classic,*" the Confucian moral primer and grammar that generations of Chinese schoolboys had to master. It contained short homilies that rhymed in Chinese and could easily be memorized: "At men's beginning their nature is fundamentally good, by nature they are similar but in practice they grow apart." This appealed to Lihua. "Even though the government said it was decadent, I thought it had a lot to teach," she said.

One of her older brothers also tried to continue his education. He had managed to save an English and a Russian dictionary when the family was exiled and he took them with him to the fields during the day. When the peasants took a break from their labor, he would go to a corner of the field to study.

"The peasants didn't understand foreign languages and didn't know what he was doing," Lihua told me later. "They accused him of maintaining illicit relations with foreign countries and being an American spy." She laughed at the memory, her large almond eyes wrinkling up and almost disappearing in the folds of her heavy eyelids. But it wasn't funny at the time. "The peasants took him to a struggle session. They beat him and took away all his notes. But they couldn't find anyone else who could read them to tell them what the notes said." After that, her brother gave up studying.

By now we were meeting once every two or three weeks. I would write her a letter setting the time, and Lihua's short, solid figure would appear at the magazine kiosk across the street from the Peking Hotel.

Chinese are always punctual; it is a mark of respect and character to be on time. But Lihua was inevitably late, the only Chinese I knew who was less punctual than I. I finally realized why. She lived on the outskirts of Peking and it took her over an hour's ride on the city's crowded bus system, with three transfers, to get into the center of town. Each ride was an adventure because she didn't have any money, and when the conductor asked for her fare, Lihua would plead that she was in Peking as a petitioner. Lihua also did not have a watch. When I discovered this, the next time I went to Hong Kong on vacation to visit my family, I bought her an inexpensive Japanese wristwatch.

Each time we met we would go for lunch in a different restaurant, hoping to avoid suspicion. Lihua would start talking, and if we managed to get a table in a quiet corner, I would scribble notes as fast as I could, holding my notebook in my lap against the waiters' prying eyes. Some days I had to wait till I got back to my office to type up my recollections. Lihua didn't mind my writing about her; in fact, she said she had kept a diary herself but her father had found it and burned it. He was worried about further retribution. But Lihua seemed to have an endless supply of grit and courage; she was already taking a giant risk by coming to Peking as a petitioner; and she wanted her story to be told. "I want people outside China to know what the Cultural Revolution was like and what the Chinese have been through," she said during one lunch.

I was curious how she had managed to get back from her village to Peking. Her father had made the first effort, she said, in 1969, three years after they had been sent out of the city. He had written to his old institute in Peking appealing for reconsideration. But the school sent his letter back to the village and the cadres had him dragged through the streets and beaten again. He himself never sought redress after that.

"People like him have ink in their stomachs," Lihua remarked. "They are learned, but have no courage."

In 1976, after Mao died and Jiang Quin, his widow, was arrested, Lihua wrote an appeal. But she discovered that the institute had by then been converted into a factory, not an unusual fate for schools during the Cultural Revolution. The officials in charge of the factory didn't recall her father's case, but they were considerate enough to dispatch two men to the village to investigate her charges. Several months later she got the reply. Her father had indeed been wronged. He would be rehabilitated. But he was now so old and weak—he was fifty-eight years old, two years short of normal retirement—that he should retire. There would be a small pension, but no financial compensation for all the years lost. Nor would the factory consider letting the family back into Peking. They had too many members for that. Government policy was to keep the size of the cities down. Therefore the officials would not give Lihua what she most wanted, a change in her *hu-kou,* the household registration certificate that is a key form of identification in China. It specified whether a person lived in the countryside or a city, and which city. A peasant could not get a job or an apartment in the cities without an urban *hu-kou,* nor could he buy grain, oil, or cloth in the cities, since these depended on city ration cards. For Lihua, a Peking household registration certificate was to become the magic talisman, "like a fortune-teller's card in the old society," she remarked. "It held your fate in its hands."

By the summer of 1979 Lihua had turned twenty and was impatient. She had heard about the petitioners coming to Peking and she decided to try herself. Her oldest brother, now thirty-three, had managed to move back to the capital because he had been sent down to the countryside separately, in a different campaign, just before the beginning of the Cultural Revolution. He was working for a construction company and lived in a tiny dormitory room. She could stay with him there temporarily. But this risked a neighbor turning her in to the police. So she developed the first of a series of stratagems, creating good, new *guan-xi.* She discovered that the neighbors needed clothes—the ready-made clothes in the stores fit poorly and Peking's few tailor shops were always busy. Lihua knew how to sew. It was a natural way to ingratiate herself.

"These days you have to do things to buy a person's humanity," Lihua commented.

Then she began making the rounds of all the government offices she thought might help: her father's old school (which had now been converted back to its original teaching function), the Public Security Bureau, the State Council, or cabinet, the High Court, and the Peking city Party Committee, where we met. I asked if she wasn't afraid of being picked up as a troublemaker and put in jail, as I knew some petitioners were.

"No," she replied. "I have no future anyway."

At her father's former institute, an official assigned to deal with petitioners invited her in to talk. They spent two hours each morning for several weeks discussing the case and drinking tea, but an investigation the official promised into her plight never took place. "To the Communists we are just like noodles in the hands of a noodle-maker, something to shape as you like," she said afterward.

One day during her rounds she met another woman petitioner. The woman had a neighbor who had a relative who knew someone in the police. "It was very roundabout, but I began going to the police officer's house. I found they needed clothes for their children, so I began to sew for them, too. They would give me the material, since I couldn't buy any myself."

There was one problem with all this sewing, however. Lihua did not have her own sewing machine. By this time Jan and I felt as caught up in her tale as she was, so we went out and bought her a Chinese copy of an early Singer.

Four months after her initial meeting with the policeman, he also felt sorry enough for her to invite her to write out her story so he might submit it for official consideration.

"I had to be very careful not to complain in explaining how my mother had been killed," she told me a few days later. "I couldn't blame the police. But who do I say is responsible? Even though nobody had done anything, I had to say I was grateful to the Party for its help." She was smiling her girlish smile again. I thought she showed a tenaciousness and sense of strategy beyond her twenty years. She was a gentle diplomat; her only resource was the sympathy she could evoke. "I hate them, but I never let it show," she once explained.

By now it was winter in Peking, and one day I dropped in to see her in the room, thirty feet square, she shared with her brother, his wife, and her younger sister and father, whom she had recently brought up from Gold Mountain. She had sent for her sister so she could get an education, but Lihua had had to use all her negotiating skills to get her into a school because of that missing household registration. Lihua also attended the parent-teacher meetings, since her father remained an invalid. Their room faced north, the undesirable vantage in Peking, letting in the cold and the wind but little light. The room was heated only by a small coal-burning stove, though to save money they didn't use it during the day and my breath showed in little puffs. It might have been forty degrees in the room. Lihua had freshly whitewashed the walls, and even the bare concrete floor she kept spotless—not a speck of dust in a city where most people seemed resigned to the daily damage visited by the dust storms from the Gobi Desert.

Their only furniture was two wide wooden planks planted on sawhorses and covered with cotton pallets the entire family used as its bed. A short wire strung along the wall near the stove was hung with newly washed laundry. On the window sill were twenty bottles of medicine and traditional Chinese tonics, testimony to Lihua's chronic ailments.

After a day's sewing. Lihua got out a low stool, spread a newspaper over the spotless sheet, and used the bed for a desk on which to study. She was trying to learn English.

Finally, the next July, a year after she had come to Peking, she received a notice from the police reporting her family could get its household registration transferred to the capital. But there was a catch. The permission would expire in three weeks and within that time she had to show they had permanent housing in Peking. That was the law: without a city household registration, you couldn't get an apartment; but without an apartment, you couldn't get a household registration.

"I am frantic," Lihua told me the next day. "China is too hopeless." She was wearing her summer costume, a white cotton blouse and yellow flowered skirt she had made herself (After Mao's death, such departures from orthodox blue were allowable.) In the winter she had one set of clothes she wore every day, in the summer another one. That was all she could afford.

She had gone to the construction company where her brother worked and asked them to write a letter saying she and her father were entitled to live in the company's housing. She promised to move out as soon as she found her own quarters. But the company refused. They were afraid she would stay, like many people in Peking. Eventually, I learned, she got a letter from her father's former school saying they would find housing for him within two months. It was a fib, but with that note she got the construction company to write to the police certifying her residence in their dormitory.

Lihua felt triumphant, but the saga was not over. The cadres in Gold Mountain wouldn't let her two remaining brothers leave. The family still owed the production team $300, they claimed. In Lihua's view, it was a debtor's trap. Because the family had long ago been labeled as landlords, half of all the work points they earned for their daily labor in the fields were deducted as "duty points." As a result, they got only half as much grain at the year-end distribution as other peasants and had to borrow money to live on. Her brothers also had to spend time cultivating land assigned to the team cadres as so-called duty labor. She deduced that the cadres didn't want to lose this form of free serf labor.

"They treated my family as criminals," she complained. In 1979, Peking had announced that the stigma of the landlord class label would be removed, but she claimed it had not been in their village. That left the cadres free to do what they liked with her family. One time she had mailed a packet of shirts and pants she had made for her brothers to Gold Mountain, but they never received the clothes. When Lihua visited the village later, she said the team leader was wearing some of her handiwork.

The situation now appeared hopeless; the three-week deadline was approaching and her brothers were still down in the village. They had to arrive in Peking before the end of July or the permit for them to live in the city would expire. Lihua made one last appeal to her father's old school. They agreed to send an official on the three-day train trip to Gold Mountain to talk with the cadres there. Finally, the team leader consented; he would reschedule the debt. The family could repay from Peking. The two missing brothers appeared a day before the deadline.

I saw Lihua a few more times after that. She was busy studying. She had spotted an advertisement for a new school set up by the city for unemployed young people. It would train them to be primary school teachers. Admission required a high school education, but Lihua spun her usual story and the head of the school agreed to let her take a test to see if she had taught herself as well as a regular school would have have. She passed.

After my wife moved to Peking and we had our own apartment, Lihua came over for lunch one day. It meant walking past the two middle-aged women who operated the elevator in our building. But that was easy for her. When the elevator women stared at her on the way up to the eleventh floor, trying to fix her description for their report to the Public Security Bureau, she smiled back and asked the polite Chinese question, "Have you eaten or not?"

She had brought a pair of tiny cotton shoes she had sewn for our baby, Sarah, and a piece of lace she had made for Barbara.

I noticed she was not wearing the watch I had given her. Now that her brothers had come, she explained with embarrassment, she was worried that they would be jealous about such an expensive item, so she had hidden it. "I don't want to cause a contradiction in my family. We have managed so far to stay together despite our problems. I don't want to spoil that."

In her modest way, she had the virtues Chinese have always prized: devotion to her family, carefully controlled emotions, a willingness to work hard, and a passion for knowledge. At the same time, she also had that ability to use people and situations, *guan-xi,* to her own advantage. In others it might have seemed manipulation; in Lihua it grew out of desperation and added to her attraction. To me she was the quintessential Chinese, proof that the Confucian character had not been wiped out.

There was another Chinese trait too—her righteous anger. Confucius taught moderation and never losing one's temper, but China did not have the moral of turning the other cheek. The last time we met I asked Lihua if, now that her family was safely in Peking, her unhappiness with the Communists had abated. No, she replied.

"People say that now that I've got my household registration, I should be happy. But I won't be happy till I die. I've never lived a good day in my life. My mother was beaten to death, my father was left senseless, and I still have to beg for everything.

"This is what the Cultural Revolution did. It is unfixable. My scars will never heal."

Suggested Readings

Literature on contemporary China is vast and rapidly growing. Roderick MacFarquhar, *The Origins of the Cultural Revolution* (London: Oxford University Press, 1974), examines the impact of the major political events from 1956 to the beginning of the Cultural Revolution. Thomas W. Robinson, ed., *The*

Cultural Revolution in China (Berkeley: University of California Press, 1971), is a collection of five articles covering events during two years, 1966 and 1967, of the Cultural Revolution. The organizations formed by China's mobilized masses during the Cultural Revolution—in particular, the youth—are examined in Stanley Rosen, *Red Guard Factionalism and the Cultural Revolution in Guangzhou* (Boulder, Colo.: Westview Press, 1982). Among the many studies of Mao Zedong's life, ideology, and political career are Edward E. Rice, *Mao's Way* (Berkeley: University of California Press, 1972); Stuart Schram, *The Political Thought of Mao Tse-Tung* (New York: Praeger, 1963); and Stephen Uhalley, Jr., *Mao Tse-Tung* (New York: Franklin Watts, Inc., 1975). Two books that offer a view of everyday life in China are Orville Schell, *In the People's Republic* (New York: Random House, 1977), and B. Michael Frolic, *Mao's People* (Cambridge: Harvard University Press, 1980). An informative study of the patterns of continuity and change in village and family life in rural China today is William L. Parish and Martin King Whyte, *Village and Family Life in Contemporary China* (Chicago: University of Chicago Press, 1978).

Leisure Time in Russia: The Timeless Approach to Life

Michael Binyon

The Western world generally perceives the Soviet Union solely in its political and military aspects. That outlook is partially rooted in the fear of and dislike for a rival system whose behavior usually is judged only in terms of Western experience and viewpoints. Most Westerners' impression of the Soviet Union is an impersonal one. Russians are viewed not as a society composed of individuals but in a collective sense as the "Soviet people." But if Westerners are truly to understand the Russian people, their human qualities and individual personalities must also be studied.

Michael Binyon's article provides just such a glimpse into the personal lives of the Soviet people. In focusing on the activities that occupy ordinary citizens during their free time, the author presents a little-known side of Russian life. Recreational activities usually reflect much of a people's environment, history, and culture; and that is certainly apparent in the following account.

Binyon points to the role played by the Russian collective consciousness in helping to determine the pattern of Soviet leisure. In Western society, leisure activities are closely intertwined with the profit motive and often serve as a distraction for the populace. The Soviet Union, on the other hand, has no comparable leisure industry, and Russians spend more time engrossed in the basic pleasures of life, such as eating, drinking, and outdoor life. Westerners often are amazed to see how contented Russians can be in doing so little. But, as the author points out, life in the Soviet Union moves at a slower pace, and activities generally are pursued for their inherent qualities and pleasures.

W hen Russians enjoy themselves, they do so to the limit. Casting aside the protective mask of formality or indifference they wear at work or in the street, they throw themselves into their pleasures with gusto. No party is complete without singing, dancing, quantities to eat and drink, tears, laughter and an almost sensuous indulgence in argument, discussion and the baring of innermost feelings. Hospitality is overwhelming: the guest is expected to stay for hours, to use the house as though it were his own, to let his hair down in spontaneous displays of affection. The Russians are wary of formal entertaining, of anything that smacks of protocol and the surveillence of the outside world. They enjoy being themselves, behaving spontaneously in the warmth of each other's company.

Leisure and free time are precious, and opportunities must be seized when they arise. The working week is still long, and the occasions limited when families and friends are all able to be together. Society provides little organized entertainment: apart from activities for children in the Pioneer's palaces and the clubs run by factories and places of work, there is no leisure industry as such in the Soviet Union. And Russians therefore depend more on each other for entertainment than do most people in the West. They enjoy the basic pleasures of life: eating and drinking, getting out of the towns into the woods and countryside, singing, talking or simply lying in the sun or beside a warm stove in winter doing nothing.

Russians are sociable people and spend their free time in the company of others. The collective consciousness, strongly reinforced by the ideological approval of the *kollektiv* and distrust of individualism, throws Russians together not only at work, in shared flats and in the crowded cities, but also determines the pattern of Soviet leisure: organized excursions, groups and clubs for enthusiasts of chess, philately, music, sport and drama, rest-homes and sanatoria where millions of workers join their colleagues from work for the annual holiday in the sun.

There is nothing a Russian likes better than getting together with friends and relatives for a good meal. Public holidays are always a good excuse: New Year, International Women's Day on March 8, May Day, and the revolutionary celebrations of November 7. But apart from New Year, which has all the trappings of the Western Christmas, these state

LEISURE TIME IN RUSSIA   From Michael Binyon, *Life in Russia* (New York: Pantheon Books, 1983), pp. 69–91.

holidays seem too official to most people. It is more personal, more satisfying, to throw a party on a whim, or in celebration of a traditional event such as a birthday, a name-day (according to Russian Orthodox tradition each saint after whom most people are named has a designated day of celebration), a house-warming or Old New Year, which now falls on January 13.

Birthdays are especially popular. The Russians organize lavish parties, and everyone brings a present. There are always toasts, and virtually every guest makes a flowery speech. Of course there is vodka, wine and Soviet 'champagne', a rather sweet but, to my taste, delicious sparkling wine that is drunk in enormous quantities and produced on special occasions. The table groans with whatever food the enterprising host or hostess can procure. For starters, or *zakuski*, there may be red or black caviar, still a favourite delicacy though hard to find nowadays and expensive, smoked salmon, tuna fish, pickled tomatoes, cold sturgeon in aspic, assorted salads with strongly tasting herbs and greens from the south, freshly baked pastry pies with meat or cabbage inside, pickled gherkins, cheese and an infinite variety of mushrooms, invariably gathered and bottled by the host and a source of special pride.

All this is just for starters, something to accompany the vodka that is downed by the glassful in one great gulp after every toast. Dinner itself begins with soup such as borsch, the typical red beetroot soup, or clear broth or perhaps a fish *solyanka* soup or, in summer, a chilled soup of vegetables or meat in a stock made of *kvas*, a kind of beer made from fermented bread. And then there might be fish in cheese sauce, or mushrooms in individual pots baked in sour cream; and after that the main course—chicken or filet or beef strogonoff with potatoes, carrots and whatever greens can be found in the private peasant markets. Dessert may be fruit compot, ice-cream, sweet dumplings filled with fruit or a home-made cake. By this time you have been sitting many hours and drunk and laughed a good deal, and everyone has been pressed to eat more than he or she can, to make a speech and to regale the guests with some good story or anecdote.

Sadly the present food shortages mean that it takes a lot of ingenuity to find all the ingredients for such a feast. But for a special gathering Russians spare no expense or effort to get enough to make their table a proud sight.

Russians eat at almost any time of the day. I could never get used to the sight or smell of other hotel guests tucking into meat and vegetables for breakfast, or finding I was expected to sit down for a hearty meal with vodka and wine at 11.00 a.m. Big meals in Russian homes take all day to prepare, and often begin at around 4.30 in the afternoon, lasting—on and off with breaks while people smoke or stroll about—until at least 10.00 at night. By that time the table has become the focal point for talk, and the subsequent discussion can go on for hours, as glasses are refilled and the room becomes a fog of smoke. Guests depart as the last buses go, or when they can get lifts in cars, or when they are ready to haggle in the street with a private motorist acting as an unofficial taxi. The last guest is usually still there at 2.00 in the morning, and many have no hesitation in dossing down for the night where they are.

No one stands on ceremony. Of course a party is an excuse to dress up, show off fashionable clothes; but there are no such things as black tie dinners in Moscow (except among the foreign diplomatic community), and jeans are just as smart as the best suit and, provided they have the right Western label, a great deal more chic.

There are some old-fashioned courtesies. Russians never arrive as guests empty-handed, and come with flowers or chocolates for the hostess, a bottle of wine, vase or some appropriate gift for the house. Many men still insist on the gallantry of bowing and kissing a lady's hand. And toasting and speechifying have an etiquette all to themselves. But the setting is never formal. Russian flats are too cramped or too untidy, and guests squeeze round the table as best they can, sitting on an assortment of different shaped chairs, elbowing each other, sharing the room with the dog or children who stay up late and are always fussed over by parents and guests alike.

Most people hanker after a little more ceremony and sense of occasion—though probably would not like it and would feel intimidated. Russians are acutely self-conscious when foreigners first come to their homes apologizing or joking about the small rooms, and seem to expect the foreigner to be used to something grander. But tact and good humour on both sides can melt this barrier, and soon the foreigner will be drawn into the talk and drinking as though he were a long-standing friend (though in his presence even drunken Russians are careful not to let slip remarks that could raise eyebrows among the other guests).

Often parties are impromptu. Friends unexpectedly descend on someone who has a birthday, bearing food and drink, records and gifts, and whatever plans he had for the evening disappear in the jollity. Someone who sees friends at the theatre or meets old acquaintances unexpectedly invariably invites them all home, dashes off to get whatever food and drink can still be bought at that late hour and spreads out the cloth on the table. In a short time there is a meal and a celebration.

Nowhere is feasting and drinking more ingrained in the national culture than in Georgia. And, being Georgia, everything is on a more lavish scale, more showy, exuberant, costly than elsewhere in the Soviet Union. I vividly remember a baptism party in Tbilisi. With typical Georgian hospitality my wife and I were invited because we were friends of friends, although we ourselves knew neither the baby boy, his parents or relations. The table, laden with fresh summer produce, seemed to stretch for ever along the upstairs balcony of a picturesque wooden pre-revolutionary house in the city centre. At the head of the table sat the *tamada*—the toastmaster—whose job it was to cap all the speeches with a toast. We were drinking fresh white wine, which tasted at first like lemonade but whose lethal kick was only apparent some time later. Two large rams' horns were passed from guest to guest, full of wine, which could not be set down before being drained. As a foreigner I was expected to make a witty speech—rather difficult after several hornfuls of wine, when my Russian was still rudimentary and all the other guests were speaking Georgian. I hardly remember how the evening ended.

The toastmaster is a key figure not only in Georgia, but in all Russia, especially at weddings. And in a move to restore some old-fashioned dignity to these ceremonies, as well as cut down excessive drinking, the Soviet authorities are discreetly trying to breed a new generation of toastmasters whose apparently contradictory task is to keep most of the guests reasonably sober.

A few years ago a special faculty to train toastmasters was opened in—of all unlikely places—the National University of Atheism in the Estonian capital Tallinn, and was promptly inundated with applications. Local factories begged the university to enrol their candidates who could then officiate at new factory banqueting halls. Letters poured in from as far away as Irkutsk in Siberia asking whether would-be toastmasters could follow the course by correspondence. Instruction consisted of lectures on how to plan receptions, organize speeches, amuse guests and—most importantly—see that everyone was so busy singing, dancing, eating and playing games that there was no time for downing too many glasses of vodka or champagne.

The revival of this traditional figure has been prompted by growing concern over the rowdiness of many weddings nowadays. The press has called them 'elaborate displays of wealth', where all the talk is of how much the dresses cost and what the presents are worth. At the other extreme, weddings are too casual—the briefest meetings on station platforms or at airports where a few friends toast the couple with quick sips of champagne before they set off on their honeymoon.

Most Russians would like a proper wedding, but are put off by the difficulties of booking a reception room, making the arrangements and getting tickets for the honeymoon. The press has reported cases of couples who were obliged to join hiking tours for their honeymoon as it was the only kind of holiday available.

Drunkenness at weddings is certainly a problem nowadays. But not only wedding guests suffer from a tide of vodka. A meal out in a restaurant usually ends with several of the guests having to be carried out and escorted home. By comparison with other nations, Russians do not eat out often: it is expensive, the choice is limited and the menu uniform. Moscow is not a city of little cafés and corner restaurants, and the quick-service 'dining-rooms', as the buffets are called, are nowhere to go for pleasure. The food is greasy, often cold, and you eat standing up at high tables.

An evening meal out in the Soviet Union is a serious business. The first problem is deciding where to go—the best restaurants are invariably full, and advance booking is essential. Moscow connoisseurs have their favourites: the Aragvi for Georgian cuisine, the Uzbekistan for Turkish-style kebabs, the Peking for Chinese-style food, the Berlin, Prague and Central Restaurants for Russian food, the Arbat and a restaurant in the Intourist hotel for a floor show and so on. Some of the best are on the outskirts of Moscow, beside the river or in the woods, where carved wooden decoration gives a more traditional and intimate atmosphere.

It is best to go with a group. Soviet restaurants seem happiest with groups, whereas individuals are usually left sitting forlornly in a corner for hours before being served. The first challenge comes when you arrive. How do you get in? The door is usually locked, with a large group of hungry people standing stoically in a queue. You have to negotiate your way past the suspicious doorman, using the diplomatic skills outlined earlier. But if these still fail to convince him you have a bona fide booking, the best way is usually a five-rouble note slipped hastily into his open palm, or a packet of foreign cigarettes.

If you regularly patronize a restaurant you can sometimes avoid this procedure. An American acquaintance was entertained in the Berlin restaurant, and was brought in round the back through the kitchens. The manageress seated him amongst senior Soviet officials. Next time he went there he again went in through the kitchens—and noticed the other diners did so also. Going to the main street door to investigate, he found it locked, with a cardboard notice stuck in the window. On one side it said 'closed'. On the back was written 'No free places'. It was turned from one side to the other according to the time of day.

Service is maddeningly slow but Russians rarely complain. They go out to celebrate, and that means taking time and having plenty to drink between courses. Placing an order is a matter of pot luck. The menu is large, but only dishes with prices marked beside them are on, and not always those. On designated days, as part of the economy campaign, many restaurants observe a fish day and do not serve any meat.

The best restaurants in hotels frequented by Western tourists have orchestras in the evenings. The repertoire generally includes Western pop music, deafeningly over-amplified, and appears to be the same in every hotel. Dancing is *de rigueur*. If the men are too preoccupied with the vodka, as they often are, the women dance together. Foreign men are just as likely to be approached by women as vice-versa.

The quality of food in all restaurants leaves much to be desired. The main problem is that it is served luke-warm. The waiters earn the same salary no matter how many people they serve. They have little enthusiasm for the job and no proper training (except in the big Intourist hotels). They tend to regard the idea of service as undignified and degrading, and food can wait twenty minutes in the kitchens before the waiters bother to collect it. Not surprisingly, Russians leave large amounts of food on their plates, but this has more to do with over-ordering and the status of showing that you are wealthy enough not to need to eat every morsel than with the cuisine itself.

Few restaurants attempt gourmet cooking. The tradition has almost been extinguished by revolution, famine, war and ideological disapproval of frivolous eating. But demand, fuelled by public grumbling, is growing, Some new restaurants, smaller than the cavernous eating halls that were favoured in Khrushchev's day, are attempting to build up individual reputations. And in the Baltic republics intimate restaurants have been opened in historic buildings in city centres, where there is something of a family atmosphere. Indeed, so successful has this proved that there is talk of licensing privately run 'family restaurants' all over the country. In Georgia most restaurants, serving better food than in the north, are virtually—though not officially—privately run already.

The best food is to be had in places not open to the general public: clubs belonging to the Union of Actors or Journalists, Writers and so on. Genuine foreign cuisine is a rarity. The head chef at the Intourist hotel does know how to prepare haggis, as groups of Scots fly to Moscow every January, bearing dozens of uncooked haggis with them, to celebrate Burns night at the hotel with members of the Soviet Burns society (who, I suspect, are sometimes there just for the free whisky). The Peking hotel does boast Chinese food, but it is not what it was. In the days when Russia and China were linked in comradely unity, the hotel was built as a monument to friendship. The restaurant ceiling was hand-painted in extravagantly beautiful Chinese style. Chinese cooks prepared the dishes with Chinese ingredients. But after the ideological break they all left. Soviet chefs now attempt to cook the same dishes using Soviet contents. And nowadays 'chicken trepang' is something all to itself. I once asked for it. 'You won't eat it,' the waiter replied. 'Why not?' I asked. 'It's disgusting,' he answered flatly. And he was right.

There are sporadic attempts to set up foreign restaurants in Moscow. There were long negotiations with a well-known American hamburger chain before the Olympics, but they foundered on Soviet insistence that Soviet meat, not considered by the Americans to be up to standard, be used in the hamburgers. Since then a Japanese restaurant—catering only to foreigners and accepting only convertible currency—has opened, and for two brief weeks in 1982 a so-called genuine Italian restaurant opened as an experiment. All the food was imported from Italy, and there was almost a crisis when the truck bringing it ran out of petrol in the Ukraine and could only be refuelled by having a truck sent all the way from Moscow to its aid. However, this did not deter some determined pasta lovers from setting up a real pizza parlour a few months later, which naturally became overnight the 'in' place to go.

The influx of tourists has had some effect in improving standards in the big cities. The main hotels in Moscow and Leningrad have had to introduce self-service restaurants, as tour groups spent so long waiting for breakfast that they missed the treasures of the Hermitage. Nowadays most hotels have set meals laid out ready for the tourists. I remember a blazing row that ensued in Samarkand when a colleague sat down and ate a breakfast apparently intended for a member of a tourist group. He was roundly chastised by the restaurant manager, the waitress, the American tour guide and the unfortunate tourist who then had to go without breakfast.

Still, the Russians themselves consider things have a long way to go. A survey in Georgia found that 87 per cent of those who went to restaurants did not like the quality of the food, 90 per cent said it was too expensive, 83 percent criticised the service, and 87 per cent did not like the atmosphere. Similar surveys in Moscow have shown similar results.

Finding a place in a restaurant is doubly difficult on public holidays, and especially at New Year, the big secular holiday that has replaced Christmas in the Soviet Union. New Year is a time for parties, family gatherings and drinking. Nowadays it has all the trappings of the Western Christmas. Several huge trees are put up in the city centres, decorated with coloured lights, glittering balls and imitation presents hanging from the boughs. A giant tree, still smelling strongly of the forest, stands inside the Palace of Congresses inside the Kremlin, admired by the thousands who stream in every evening to watch the Bolshoi Ballet perform there. Throughout Moscow, officials boast, about 50,000 trees go up in shops, offices and on street squares.

In Russia, as elsewhere, the Christmas tree tradition has been borrowed from Germany, but by now it is firmly established. Every home tries to get a tree, and for the ten days before New Year people mill around the markets where trucks deposit about 700,000 small pines from the state plantations. In the evenings you see people hurrying down the metro escalators clutching their prizes tied up with string. There are still not enough trees to satisfy demand—a third of all buyers go away empty-handed or have to make do with plastic ones. And those lucky enough to get hold of a *yolka*, as the traditional shaped tree is called, queue at least two hours, and often up to eight according to one newspaper survey, many doing so in working hours.

Every year some entrepreneurs sneak off into the forests to poach trees. The fine has now been increased to 100 roubles (about £63), but the papers annually report such cases as that of the man who chopped down a tree in the avenue outside his flat—for which he had to pay an extra 45 roubles replanting costs—or the man in Siberia who was sent to jail for three years for cutting down a rare cedar. The authorities estimate the annual damage inflicted by illegal cutting at 120,000 roubles.

New Year is the time for Grandfather Frost, the Soviet Santa Claus. He comes naturally in boots, a red fur-trimmed costume and a flowing white beard, and nowadays he is as commercialized in Russia as in the West. Down in Kirghizia, where snow rarely settles and Grandfather Frost is as far removed from Central Asian customs as Muslim customs are from Moscow, the men in beards and boots nevertheless have a busy time. As everywhere in the country, they use the occasion to promote feelings of public gratitude to the state and party, opening shops and cinemas, and presenting the lucky owners in the big towns with keys to flats, holding sessions in the palaces of culture and entertaining children.

In Moscow Grandfather Frost does his stint at the main toy shop Detsky Mir ('Children's World') just across the road from the headquarters of the KGB. But he also has a plan to fulfil—and there are sometimes complaints that he only spends forty-five minutes a day in the shop. On New Year's Eve thousands of Grandfather Frosts—selected after a tough examination by a special commission, according to *Pravda*—take part in Moscow's 'Dial-a-Santa' service. For a fee of 5 roubles one will appear at your door, fill up his sack with the presents you quickly hand him, and then delight the children by delivering their toys. The only hazard is hospitality—after a glass of something warming at each of the first ten flats, Grandfather Frost tends to radiate something more than seasonal jollity. It needs the icy eye of 'Sneguruchka', the Snow Maiden, who usually accompanies him dressed as a maiden in comely white, to keep things in control.

The toy shops do a brisk trade before the holiday, and by New Year's Eve almost all the shelves are bare. The best toys are East German—well-made electric trains, stuffed animals, jigsaws, construction kits and so on. The worst, by a long chalk, are locally made Soviet toys, which have an uncanny ability to fall to pieces in five minutes or simply do not work at all. Toy trucks cut your fingers with their sharp edges, wheels fall off the plastic tractors and even the imitation machine-guns—a great favourite despite offical propaganda which maintains that unseemly war toys are sold only in the West—are considerably shorter lasting than the real thing. A friend once saw a mother complaining that the radio-controlled toy tank she had bought for her son did not work. The shop assistant took another. That too would not move, so she threw it in the corner, and took another. That also ended up in the corner. She took another and then another, until about the twelfth worked and the corner was full of useless toys. 'Let's hope the real ones work better,' some wag remarked who had watched the sorry scene.

The press has often criticized the poor standard of toys. The problem is that there is no single ministry of toy-making. Toys are made by 950 factories working under a dozen different ministries. Despite exhortations for more Meccano-type construction kits, tool sets, model lathes and toys to instil a love of industry and work, anything produced is snapped up by adults who cannot get hold of real tools and make do with toy versions. The papers once recounted how one ministry decided on its own initiative to invent a toy suitable for handicapped children. It devised a rattle for deaf children that flashed a light instead of making a noise. When the All-Russian Society for the Deaf received a sample, it sent out a letter to let parents know about it. Not one person ordered the flashing rattle.

The New Year break is a favourite time for winter sportsmen and outdoor skaters. Many people go into the woods cross-country skiing, or ice-fishing on the frozen lakes. Hardy swimmers known as 'seals' brave sub-zero temperatures, cut a hole in the ice and plunge in. Children can go on special troika rides at Moscow's Permanent Exhibition of Economic Achievements. There, for a fee, they can whirl through the snow in a sleigh pulled by three steaming horses and pretend the old days live on.

Russians are hardy, outdoor people, and for many the greatest pleasure is being outside, close to nature in winter and summer. Nothing typifies the Russian character better than the national passion for mushrooming. When the summer comes and the sun lights up the damp woods, people in their thousands flock out with baskets and sharp knives to go mushroom hunting. Enthusiasts set off in the small hours in hired buses, and many make a weekend of it, taking the late night suburban trains into the villages on Fridays. They take a short nap in the stations—the hardier venturing to camp in the woods—and at first light they begin.

To go mushrooming you need sharp eyes, waterproof boots, old clothes and a stout stick. Experts know the best ground for the various fungi—spongy and damp for some, and a little drier and near birch trees for some of the tastiest. You need the stick to poke at the fallen leaves, as some of the commonest fungi look just like yellow leaves. Or if you lift up the branches of small pines you can find a variety of mushrooms sprouting in the sheltered gloom.

There are up to forty varieties of edible mushrooms commonly found around Moscow. Generally considered the best are the *belyie*—white ones—but also common are *chernushki*—black ones—and *lishichki* (little foxes). Others have picturesque names like 'Under the Aspens', 'Under the Birches', 'Little Pigs', 'Caesar's Mushroom', and a popular sort call *opyata,* meaning 'Round the Tree Trunks'. Mushrooming is hard work. You wander from glade to glade, poking, bending, picking and scrabbling through the trees. In some places there are little colonies of bright red button-shaped mushrooms; in others you find a large, gnarled-looking, yellowish-brown one standing on its own or half hidden under the soil.

In the excitement of the chase you can go on for hours and get completely lost. People go in groups and call to each other now and then so as not to get parted. Or else they call over their friends to work a particularly productive patch or to view a giant mushroom (newspapers regularly report the finding of mushrooms several feet across). Of course, not everything is edible. As a rough rule anything with a thin stem is an inedible toadstool. The Russians call these *poganki,* from the old world *pogani* meaning foul. Some toadstools are well-known in Britain—the bright red one with white spots, called in Russia 'fly poison' (fly agaric in English), or the temptingly smooth white ones (avenging angels in English) so similar to common field mushrooms.

Most *gribniki,* as mushroom hunters are called, know the difference between good and bad, but unfortunately not all. Every year there are cases of poisoning, sometimes fatal. Hospitals prepare for a rush of cases when the season starts in early summer. For people's guidance many booklets and pamphlets are published on the attributes and characteristics of fungi. Children learn about them at school. Large illustrations are put up beside market stalls where huge heaps are on display, all shapes and colours, waiting to be bottled, preserved, salted, fried, baked or eaten raw by those who have not had time to gather their own.

At the end of the day the *gribniki* sort out their baskets of fungi, rejecting the bad or very dirty. The laborious task of cleaning them properly begins at home. It is usually work reserved for women, while the men discuss their finds, like anglers boasting about a good catch. Russians love mushrooming because they feel they have enjoyed nature to the full. But this enjoyment is only complete when it involves suffering. When Russians walk, ski, fish or go mushrooming, they go on for ten or twelve hours until it hurts; otherwise they feel the day has not been properly exhausting. The reward is warmth at home later, or several glasses of vodka with pickled mushrooms from an earlier crop, or a visit to the steam baths to relax.

Even in the cities older enthusiasts can be found mushrooming on the grass medians that separate the dual carriageways, or in the the little parks between Moscow's boulevards. Russians do not lose their mushrooming instinct when abroad. If you get up early enough, you can sometimes see Soviet diplomats hunting for mushrooms in London's parks, amazed that such delicacies are neglected by the natives.

Russians have an almost mystical belief in the value of fresh summer air. For six months of winter they seal themselves off from the freezing world outside, swaddling themselves in layers of padded clothing. They nail shut the windows and seal every crack with strips of sticky paper, heat up their buildings to an extraordinary degree and live in a fetid fug from November till May. By spring everyone is pale and coughing, and most have had several bouts of flu. When summer comes at last, the one thought is to get outside, fill the lungs with country air, get back to the rural roots that still bind even city dwellers so closely to the land.

Those who have money, position and influence usually have dachas—country cottages which have sometimes remained in the family for generations. Nestling in woods or near rivers, these slightly shabby painted wooden structures look like stage sets for a Chekhov play. Those belonging to writers, artists and intellectuals are virtually unchanged inside. The Revolution, instead of abolishing these country seats for the privileged, simply made them communal. Many of the best dachas, formerly belonging to the nobility, are now owned by factories, newspapers and trade unions which let their members use them in turn. But it is still everyone's dream to have his own dacha, and all round the big cities hundreds of privately owned cottages, some no more than two-room huts, are clustered in woods and fields. The lucky owners pack up on Friday nights, take the suburban train to the outskirts of Moscow or Leningrad and relax on their country plots all weekend. Some even commute daily from their dachas throughout the summer. On the hills around Tbilisi, the Georgian capital, the dachas are minor palaces—all marble and stone and sumptuously decorated. The wealthy are still building their retreats. 'It's our millionaires' row,' remarked a local official who took me on a tour of the area.

Recently the state has tried to entice people back to the land by giving grants to build modest dachas on condition they cultivate the surrounding land and put in a stint in the communal orchards. These 'orchard cultivation co-operatives' are so popular that there is a waiting list to join.

The British embassy, like other western embassies, has a dacha, rented from the state in prime dacha land where the Bolshoi Ballet, Soviet ministries and other top bodies have their retreats. It is a cosy, rather dilapidated, rambling wooden house near the Moscow River. It has a big room for parties, several bedrooms, a sitting-room with an open wood fireplace, deep old sofas and piles of well-thumbed magazines. Long ago the heating stoves, built into the walls, used to work, but now they are sealed up and radiators keep it snug when the snow piles up outside.

Only a fraction of Moscow's 8 million people can get out to dachas. And when it is hot and sultry, as it often is in summer, many just go to the nearby lakes, reservoirs and rivers. A favourite place is Seryebroni Bor ('Silver Wood') on the Moscow River. Only about thirty minutes from the city centre by trolleybus, it is quiet, green, fresh, and a world away from the rush and squash of the city. It is just beyond the diplomatic dachas, so Russians have to leave their cars far away and take a bus down to the river. Foreigners, of course, ignore the 'No entry' sign and drive down to the beach.

There *is* a beach, and a seaside atmosphere, although it is 400 miles to the nearest coast. On a Saturday afternoon Silver Wood is crowded with ordinary people enjoying themselves. They sit around on wooden benches playing cards, drinking beer, and munching dried fish wrapped in old copies of *Pravda*. Someone has usually brought a transistor, tuned to Radio Moscow's 'World Service'—not because he wants to practise his English, but because it is the best way to hear the latest Russian or even Western pop music. (Taxi drivers who speak no word of English usually have a stream of impeccably American English from this service pouring out of their radio.) Here and there a cassette recorder is playing the Bee Gees. Someone sporting a black market T-shirt with 'Pop City Music' printed on it strolls past.

Families are tucking into sardines or boiled eggs bought from the pavilion, a dilapidated wooden hut that is open only about ten weekends a year—though not during the lunch hour—and sells lemonade, beer, assorted snacks and those peculiarly Russian cigarettes *(papyrosi)* with an inch of strong, sweet tobacco at the end of three inches of hollow cardboard tubing. Corpulent grandmothers with no inhibitions entrust their voluminous bodies to garish and outsize bikinis and manufacture triangular paper hats from old copies of *Pravda*. (This organ of the Communist party appears to have a hundred more useful functions than purveying the daily party line). They fuss over little children, who also wear floppy hats. As soon as it is warm enough to remove the woolen bonnets that envelop children all winter, the grandmothers insist on a sunhat in case of sunstroke.

Some romantic young couples lie speechless and supine in the the sun. Many more take part in organized games of volleyball, punching the ball around in a group with a lot of laughter and shouting. There is always a match going on at the two old table tennis tables near the entrance to the beach enclosure. A group of fifteen-year-olds are horsing around, burying each other in sand and trying to smoke illicit cigarettes undetected.

In mid-summer you can hire rowing boats for 47 kopecks (30p) an hour, but police launches cruise up and down and a stentorian voice bellows through the megaphone at any citizens who row their boats beyond the marker buoys. Now and then an enormous barge, laden with coal or pig iron, is tugged along in the direction of the city. My young son and I and a Russian friend once hired a boat during the Falklands crisis. We rowed about in circles very ineptly for a while, almost being run down by a large pleasure steamer, and then attempted to steer back to the bank. The man in charge must have heard us speaking English, for he shouted out as we approached: 'Falklands Islands, over here!'

Naturally there are rules: no Russian place of enjoyment is complete without instructions on how to enjoy yourselves. 'Citizens!' say the placards, with appropriate cartoons, 'observe the following rules! Don't jump into the water from ice, benches, car tyres or floating objects. Don't swim too far from the bank or overestimate your strength. Don't let children play unsupervised. Don't play around in an unsober state. Don't swim near oncoming boats. Don't remove the life belts from the stands . . .' and so on. No one takes much notice of these eminently sensible regulations—that is the way with all rules in the Soviet Union.

The families and groups of friends stay till dusk when they queue for the trolleybuses home. By evening the place is usually deserted. In the distance can be seen two of Stalin's gothic wedding cakes, markers of the city skyline. Nearby is an old church with gleaming cupolas. On the opposite bank thick trees hide what must be a more exclusive area closed to the public. Under the silver birch trees behind the beach, people wander down the paths, while old women in headscarves gossip on benches in clearings.

Despite their love of the open air, Russians have little interest in gardening—unless it is for profit. Most city dwellers do not have a garden, and the communal gardens in the courtyards of apartment blocks are a pathetic sight; a few straggling flowers are planted in the early spring, but they are quickly forgotten as they are surrounded by weeds. Dacha gardens are not tended and trimmed as the English would have them. For the Russians, nature is meant to be enjoyed *au naturel,* and the ideal garden is one that most closely resembles a jungle. Grass should be a meadow, thick and lush, flowers should ramble wild and trees should have that forlorn, untamed look that features in every painting of the Russian landscape.

This outlook is convenient in a country where a lawnmower is almost unknown and where the idea of disciplined work with a trowel in your free time seems idiotic. You have to go to Estonia to find more Teutonic order and tidiness. But the unkempt look is not so suitable for the big parks. Here gardening has been refined to a semi-industrial art. A planting brigade goes out in spring and huge beds appear to bloom overnight. I have watched a street-washing lorry water all the flowers outside the hotel in Yalta with admirable economy of time and labour. The driver directed a high-pressure hose on to each tub, and within ten seconds it was inundated, with spatterings of mud and flowers on the ground as evidence of speedy delivery.

Growing for profit is a different matter, however. With the increasing shortage of fresh fruit and vegetables, more and more city-dwellers are turning—with official encouragement—to the cultivation of private plots. Books on kitchen gardening are in demand, and translations of Western manuals on running your allotment are even circulating in *samizdat* copies. At the markets peasants sell home-collected seeds in little newspaper cones with gaudy handpainted cards beside each pile illustrating sumptuous marrows or succulent tomatoes. I know of one man who set up a hothouse in his flat. He filled an entire room with trays and earthbeds, and in spring was able to offer tulip bulbs and vegetable seedlings at prices that quickly made him very rich.

Flowers are easily the most profitable thing to grow, and inhabitants of the sunny south, especially Georgians, used to book up all the seats on Aeroflot every spring and fly north with suitcases of flowers (though this has recently fallen under official disapproval). The demand is insatiable—flowers are essential not only for weddings and banquets, but to greet delegations at stations and airports, to throw on stage at your favourite theatre or ballet star, present to your teacher on the first day of school and to take round to friends in hospital or entertaining at dinner. Roses and gladioli sell for a minimum of 3 roubles (£2) a bloom. There is a well-known joke about the flower trade; an airliner from Georgia to Moscow was hijacked and ordered to fly to Paris. Suddenly two passengers sprang up, overpowered the hijackers and told the pilot to continue to Moscow. On landing the Georgians were fêted with a heroes' welcome, but a friend took them aside and asked why they had done it when they could otherwise have been in Paris. 'But,' replied one Georgian, 'what are we going to do with 2,000 daffodils in Paris?'

The one area where urban Russians excel is indoor gardening. Potted plants have become voguish, with huge palms adorning hotels and private homes. One of the best displays I remember used to be in the cashier's office of the Moscow customs house. I was pleased to discover the cashier's penchant, and once took her a particularly nice plant when I knew a consignment of mine arriving from Finland bore a rather steep duty. She was delighted, and with rare and infuriating Soviet rectitude accepted the gift and charged me the full duty.

The Russians know the English as keen gardeners. But English people are also celebrated as dog-lovers, and the typical Englishman in Soviet films and popular imagination always has one or two dogs in his home. Nowadays the description applies equally to the average Muscovite. A mania for dogs, cats, birds and pets of all kinds is gripping the country. Almost every household boasts some four-legged creature.

Dogs are especially fashionable. At any time of the day or night you can see young men exercising their dogs in the parks or pensioners walking them in the yards beside each block of flats. As you go up the staircase in almost every block you can hear barking and yapping coming through the usual black, supposedly soundproof padding on people's front doors. All breeds can be found: poodles, terriers, wolfhounds, Alsatians, St Bernards, collies and English sheepdogs. Especially popular, in spite of a natural and somewhat embarrassing disadvantage in the winter snow, is the dachshund. Indeed at the moment the dachshund is in short supply. Ten years ago there were plenty to be had. Now you have to wait years if you apply for one at a recognized kennel club.

A dog has become a prestige symbol, a sign of money and good taste which can be trotted out daily to be shown to the neighbours. It is a far cry from the postwar years when most Russians could hardly feed themselves, or from the terrible 900-day siege of Leningrad during the war when dogs were eaten to keep a starving population alive. The bigger the dog, the greater the prestige, and people will go to inordinate lengths to acquire the right status symbol. I know of a couple who live in Yakutsk, in eastern Siberia, where the winter temperature can fall to minus 50 degrees, who travelled 4,000 miles to Moscow to collect a huge Afghan hound which they took back to share their one-room flat together with a child and mother-in-law.

A good pedigree dog can be quite expensive—up to 100 roubles— and breeders make a fortune. The Moscow pet market is one of the most fascinating places to visit. Every Saturday and Sunday it is thronged with pigeon-fanciers, fish-breeders, peasants from the countryside with rabbits, hamsters, canaries, coypu and other creatures for sale. A huge crowd jostles and pushes round the stalls, prodding, peering, filling up old pickle jars with brightly coloured miniature fish or spooning out birdseed from a sack into newspaper cones.

Dogs are not officially meant to be sold in the market, but there are plenty around. Usually their owners hang about the entrance, carrying large baskets covered with a blanket from which you occasionally see a wet, black nostril poking out. Big dogs sit on the ground under the trees, looking rather forlorn, especially in midwinter when only a bit of straw or old newspaper is put down for them on the snow. Many sellers, on the lookout in case they are moved on by the police for trading without a licence, keep their puppies tucked inside their jackets. As you walk past they flash open their coats, with a furtive 'psst' like dirty postcard sellers, to reveal a trembling, furry face.

All dogs should be officially registered with the local veterinary authorities and are given a number or address tag which they have to wear on their collars at all times. They are inoculated against rabies and the owners are told to look after them. Most Russians are fanatically proud of their dogs and eagerly take part in the shows and competitions organized for kennel club members. The winning dogs are awarded certificates and medals, and sometimes their owners take them for Sunday walks with all their medals and ribbons strapped to the animals' chests.

There is a sad side to the present explosion in the canine population. More and more people buy dogs out of caprice and do not look after them, turning them loose when they tire of them or move into a new flat, and the number of strays has increased alarmingly. In 1981 the press began a vigorous anti-dog campaign aimed at preparing people for the introduction of a dog licence of up to 200 roubles, a colossal sum which would have meant millions of dogs having to be destroyed. *Pravda* said the state spent 1,500 million roubles a year in subsidies on meat eaten only by dogs. A draft law was prepared enabling local authorities to ban the keeping of dogs in flats near kindergartens, and spoke of the diseases spread by dogs. But news of this leaked out, and such was the outcry, especially from pensioners, that the draft never became law.

Even attempts by municipal dog-catchers to round up strays have been hampered by angry citizens attacking them, smashing their vans and screaming abuse. But the strays are now a real danger in some cities. One pack made its home among the scenery and discarded props of the main Moscow film studios. Becoming hungry, they attacked people working there and killed four black swans which were the studio's pride. When they were finally put down there was such an outcry that the local authorities had to set up a special inquiry.

Another campaign began recently to suppress the latest fad: exotic pets. Many people have started keeping wild animals in their flats— monkeys, foxes, badgers, snakes and even lions. There was a tragic case in Baku of a family whose lion killed the child and then attacked the mother, and this was given great prominence in the press as a warning.

The Russians do not have organized greyhound racing, as in England, but they do have a strictly limited form of another Western sport, horse racing. I once went to the Moscow hippodrome to see what it is like. Built in 1955, the hippodrome is an extraordinary edifice looking like an imitation classical Greek building. The cream-coloured façade is topped with a spire and surrounded by statues of prancing horses. The entrance is through a marbled hall with a vaulted ceiling, and the two-tier grandstand is all columns with decorated capitals, painted ceilings, plaster frescoes of horses in Elysium.

In this classless society there are three classes of seating. For 30 kopecks you can go to the main stand with its wooden seats and high railings. For the top price you can go into the emptier, smarter section with its elaborate covered stand, stained glass windows (again of horses) and decorative canopies. Inside, the betting hall looks like a railway waiting-room, with women bookies (the word in Russian is *bukmaker*) sitting behind a wire grille. It is all a bit shabby, worn down by countless people and too little maintenance. And the attempt at grandeur is at odds with the eager, jostling, smoking, garlic-smelling crowd.

Racing begins at 1.00 on Sunday afternoons. The first thing to do is to queue up for a programme. The twenty-page booklet lists all the horses for each race, their age, parentage, times and placings in previous outings to give an idea of form, and the names of the jockeys and their colours.

Actually they are not really jockeys because on most days the events are trotting races, with the riders being pulled along in two-wheeled buggies. The flat racing season opens in the middle of summer, and on one grand day there is the equivalent of the Grand National, the Derby and Ascot all rolled into one. But usually on the three racing days—Wednesday and Saturday evenings and Sundays—it is trotting.

I arrived too late to get a programme, but persuaded one of the plump and friendly bookies to give me hers. She explained the betting: you have to pick the winning two horses. There is no place or show option, and the basic stake is a rouble. You get a cardboard ticket with the choice scribbled on. Of course all betting is on the totalizator system—there are no private bookmakers, at least not officially. In theory the odds are worked out before each race and the payouts vary accordingly. But there was no way of finding out the odds, and people say the winnings are suspiciously uniform and never more than a few roubles.

All types go to the races: actors, artists, rugged workers in rough clothes, the smart and fashionable sporting anoraks and T-shirts with familiar Western emblems on them, war veterans in their Sunday best with medals on their chest, leather-jacketed youths, swarthy mustachioed faces from the south, a few old women and the occasional blonde bombshell.

In the depths beneath the stands are more betting booths, beer bars, a smell of shashlik and the lavatories. Loudspeakers play oompah music. There is a happy, relaxed atmosphere. Even the police lounge against the fence and chat with the spectators.

For the 3.00 race I bet on a horse with the unlikely name of Cardiff. He had a promising lineage—born of Ideal and Culture. I wagered that Kashma would come in second. A bell rang three minutes before the race. Already a tanker truck, of the kind used for washing the streets, had been round the course spraying the dusty track. In the in-field was a large banner proclaiming 'Glory to work', a large illuminated indicator that did not work, a few heaps of sand and two clocks, one stopped at 12.00 and the other at 2.00. The finishing post—*finish* in Russian—was opposite the most expensive part of the stand.

The horses and buggies lined up beside a truck carrying a gate that stretched out across the track. The truck led them trotting down to the start, and then sped on ahead, drawing in the folding gate like wings and turning off the course as the horses raced on round. People cheered their favourites. Cardiff was meant to be number one, but there seemed to be three other horses also marked number one, which was confusing. The commentator seemed more laconic than his Western equivalents, but Cardiff was clearly in the lead. In the smart stands the enthusiasts were looking through binoculars. A few were squinting down telescopes.

They trotted round once, and Cardiff won. I pushed back through the throng to my friendly bookie to claim some money. She explained I had not understood the system: Kashma came in fourth instead of second as I had wagered. 'But I wish you'd won,' she said kindly, as she took my money for the next race. They went round again, the riders in their coloured plastic helmets and striped jackets, the horses stepping high with a few laggards breaking into an illegal gallop as the jockeys restrained them (a notice in the programme announced that there would be no payouts on any horse that galloped). Unfortunately Dialogue and Kamchatka, my next choices, came in second and third instead of first and second. My betting ticket joined the thousands of others littering the ground.

Russians have a passion for gambling. Perhaps that is why it is so carefully controlled. There have been scandals from time to time that the jockeys fix the races. I know of one man who used to put large sums with illegal private bookmakers (who operate with a few winks and nods). He even gave in his party membership card and his internal passport as guarantees when his request for credit was denied. In the end he literally laid his suit on a horse then and there in mid-winter, caught pneumonia and died.

From time to time the authorities have twinges of conscience that horse racing is not really suitable for good communists. There was considerable debate over the building of the hippodrome to replace an earlier one that was burnt down. In the early seventies the press waged a long but fruitless campaign against racing. And there are still invectives against gambling. But the state makes millions of roubles out of the legal outlets, especially from the many and various national lotteries.

Buying a lottery ticket from a street kiosk and scanning the papers for the winning number is a national pastime which, in the absence of football pools and off-track betting, occupies a central position in many people's lives. The main lottery is held every six weeks, and is called, rather prosaically, 'Money and Things Lottery'. A ticket costs 30 kopecks, and the prizes include cars, carpets, motor cycles, refrigerators, cameras, vacuum cleaners and so on. Or the winner can choose the equivalent in money.

In the draw in the Russian Republic's lottery (each republic runs its own) about 12,000 consumer items are offered in prizes, and some

5 million money prizes totalling about 10 million roubles—a considerable sum and a good indicator of the popularity of this form of gambling.

One of the most popular lotteries is called Sportlotto. There are two kinds, the commoner being the regular weekly draw on Wednesdays. The system is rather like bingo: at a cost of 30 kopecks entrants have to cross out six numbers on a card of forty-nine numbers, and the completed section is sent in and the competitor keeps a copy. The winning numbers are published in the press and announced, like football pools, in a ten minute television programme on Wednesday evenings. Sportlotto kiosks can be found in all the main streets, plastered with details of the winning prizes and slogans wishing all entrants good luck. Metro stations often have tables outside (inside in winter) where tickets are sold. The lottery has little connection with sport, though one version substitutes the names of sports for numbers and the competitor again has to pick the winning combination. There are also at least half a dozen other specialized draws. The art lottery, for example, offers pictures, vases, carpets and such objects as prizes, and tickets are sold mainly in art shops. There is no choice of prizes: it is just bad luck if the winner does not like his picture or sculpture.

The gaming instinct is manifest not only in gambling but in the Russian enthusiasm for sport of all kind. Even more than in the West, sport is the opiate of the Soviet masses. Football matches draw capacity crowds, and fans follow their clubs with fanatical devotion. When Tbilisi won the national cup one year, there were unprecedented scenes in the Georgian capital as thousands upon thousands of people poured into the streets, dancing, cheering and creating such a commotion that the authorities, ever nervous of spontaneous demonstrations, were on the point of intervening to break up the huge gatherings. During football matches, the police take no chances with rowdyism. The sale of alcohol is forbidden and throughout the game a steel cordon of soldiers rings the pitch, facing outwards up at the crowd.

Ice-hockey is however the real national game, and emotions run high during all matches. Brezhnev himself was a keen fan, and even when his health did not permit him to carry out state ceremonial functions, he was occasionally spotted at matches. When the Soviet national team plays the Canadians or the Americans, the streets are deserted as everyone makes for the nearest television set. Indeed so sure are the authorities of the popularity of hockey and football that the party has interrupted sports programmes when it has an announcement it wants seen by the largest possible audience—such as denials of rumours that food prices are to rise.

Almost everyone follows some kind of sport. In winter improvised rinks in courtyards are crowded with youths practising ice-hockey shots, and supporters' clubs are often the central focus of young people's lives.

The initials and emblems of different clubs are daubed on walls and staircases, and youth gangs are formed on the basis of team loyalties. Sport is the instant topic of conversation with foreigners, the only part of the evening television news people watch. Sports stars in the limelight are allowed a certain amount of personal publicity—something rigorously denied most public figures.

Like the Americans, the Russians play to win, and pressure on clubs and sports stars to succeed are enormous—so much so that regular cases of corruption are uncovered. Partisanship is intense, and never more so than when a national team is playing another country. The communist party plays skillfully on this emotion, appealing to deep-seated patriotism, using sport to cement national feeling and portraying success as the result of ideological rectitude and the communist way of life. The Kremlin clearly had every intention of exploiting the 1980 Olympics to the full for their propaganda value, and was therefore that much more chagrined by the American-led boycott.

In such an atmosphere the penalties for failure, especially on a national level, are severe: instant public oblivion and an almost total silence in the media. But success, especially if it has an ideological overtone, brings stardom. Perhaps no one better demonstrates this than Anatoly Karpov, three times world chess champion. A brilliant, cold, slight man with prominent cheek bones and a high-pitched voice, he has willingly played the roll required of him in a sport where the Russians have long dominated the world stage. He has effusively praised former President Brezhnev, the party and the Soviet system, and demonstrated an icy dignity in the bitter personal feud with Viktor Korchnoi while managing to imply disdain for the defector's politics. He received in return the Order of Lenin, the highest civilian award, is chairman of the Soviet Peace Fund, lives in considerable luxury and is frequently in the public eye. He has even been featured on a Soviet postage stamp—a rare honour for a living person.

Using his position, Karpov does much to encourage chess in the Soviet Union. The game is in little danger of losing its appeal however. Russians play chess at almost every opportunity—in trains, in corners of public parks set aside for enthusiasts, in clubs and palaces of culture, on picnics and at the seaside, and of course at home. Chess newspapers and journals have a vast circulation, millions take part in national tournaments and every opportunity is given to those showing particular promise at a young age. Because of the prestige a string of Soviet successes has brought them, the Russians take the game with a patriotic earnestness and determination that suggests it is viewed as more than just a hobby: it is a fundamental part of the Soviet way of life.

In chess, as in every worthy freetime activity, the authorities see it their job to promote and organize, claim credit for successes and direct people's energies into edifying pursuits. But often it is all to no avail.

For millions of people have no interest in any of these constructive activities. To them leisure means doing nothing—absolutely nothing. Western Europeans, particularly those conditioned by the Protestant work ethic and the feelings of guilt that idleness arouses, find it hard to understand how Russians can be so happy doing so little. But they are. Soviet society has much that is Oriental about it and, like Oriental people, Russians can sit for hours watching the world go by, or waiting for a fish to bite, or simply sleeping. They complain they have enough to do at work, where the constant urgings-on, the exhortations for greater heroic toil, go against the Russians' timeless approach to life; they feel, and believe, they are worn out after a day's work—and often are. What nicer than simply resting at home, or in the sun, or anywhere. It is an attitude that leads activists to despair about ever getting the country to bestir itself. But I sometimes had a sneaking feeling that it was not so bad after all.

Suggested Readings

Two books that offer an insight into everyday life in Russia are William Mandel, *Russia Re-Examined: The Land, the People and How They Lived* (New York: Hill and Wang, 1964), and Hedrick Smith, *The Russians* (New York: Ballantine Books, 1976). A look at contemporary Soviet society, including a brief survey on leisure, is provided in Basile Kerblay, *Modern Soviet Society,* trans. Rupert Swyer (New York: Pantheon Books, 1983). The third and final section of Jenny Brine, Maureen Perrie, and Andrew Sutton, eds., *Home, School and Leisure in the Soviet Union* (London: George Allen & Unwin, 1980), is concerned with various aspects of leisure, in particular recreational facilities, sports, and reading.

Human Waves

Leon F. Bouvier

Today's rapidly growing global population is one of the world's major problems. By the year 2000, the population worldwide is expected to exceed 6 billion. Practically every economic, political, and social issue challenging our contemporary society will be significantly affected by the enormous number of individuals soon to occupy the earth. One of the major concerns we face today is the distribution of the dramatically increasing population. Economic factors, in particular, are forcing sizable movements of people from under-developed to advanced countries.

The following selection by Leon F. Bouvier is a frank discussion of the questions raised by increased international migration. Chief among those questions is whether a nation has the right to determine its own demo-graphic and cultural characteristics. Continued migration, according to the author, will lead to the rapid growth of minorities in advanced countries and to a marked change in the composition of national populations. The traditional cultural identities of developed countries, such as the United States, could be significantly altered, and a multicultural, integrated society might be the result.

When the problem of worldwide population growth is mentioned, attention is almost always focused on fertility rates. Yet another side of the population problem is causing mounting concern—

the movement across national borders of millions of people in search of a better life. People have always dreamed of moving to greener pastures, but never in recorded history have migration levels approached those of today. The rising tide of migrants is raising legal and ethical questions that nations have not previously had to face.

Some thirty-five years ago, American sociologist-demographer Kingsley Davis wrote:

> Not only is the earth's total population increasing at the fastest rate ever known, but the increase is extremely unequal as between different regions. Generally the fastest growth is occurring in the poorest regions; the slowest growth in the richest. . . . Between the two kinds of areas the differences in level of living are fantastic. What is more natural than to expect the destitute masses of the under-privileged regions to swarm across international and continental boundaries into the better regions?. . . One wonders how long the inequities of growth between major regions can continue without an explosion that will somehow quickly restore the imbalance.

Davis's prediction is beginning to be realized. People do not move simply because they are crowded; they move because there is not enough food, jobs are scarce, and wages are low in their home countries. If population growth levels had been falling instead of rising during the 1950s and 1960s, conditions would be far less difficult in most countries. Unfortunately, nothing can be done about past demographic behavior. We are just now beginning to witness the impact of the decline in mortality that occurred during the 1950s and 1960s, particularly infant and child mortality, while fertility remained high. Those fifties and sixties babies are now entering adulthood, moving to cities, and forming their own households and families. That is why, in Mexico, for example, despite the decline in fertility among individual women, the country's current population of 75 million will surpass 175 million in less than fifty years. There, and in many other less developed countries, the sheer numbers of women entering reproductive age will keep the overall rate of natural increase high. So while we must reinforce our efforts to lower fertility, that will not solve the problem of millions upon millions of young adults seeking a better way of life now.

For years, many demographers saw the 3 percent rates of growth—meaning a doubling of the population in less than twenty-five years—as problems only for underdeveloped nations. We expressed the opinion that such unprecedented growth could not continue for very long—death rates would soon climb as a rapidly growing population encountered a dwindling supply of resources. But now that the beneficiaries of declining infant and child mortality have come of age, the true im-

HUMAN WAVES   By Leon F. Bouvier, from *Natural History,* August 1983, pp. 6–13.

pact of the population explosions in the developing countries is being felt not only in those countries but also in the advanced countries, as immigration levels swell.

In 1940, 65 percent of the people on the earth lived in developing countries; today the number approaches 75 percent of the 4.6 billion world population. In a short seventeen years it will surpass 80 percent of some 6.1 billion people. Increasingly, residents of the poorest nations are making the decision to move across international borders in an attempt to improve their lives. But with the emergence of nation-states and political barriers, migration has become subject to control. To people facing the prospect of staggering poverty at home, the spectacular advances in communications and transportation have made the possibly dire consequences of migration seem less risky than staying put. This is becoming evident all over the planet as people move from Mexico and Central America to the United States; from Guinea to the Ivory Coast; from Colombia to Venezuela; even from such small islands as Saint Vincent and Saint Lucia to Barbados. Some are legal migrants whose decision to move results from considerable discussion and thought; some 13 million are refugees forced to abandon their homelands for political reasons; some are illegal migrants who enter a country surreptitiously and lead guarded lives for fear of apprehension. The effects of these movements across borders are awesome and differ substantially from one region to another.

When Third World countries exhibit rapid industrial growth, as some OPEC nations have in recent years, they attract residents from less fortunate neighboring states. Thus in Kuwait and the United Arab Emirates, 75 to 80 percent of the population are immigrants—temporary residents who are not citizens and in all likelihood will never become citizens. Illegal immigrants from such impoverished countries as Colombia and Ghana have swarmed to Venezuela and Nigeria. The recent forced exodus of Ghanaians from Nigeria uncovered hundreds of thousands of illegal migrants. Some half a million Colombians may be living clandestinely in Venezuela. About 25 percent of the population of the Ivory Coast are foreigners, many having migrated from Upper Volta and other Sahelian countries.

What happens when the economic bubble bursts and there is no longer any employment for foreign workers, when there is not even enough work for the native-born citizens of the country? Nigeria has provided one answer with its sudden mass expulsion of Ghanaians. The arbitrary and cyclical nature of economic differences between countries is pointed up by Ghana's explusion in 1969 of all aliens without residential permits, forcing some 200,000 persons, mostly Nigerians, to leave. The recent massacres of Bangladeshis residing in Assam, a state of India, is still another example of what may happen when a large immigrant population competes with natives for insufficient land or jobs.

Such solutions may well be repeated again and again in other parts of the world.

In the United States there is increasing concern with immigration issues involving refugees and both legal and illegal immigrants. Since the mid-1970s we have accepted well over 100,000 refugees every year, and given the unstable political situation in many regions of the world, one can only speculate as to the demands in future years. Since 1980, legal immigrants to the United States have averaged more than 600,000 per year. To that we must add the untold hundreds of thousands of clandestine immigrants who enter the country without legal documents. Their number is simply not known. Some illegal immigrants return home each year so that estimates of net illegal migration range from as low as 100,000 to upward of 500,000 per year. In particular, the number of clandestine entrants across the 2,000-mile border between the United States and Mexico is increasing as economic and political conditions deteriorate in parts of Latin America.

The situation in Western Europe is somewhat different. In Switzerland, Sweden, West Germany, and France, the 1960s and early 1970s saw a growing need for unskilled workers from other countries. Between 1960 and 1974 every major country in Western Europe had a positive net migration of legal "guest workers." France accepted 3.8 million workers; West Germany, 6 million. The early movements tended to come from countries such as Spain and Italy, but by the late 1960s and early 1970s the sources of immigration had changed dramatically. Poorer countries such as Morocco, Tunisia, Turkey, Yugoslavia, and Portugal had become the main sources of workers for France. In West Germany, over the same period, the Yugoslav and the Turkish proportion of immigrants increased so that by the early 1970s, Turks accounted for 39 percent of net immigration. Many of these workers came without their families. After 1973, economic conditions worsened in Germany and elsewhere and the demand for labor lessened. Under these economic conditions, some nations attempted to repatriate "temporary" workers to their home countries. Those efforts usually took the form of financial incentives often made only on the condition of permanent exile. Such repatriation programs have not been very successful. Guest workers have become permanent legal residents, and European governments have allowed some family reunifications. Nevertheless, the question remains: What does a country do with the foreign workers already there, particularly in a depressed economic situation?

Another very touchy issue has arisen in the more developed nations. Fertility has fallen to historical lows in almost every one of these countries. Women in West Germany are averaging 1.4 births; in Sweden 1.6; in Great Britain 1:7—all well below the level needed to replace the population. Without immigration the populations in these countries will soon begin to decline. Such a decline has already begun in West

Germany, Denmark, and Sweden, and a number of other Western European countries are expected to begin losing population by the year 2000. With immigration, or at least with the higher fertility of the immigrants already there, the total populations may not decline, but within fifty to seventy-five years what were once homogeneous nations will hardly be recognizable. The Turks and Yugoslavs in Germany and Sweden, the Portuguese and North Africans in France, the West Indians in England, will all become significant minorities in these countries. This could result in new kinds of assimilation. More likely, however, rivalries between groups will become more intense and bitter, possibly leading to major disturbances.

In the United States, fertility has remained well below the population replacement level for more than a decade. Without continued immigration the population would begin falling after the year 2020. If the current pattern of migration were to continue for a century, the former so-called white non-Hispanic majority would make up less than 50 percent of the population. This country is a "nation of immigrants," and at the turn of the twentieth century it experienced major ethnic changes in its white population as the main source of immigration shifted from northwest Europe to southern and eastern Europe. As we approach the twenty-first century the nation is faced with a new challenge: accepting millions of newcomers, this time of predominantly Asian and Hispanic backgrounds. Whether orderly assimilation will take place or increased racial conflicts will occur remains to be seen. One thing is certain: in the emerging era of high international migration, the concept of the nation-state and its cultural identity will be called into question. Emerging trends are forcing upon us some difficult ethical questions for which there are no real historical precedents.

Does an independent nation have the right to block immigration or to expel recent and not-so-recent immigrants if their presence is perceived as jeopardizing the economic well-being of the native inhabitants? The overtly inhumane and violent measures taken in Nigeria and Assam are merely drastic examples of more extensive problems.

We have noted the repatriation attempts made by Western European nations. In the United States more than one million apprehensions of those engaged in illegal entry occur every year. These people are sent back to their home countries, but many return again and again. The U.S. Congress is currently wrestling with the issue of amnesty. Should the millions of residents who have lived and worked here for years without documentation be granted the legal right to remain or should they be repatriated?

Many in the United States feel that numerical increase should come to an end and be followed by an era of zero population growth at perhaps 275 or 300 million. Even with our very low fertility the population will, if immigration continues at recent rates, approach 350 million within a hundred years and will still be growing. Furthermore, the existing culture of the nation will be altered by the increasing proportion of immigrants and their descendants in the population. Thus ethical considerations are raised that go far beyond the matter of competition for jobs. Does a nation have a right to determine its own demographic and cultural characters?

The problems are not limited to countries with a long history of receiving immigrants. Tiny Belize, with a population of fewer than 150,000 people and independent of Great Britain only since September 1981, is faced with massive refugee and immigrant movements from El Salvador, Guatemala, and Nicaragua. Predominantly black and English speaking, Belize could easily become Hispanic through immigration. Barbados, population 250,000 with fertility below replacement, is concerned about current immigration from neighboring, poorer islands; some Barbadians are worried that their nation's culture will be changed by the incursion of East Indians. Such agonizing issues face many nations. Is it proper for a nation to insist that its culture remain as it is? If the answer is yes, is this a subtle new form of racism or is it a laudable expression of cultural identity?

The Universal Declaration of Human Rights adopted by the United Nations General Assembly in 1948 states unequivocally: "Everyone has the right to leave any country including his own and to return to that country." This "right" is hardly honored by many countries—witness the tragic plight of Jews trying to leave the Soviet Union. But even if all the members of the United Nations were to uphold the right of emigration, of what value would it be if no concomitant right of immigration had been agreed to? As a U.N. document reports, "There are few countries which have not placed restriction on the number of immigrants who may enter or upon the activities of the immigrants after arrival."

While there are no easy answers, I believe that action on a variety of fronts might help to reduce the future political and social stresses that will be caused by international migration. For one thing, massive economic as well as family-planning assistance must be supplied to developing nations if both population growth and emigration are to be curtailed. Assistance that contributes to labor-intensive rather than capital-intensive industry and agriculture should be emphasized. As countries like the United States and Japan become increasingly technologically oriented, more assembly-line work should become available in developing countries. To the extent that residents of these nations are able to share in global economic growth without leaving their homes, migration pressures will be reduced.

I believe that the developed countries must be prepared to accept changes in the age and ethnic composition of their populations. Even with increased economic and family-planning assistance to developing nations, any substantial reduction in the level of migration cannot be assumed for the near future. As a result, those of us in the developed countries must prepare for major changes in the composition of our future populations. We will be older societies simply because of our low fertility rates, and we will be more heterogeneous because of continued migration. Sweden may not be as Swedish in fifty years as it is today; West Germany may not be as German. The United States may be on its way to becoming a truly multiracial society, with no single population group constituting a majority. Such changes will occur, but they should not be allowed to come about so abruptly as to make a nation unrecognizable in a mere half century or even a century. Immigration must be limited to some reasonable level; nevertheless, it is important that the receiving nations consider innovative approaches to the acculturation of their newest residents.

The American people, while accepting continued immigration, must decide if they prefer a multicultural, integrated society, with perhaps two or more working languages, or whether every effort should be made to assimilate the newest immigrants into what many have traditionally considered the American culture to be—an Anglo-Saxon umbrella covering a limited variety of customs. Similarly, the heretofore homogeneous societies of Europe must decide whether they will assimilate their newest residents or maintain ethnic enclaves, where the residents, while integrated in some respects, will remain Turkish or Moroccan or whatever, and not become German or French.

Finally, the very size of international population movements of all kinds begs for a reexamination at the global political level of the issues involved. No nation has an open-door policy today. Yet migration is bound to increase in the future into precisely those nations that now exercise restriction on how many and what kinds of people are to be permitted to enter. The international community must seek some agreed norms of conduct in a world that combines increased disparities with increased mobility. Conflict and suffering are inevitable, but we must do what we can to hold them to a minimum.

Suggested Readings

A good survey of population growth from the late seventeenth century to the present Thomas McKeown, *The Modern Rise of Population* (London: Edward Arnold, 1976). Rafael M. Salas, *Reflections on Population,* 2nd ed. (New York: Pergamon Press, 1985), is a very informative presentation of current population problems, including migration. Georgia Lee Kangas, *Population and Survival* (New York: Praeger, 1984), provides insight into both the failures and the successes of family planning during the last 20 years. Michael D. Bayles,

Morality and Population Policy (University: University of Alabama Press, 1980), examines the moral issues in population control, in particular national populations, international assistance, and migration policies. Three surveys treating development problems in Third World countries are Paul Harrison, *Inside the Third World: The Anatomy of Poverty* (Sussex, England: Harvester Press, 1980); Edward G. Stockwell and Karen A. Laidlaw, *Third World Development* (Chicago: Nelson-Hall, 1981); and Lloyd G. Reynolds, *Economic Growth in the Third World, 1850–1980* (New Haven and London: Yale University Press, 1985).

Robots and Japan: The New Breed

Robert C. Christopher

Japan's economy has experienced phenomenal growth in the last 30 years. Prior to the mid-1950s it was a struggling, developing economy. Since then it has been transformed into an economy that is internationally both respected and envied. Most Westerners, when they think of "Japanese industry," generally associate the phrase with such huge, efficient corporations as Toyota, Sony, or Nippon Steel. Despite that image, most of Japanese industry is carried on in small and medium-sized enterprises, which account for more than 50 percent of Japan's total industrial production.

The small factory or workshop is, in many ways, more characteristic of Japan's economic life than the large corporation is. The small concerns belong to Japan's past and are a remnant of the traditional Japanese economy. The present economic "dualism" of large corporation and small factory has given the Japanese economy a unique blend of old and new. This highly successful merging of modernity and tradition is, in part, responsible for Japan's emergence as an economic superpower.

Japan's small factories, however, are undergoing radical changes in their labor practices. A current shortage of competent and affordable workers increasingly has forced Japan's small manufacturers to switch from human labor to robots. This selection by Robert C. Christopher examines the nature of small manufacturing in Japan and analyzes the reasons for the replacement of individuals by robots. The contrast in Western and Japanese attitudes toward robots—and toward technology in general—is apparent in the author's treatment of this new addition to one of Japan's traditional economic institutions.

T oshio Iguchi, a compact, square-faced man of thirty-one, is in many ways the kind of "modern" Japanese husband featured in TV commercials for barbecue grills and the like. He and his wife have the ideal Japanese family in terms of size and sex—one girl, one boy— and live in solid middle-class comfort on the outskirts of Tokyo in a pleasant house graced with a handsome rock garden. There are, in fact, only two respects in which the Iguchis' life-style departs a bit from the norm: their yard is an unusually large one, and unlike the majority of Tokyoites, Toshio doesn't commute to work.

Both these circumstances stem from the fact that Toshio is his own boss. Under the corporate name of Iguchi Seisakujo, he is a sub-contractor for a company that manufactures toy watches for children. His "factory"—which is actually a large metal shed set in one corner of his yard—consists basically of three injection-molding machines with which he produces plastic parts for the kiddie watches.

At one time, Toshio employed four workers to tend his molding machine. This, he confessed to *New York Times* correspondent Henry Scott Stokes, wasn't a totally satisfactory arrangement, since he could never be sure that his workers would actually show up when they were supposed to. Nevertheless, it was a real blow when the oldest of the four—and the only skilled hand among them—was lured away by another company in the same business. Then, to make matters worse, Toshio's younger employees began drifting off to better jobs in offices and coffee bars, and by the spring of 1980 he was left with no workers at all.

At one time that probably would have been the end of Iguchi Seisakujo. But no longer. To solve his problem, Toshio turned to Japan's newest labor pool: robots. In the rapidly developing technology that the Japanese have christened "mechatronics"—a word coined to describe the marriage of electronics and mechanical engineering—the robots that Toshio acquired to run his molding machines represented a rather primitive stage. Unlike the most advanced robots, which are controlled by computer tapes, Toshio's are operated by a fixed sequence of electrical switches and hence cannot easily be "reprogrammed." Even these relatively simple machines carry a price tag too steep for a company with a total capitalization of less than $40,000. Fortunately, however,

ROBOTS AND
JAPAN

361

ROBOTS AND JAPAN: THE NEW BREED   From Robert C. Christopher, *The Japanese Mind* (New York: Linden Press/Simon & Schuster, 1983), pp. 285–94.

Toshio was able to lease the equipment he needed from a company named Japan Robot Lease—and to do so at a cost that represented only a fraction of the wages he used to pay his human workers.

Becoming a one-man band has simplified Toshio Iguchi's life considerably. All he has to do these days is keep the molding machines fed with plastic, collect the parts the robots make and package them for shipment to the assembly plants. He no longer has to worry about absenteeism and keeping track of wages, the robots never make mistakes and, because his costs are lower, his company is more competitive. "This," he says, "is certainly the most effective way to deal with the present labor situation."

But expensive and unreliable as his human workers were, Toshio has to admit that he misses their companionship—and the fact that he can now spend more time than he used to with his family somehow doesn't totally fill that void. So just to have other men to talk to, he has taken to playing golf quite a lot.

Inevitably, the hundreds of thousands of small and medium-sized manufacturing companies scattered around Japan differ vastly in what they make and how they make it. Perhaps 10 percent of them are still engaged, like the Tamayama copperware shop in Tsubame City, in the hand production of traditional goods ranging from rice paper to porcelains. At the other end of the scale are firms such as the Mitsumi Electric Company near Tokyo, which uses high-precision equipment to turn out extremely sophisticated integrated circuits.

Whatever they make, however, Japan's small manufacturing enterprises tend to be family businesses or firms controlled by a single man. And the majority of them—an estimated 60 percent—do not make finished consumer products but, like Toshio Iguchi, are subcontractors who manufacture parts that are subsequently assembled by larger firms. Like the Japanese distribution system, manufacturing in Japan is often a highly complex affair involving many invisible hands: an item that bears a famous brand name is very apt to be in reality the composite product of layer upon layer of subcontractors.

In many cases, these small subcontractors sell all or virtually all of their output to a single bigger company and, in effect, become a part of its industrial "group." For the subcontractor this has the advantage that it eliminates the expense and uncertainties of marketing. But it also leaves him little alternative but to comply when his sole customer presses him to cut the price and improve the quality of his product. "This isn't a matter of give-and-take," says Dodwell's Mark Popiel. "The big company simply sets the terms. It pays the subcontractor a price just high enough to enable him to survive if he cuts costs to the bone. A big company won't push one of its subcontractors over the edge if it can help it—but it will push him right to it."

For the great Japanese corporations that have flooded the world with their exports this arrangement constitutes an invaluable economic cushion—and one of which they take maximum advantage. Where Ford and General Motors, for example, produce about two-thirds of what goes into their cars themselves and rely on subcontractors only for the remaining third, Toyota and Nissan operate on exactly the reverse ratio.

In a variety of ways, this heavy reliance on subcontractors helps Japan's industrial giants to keep their costs in check. To begin with, it permits them to operate with far smaller parts inventories than most major U.S. corporations. This, in turn, means that they don't have to tie up as much capital in warehouses and real estate or pay the wages of as many stock clerks and transport personnel. Instead, these functions are in large part farmed out to smaller firms that can perform them more cheaply.

In general, in fact, the subcontracting system allows a major Japanese company to operate with minimal staff of its own and to get much of the work that goes into its finished products performed by relatively low-cost outside labor. For unlike the country's big corporations, Japan's small subcontractors do not seek to attract the cream of the work force through guarantees of lifetime employment and other expensive benefits. Rather, they tap the lower levels of the national labor pool, often relying heavily on so-called part-time workers. (Somewhat confusingly, hundreds of thousands of the latter are what is known as "full-time part-timers"—people who actually work an eight-hour day five or six days a week, but who are less well paid than they would be if they were technically classified as full-time employees.)

Still another advantage of the subcontracting system from the point of view of Japan's big corporations is that in times of trouble it provides them with a built-in—and to them, more or less painless—cost-reduction mechanism. "When a recession strikes or the competition gets really tough," says Mark Popiel, "the first thing a big corporation in this country does is put the squeeze on its subcontractors." Simply by decreeing a reduction in the prices it will pay its captive suppliers for parts and services, the big corporation can instantly chop its costs without inflicting morale-destroying wage cuts on its own personnel.

This system makes it possible for Japanese companies to respond quickly to changes in the economic climate and at the same time serves to inhibit the kind of suicidal wage inflation that has sapped the competitiveness of so many U.S. industries. Perhaps equally important, extensive use of subcontractors and the disproportionate number of small manufacturing firms in Japan have helped the Japanese escape some of the rigidities that tend to characterize big business elsewhere in the world. With no hint of complaint, Masato Tsuru, managing director of Nippon Oil Seal, one of Japan's biggest subcontracting firms, pointed out to me that a big manufacturer can often exact improvements in product quality more easily from an outside supplier than from his own employees. Similarly, when the demands of the market dictate a change in product design, it is often easier to turn around a number of small firms than a single big one with its elaborate managerial hierarchy. And of necessity, small firms are more prepared than huge ones to gamble their entire existence on a product that may or may not prove successful.

Often enough, of course, such gambles fail. In 1981, in fact, more than 17,600 Japanese companies with total liabilities of nearly $12 billion went bankrupt. From an economist's point of view, that was not necessarily cause for unalloyed sorrow: in theory, as MITI's Masahisa Naitoh notes, it is almost as important for "senescent" or uneconomic industries to die as for promising new ones to be born. But however desirable that process may be in overall economic terms, the death of an industrial giant inevitably causes great social disruption. Here again, Japan is well served by its abundance of small enterprises: it is they rather than the country's major enterprises that do virtually all the dying—a fact which considerably mitigates the social costs involved.

In human terms, the environment in which Japan's small manufacturers and their employees exist is a difficult one at best, and not infrequently downright harsh. Without disputing that, many Japanese will nonetheless argue that it has played a key role in their country's emergence as an economic superpower. "It provides a sort of vitality that we must retain in order to keep our country competitive," insists Masaru Yoshitomi. And the most enterprising of Japan's small manufacturers now quite clearly constitute the vanguard of a revolution that seems likely to infuse even greater vitality into the Japanese industrial structure.

Though never so heavily overmanned as the country's farms and distribution system, Japan's small manufacturing enterprises have also in a sense been part of the informal welfare system. Specifically, they have served as a source of employment for the nation's less desirable workers, those who because of age, lack of education or some other handicap—such as simply being married and female—could not find a place in a big company. To some extent, this is still true, but it is becoming less and less true every day. At a very rapid pace, Japan's small factories are radically changing their labor patterns.

Two factors—one economic and the other primarily social—have conspired to produce this change. The relentless pressure big corporations have put upon their subcontractors to reduce costs and simultaneously improve the quality and reliability of their goods has necessarily driven the smaller companies to seek greater worker productivity. And this, quite clearly, is a goal most likely to be achieved through the use of energetic and relatively well-educated workers—which is to say young people with high school diplomas.

But even as the demand for productive young workers has mounted, Japan's birthrate has been falling: where the average Japanese woman in the 1960s had 2.1 children, today she has only 1.7. As a result, the percentage of young people in the overall Japanese population is steadily diminishing. Inevitably, this has increased the competition for their services and made them less willing to accept the inferior wages and working conditions that generally prevail in small companies.

The upshot of all this has been that in recent years more and more of Japan's small manufacturers began to face the same problem that Toshio Iguchi did: an intractable shortage of effective and affordable workers. But at this point, characteristically, the Japanese Government stepped into the picture. With a little courteous arm-twisting here and there, Tokyo's mandarins persuaded nearly three dozen of Japan's burgeoning robot manufacturers to set up a joint company to lease their products. For the robot makers this had the advantage that it significantly expanded their potential market. Even more important for the overall economy, however, it enabled a small manufacturer who could not afford to buy, say, a $45,000 robot outright to lease one for as little as $750 a month. What's more, it gave him the assurance that he could freely trade his robots in for new and improved models as they come along.

With the way thus paved, throngs of small Japanese entrepreneurs like Toshio Iguchi have now switched—at least in part—from human labor to robots. While Americans still tend to think of robots as complex devices suitable only for giant operations like an automobile assembly line, it has now become routine for small Japanese firms to use them for such tasks as welding, spray painting and metal grinding. As of 1980, an estimated 41 percent of all Japanese companies with between 30 and 100 employees were already employing at least some robots, and that figure seems certain to snowball as companies that have not yet "robotized" begin to find themselves unable to compete with those that have. Though he laughed as he said it, Masaru Yoshitomi clearly was not joking when, in the spring of 1982, he suggested to me that in the typical Japanese family enterprise of the future, Mom will keep the books, Pop will tend the robots and Junior will do the programming for them.

Besides manufacturing, there is at least one other sector of Japan's traditional economy where robotization is likely to have dramatic impact. Sooner or later—most probably within the next generation—some of Japan's service trades too seem virtually certain to be revolutionized by robots.

Historically, service jobs in Japan have been what the economists like to call labor-intensive. As anthropologist Lionel Tiger pointed out in a paean to Japanese food a few years ago, to prepare and serve Japan's seemingly simple traditional cuisine properly involves far more human labor than is required for anything short of haute cuisine in the

West. Similarly, Japanese businesses of every description have tradition-ally maintained serried ranks of receptionists, gofers, tea makers and assorted other spear carriers of various types. In all my time in Japan, I cannot recall ever having visited a business establishment that did not immediately dispatch one of a corps of demure maidens to fetch me tea, juice or coffee—and not infrequently, all three in succession. And on a fair number of occasions, I have had a car and chauffeur pressed upon me to ferry me to my next appointment.

But while it lends a welcome graciousness to what in the West are often brusque and impersonal transactions, this profligate use of human resources has become too expensive to maintain in many areas of the contemporary Japanese economy. So, in an effort to preserve the form if not the substance of their traditional behavior patterns, the Japanese have once again turned to robots. As early as the mid-1970s, robot "greeters" clad in kimono or waitress costumes began turning up in stores and restaurants. And instead of straightforward automatic signals, robot flagmen and traffic cops became a familiar sight on Japan's highways.

All signs are that these are only the first modest steps in the de-humanization of services in Japan. In late 1981, in a deadly serious article in the respected publication *Ekonomisuto,* a university professor named Tetsuo Ihara conjured up a vision of Japan in which people will have their hair attended to by robot barbers and beauticians and will get their washing done at "a robot-operated laundromat that re-turns the dirty clothes fed into it as cleanly and neatly as your local laundry service now does." And when the Tokyoite of tomorrow de-cides to dine out, Ihara suggested, he may well go to a "tastefully dec-orated" restaurant in his own apartment building where robot chefs will "cook whatever dish you command by the insertion of an order card."

To many Westerners, the world Professor Ihara envisages will surely sound depressingly sterile and dehumanized. But this is not a concern most Japanese would share. Japanese in general actively like robots. A few years ago at a seminar in Tokyo, Ichiro Shioji, the head of Japan's watered-down version of the United Auto Workers, noted that the humans who labor on Japan's automobile assembly lines treat the robots they work with like partners. "They talk to their robots, pat them on the arm and even give them affectionate nicknames," Shioji said with an indulgent smile. At that, some of the Europeans and Americans present exchanged quizzical glances, but their skepticism was unwarranted: a subsequent visit to a big auto plant demonstrated to me that Shioji was simply reporting literal fact.

Japanese sociologists and psychologists like to attribute their coun-trymen's receptivity to robots to the influence of Buddhism—which, unlike Christianity, does not place man at the center of the universe and, in fact, makes no particular distinction between the animate and inanimate. As a result of this outlook, the theory goes, Japanese do not instinctively feel threatened by machines with human attributes as Westerners tend to do.

There is probably a large element of truth in this explanation. But whatever special psychological affinity the Japanese may have for robots has surely been reinforced by the fact that up until now robots have to a great extent been employed in Japan to perform jobs that human workers find unusually arduous or distasteful. More important yet, the introduction of robots has not so far thrown any significant number of Japanese out of work. At the moment, in fact, robotization is not even meeting the overall requirements of the Japanese economy for additional labor. As of 1981, Japanese industry was creating new job openings at the rate of 600,000 a year while robot production amounted to only about 20,000 units a year—and while "intelligent robots" that will perform the work of two or three men are in the offing, the general rule of thumb in Japan is still that it takes one robot to fill the shoes of one human.

If the optimists are right, moreover, there is no reason to expect that robotization will ever create widespread unemployment in Japan in the foreseeable future. From an overall economic point of view, the optimists argue, the results of robotization in Japan will be like those of the Industrial Revolution in nineteenth-century Europe: it will create economic growth matching—or more than matching—the increases it makes possible in labor productivity. This, in turn, will lead to increased demands for goods and services and hence to a general increase in employment opportunities.

By no means all Japanese are totally convinced that things will work out that neatly. For one thing, the Doubting Thomases point out, the world economy in general shows worrisome signs of becoming a zero-sum game in which demand cannot be expected to expand automatically; and although the Japanese economy is still growing, it is now doing so at a far slower rate than it did in the go-go 1960s. And in any case, no matter how rosy Japan's overall employment picture may remain, an overly rapid mass resort to robots by Japan's small manufacturing and service enterprises could well cause a great deal of individual hardship and disruption. For while Japan's big corporations can—and do—retrain workers replaced by robots for other jobs, no such safety net exists for the millions of Japanese employed by little companies.

On balance, though, the prevailing Japanese attitude on this issue appears to be that expressed by economic journalist Keiji Ikehata: "Too much brooding over the impact of the spread of robots . . . will probably lead to groundless fears." Just as it has protected farmers and shopkeepers against the ravages of unrestrained competition, so the Japanese Government would almost certainly intervene if the robotization of small factories and service enterprises clearly threatened to cause excessive economic and social disruption. So far, however, the enthusiasm with which Toshio Iguchi and his counterparts all over Japan have embraced robots has been an almost unalloyed blessing: its key effect has been to enhance the efficiency and flexibility with which Japan's small entrepreneurs serve the great corporations that constitute the cutting edge of the nation's economy. Robotization, in short, is bringing the productivity of the Japanese work force as a whole closer to the U.S. level and may indeed herald the day when the only economic advantage the United States has over Japan will be as a producer of food and raw materials.

Suggested Readings

Gerard K. O'Neil, *The Technology Edge* (New York: Simon and Schuster, 1983), examines the strengths and weaknesses of United States and Japanese industry. Of particular interest is a comparison of robotics in Japan and the United States.

The Japanese economy has been extensively studied. Notable among the vast number of books dealing with it are M. Shinohara, *Industrial Growth, Trade, and Dynamic Patterns in the Japanese Economy* (Tokyo: University of Tokyo Press, 1982); Takafusa Nakamura, *The Postwar Japanese Economy,* trans. Jacqueline Kaminski (Tokyo: University of Tokyo Press, 1981); Hugh Patrick and Henry Rosovsky, eds., *Asia's New Giant: How the Japanese Economy Works* (Washington, D.C.: The Brookings Institution, 1976); and G. C. Allen, *The Japanese Economy* (London: Weidenfeld and Nicolson, 1981).

An analysis of the elements likely to dictate Japan's future development is Lewis Austin, *Japan: The Paradox of Progress* (New York: Yale University Press, 1976).

High Tech/High Touch

John Naisbitt

The rapidly increasing rate of scientific and technological development and the practical utilization of its discoveries have had a revolutionary impact on contemporary society. The pace at which new technology presently is being introduced shows no signs of decreasing—and is actually accelerating even faster. As more and more of this technology enters our lives, we are forced to discover new ways to accommodate and shape it. The nature of our response to technological development certainly will dictate the future of civilization.

This book's final selection, a brief excerpt from the often controversial best seller Megatrends *by John Naisbitt, examines the manner in which humans adapt to technology. Naisbitt maintains that whenever new technology is introduced into society it creates a need for a counterbalancing human response. If that need is not fulfilled, the technology is rejected. It is this human compensation that balances the impersonal nature of technology. Naisbitt provides a provocative analysis of several innovations—including television, the pill, and the computer—to substantiate his claims. His conclusions offer hope that, no matter to what extent and at what rate technology enters our lives, the desire for human interaction will allow us to deal successfully with its complexities.*

High tech/high touch is a formula I use to describe the way we have responded to technology. What happens is that whenever new technology is introduced into society, there must be a counterbalancing human response—that is, *high touch*—or the technology is rejected. The more high tech, the more high touch.

The parallel growth of high tech/high touch took place during the last three decades, a period that appeared chaotic, but that really had its own rhythm and sense.

The alienation of the 1950s was a response to the most intensely industrialized period in our history. During this decade of the gray flannel suit and the organization man, fully 65 percent of our workforce were in industrial occupations, many in assembly-line regimentation. More workers, 32 percent, were unionized than would ever be again.

During both the 1950s and the 1960s, we mass-marketed the products of that industrial era—products whose regimented uniformities mirrored their industrial base. High tech was everywhere—in the factory, at the office, in our communication, transportation, and health care systems and, finally, even in our homes.

But something else was growing alongside the technological invasion. Our response to the high tech all around us was the evolution of a highly personal value system to compensate for the impersonal nature of technology. The result was the new self-help or personal growth movement, which eventually became the human potential movement.

Much has been written about the human potential movement, but to my knowledge no one has connected it with technological change. In reality, each feeds the other—high tech/high touch.

Now, at the dawn of the twenty-first century, high tech/high touch has truly come of age. Technology and our human potential are the two great challenges and adventures facing humankind today. The great lesson we must learn from the principle of high tech/high touch is a modern version of the ancient Greek ideal—*balance*.

We must learn to balance the material wonders of technology with the spiritual demands of our human nature.

High Tech/High Touch: TV, the Pill, and Hospices

Perhaps the most powerful technological intrusion was television, far more vivid and more engaging than either radio or the telephone.

HIGH TECH/HIGH TOUCH   From John Naisbitt, *Megatrends* (New York: Warner Books, 1984), pp. 35–52.

At almost exactly the time we first introduced television, we created the group-therapy movement, which led to the personal growth movement, which in turn led to the human potential movement (est, TM, Rolfing, Yoga, Zen, and so forth—all very high touch). Television and the human potential movement developed almost in lockstep, much of both in the bellwether state of California.

The first real television generation, the baby boomers, who started out in life with *The Howdy Doody Show* and who mellowed into *The Mickey Mouse Club* and *American Bandstand,* are without a doubt the strongest proponents of the human growth movement. The need to compensate for the years of being technologically bombarded is part of the unfolding of this high-touch phenomenon.

The gee-whiz futurists are always wrong because they believe technological innovation travels in a straight line. It doesn't. It weaves and bobs and lurches and sputters.

We show no signs of lessening the pace with which we introduce even more technology into our society—and into our homes. The appropriate response to more technology is not to stop it, Luddite-like, but to accommodate it, respond to it, and shape it. In the interplay of technology and our reaction to it, technological progress does not proceed along a straight course. That is why the gee-whiz futurists who said we are all going to pilot our own helicopters, or that home hook-ups will replace the newspaper, were mistaken. Technological innovation rarely goes the way of straight-line extrapolation, but proceeds as part of a lurching dynamic of complicated patterns and processes.

Examples of the high-tech/high-touch phenomenon are all around us.

- The high technology of heart transplants and brain scanners led to a new interest in the family doctor and neighborhood clinics.
- Jet airplanes, as far as I can tell, have led only to more meetings.

The pill is a good example of high tech/high touch. The high technology of chemistry and pharmacology led to the development of the pill, which in turn led to a whole revolution in lifestyles. Societal taboos against premarital sex are of course partly pragmatic since becoming pregnant can lead to all kinds of complications; the advent of the pill initiated widespread experimentation and adventurism, including living together, which became very widespread. Although marriage is coming back in the 1980s, during the 1970s there were days when I was sure that the only people in this society who *really* wanted to get married were priests.

The introduction of the high technology of word processors into our offices has led to a revival of handwritten notes and letters.

A very poignant example of what I mean by high tech/high touch is the response to the introduction of high technology of life-sustaining equipment in hospitals. We couldn't handle the intrusion of this high technology into such a sensitive area of our lives without creating some human ballast. So we got very interested in the quality of death, which led to the hospice movement, now widespread in this country.

The more high technology we put in our hospitals, the less we are born there, dying there—and avoiding them in between.

The health field offers still more examples of high tech/high touch. The high-tech side has brought heart transplants into the medical mainstream; microsurgery to reattach severed limbs, and, recently, artificial pancreata; and "walking dialysis" to replace expensive and confining hemodialysis. At the same time there is a trend toward less surgery and less radical surgery.

And medical care is becoming far more high touch. Home care and home births are becoming increasingly popular, while in hospitals the staff is attempting to create a more homelike atmosphere. New low-tech birthing rooms are being added to hospitals, and freestanding birthing centers, similar to hospice centers, are proliferating. Primary nursing, for example, where a nurse is responsible for the total care of a few patients, is very high touch.

The immensely popular *Star Wars* saga is very high tech/high touch. It portrays a contest between characters who have used technology within human control and scale and others who have been dominated by it. The good guys are not antitechnology: When Luke Skywalker flies in on that final run, the Force with him, he turns off his computer, but not his engine.

The Computer as Liberator

I had thought earlier that we might rebel against the computer for dehumanizing us. But now I think we are beginning to understand just how liberating the computer is in a high-tech/high-touch sense. For example, a company with 40,000 employees has treated those employees pretty much the same for generations. It had to because that was the only way to keep track of them. With the computer to keep track, the employees can be treated differently, with a unique contract for each of the 40,000. We are all slowly moving in that direction. In addition, companies are now offering a "cafeteria of compensations," for example American Can and TRW. An employee can now decide to have a certain combination of salary, pension, health benefits, insurance, flexitime, job sharing, vacation arrangements, and job objectives.

The technology of the computer allows us to have a distinct and individually tailored arrangement with each of thousands of employees.

Even pension plans are moving in this direction: Because we have the computer to keep track of it, an individual contributor to the pension plan can decide where that contribution is going to be invested. And that is one of the key reasons that unions are out of tune with the new computer-rich information society. The basic idea of a union is to ensure that everyone is treated the same. But now we all want to be treated differently.

It is important to think about the computer as a tool that manages complexity, because just as surely as highways only encourage more cars, having a tool that manages complexity invites more and more complexity into the society.

High-Tech Backlash

Whenever institutions introduce new technology to customers or employees, they should build in a high-touch component; if they don't, people will try to create their own or reject the new technology. That may account for the public's resistance to automation and electronic accounting.

In 1975, when automatic payroll deposits were instituted at Spartan Industries in Detroit, three women assembly-line workers sued the company over the issue. They charged that they were fired for refusing to participate in the computerized system. Electronic Funds Transfer faced a far more substantial and widespread backlash. The vice president of the Bank of Hawaii, David Cheever, explains it this way: "We've done a lot of research and the customer simply feels better writing checks himself, knowing it will get done."

There is no high touch in the high tech of electronic funds transfer, so bank customers are rejecting it everywhere. The banks offering it are essentially saying, "We used to do business one way and now we are all going to do it another way—electronically."

The problem is with the customers. Some of us *want* to go to tellers. In fact, some of us want to go to *the same* teller every time. I don't know about you, but I feel outrageously virtuous writing out my own checks every month—and the banks want to take that away from me.

The banks are offering what amounts to an either/or formulation rather than an option. In a highly diversified, highly segmented society, options succeed and either/or formulations fail miserably. Also, interiors of banks are being re-designed to provide (high touch) lounge areas for cozy discussions about loans.

When high tech and high touch are out of balance, an annoying dissonance results. There are many examples of high-tech dissonance:

- The backlash against high-tech polygraph tests, which were labeled "dehumanizing" and subsequently outlawed in nineteen states and the District of Columbia.

- The widespread concern about personal privacy that erupted just as computers were becoming widespread in society.
- Another example is as mundane as the telephone. You use the high technology of the telephone to dial 411 to get a phone number and, instead of a high-touch response, what you get is more technology: a record upbraiding you for not checking your directory.

High-tech dissonance infuriates people. It's even worse when you again use the technology of the telephone to call a warm friend and instead get more technology: "Hi there, I've gone out for a little while. . . ." That's why so many improbable messages are left recorded on those machines.

Many of us instinctively feel the metric system is too high tech. To make matters worse, it was imposed on us top-down by some Metric Council or other (presumably in Washington, D.C.) and consequently we do not want very much to do with it.

"Metric will be about as successful as Esperanto." That prophetic statement was made by Steward Brand, the editor of *CoEvolution Quarterly* and head of California's Metric Council. The high tech of metric is being imposed on people without any high-touch tradeoffs and in the face of the comfortable, high-tech/high-touch balance of measures like the inch and quart. The inch, we all know, is about the size of the middle joint of our fingers, and the quart has been the traditional container of the ultimate higher-touch beverage—milk.

The genius of customary measure is its highly evolved interrelationship of hand and eye. Metric works fine, technically. But when you try to cook, carpenter, or shop with it, as Brand has pointed out, metric fights the hand. In Japan, which has been trying to go metric for forty years, architects design in metric and the contractors blithely build (even skyscrapers) by the traditional shaku-sun measure.

The high touch of traditional measure is simply too well-ingrained for us to want to change without good reason to do so. High-tech metric has gone as far as it is going to go.

High Touch: The Need to Be Together

High tech/high touch. The more technology we introduce into society, the more people will aggregate, will want to be with other people: movies, rock concerts, shopping. Shopping malls, for example, are now the third most frequented space in our lives, following home and workplace.

About nine years ago, in 1975, after we invented those huge screens that you could have in your living room to watch movies, Arthur D. Little issued a report suggesting that by the year 1980 there would be almost no movie theaters in the United States. What they didn't understand was high tech/high touch. You do not go to a movie just to see a movie. You go to a movie to cry or laugh with 200 other people. It is an event.

Perhaps it is the high-touch need to be together that enables us to tolerate the high levels of density we experience in many crowded cities.

And what could be more high tech/high touch than an impossibly crowded nightclub dance floor with flashing strobe lights circling above?

Because we want to be with each other, I don't think many of us will choose to work at home in our electronic cottages. Very few people will be willing to stay home all of the time and tap out messages to the office. People want to go to the office. People want to be with people, and the more technology we pump into the society, the more people will want to be with people. It is good for emergencies (like Mondays) and to be able to stay home on some days and deal with your office and work through a computer is an attractive occasional option. During certain specific periods—the late stages of a pregnancy, for example—it is useful to be able to continue work via a computer. But for the most part, we will seek the high touch of the office.

The utilization of electronic cottages will be very limited: People want to go to the office; people want to be with people.

The same may be said for electronic marketing. The same people who predicted we would all fly helicopters (those captives of straight-line, technological extrapolation) now say that with computers at home we will shop electronically and stores will become extinct. We will eventually do some shopping by computer, but only for staple items of which we have a very clear sense and experience. It will be no substitute for the serendipity and high touch of shopping for what we want to be surprised about.

Computer buying will never replace the serendipity and high touch of shopping for what we want to be surprised about.

Teleconferencing. That is another trend that will not happen. Talking with people via television cannot begin to substitute for the high touch of a meeting, no matter how rational it is in saving fuel and overhead. If it is of little importance, use teleconference. Be appropriate. But we have to face it: There is no end to meetings.

Teleconferencing is so rational, it will never succeed.

On the other hand, videotechnology works wonderfully in a high-touch situation:

- A Tahoe City realtor told the *Los Angeles Times* that videotapes are proving a useful marketing tool for vacation property: The tapes can be mailed to prospective buyers, who can then decide whether the property is worth the trip to see it.

- A Rockville, Maryland, talent agency shows engaged couples video-tapes of the bands available to play at their wedding.
- A Washington, D.C., woman offers what amounts to "shrink selection service" whereby prospective patients can view psychologists and psychiatrists, taped at their offices, talking about themselves and their theories.
- Then, of course, there is the proliferation of videodating services. Not everyone's cup of tea, perhaps. But the services do appear successful.

High Touch: In the Schools

Readers of the *Trend Report*'s education section noticed a curious phenomenon for volume two of the 1980 report. During the exact same time period that articles on education appeared throughout the nation reporting widespread use of the computer in the schools, a wave of stories appeared about either reviving religion in the schools or about teaching values.

Twenty-five states were debating the questions of voluntary prayer, posting the Ten Commandments, and silent meditation at school.

And many schools incorporated values discussions into the regular curriculum:

- A Denver, Colorado, elementary school program seeks to "break sexual stereotypes limiting career opportunities."
- At a Kansas City, Missouri, school, students discussed whether or not a friend should turn another friend in for shoplifting.
- In Scarsdale, New York, moral questions are used to teach an "argumentative writing course."
- In Tulsa, Oklahoma, an elementary school is testing the positive-thinking theories of former Dallas salesman Zig Ziglar. The course's motivational message is "I canness."

Conclusion? Again it is high tech/high touch. As computers begin to take over some of the basics of education, schools will more and more be called upon to take responsibility for teaching values and motivation, if not religion.

High Tech/High Touch: Home and Factory

The need for compensatory high touch is everywhere. The more high tech in our society, the more we will want to create high-touch environments, with soft edges balancing the hard edges of technology.

As we moved through the 1970s, industrialization and its technology moved more and more from the workplace to the home. High-tech furniture echoed the glories of an industrial past. Kitchen tech, whose high point was Cuisinart, industrialized our kitchens as minimalism dehumanized our living rooms. And of course the ultimate intrusion of home-style high tech is the personal computer.

But the brief period of interest in high-tech furniture and minimalist design was just that—brief. It is now behind us. Ahead of us for a long period is an emphasis on high touch and comfort to counterbalance a world going mad with high technology.

Among other things, this means soft colors—pastels are becoming quite popular—coziness, plumpness, the unconstructed look, and links to the past. Folk art is the perfect counterpoint to a computerized society. No wonder handmade quilts are so popular. Even country music's popularity is partly a response to electronic rock.

Uniformity in style, whether it is traditional or modern, will give way to a great eclectic mix. Mixing furniture styles, accessories, and art can be a bold statement of individuality. The same goes for original art and one-of-a-kind furniture.

Granted, at this point few of us appear terribly original, what with our need to have a designer's initials on all our clothing, fabrics, sheets, towels. And now even chocolates.

But it is all part of a transition. We needed to buy designer this and designer that because we were not yet confident of our own ability to make an individual statement.

Even insecurity does not last long in a fast-changing world.

Now we are moving in the direction of putting our own imprimatur on our environment, allowing personal visions amid the technology.

High-tech robots and high-touch quality circles are moving into our factories at the same time—and the more robots, the more circles.

In our factories we are also moving in the dual directions of high tech/high touch: high-tech robots and high-touch quality control circles—groups of workers who discuss work-related problems and solutions.

As we restructure from an industrial to an information society, we are moving more information and more technology, in the form of quality circles *and* robots, into our factories. And (high tech/high touch) the more robots, the more quality circles.

Similarly, when we moved from an agricultural to an industrial society, we moved more industry into our farms. In about 1800, 90 percent of our population produced 100 percent of the food. Today only 3 percent of our population produces 120 percent of the food we need. The surplus is stored or exported.

That is the direction our industrial production is going. As part of this process, we will increasingly run our factories with information rather than laborers. Robots will play a big role in bringing this about. Conservative estimates predict that by 1990 we will be producing 17,000 robots per year and that the total robot workforce will reach 80,000. Most experts would double those figures.

Needed: High-Tech Skills

The skills to maintain high-technology systems are becoming as important as the creative skills that design the systems.

All across the country, buses, planes, utilities, even sewage treatment plants, miracles of modern science, are breaking down and proving unusable because we are unable to provide the companion miracle of modern maintenance.

The lack of skilled workers is most alarming in the area of nuclear power. Everyone is familiar with Three Mile Island, but numerous other dangerous incidents have been caused by carelessness or ignorance. In Virginia, the North Anna One nuclear plant was shut down when a worker's shirt snagged a circuit breaker; previously, employees at the same plant had jammed an emergency switch with a pencil and paper clip. At Florida Power's Crystal River plant, a potentially serious leakage of radioactive water may have been unknowingly caused by an electrician. At the Rancho Seco plant in California a similar incident occurred several years ago when a technician dropped a console light bulb into the wiring.

New safety requirements in the nuclear industry have created a need for more engineers and other technicians, while the fear of another Three Mile Island has led to greater emphasis on hiring qualified workers. But as the need has grown, the number of workers has not. The unpopularity of nuclear power on college campuses and its uncertain future have discouraged many students from entering the field. Between 1978 and 1981, there was a 25-percent drop in the number of students receiving a bachelor of science in nuclear engineering, and a 43-percent drop in those taking a master's. Regulators fear that plants, unable to find qualified workers, will lower their safety standards; in fact, one of the Nuclear Regulatory Commission's regional offices recently ordered Toledo Edison Company to retract a series of promotions at its Davis-Besse nuclear plant. The promotions had gone to unqualified workers, they said, making the plant unsafe.

The panel studying the crash of the DC-10 in Chicago in 1979, which killed 273 people, listed improper maintenance as the starting point for the failures that led to the crash. That and similar findings have led the airline industry to worry that too many functions are being taken over by unqualified workers.

Both Houston, Texas, and Baltimore, Maryland, have plans to renovate old buses, at considerable expense, because the new "advance design buses" manufactured by both General Motors and Grumman's Flxible Industries (the only type currently available in the United States) have proved too difficult and expensive to maintain. In Connecticut electrical fires have started in the engine boxes of five Grumman Flxible's buses. Miami's new air-conditioned buses broke down when the air conditioning was turned on. Houston has 150 of the General Motors buses, which have lifts for the handicapped, wide seating, air conditioning, and windows that don't open. The city found itself in a crisis situation during the summer of 1981 when the air conditioning on dozens of the new buses broke down, making them unusable. Authorities solved the problem by removing the windows on forty of the buses, a short-term solution at best.

In 1979 a new sewage treatment plant at San Jose, California, broke down, flooding a billion gallons of partially treated sewage into San Francisco Bay and wiping out marine life. Floating bacteria had clogged the screens, and the bacteriologist, who might have corrected the problem, had resigned and not been replaced. In all, there were nineteen vacancies on the operating staff. Between September 1979 and March 1980, the state of Maryland ordered 24 malfunctioning treatment plants to cut back the flow of sewage. And when the Environmental Protection Agency checked 100 new sewage plants, it found 20 operating poorly at times. "It takes a lot of judgment to run these plants, but finding good operators is a nationwide problem," said Laurence D. Bory of the American Consulting Engineers Council. In an increasingly complicated area, one with the potential for causing massive pollution, the level of salaries is incredibly low, in some parts of the country falling under $10,000 a year. It's not surprising that a study conducted for the Water Pollution Control Federation shows operators often lack the experience and training to understand how the plants operate. "Operators are no longer people who should be thought of as coming to work in T-shirts," says Bill Parish of Maryland's sewage plant compliance section. "They need mechanical engineering and biological backgrounds."

Even the family automobile is becoming too complicated for most of us to fix. "There is already a competency crunch among the nation's 525,000 automechanics," says the president of the National Institute for Automotive Service Excellence, which certifies mechanics. "We may already have passed the day when an individual could work on his own car," asserts John Betti, a Ford vice president.

What's going to happen when we get artificial hearts? Unless we begin to fill the need for skilled technicians, we will be forced to abandon much of our technological infrastructure and return to older, simpler methods. Barney Clark gave all of us a new sense of high touch.

The high-tech repair problems we already face are testimony to the need for mechanically skilled engineers, technicians, and repair people. All of these are good occupational bets for the next twenty years. But better incentives will have to be created to attract and develop the skills needed to keep our technology viable.

Living in a High-Tech World

Generally speaking, most of us will want to develop our own ways to compensate for the high-tech influence of the computer in our work and home environment. Soft shapes and colors are some of the design responses possible. And parents will have to watch to see that children don't become completely wired to the computer (remember television?).

We will have a greater need to compensate for technology by being out in nature more often, going camping, going to the seashore. You may have to drag your children away from the computer or video games to take them fishing or bicycling.

In a high-tech information world, where we use our brainpower instead of performing physical labor, as did the factory workers of the industrial era, we will want to use our hands and bodies more in our leisure activities to balance the constant use of mental energy at work. You can see this already in the popularity of gardening, cooking, and home repair and renovation.

The balance between the high tech and high touch is one way to evaluate the usefulness and lasting value of the many high-tech (and high-priced) consumer gadgets that fill the marketplace. I for one wish I had not bought a food processor. I use it infrequently, preferring the high touch of chopping foods by hand, even though it takes longer.

The food processor is only one high-tech temptation, and there will be many more. We can probably all do with a little less enthusiasm for the latest technological wonder vying for our attention and our wallets, and seek a little more high-touch balance in our lives.

The Danger of the Technofix Mentality

"Man is a clever animal. There is no way to keep him from devising new tools. The error lies in thinking that new tools are the solution. It could be a fatal error," writes John Hess in a *GEO* magazine article entitled "Computer Madness."

When we fall into the trap of believing or, more accurately, hoping that technology will solve all our problems, we are actually abdicating the high touch of personal responsibility. Our technological fantasies illustrate the point. We are always awaiting the new magical pill that will enable us to eat all the fattening food we want, and not gain weight; burn all the gasoline we want, and not pollute the air; live as immoderately as we choose, and not contract either cancer or heart disease.

In our minds, at least, technology is always on the verge of liberating us from personal discipline and responsibility. Only it never does and it never will.

The more high technology around us, the more the need for human touch.

That is why the human potential movement that advocates both discipline and responsibility is such a critical part of the high-tech/high-touch equation. By discovering our potential as human beings we participate in the evolution of the human race. We develop the inner knowledge, the wisdom, perhaps, required to guide our exploration of technology.

With the high-touch wisdom gained studying our potential as human beings, we may learn the ways to master the greatest high-tech challenge that has ever faced mankind—the threat of total annihilation by nuclear warfare.

High tech/high touch. The principle symbolizes the need for balance between our physical and spiritual reality.

Suggested Readings

E. P. Velikhov, J. M. Gvishiani, and S. R. Mikulinsky, eds., *Science, Technology and the Future* (New York: Pergamon Press, 1980), provides a comprehensive analysis of current scientific and technological tendencies and their influence on socioeconomic development. Gerard K. O'Neil, *The Technology Edge* (New York: Simon and Schuster, 1983), studies six new high-technology areas. Alvin Toffler, *Future Shock* (New York: Random House, 1970), examines change and the ways in which people adapt—or fail to adapt—to the future. Robert L. Heilbroner, *An Inquiry into the Human Prospect* (New York: W. W. Norton and Co., 1980), takes a look at the future from a socioeconomic perspective. Additional studies on the relationship between technology and social change are Charles A. Thrall and Jerold M. Starr, eds., *Technology, Power and Social Change* (Lexington, Mass.: Lexington Books, 1972), and Daniel Bell, ed., *Toward the Year 2000* (Boston: Houghton Mifflin Co., 1968). For a critical look at John Naisbitt's *Megatrends,* see the pamphlet *All One System* (Washington, D.C.: Institute for Educational Leadership, 1985).

DISCUSSION QUESTIONS:
THE TWENTIETH CENTURY

1. Entertainment often responds to social needs greater than a simple desire for individual diversion. After reading "Depression America and Its Films," to what needs do you feel the Hollywood comedies of the 1930s were responding? Were these films an instrument of social change, or did they serve some other function? We often talk about how the media shape public opinion. To what extent do you think that public opinion shapes the media? What social similarities do you see between these film comedies and the Tokugawa Kabuki discussed in Part I?

2. We have seen in "Depression America and Its Films" how the Great Depression shook popular confidence in traditional institutions and values. And yet, "Democracy and Hypocrisy" shows us that racism was as strong as ever. Why had the confidence of the majority in that particular "value" not diminished? Why did the government not consider interning Americans of German or Italian birth? What factors had been acting to preserve racism in America, and what factors were now at work to diminish it?

3. In virtually every industrialized nation except South Africa, official racism and discrimination are on the decrease. As we can see from "Apartheid: Its Origin and Nature," they have been institutionalized and are, in many ways, fundamental to the South African society and government. Why do the South Africans cling so fiercely to racism and discrimination? How have they been able to do so in the face of almost universal disapproval? In what ways have the problems of race differed in South Africa and the United States?

4. In "Lihua: A Young Woman's Experience with China's Cultural Revolution," Lihua says, "I've never lived a good day in my life." How does her life—and most particularly her personality—compare with that of woman Wang in "The Death of Woman Wang" in Part I? The Cultural Revolution was not intended to produce such a determined personality as Lihua had. Why did it do so? What is the difference between the daily want and turmoil of Lihua's Cultural Revolution and life in woman Wang's village, and why did the two environments produce two such different people?

5. Many of the leisure activities portrayed in "Leisure Time in Russia: The Timeless Approach to Life" are similar to those of Americans, whereas others are different. What are the differences, and why do you think they exist? Some scholars believe in "convergence"—the theory that Russian and American society will grow more and more similar over time. To what extent does this reading support that view? How valid do you think the theory is?

6. In "Human Waves," the author presents the phenomenon of the international movement of people in dramatic fashion, but such movements have been a normal feature of international relations since the 1500s. "The African Slave Trade," "The Response of Slaves," and "Irish Ser-

vant Women: The Irish 'Biddy,' " in earlier parts of this volume, all deal with similar movements in earlier times. How does the present situation differ from that of the past? Are the differences merely quantitative, or are they qualitative also? In what ways are these migrations another effect of the Industrial Revolution? Why did unchecked population growth not continue in the developed countries? Does your answer suggest possible solutions for the problem?

7. The author of "Robots and Japan: The New Breed" describes with some admiration the advantages of the Japanese manufacturing system's reliance on numbers of small manufacturers. Compare this system with that of Britain in the early modern period, as described in "Cottage Industry and the Factory System." To what extent are the two systems alike? Are their inherent advantages similar? Was there a weakness in the British system? Why did it eventually evolve into the factory system? How do you think the Japanese system will develop in the future? Would the Japanese type of manufacturing organization work in the United States? Why, or why not?

8. Marxist historians would argue that history—that is, the sum total of human actions—evolves according to economic laws. According to that view, human beings are not really in control of their destinies. How would a Marxist historian view the optimism of the author of "High Tech/High Touch"? To what extent is the author dealing only with superficial aspects of technological development? How might he think society would deal with the greater efficiency and lower cost of robotics as described in "Robots and Japan: The New Breed," or with the demographic problems of "Human Waves"? Is his optimism justified? In short, to what degree are we in control of the way our society is changing?

9. "Human Waves," "Robots and Japan: The New Breed," and "High Tech/High Touch" all deal with the prospect of basic changes in our society as a result of technological innovation. "An Early Energy Crisis and Its Consequences," "Two Parsons," "Cottage Industry and the Factory System," and other earlier selections discussed previous eras of change. How have humans in the past reacted to the prospect of basic change? How do you account for our general attitude of admiring progress and at the same time clinging to traditional values?

10. Some thinkers have suggested that one great problem of the modern world is that it has emphasized technological progress and ignored moral advancement. Consider "Democracy and Hypocrisy: The American Homefront During World War II," "Apartheid: Its Origin and Nature," and "Lihua: A Young Woman's Experience with China's Cultural Revolution," and compare them with such earlier readings as "The African Slave Trade" and "Cottage Industry and the Factory System." Have a sense of justice, a regard for individual integrity, and basic humanity increased in the world? To the extent that they have, to what can you attribute the advance? To the extent that they have not, what do you think are the deterring forces?

Copyrights and Acknowledgments

For permission to use the selections reprinted in this book, the author is grateful to the following publishers and copyright holders:

ANDREW BERGMAN   For "Depression America and Its Films: The Marx Brothers and W. C. Fields," from *We're in the Money: Depression America and Its Films*, copyright © 1971 by New York University Press. Reprinted by permission of the author.

DOUBLEDAY & COMPANY, INC.   For "The African Slave Trade," from "The Era of the Slave Trade" in *Africa and Africans* by Paul Bohannan and Philip Curtin. Copyright © 1964 by Paul Bohannan. Copyright © 1971 by Paul Bohannan and Philip Curtin. Reprinted by permission of Doubleday & Company, Inc.

W. H. FREEMAN   For "An Early Energy Crisis and Its Consequences," by John U. Nef. First published in *Scientific American*, November 1977. Reprinted by permission of W. H. Freeman and Company.

HARCOURT BRACE JOVANOVICH, INC.   For "Two Parsons," from *The Second Common Reader* by Virginia Woolf, copyright © 1932 by Harcourt Brace Jovanovich, Inc.; renewed 1960 by Leonard Woolf. Reprinted by permission of the publisher.

HISTORY TODAY   For "Woodes Rogers: Privateer and Pirate Hunter," by M. Foster Farley, first published in *History Today*, 1979. For "The Response of Slaves," by Gad Heuman, first published in *History Today*, 1984. For "Cottage Industry and the Factory System," by Duncan Bythell, first published by *History Today*, 1983. All reprinted by permission of *History Today*.

INDIAN ECONOMIC & SOCIAL HISTORY REVIEW   For "The Business World of Jamsetjee Jejeebhoy," by Asiya Siddiqi, copyright © 1982. Reprinted by permission of Indian Economic & Social History Review.

MACMILLAN   For "Universities and the Scientific Revolution," from *Technology and the Academics* by Eric Ashby. Reprinted by permission of Macmillan, London and Basingstoke. Footnotes omitted by permission.

NATURAL HISTORY   For "Human Waves," by Leon F. Bouvier with permission from *Natural History*, Vol. 92, No. 8; copyright the American Museum of Natural History, 1983.

OXFORD UNIVERSITY PRESS   For "Quinine and the European Conquest of Africa," from *The Tools of Empire: Technology and European Imperialism in the Nineteenth Century* by Daniel Headrick. Copyright © 1981 by Oxford University Press, Inc. Reprinted by permission. Footnotes omitted by permission.

PANTHEON BOOKS   For "Leisure Time in Russia: The Timeless Approach to Life," from *Life in Russia* by Michael Binyon. Copyright © 1983 by Michael Binyon. Reprinted by permission of Pantheon Books, a Division of Random House, Inc.

PUTNAM PUBLISHING GROUP   For "Democracy and Hypocrisy: The American Homefront During World War II," from *The Homefront: America During World War II* by Mark Jonathan Harris, Franklin Mitchell and Steven Schechter. Copyright © 1984 by G. P. Putnam's Sons. Reprinted by permission of the publisher.

RANDOM HOUSE, INC.   For "Apartheid: Its Origin and Nature," from *The Africans* by David Lamb. Copyright © 1983 by David Lamb. Reprinted by permission of Random House, Inc.

ROWMAN & ALLANHELD   For "The Emergence of Team Sports: Baseball's Early Years," from *Sports in the Western World* by William J. Baker. Totowa, N. J.: Rowman and Littlefield, © 1982, pp. 138–150. Reprinted by permission of the publisher.

SIMON & SCHUSTER   For "Robots and Japan: The New Breed," from *The Japanese Mind* by Robert C. Christopher. Copyright © 1983 by Kriston Corporation. Reprinted by permission of Linden Press, a division of Simon & Schuster.

STANFORD UNIVERSITY PRESS   For "Skills and Resources in Late Traditional China," by Mark Elvin. Reprinted from *China's Modern Economy in Historical Perspective*, edited by Dwight H. Perkins, with permission of the publishers, Stanford University Press, © 1975 by the Board of Trustees of the Leland Stanford Junior University.

TIMES BOOKS   For "Lihua: A Young Woman's Experience with China's Cultural Revolution," from *China: Alive in the Bitter Sea* by Fox Butterfield. Copyright © 1982 by Fox Butterfield. Reprinted by permission of Times Books, a Division of Random House, Inc.

385

Illustration Credits

A 6
B 7
C 8
D 9
E 0
F 1
G 2
H 3
I 4
J 5